Springer Series in Information Sciences 6

Editor: King-sun Fu

Springer Series in Information Sciences

Editors: King-sun Fu   Thomas S. Huang   Manfred R. Schroeder

Volume 1   **Content-Addressable Memories**
By T. Kohonen

Volume 2   **Fast Fourier Transform and Convolution Algorithms**
By H.J. Nussbaumer   2nd Eidition

Volume 3   **Pitch Determination of Speech Signals**   Algorithms and Devices
By W. Hess

Volume 4   **Pattern Analysis**
By H. Niemann

Volume 5   **Image Sequence Analysis**
Editor: T. S. Huang

Volume 6   **Picture Engineering**
Editors: King-sun Fu and T. L. Kunii

Volume 7   **Number Theory in Science and Communication**
With Applications in Cryptography, Physics, Biology
and Digital Information
By M. R. Schroeder

Volume 8   **Self-Organization and Associative Memory**
By T. Kohonen

Volume 9   **An Introduction to Digital Picture Processing**
By L. P. Yaroslavsky

Volume 10 **Probability, Statistical Optics, and Data Testing**
A Problem Solving Approach
By B. Roy Frieden

Picture Engineering

Editors: King-sun Fu and T. L. Kunii

With 166 Figures

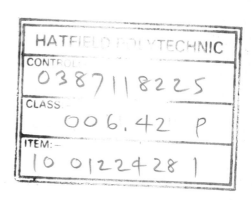
Springer-Verlag Berlin Heidelberg New York 1982

Professor King-sun Fu

School of Electrical Engineering, Purdue University,
West Lafayette, IN 47907, USA

Professor Tosiyasu L. Kunii

Department of Information Science, Faculty of Science,
University of Tokyo, Bonkyo-ku, Tokyo 113, Japan

Series Editors:

Professor King-sun Fu

School of Electrical Engineering, Purdue University,
West Lafayette, IN 47907, USA

Professor Thomas S. Huang

Department of Electrical Engineering and Coordinated Science Laboratory,
University of Illinois, Urbana, IL 61801, USA

Professor Dr. Manfred R. Schroeder

Drittes Physikalisches Institut, Universität Göttingen, Bürgerstraße 42–44,
D-3400 Göttingen, Fed. Rep. of Germany

ISBN 3-540-11822-5 Springer-Verlag Berlin Heidelberg New York
ISBN 0-387-11822-5 Springer-Verlag New York Heidelberg Berlin

Library of Congress Cataloging in Publication Data. Main entry under title: Picture engineering. (Springer series in information sciences; v. 6). Includes bibliographical references and index. 1. Image processing. I. Fu, K. S. (King-sun), 1930– . II. Kunii, Toshiyasu. III. Series. TA1632.P525 1982   621.36′7   82′10637

Offset printing and bookbinding: Brühlsche Universitätsdruckerei, Giessen
2153/3130-543210

Preface

This book seeks to elucidate picture engineering as a new discipline for handling the entire scope of picture processing in a systematic manner. Picture engineering as a discipline has three aspects, the first of which is methodological, technical, and architectural. The second consists of pattern analysis and recognition of pictorial input, picture database management, including picture data structure and data representation for picture storage and transformation, and computer graphics for picture output and display. Versatile applications such as computer-aided design, manufacturing and testing (CAD/CAM/CAT), office automation (OA), robotics, and fancy computer arts comprise the third aspect. This book covers all three aspects in original papers by leading experts in the discipline.

The book is divided into six parts. Part I covers the central topic of pictorial database management in three papers. The first, by Yamaguchi and Kunii, presents a data model for designing a picture database computer. The second, by Klinger, discusses the organization of computers for handling pictorial data. In the third paper, Shi-Kuo Chang treats the indexing and encoding of pictorial data.

Part II is devoted to picture representation. First, a general approach to picture analysis using both syntactic (structural) and semantic information is described by Fu. This is followed by an in-depth explanation of various 3-D shape representation methods by Ikebe and Miyamoto. Schumaker elaborates polar spline representation of 3-D objects, and finally, Enomoto, Yonezaki and Watanabe describe a unique method of characterizing 3-D surfaces by structure lines.

Part III is on picture computer architecture. It presents concrete examples on how to implement various methods and techniques of picture engineering in hardware. All picture computers presented here are based on multiprocessor architecture. Giloi and Bruening explain the use of configurable architecture in building high-performance picture computers which satisfy contradictory application requirements, and Agrawal and Jain extend picture computer architecture to cover moving pictures. Architecture on VLSI arrays with a control structure for optimal throughput is discussed by Young and Liu.

Parts IV and V cover aspects of picture engineering for advanced automation in business and engineering offices. Automation in business offices is becoming a booming field, and is now termed office automation (OA). This field is treated in Part IV, which consists of three papers. The first, by Saigusa and Takeshita, illustrates a high-level programming support for color graphic report generation. In the second paper, Takao presents an image-editing and filing technique, and in the third, Ni, Wong and Lee describe a multiple microprocessor system for office image processing. Part V covers computer-aided design (CAD), a very important field for supporting the automation of engineering offices. Hiraishi and Yajima discuss electronic circuit design, and Matsuka covers the use of CAD for architectural design.

Part VI concludes the book with a description of a picture engineering approach to computer art. Sasaki and Sasaki take a statistical approach to computer art, and present various attractive test examples.

The authors of the papers on the architecture of picture computers were invited from among the contributors to the IEEE Computer Society Workshop on Computer Architecture for Pattern Analysis and Image Database Management held at Hot Spring, Virginia, November 11-13, 1981. Most of the authors of the papers on the other areas were invited from among the contributors to the 15th IBM Japan Computer Science Symposium on Picture Engineering held at Amagi, Shizuoka, September 8-10, 1981. The editors are grateful to IBM Japan for its support in making the updated version of several papers available for the book.

West Lafayette, IN, USA   *King-Sun Fu*

Tokyo, Japan   *T.L. Kunii*

Contents

Part I **Pictorial Database Management**

PICCOLO: A Data Model for Picture Database Computers
By K. Yamaguchi and T.L. Kunii (With 10 Figures) 2

Computer System Organization for Pictorial Data
By A. Klinger (With 3 Figures) 24

A Methodology for Picture Indexing and Encoding
By S.-K. Chang (With 3 Figures) 33

Part II **Picture Representation**

A General (Syntactic-Semantic) Approach to Picture Analysis
By K.S. Fu (With 7 Figures) 56

Shape Design, Representation and Restoration with Splines
By Y. Ikebe and S. Miyamoto (With 23 Figures) 75

Computer-Aided Design of 3-D Objects Using Polar Spline
Representations. By L.L. Schumaker (With 2 Figures) 96

Application of Structure Lines to Surface Construction and
3-Dimensional Analysis. By H. Enomoto, N. Yonezaki, and
Y. Watanabe (With 26 Figures) 106

Part III **Picture Computer Architecture**

A Configurable Micro Array Computer for Signal and Image
Processing. By W.K. Giloi and R. Bruening (With 3 Figures) 140

A Multiprocessor System for Dynamic Scene Analysis
By D.P. Agrawal and R. Jain (With 8 Figures) 152

VLSI Array Architecture for Picture Processing
By P.S. Liu and T.Y. Young (With 10 Figures) 171

Part IV **Office Automation**

High-Level Programming Support for Color/Graphics Reports
By K. Saigusa and T. Takeshita (With 18 Figures) 188

An Approach to Image Editing and Filing
By Y. Takao (With 7 Figures) 210

A Multiple Microprocessor System for Office Image
Processing. By L.M. Ni, K.Y. Wong, and D.T. Lee
(With 7 Figures) 232

Part V   Computer-Aided Design

Logic Diagram Editing for Interactive Logic Design
By H. Hiraishi and S. Yajima (With 17 Figures) 248

Extended Graphic Functions of the A-IDAS System
for Visual Design. By H. Matsuka, S. Uno, K. Sugimoto,
and J. Takama (With 15 Figures) 268

Part VI   Computer Art

Towards an Intelligent Computer Art System
By M.K. Sasaki and T. Sasaki (With 7 Figures) 286

Index of Contributors 303

Part I

Pictorial Database Management

PICCOLO: A Data Model for Picture Database Computers

K. Yamaguchi and T.L. Kunii

Department of Information Science, Faculty of Science
The University of Tokyo, Hongo, Tokyo 113, Japan

Abstract

A picture data model for use as the architectural basis of picture database computers is investigated. For a picture database, it is required to manipulate varieties of data structures efficiently. In this paper, an extension of the relational model named PICCOLO is proposed. Operations of PICCOLO are more powerful than a relational algebra or QBE(Query By Example); the graph isomorphism can be checked by the operations of PICCOLO. The operation can be specified in a structured way and shared among users. For a picture database, it is also required to carry out operations in parallel in order to accelerate the execution. It is shown that the data operation of PICCOLO can be performed in a highly parallel way.

1. Introduction

Recently, very large picture databases are accumulated through various applications such as LANDSAT image processing, computerized tomography and geographical data processing. Also advanced automations require picture databases for shared use of engineering drawings, business forms and illustrations through graphic terminals.

Increasing number of systems have been developed to manage picture databases. They include INFADS and related results by Kunii [1, 2], GADS by Carlson [3], GRAIN by Chang [4] and Query-By-Pictorial-Example by Fu [5]. Every picture database management system already constructed can handle only one or two picture data structures such as a two dimensional array of pixels for computer graphics applications. One of the drawbacks of this limitation is the restriction of the data structures which can be used for picture processing applications. Very large volume of picture database makes efficiency another important factor. For certain applications such as image analysis, a quad tree [6] and several graph representations, for example a minimum spanning tree (MST) [7], are proposed and applied to process pictures efficiently.

Breakthroughs have been emerging recently: a data model research advancement, including the ANSI/X3/SPARC 3 shema model [8] and the extensions of the relational model, and the recent hardware technology advancement, as typically seen in the VLSI technology. In order to manage varieties of application dependent data structures of pictures without making the data model complicated, the idea is that various application

2

dependent data structures and their operations named external data models by ANSI are represented by a generalized common data structure and its operations named PICCOLO which correspond to the ANSI conceptual data model. The implementation of the conceptual models in hardware significantly increases the performance of data management systems without complicating the data models. This is along the line of the language directed machine architecture [9]. Fig.1 illustrates this architecture.

PICCOLO Architecture		ANSI/X3/SPARC Architecture
Application dependent data model* e.g. pixel arrays for computer graphics	<->	External data models
PICCOLO as a generalized common data model*, implemented in hardware	<->	Conceptual data models
Performance dependent data model*	<->	Internal data models

*Data Model = Data Structure + Data Operations

Fig.1 PICCOLO as a generalized common data model

The VLSI technology advancement enables us to further overcome the problem of the execution speed by allowing us to produce a highly parallel processor to process pictures at a reasonable price.

To utilize these technologies, especially the VLSI technology, our approach starts from deciding a computer system including not only software but also hardware and firmware which are suitable to handle pictures. In this paper, we explain a picture data model PICCOLO which is defined to support various application dependent and performance dependent picture data models. Also we explain the execution mechanism of the operations of PICCOLO which is suitable for VLSI implementation. In Section 2, the requirements for a picture database system are elaborated. Section 3 discusses the framework of a system and the definition of PICCOLO. In Section 4, a generic representation is introduced. The generic representation is a key feature of such a picture database in which a repeated and regular pattern appears frequently. Section 5 shows the parallel execution of operations. Section 6 is devoted to examples to show how varieties of data structures and their operations are represented. Section 7 concludes this paper.

2. Requirement Specification

For the utilization of the VLSI technology, first we start to design a computer which is suitable to the picture database. We call the computer picture computer. The requirements for the picture computer which are sketched roughly above are refined into six assertions as follows:

3

<u>Requirement.1 The uniformity in representation of pictures is realized as
much as possible.</u>

A picture database has multiple representations.   For example, a picture
which consists of a two dimensional array of pixels may be painting objects
such as trees and humans, and their relationships such as "on the right of"
and "below".   A picture represented as pixels is an example of a <u>physical
picture</u>. A picture represented as objects and relationships is an example
of a <u>logical</u> <u>picture</u>. These terms are relative, and a two dimensional array
may become a logical picture in some situations. The relationship between
logical pictures and physical pictures, and an entire architecture of the
picture database are shown in Fig.2.

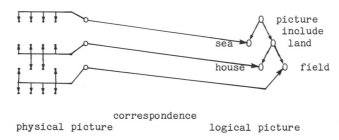

correspondence

physical picture   logical picture

<u>Fig.2</u> An architecture of a picture database

For any given picture, there are many representations even if only a
physical picture is considered. For example, a two dimensional array of
pixels, a quad tree [6], and an MST(Minimum Spanning Tree) [7] are just a
few of popular physical representations.   If we can find a formalism or
logic to accommodate these varieties of picture representations, only a
single hardware architecture (and design) is required for the picture
computer. Considering that a mask pattern design for the VLSI occupies the
major part of the cost of the VLSI chip, the cost of the VLSI chip is
decreased significantly, by reducing the number of hardware design and hence
increasing the production volume for each design.

<u>Requirement.2 The operation is executed concurrently as much as possible by
employing identical processors.</u>

The number of processors on a single VLSI chip does not necessarily increase
its cost drastically.   Once the mask pattern has been designed, the
production cost is rather low. Since picture processing generally consists
of highly independent operations such as the update of color values at very
many picture points, the time necessary for executing the operation is
significantly saved by designing a highly parallel processor chip without
much increasing the cost.

<u>Requirement.3 Representations and their relationships are treated within
the same framework.</u>

As shown in Fig.2, it is generally the case that a logical picture and a
physical picture need to be mutually related somehow. For example, in case
of an image analysis (or pattern recognition) application, it is required to
create a logical picture from a physical picture. In case of a computer

graphics application, it is required to generate a physical picture from a logical picture. Hence, it is required that <u>a physical picture and a logical picture, and their relationships are handled easily by the picture database</u>. It is also possible to derive new information of a logical picture such as the distance of objects which is not stored in the logical picture from the physical picture by utilizing the correspondence between two pictures. Also important is non-pictorial data such as an owner's name, date, object names, and so forth. By treating non-pictorial data and the correspondence among the data and pictures within the same framework, we need no additional hardware to bridge them.

<u>Requirement.4 Any algorithmic query such as the connectedness of regions and the graph isomorphism is manageable within the framework</u>.

A boundary following is an example of popular picture processing operations. Suppose the boundary following operation is not handled within the framework. Then it is necessary to transfer the picture data to other systems in which the boundary following operations are available. If the transfer takes much time, the parallel processing capability of the picture computer is not at all utilized. So it is desirable that the computer has the capability to handle any algorithmic query on pictures.

<u>Requirement.5 A query form is stored in a database and utilized in a simple way</u>.

By sharing a query form, the cost to specify query form is reduced. In a picture database case, the query form is much more complicated than that in a business database case. For example, a query to find the connectedness of regions is not an easy query to describe. If the query form is stored and can be utilized in a simple way, a user can describe a complicated query easily and systematically.

<u>Requirement.6 Display forms are controlled and produced within the same framework</u>.

For a picture database, display forms are of considerable value. Because varieties of data structures are usually required to be represented in PICCOLO, it is usually desirable for the picture computer to have a mechanism that a user can define an interface tc translate data from one form into some other application dependent forms such as a graph representation or a tree representation. By sharing the most part of the interface which is described in a query form, much interfacing cost can be saved.

3. Determination of the Framework

In this section, a logical framework of a picture database is discussed and defined.

Relationships in a physical picture

To achieve the uniformity of a picture representation (Requirement.1), we introduce here a representation of a physical picture by objects and relationships. A pixel can be regarded as an object. It is easy to see that pixels have relationships with each other. For example, a pixel is "on the right of" its left pixel as illustrated in Fig.3.

```
0→0→0→0           O    a pixel
↓  ↓  ↓  ↓
0→0→0→0           ↓    a "below" relationship
↓  ↓  ↓  ↓
0→0→0→0           →    an "on the right of" relationship
↓  ↓  ↓  ↓
0→0→0→0
```

Fig.3 A two dimensional array of pixels represented by objects and
        relationships

Assuming the pixels are located on two dimensional grid points, it is
obvious that the objects, and the "on the right of" and "below"
relationships represent two dimensional array of pixels correctly. By
representing a pixel by an object, a physical picture is considered to
consist of objects and relationships, and the uniformity required by
Requirement.1 is attained. In the following, in order to treat both
physical and logical representations of pictures in the same framework, we
use the term object as a generic term of an object in a logical picture such
as a pattern and an object in a physical picture such as a pixel. When we
refer to an object in a logical picture and that in a physical picture, we
call them a logical object and a physical object, respectively.
Analogously, we use the term relationship as a generic term.

     From Requirement.3, it is necessary to represent the correspondence
between a physical picture and a logical picture. Thus, we need the
capability to represent relationships among the relationships in addition to
that to represent objects and relationships. A relationship among
relationships is called relationship relationship.

Extension of the relational model to satisfy Requirement.3.

To represent an object, a relationship and a relationship relationship, the
relational model proposed by Codd [10] was extended and named PICCOLO. The
advantages of extending the relational model is that the relational model is
defined on a formal basis and the model itself has no specific structures in
it. In the extended relational model, an object, a relationship or a
relationship relationship is represented by a tuple. In our previous paper,
we extended the relational model and defined ELF [11] in which objects and
relationships can be represented and manipulated. PICCOLO is a further
extension of the model so that relationship relationships can be
represented.

Definition of PICCOLO

A relation R in PICCOLO is defined as follows:

$$R \in N \times N_1 \times R_1 \times N_2 \times R_2 \times \cdots \times N_k \times R_k \times D_1 \times D_2 \times \cdots \times D_m$$
   where N, N_i are tuple id domains,

       R_i is a set of relation names, and

       D_i is a domain.

     Suppose that $t=(n,n_1,r_1,n_2,r_2,\ldots,n_k,r_k,d_1,d_2,\ldots,d_m) \in R$. Then, n is a
tuple id given to the tuple t, n_i and r_i are used as a pair to specify

6

another tuple of a relation r_i with a tuple id n_i, d_i is a value associated with the tuple t. The tuple t represents a k-ary relationship among tuples which are specified by (n_1,r_1), (n_2,r_2), ..., and (n_k,r_k). From the uniqueness of the tuple id in a same relation, the next condition has to hold:

$$\forall t, t' \in R((n,...)=t \wedge (n',...)=t' \wedge n=n' \rightarrow t=t').$$

Here, we do not impose stronger condition that asserts the uniqueness of the tuple id in different relations:

$$\forall t \in R \quad \forall t' \in R'((n,...)=t \wedge (n',...)=t' \wedge n=n' \rightarrow t=t' \wedge R=R').$$

That is, a tuple id is not unique in the database except within one relation. Hence, it is necessary to use a pair (n_i,r_i) to specify a tuple in the database. By defining tuple ids relative to each relation, the modularity of the system increases.

In the following, a relational calculus by Codd [12] is employed to describe an operation. An extended part of the calculus is explained when it is used.

Representing varieties of image representation techniques uniformly in PICCOLO

We show a few examples to represent image data structures in PICCOLO below.

A quad tree
A quad tree is represented in PICCOLO as in Fig.4.

O   a pixel

↗   a NW relationship

↙   a SW relationship

↘   a NE relationship

↘   a SE relationship

Fig.4   A quad tree represented by PICCOLO

An MST
A more interesting data structure is an MST. An MST is generated by the following operation.

For each pair of adjacent pixels (p,p') do
    if |gray level of p - gray level of p'| < criteria
    then p is connected to p'.

7

MST operations generate connected relationships between pixels from the two dimensional array of pixels. The operation is described in the relational calculus:

CONNECTED(NID1,RNAME1,NID2,RNAME2)={(n1,PICTURE,n2,PICTURE)|
   (n1,v1),(n2,v2)∈ PICTURE,
   (an1,PICTURE,an2,PICTURE)∈ ON_THE_RIGHT_OF,
   (bn1,PICTURE,bn2,PICTURE)∈ BELOW,
   ((n1=an1 ∧ n2=an2) ∨ (n1=bn1 ∧ n2=bn2)) ∧ abs(v1-v2)<c}.

Here, we describe a relation A with attributes a_1, a_2,..., a_n as $A(a_1, a_2,..., a_n)$. The result of this operation is illustrated in Fig.5.

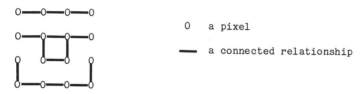

O   a pixel

——   a connected relationship

Fig.5   An MST represented by PICCOLO

Generating a logical picture from a physical picture.

As mentioned previously, PICCOLO is defined so that it can represent logical and physical pictures and their correspondence. The logical picture generation progresses in three steps.

The first step is to generate an MST from the physical picture already explained. The second step is to generate the region representatives for each region explained in Section 6. The third step is to generate a logical picture by generating an object for each region representative and to associate the region and the object interactively. The result is shown in Fig.2.

4. A Generic Representation of Relations

- Another extension to increase flexibility -

In order to provide the PICCOLO system with more flexibility, we introduce a generic representation of relations. Let us think about the case that a logical picture of a sheet of cloth in a flat weave woven by interlacing white and black threads is described in the PICCOLO. By utilizing the pixel ids of Fig.6, we can derive the gray level of the pixel v from the pixel id n by an expression: v=(n+(n div 4)) mod 2.

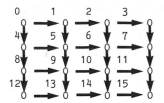

A number marked on the upper left corner of each square
(pixel) is a pixel id.

Fig.6 A pixel id

We assume here that the gray level of a white thread is one and that of a
black thread is zero. By utilizing the expression, pixels are represented
by one tuple of a relation named a "picture" object as shown in Fig.7.

NID	GRAY_LEVEL	COND
n	v	$v=(n+(n \text{ div } 4)) \text{ mod } 2$

A "picture" object

NID1	RNAME1	NID2	RNAME2	COND
n	picture	n+4	picture	$n<12 \wedge n\geq0$

A "below" relationship

NID1	RNAME1	NID2	RNAME2	COND
n	picture	n+1	picture	$n<16 \wedge n\geq0 \wedge ((n+1) \text{ mod } 4)=0$

An "on the right of" relationship

Fig.7 Generic representations of relations

This tuple is called a generic tuple and the table is called a generic
table. In this tuple, n is a variable which runs over pixel ids. COND is a
flag associated to each attribute, and the COND flag which is true means
that a value in the attribute is used as a predicate to test what values the
variables in the tuple can have. Thanks to variables and COND flags, the
single tuple in the "picture" object represents a set of tuples {(n,(n+(n
div 4)) mod 2)|$0\leq n \wedge n<16$}. We call the process to obtain the set of tuples
(0, 0), (1, 1), (2, 0), ..., (15, 1) from the generic tuple an evaluation.
Similarly, two relationships "on the right of" and "below" in Fig.3 are
represented in Fig.7 as two tuples. One generic tuple of a relation to
describe the "below" relationships is equivalent to a set of tuples {(n,
picture, n+4, picture)|$0\leq n \wedge n<12$}, and another generic tuple to describe the
"on the right of" relationship is equivalent to a set of tuples {(n,
picture, n+1, picture)|$0\leq n \wedge n<16 \wedge ((n+1) \text{ mod } 4)=0$}. Hence, a compact
representation of relations is achieved in PICCOLO by this extension.

Derivation of logical picture data from physical picture data
PICCOLO supports the derivation of a logical picture data from a physical
picture data. We show an example of the derivation of an adjacency
relationship of objects in a logical picture of Fig.8 from the adjacency of

9

regions in the physical picture. This derivation process is presented by three terms:

$$ADJ(NID1,RNAME1,NID2,RNAME2,COND)=\{(u,p,v,p)\mid$$
$$(x,p,y,p)\in r(NID1,RNAME1,NID2,RNAME2),(r="ON\_THE\_RIGHT\_OF"\vee r="BELOW")$$
$$\wedge((u=x\wedge v=y)\vee(u=y\wedge v=x))\}.$$
$$RADJ(NID1,RNAME1,NID2,RNAME2,COND)=\{(w,p,x,p)\mid$$
$$(w,p,u,p),(x,p,v,p)\in REGION(NID1,RNAME1,NID2,RNAME2),$$
$$(u,p,v,p)\in ADJ(NID1,RNAME1,NID2,RNAME2)\}.$$
$$OADJ(NID1,RNAME1,NID2,RNAME2,COND)=\{(y,q,z,q)\mid$$
$$(y,q,w,p),(z,q,x,p)\in CORRESPONDENCE(NID1,RNAME1,NID2,RNAME2),$$
$$(w,p,x,p)\in RADJ(NID1,RNAME1,NID2,RNAME2)\}.$$

The result is as follows:

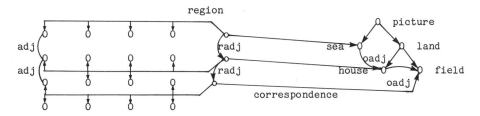

Fig.8 Adjacency relationships in a logical picture derived from the adjacency relationships of pixels in a physical picture

A generic representation versus QBE

We show here that a generic representation is more powerful than QBE by Zloof [13] in the following points.

(1) One tuple in a generic representation can describe a query form of QBE. And the same result as the query form of QBE is obtained by referring to the generic tuple. Thus, the external schemas of ANSI/SPARC model which are usually described each time by query languages such as QBE and SQL of system R can be stored as a part of the database and hence can be repeatedly used.

(2) A generic tuple can represent a set of tuples by one tuple. Thus, it can save storage spaces, and the meanings of the data are explicit and hence clearer than represented by the occurrences.

An Evaluation of a Generic Tuple

We explain how a generic tuple is evaluated. A simple domain D_i and a pair of a tuple id N_i and a relation name R_i have the COND flag. Suppose that a tuple $t = (t_1, t_2, \ldots, t_n, t_{n+1}, \ldots, t_m)$ in a generic table with attributes a_1, a_2, $\ldots$, a_n, a_{n+1}, $\ldots$, and a_m where a_1, a_2, $\ldots$, and a_n have false COND flags and a_{n+1}, a_{n+2}, $\ldots$, and a_m have true COND flags. If a domain D_i has a true COND flag, then the value in D_i is considered as a predicate. If domains (N_i, R_i) has a true COND flag, then the value in (N_i, R_i) is used to specify a tuple and the value in the domains is replaced by

10

the tuple when the tuple is evaluated. This indirection is attractive when
there are frequently used predicates. For example, "below" relationships
can be represented utilizing the indirection as in Fig.9.

BELOW	NID1	RNAME1	NID2	RNAME2	NID3	COND	RNAME3
	n	p	n+4	p	m		CONDITION

CONDITION	NID	PREDICATE
	m	$n<12 \wedge n \geq 0$

Fig.9 An example of an indirect COND representation

After this replacement of the indirection, the tuple is evaluated as a set
$\{(t_1,t_2,\ldots,t_n) | t_{n+1} \wedge t_{n+2} \wedge \ldots \wedge t_m\}$ by regarding t_{n+1}, t_{n+2}, $\ldots$,and t_m as
predicates. There are cases to handle these tuples without evaluating them
such as to insert a generic tuple into a generic table. In such a case,
" ε " is used instead of " $\in$ " in the calculus.

5. Operations and Executions

Definition of operations of PICCOLO

Operations are based on a relational calculus.
From the following two reasons, we selected a relational calculus [12] as
the basis of the operations of PICCOLO.

(1) The extension based on a relational calculus is simple. For example,
    the operation to join a relationship and objects specified by the
    relationship is illustrated in Fig.10.

A	B
D	nD
E	nE

a relationship
relation Z

B	C
nD	a
nD'	a'

an object
relation A

B	C
nE	b
nE'	b'

an object
relation B

A	B	C
D	nD	a
E	nE	b

the resultant object
relation R

$R=\{(t.A,t.B,u.C) | t \in Z, r=t.A, u \in r, t.B=u.B\}$
The operation described in the calculus

Fig.10 A kind of a join operation through a tuple id and a relationship
        name

(2) Because a relational calculus automatically navigates in the database,
    a high level of operations are allowed for the user.

Definition of operations based on a relational calculus
Operations to manipulate PICCOLO are defined in the following. The syntax
of the operations is defined in a BNF [14] and then the semantics of the
syntax is explained. In the definition, a notation <a>b is used to stand
for a symbol which is of the type <a> and identified by b.

11

```
<term>::=<constant>|<variable>|<function>(<arg>)|<term>.<term>|
        <term> ∈<term>|<term> ε <term>|
        <quantifier>(<term><term>)|(<term>)
<arg>::=empty|<arg><term>
```

An *empty* and an *undef* are reserved values.

A <value> is a meaningful unit such as a boolean value, a character string, a binary number, or a relation name, and their meanings are implementation specific. The boolean values, namely, *true* and *false*, are also reserved.

A <variable> is a symbol, and is either free or associated with a value. The values are called to *satisfy* a term if and only if, by associating the values to variables of the term, the term becomes *true*.

A <function> is a function such as an arithmetic operation and its meanings are implementation dependent.

The <term>s <term>.<term>, <term>∈<term>, and <term>ε <term> are special cases of the <term> <function>(<arg>), but because they have database-oriented meanings in PICCOLO, we treat them separately.

<term>t_1.<term>t_2 gives a value in an attribute t_2 of a tuple t_1.

<term>t_1 ∈<term>t_2 gives *true* if and only if a tuple t_1 is a tuple of a relation t_2, where a tuple of a relation t_2 is evaluated as a generic tuple.

<term>t_1 ε <term>t_2 gives *true* if and only if a tuple t_1 is a tuple of a relation t_2, where a tuple of a relation t_2 is not evaluated as a generic tuple.

<quantifier>(<term>t_1<term>t_2) gives a value evaluated from all the values of a term t_2 on the condition that a variable-value association satisfies a term t_1. The meaning of the <quantifier> is implementation dependent.

Implementation of the execution mechanism of the extended relational calculus by an abstract machine

The method to execute the operation defined previously is shown by defining an abstract machine, an eval, which is defined recursively in the following. In order to associate a <variable> with a <value>, an *association list* is defined as:

```
<list> ::= empty|<list> <variable><value>
```

We use this list so that the rightmost pair is the most recent one, that is, when two <variable><value> pair appears with the identical <variable> in the list, the <value> associated with the <variable> is the rightmost one. To utilize the list, a function which returns a value associated with a variable v is defined as follows:

```
assoc(v,list):=
    if list=empty then return undef
    else if list=<list>nlist <variable>x<value>y then
              if v=x then return y
          else return assoc(v,nlist)
    else error
```

By utilizing the the list, the function of the eval is defined below in a
language PASCAL [15] (this is actually a further extended version of
concurrent PASCAL [16]) recursively. The meanings of the notations such as
a cobegin are explained at the end of this definition.

```
eval(<term>,list):=
    if <term>=<constant>c then return c
    else if <term>=<variable>v then return assoc(v,list)
    else if <term>=<function>f(<term>a_1<term>a_2...<term>a_n) then
      begin
        cobegin
          t_1:=eval(a_1,list);

          t_2:=eval(a_2,list);

                    .
                    .
                    .

          t_n:=eval(an,list)

        coend;
        return f(t_1,t_2,...,t_n)
      end
    else if <term>=<term>t_1.<term>t_2 then
            begin
              cobegin
                u_1:=eval(t_1,list);

                u_2:=eval(t_2,list)

              coend;
              return t_1.t_2
            end
    else if <term>=<term>t_1 ∈ <term>t_2 then
        begin
          cobegin
            u_1:=eval(t_1,list);

            u_2:=eval(t_2,list)

          coend;
          if u_1=undef then

            if t_1=<variable> then

              for each v∈u_2
                 begin
                    list:=list t_1 v;
                    return true
                 end
            else error
          else return u_1∈u_2
```

13

```
                      end
          else if <term>=<term>t₁ ε <term>t₂ then
                  begin
                    cobegin
                       u₁:=eval(t₁,list);

                       u₂:=eval(t₂,list)

                    coend;
                    if u₁=undef then

                       if t₁=<variable> then

                          for each v ε u₂
                             begin
                                list:=list t₁ v;
                                return true
                             end
                       else error
                       else return u₁ ε u₂
                  end
          else if <term>=<quantifier>q(<term>t<term>p) then
                  begin
                    set:=empty;
                    cobegin
                       if eval(t,list)
                          then set:=set eval(p,list);
                    allend;
                    return q(set)
                  end
          else error
```

Explanations

(1) A term $t_1 \in t_2$ gives _true_ if and only if t_1 is an element of t_2. If t_1 is a variable and no value is associated with it, then we regard this to mean that t_1 may be associated with any value in t_2. For example, suppose that we execute an eval operation for the term $(x \in A)$ where $A=\{a,b,c\}$. Then, $eval((x \in A), \underline{empty})$ returns _true_ 3 times with an association list (x a), (x b), (x c) for each time.

(2) A block of the statements enclosed by _cobegin_ and _coend_

```
        cobegin
          P₁;

          P₂;

          ·
          ·
          ·
          Pₙ
        coend(or allend)
          Pₙ₊₁
```

is executed as follows:

((1)) P_1, P_2, ..., P_n are executed concurrently, when all the statements

P_1, P_2, ..., P_n have been finished, the following statement P_{n+1} is executed.

((2)) If any P_i returns an <u>undef</u> and an association list is modified in course of execution by some P_j (here, $1 \leq i, j \leq n$), P_i is tried once again with the modified list.

((3)) If there remains any P_i which returns an <u>undef</u>, an <u>undef</u> is returned by the block and the whole program is terminated. Otherwise, the execution continues from the next statement P_{n+1}.

We now explain the <u>allend</u> statement. As we have seen, in course of the execution of P_i, P_i may return the results several times such as in the execution of $x \in A$. In this case, if the <u>coend</u> statement is used, in our PICCOLO scheme, the execution of P_i employs as many number of processors as the returns have occurred. On the other hand, if the <u>allend</u> statement is used, no extra processers are employed by P_i than those employed by the previous statements.

6. Data Structures and Data Operations

To accommodate multiple data structures such as a tree and a graph to reside in the system, it is necessary to represent data structures in another data structure. We call the former a <u>represented data structure</u> and the latter an <u>underlying data structure</u>. As an example of the represented data structure with its underlying data structure, let's represent a graph in the relational model. By giving each node and arc a unique identifier, a directed graph can be represented by a set of triplets (arc identifier, initial node identifier, terminal node identifier) and a set of node identifiers. In this section, we examine several data structures and operations to them.

First, several terminologies are introduced in order to give a mathematical foundations. A set of data structures A (a set of data which have the data structures) is called <u>represented</u> by a set of data structures B iff there is a surjective partial function $g:B \rightarrow A$.

The fact that a data structure A is represented in a data structure B does not mean that the operations to A can be simulated by operations to B. For example, consider an operation to insert a node or an arc into a graph. By giving unique identifiers to a node and an arc, it is possible to represent a graph in the relational model. However, a node insertion requires a generation of a unique identifier which cannot be performed by a relational algebra itself without utilizing additional operations to an identifier. For a picture computer case, a broad class of operations are required. So the study of the hierarchy of operations is very important, because once the primitive operations are fabricated in a VLSI chip, it is impossible to expand the range of the executable operations.

An <u>operation</u> on a data structure D is defined as a set of functions O where $o \in O$ is a function $o:D \times D \times ... \times D \rightarrow D$. An operation O is called <u>closed</u> if $\forall o, o_1, o_2, ..., o_n \in O$ ($o \cdot (o_1 \times o_2 \times ... \times o_n) \in O$). An operation which is minimum and closed including O is called a <u>closure</u> of the operation

O denoted as $\bar{O}$. A set of operation O_1 is called <u>simulated</u> by an operation O_2 iff there is a mapping $f:O_1 \to \bar{O}_2$ such that for any o in O_1 the schema below commutes.

$$D_1 \times D_1 \times \ldots \times D_1 \xleftarrow{g \times g \times \ldots \times g} D_2 \times D_2 \times \ldots \times D_2$$

$$o \downarrow \qquad\qquad f(o) \downarrow$$

$$D_1 \xleftarrow{\quad g \quad} D_2$$

where a function $g:D_2 \to D_1$ is a mapping by which a data structure D_1 is represented by D_2.

We use notations RA, RC, QBE and PICCOLO to stand for the closure of a relational algebra operation, that of a relational calculus operation, that of QBE operation without arithmetic, MAX nor COUNT operations, and that of PICCOLO operation, respectively. By Codd [12], it was shown that RA = RC. Apparently QBE includes RA.

In the following, we consider several data operations which are frequently used for picture processing.

L Operator of QBE
QBE$\neq$RA because RA cannot simulate the L operator which is used to specify an entity of a tree structured table in a variable level as shown below.

PARENT	CHILD
a	b(nL)

=

PARENT	CHILD
a	b_1
b_1	b_2
.	.
.	.
.	.
b_{n-1}	b

One of the application of this operation is to calculate a transitive closure of the given set. PICCOLO can simulate this operation. In PICCOLO the descendents in the n-th level are obtained by the following generic representation. Here, $(a,b,n) \in A^*$ means that b is the n-th level descendent of a.

$$A^* = \{(a,b,n) \mid (n=1 \to (a,b) \in A) \lor (n \neq 1 \to (a,c) \in A \land (c,b,n-1) \in A^*)\}.$$

Recursive Function
A function $v'=f(v)$ is represented as a generic tuple $(v,v',v'=f(v))$ where $v'=f(v)$ is a predicate with a true COND flag in the attribute. It is remarkable here that there is no restriction to a predicate $v'=f(v)$, so it is possible to define a recursive function by a generic tuple. For example, the Fibonacci sequence is calculated by an operation:

$$F(V,N,COND) = \{(v,n,(n=0 \to v=1) \lor (n=1 \to v=1) \lor$$
$$(n \neq 0 \land n \neq 1 \to (v1,n-1) \in F \land (v-v1,n-2) \in F)\}.$$

Here, "$\to$" is a quantifier which evaluates the left hand side, and then evaluates the right hand side if the result is true. It is noteworthy that for a set of values of n this operation can be executed in parallel. This is because a generic tuple is used as "a pure procedure". A dynamic operation which is defined below has not this property. RA and QBE do not have the capability to calculate a recursive function.

Graph Node Deletion
In case of a graph node deletion, a graph consistency maintenance condition requires executing not only an operation to delete the specified node but also an operation to delete arcs which have the deleted node as their ends. This is described in a generic tuple as:

DELETE_NODE(NODE_RELATION_NAME,ARC_RELATION_NAME,NODE_ID,COND)=
$\{(r,a,n,(DELETE(r,\{(n)\}),DELETE(a,\{(at,ni,nt)\mid$
$(at,ni,nt)\in a,(ni=n \vee nt=n)\})))\}$.

RA and QBE do not have this capability by themselves.

Graph Node Insertion
A graph node insertion requires an operation to generate a unique identifier. Apparently, RA, QBE and PICCOLO can not perform this operation. By representing an identifier by a natural number and allowing comparison and addition operations to it, QBE and PICCOLO can insert a node into a graph, while RA cannot. This is because RA does not have an iteration mechanism, while QBE has an iteration mechanism, that is, ALL command. The method to generate a unique identifier here is to find the maximum number already used by utilizing an order among numbers and to add one for generating the next element. By utilizing the value of the inserted data, QBE and PICCOLO can insert nodes into a graph. The operation to perform unique identifiers for inserting a set Y(VALUE) into a set X(ID,VALUE) is described as a term:

$X=X^{\cup}\{(i+v.VALUE+1,v.VALUE)\mid i=t.ID,t\in X, \forall u\in X(i\geq u.ID),v\in Y\}$.

Numbering
Numbering is an important function which is frequently used for renumbering identifiers. This operation is carried out by COUNT operations as:

$N=\{(i,v)\mid i=COUNT(\{u\mid(v),(u)\in V,u<v\})\}$.

Generating a Region Representative
Suppose that a graph is represented by two tables. One table N is a set of node identifiers. The other table A is a set of triples where a triple (a, n_1, n_2) of a table A means that there is an arc a from the node n_1 to the node n_2. For generating the representative of a region, it is necessary to choose one element from a given set. As easily proven, RA, QBE and PICCOLO cannot choose one element from a set by themselves. By representing an identifier by a natural number, it is possible to do this operation utilizing a comparison operation of a natural number by QBE or PICCOLO. Generating a table "REGION" whose elements are representatives of connected regions is performed as:

$REGION=\{(t)\mid(t,v)\in CONNECTED, \forall(t,u)\in CONNECTED^{*}(t\geq u)\}$.

The graph is connected iff COUNT(REGION)=1.

Multiset
RA, QBE and PICCOLO are defined on a set basis. However, in the course of the execution of a relational calculus, a multiset [17] is actually used. For example, SEQUEL adopts an "impure" approach such that a duplicate

elimination is carried out only when a user specifies it by an operation
UNIQUE, which eliminates duplicates of the data. The reason why an impure
approach is taken is that the duplicate elimination is a costly operation
and also that it is necessary to leave duplicates as they are for carrying
out a certain kind of operations such as summation. In the following, we
denote data, data structures and data operations with a suffix "m" when they
are defined on a multiset basis. A multiset is represented by a set by
giving each data a unique identifier. A multiset $\{$ a, a, b, c, c, c $\}_m$ is
represented by a set $\{$ (0,a), (1,a), (0,b), (0,c), (1,c), (2,c) $\}$. This is
a simple case of a graph without arcs. The set operations such as union or
difference for a multiset are simulated by the graph node manipulation
operation. The UNIQUE operation can be simulated by projecting the
represented data to the second element, and then take a Cartesian product by
the set $\{0\}$.

Cartesian Product
An extended Cartesian product allows no column nesting while an original
Cartesian product allows column nesting. A Cartesian product $(A \times B) \times C$ and
$A \times (B \times C)$ are not equal while an extended Cartesian product $(A \times B) \times C$ and
$A \times (B \times C)$ are equal. The relational model adopts an extended Cartesian
product as its basis, and QBE and PICCOLO follow it. A column nesting can
be described by additional data which represents a tree structure of the
columns. For example, $(A \times B) \times C$ is represented by two triplets (ROOT,*,C)
and (*,A,B) and $A \times (B \times C)$ is represented by two triplets (ROOT,A,*) and
(*,B,C). By this additional table, a projection to the first element is
simulated by allowing variables to appear as table names and attribute names
as follows:

    Y(TUPLE_ID,a)={(b,c)|(b,c)∈ X(TUPLE_ID,a),
                    (ROOT,b)∈ X'(PARENT,FIRST),
                    (b,a)∈ X"(PARENT,CHILD)}.

X' is a relation associated to the relation X which describes the column
structure and X" is a transitive closure of the relation X' eliminating the
distinction between the first element and the second element. This
simulation of the original Cartesian product is not possible in case of QBE,
because it does not have the capability to manipulate through tables and
attributes.

Aggregation and Generalization
Aggregation and generalization are introduced by Smith [18] to capture more
meanings. An example of aggregation is that an employee data consists of
emp.ID, name, age, and employee-type. An example of generalization is that
a vehicle is classified into an air vehicle, a land vehicle and a water
vehicle. This information are represented by relationships between the
relation names, and stored in a binary relation. Codd classified the
aggregation and generalization and introduced more semantics [19]. These
data are also represented by relationships among relations. Because these
relationships do not depend on the occurrences, this is the easiest case of
the relationships in PICCOLO. For example, Cartesian aggregation is
supported by the Cartesian product which was already explained above.

Dynamic Operation
An update operation which stores the result in a temporary storage and does
not rescan the result while executing the operation is called static update.
In contrast to this update operation, an update operation which rescans the
result repeatedly until no more change occurs is called dynamic update. A

dynamic update is more powerful than the static one, because the dynamic update allows a query to be processed iteratively. If it is needed to show which operation is considered, we label the operation that is executed statically or dynamically with a suffix "static" or "dynamic", respectively. Although the dynamic update enables us to calculate larger class of operations, it is difficult to execute the operations as in parallel as the aforementioned generic tuple approach. For example the Fibonacci number calculated by a dynamic update as shown below cannot be carried out in parallel for a set of numbers, because the table which defines the operation itself is used to hold the temporary values.

$$N=N\cup\{(i+j,k)|(i,k-1)\in N,(j,k-2)\in N,k\leq n\}_{dynamic}.$$

where initially $N=\{(1,0),(1,1)\}$.

The L operator of QBE can be applied only to a tree structured relation and an arbitrarily iterating operation as above cannot be described. A generic representation can simulate a dynamic execution by executing the same operation recursively until no more change occurs.

Non Atomic Value

A set whose element is a set is not supported by RA and QBE, because an element of a domain is limited to a simple (atomic which is not decomposable) value. In PICCOLO, a relation name is allowed for a value, so a non atomic value can be represented and the operations on it can be simulated. For an example to simulate non atomic values, we explain an operation to generate a power set 2^A from a given set A.

$$2^A=\{(y),(y+COUNT(A))|(COUNT(A)\neq 0\rightarrow x=max(A)\wedge y\in 2^{(A-\{x\})}\wedge$$
$$CREATE\_RELATION(y+2^{COUNT(A)},y\cup\{x\})\vee$$
$$(COUNT(A)=0\rightarrow y=0\wedge CREATE\_RELATION(0,\{\}))\}.$$

Here a natural number is employed as a relation name so that new relation name are generated mechanically.

User Interface

A user interface is an important part of a real system. User interfaces of existing systems are not flexible and the display format cannot be changed. For example, QBE has a fixed table format which cannot be modified. From Requirement.6, it is required that a system for a picture database has the capability to control a display form. To allow a procedure call of the graphic system to be described in PICCOLO, prepare special tables with the names of procedure names such that whose attributes are used to stand for the parameter names of the corresponding procedures. For example, a flat weave having a 256×256 mesh in the previous example can be displayed by updating color values in the table "PLOT" as:

$$PLOT(X\_POSITION,Y\_POSITION,COLOR\_CODE)=\{(x,y,v)|$$
$$0\leq x<256,0\leq y<256,v=(x+y)\bmod 2\}.$$

By this operation, a flat 256×256 weave appears on the screen.

View Control

A view control which allows multiple users to perceive the same, shared data in different ways is important in a database environment. For a picture database case, the view control is important not only for multiple users but also for a single user. This is because a picture has many structures and hence one user may need to handle multiple structures simultaneously. In PICCOLO, the view control is accommodated by a generic representation by defining another table as a virtual table which can be shared among users.

By this definition, insertion or deletion operations to several tables are represented simply as one insertion of a tuple into a generic table. For example, if the original table P is a two dimensional array of pixels in the 256×256 resolution and you are manipulating a virtual table P' which is also a two dimensional 128×128 array of pixels. Here, we assume that 2×2 pixels in P correspond to the 1×1 pixel in P'. Then, by defining the table P' as shown below, retrieval operations to the table P' can be simulated as if it were existing actually.

P'(ID,GRAY_LEVEL,COND)={(n,v,((n1,v1),(n1+1,v2),(n1+256,v3),
   (n1+257,v4) $\in$ P(ID,GRAY_LEVEL) $\wedge$
   n1=(n div 128)*2*256+(n mod 128)*2 $\wedge$ v=(v1+v2+v3+v4) div 4)}.

Zoom-in and Zoom-out

Zoom-in and zoom-out are operations which control the display detail. Here, a "STRUCTURE" table stores a hierarchical structure of pixels and a "COLOR" table associates pixel ids and their RGB values. A "DISP" table memorizes the currently displayed pixel ids, and a generic table "PLOT" is used to control the display. Then the zoom-in operation is performed by:

PLOT=PLOT $\cup$ {(n2 mod 256, n2 div 256, v)|
   (n1,n2) $\in$ STRUCTURE(PARENT,CHILD),
   (n2,v) $\in$ COLOR(ID,VALUE),(n1) $\in$ DISP}
DISP={(n2)|(n1) $\in$ DISP,(n1,n2) $\in$ STRUCTURE(PARENT,CHILD)}.

Graph Isomorphism

We call graphs $G_1 = (N_1, A_1, f_1)$, $G_2 = (N_2, A_2, f_2)$ are isomorphic if there are bijections g_N and g_A such that $g_N(N_1) = N_2$, $g_A(A_1) = A_2$ and $f_2 = (g_N \times g_N) \cdot f_1 \cdot g_A^{-1}$. The isomorphism of given two graphs is decided by a query form:

A={a|a $\in 2^{A_1 \times A_2}$,COUNT(a)=
   COUNT({(a$_1$)|(a$_1$,a$_2$) $\in$ a})=COUNT({(a$_2$)|(a$_1$,a$_2$) $\in$ a})=
   COUNT(A$_1$)=COUNT(A$_2$),
   N={(n$_1$,n$_2$),(n$_1$',n$_2$')|(n$_1$,n$_1$') $\in$ a$_1$,(n$_2$,n$_2$') $\in$ a$_2$,(a$_1$,a$_2$) $\in$ a},
   $\forall$n$_1 \in$ N$_1$(COUNT({(n$_2$)|(n$_1$,n$_2$) $\in$ N}) $\leq$ 1),
   $\forall$n$_2 \in$ N$_2$(COUNT({(n$_1$)|(n$_1$,n$_2$) $\in$ N}) $\leq$ 1),
   COUNT(N$_1$)=COUNT(N$_2$)}.

The given two graph is isomorphic if A $\neq \phi$.

LENGTH-L of QBPE

A length-L operation of QBPE by Fu [5] is executed if a line is represented by two end points coordinates in a relation.

L={ $(\sqrt{((x_1-x_2)^2+(y_1-y_2)^2)})$ |(n$_1$,x$_1$,y$_1$) $\in$ ROAD,(n$_2$,x$_2$,y$_2$) $\in$ ROAD}.

Remarks

In this section, we listed several operations which are frequently used in picture processing case. The relational algebra can not perform most of the operations listed in this section and so it is not adequate for the picture database computer. QBE can perform a few of them with the help of arithmetic operations and the L operator. PICCOLO can perform most of the operations with the help of arithmetic operations. QBE and PICCOLO differ in the following points.

(1) QBE does not allow variables to appear in attribute names and relation names, while PICCOLO allows them. Thus, operations such as the column nesting can be supported only by PICCOLO.

(2) QBE has only the L operator for a repeating mechanism, while PICCOLO allows a recursive definition of operations. Thus, the power set 2^A can be generated from the given set A by defining it recursively by PICCOLO.

7. Conclusion

A picture computer PICCOLO is designed in this paper. Because the approach is based on a requirement driven method, most of the advantages of the design are known a priori before the design has finished. The advantages and disadvantages of PICCOLO are summarized here.

Advantages of PICCOLO

(1) PICCOLO has a uniform structure which are applicable to most picture data processing cases. Hence only a small number of hardware designs are needed in PICCOLO. This makes PICCOLO suitable to the implementation by the VLSI which requires a fairly large volume of production for each design.

(2) PICCOLO treats a logical picture, a physical picture and also their correspondence within the same framework. Thus, once a physical picture is loaded into the system, all the manipulations to generate a logical picture through image analysis are processed by PICCOLO. The inverse manipulations to generate a physical picture for graphics display from the logical picture description can also be handled. Further complex manipulations can be processed through the correspondence between logical and physical pictures.

(3) PICCOLO possesses a capability to represent a generic tuple. This reduces the storage requirements significantly. Also, this mechanism is used to derive the features of logical and/or physical pictures through the picture database search. Recursive definitions of operations are allowed by the generic representation. This enables a user to describe a complex query.

(4) PICCOLO executes an operation concurrently utilizing a large number of the same type of hardware devices. This extremely accelerates picture processing and database operations.

Disadvantages of PICCOLO

(1) The architecture and design are not dedicated to a specific structure of picture data. Thus, it is possible that the efficiency which can be gained by employing a specific structure-dependent logic may be sacrificed in some applications.

(2) PICCOLO is not specifically oriented toward sequential operations such as a boundary following, and hence it may not be superior to conventional computer architecture/design in such limited applications.

However, in a multiple user case these sequential operations are executed in parallel. Thus the total throughput is better that the conventional mechanism even in processing the sequential operations.

The capability of PICCOLO is open because the <function> and <quantifier> actually implemented in the computer decide the capability of the computer. To simulate many picture data operations, arithmetic operations are required and also sufficient. This is because the PICCOLO framework allows an effective combination between the additional operations and the original operations by the generic mechanism.

References

1 T. L. Kunii, et. al.,
"An Interactive Fashion Design System INFADS,"
Proc. of Conference on Computer Graphics and Interactive Techniques, 1974.

2 T. L. Kunii, S. Weyl, and J. M. Tenenbaum,
"A Relational Data Base Schema for Describing Complex Picture with Color and Texture,"
Proc. of Second International Conference on Pattern Recognition, 1975.

3 E. Carlson and P. Manty,
Tech. Reports from IBM San Jose Research Laboratory.

4 S. K. Chang, J. Reuss, and B. H. McCormick,
"An Integrated Relational Database System for Pictures,"
Proc. of IEEE Workshop on Picture Data Description and Management, IEEE Computer Society, 1977, pp. 49-60.

5 N. S. Chang and K. S. Fu,
"Query-by-Pictorial-Example,"
Proc. COMPSAC 79, Chicago, November, 1979, pp. 325-330.

6 N. Alexandridis and A. Klinger,
"Picture Decomposition Tree Data-structures, and Identifying Directional Symmetries as Node Combinations,"
Computer Graphics and Image Processing, 8, 1978, pp. 43-77.

7 N. Ohbo, K. Shimizu, and T. L. Kunii,
"A Graph-theoretical approach to region detection,"
Proc. IEEE Computer Society's Third International Computer Software & Applications Conference, Chicago, Nov., 1979, pp. 751-756.

8 ANSI/X3/SPARC Study Group on Data Base Management Systems Interim Report, 75-02-08, FDT-Bulletin of the ACM SIGMOD, Vol. 7, No. 2, 1975.

9 "Directions in Computer Architecture",
IEEE Computer, Oct., 1980.

10 E. F. Codd,
"A Relational Model of Data for Large Shared Data Banks,"
Comm. ACM 13, 1970, pp. 377-387.

11 K. Yamaguchi, N. Ohbo, T. L. Kunii, H. Kitagawa, and M. Harada,
    "ELF: Extended relational model for Large, Flexible picture databases,"
    Proc. IEEE Workshop on Picture Data Description and Management,
    Asilmar, California, Aug., 1980, pp. 95-100.

12 E. F. Codd,
    "Relational Completeness of Data Base Sublanguages,"
    in Data Base Systems, ed. R. Rustin, 1972, Prentice-Hall, pp. 65-98.

13 M. M. Zloof,
    "Query by Example,"
    Proc. AFIPS, NCC, Vol. 44, 1975, pp. 431-438.

14 J. E. Hopcroft and J. D. Ullman,
    "Introduction to Automata Theory, Language, and Computations,"
    Addison-Wesley, 1979.

15 K. Jensen and N. Wirth,
    "PASCAL User Manual and Report,"
    second edition, Spring-Verlag, 1975.

16 P. B. Hansen,
    "Concurrent PASCAL,"
    IEEE Trans. Software Eng., SE-1, 1975, pp. 199-207.

17 D. E. Knuth,
    "The Art of Computer Programming, Fundamental Algorithms,"
    second edition, Vol. 1, Addison-Wesley, 1973.

18 J. M. Smith and C. P. Smith,
    "Database Abstraction: Aggregation and Generalization,"
    ACM Transaction on Database Systems, Vol. 2, No. 2, June 1977, pp.
    105-133.

19 E. F. Codd,
    "Extending the Database Relational Model to Capture More Meaning,"
    ACM Transaction on Database Systems, Vol. 4, No. 4, June 1979, pp.
    347-434.

Computer System Organization for Pictorial Data

A. Klinger
University of Los Angeles, Los Angeles, Cal., USA
and The Aerospace Corporation

Abstract

This paper concerns 1) recent extensions of computer capabilities
that relate to processing two-dimensional data, and 2) concepts
of how computer technology will be applied in the future to
images. The first section describes the nature of image data
and the main approaches that have been taken to handle it.
Image processing, computer graphics, and pattern recognition
methodologies all contribute substantially to the body of techniques available today. We discuss engineering approaches used
now and the potential directions for extending these approaches
to take advantage of new technologies and to meet real-world
needs. The newer systems discussed include 1) cellular processors, 2) conventional computers as "host" with a peripheral
array processor, and 3) "supercomputers" (fast, large machines
which employ pipelining and parallelism).

1. Introduction

Major changes in computer architecture and organization are taking
place due to the availability of lower cost processors. Highly
effective parallel processing systems are now commercially available while only a few years ago they were expensive and only
partially-implemented research tools. Little experience is
available in running existing image processing algorithms on
such devices and less experimentation has occurred than should
have, considering their potent capabilities, due to a combination
of high system cost and relatively low funding for research hardware acquisition.

This paper concerns 1) such recent extensions of computer
capabilities as they relate to processing two-dimensional data,
and 2) concepts of how computer technology will be applied in the
future to images. The first section describes the nature of
image data and the main approaches that have been taken to handle
it, along with the main engineering methods and systems used now.
The potential directions for extending these systems to take
advantage of new technologies and meet real-world needs is the
subject of the remainder of this paper.

The next section discusses image processing systems and
operations. Then we describe different computer architectures

24

for large-array data-handling. Cellular devices and the programming tasks that remain for them and other image handling systems are discussed next. Then we deal with the general state of technology related to image processing. We next discuss software: data structures and data bases; to handle imagery. Then we expand on this to describe image processing software. The last section is a summary and conclusion.

Several problems encountered in applications involving image data emphasize the distance between what has been done and what needs to be accomplished before computers can have the same kind of impact on image data that they have had already on numeric data.

2. Characteristic Approaches to Image Data

Several large bodies of literature discuss ways to compute aspects of images. The standard works in image processing, PRATT (1978), ROSENFELD and KAK (1976), present much of the extensive material in that field. The field emphasizes image coding, compression, enhancement, and restoration, so the orientation of this kind of computing on image data is to very narrow technical goals. Resultant images are entities to be viewed, not source datasets for computerized representations of the knowledge present there, and human participation is of the essence at later stages. By contrast, pattern recognition (see e.g. DUDA and HART (1973) deals with use of computing to decide either what is present in an image (scene analysis, image understanding) or to which, out of several classes, a pictorial record belongs. Unlike image processing (enhancement/bandwidth/compression/etc.), pattern recognition operations ideally concern evaluating specific attributes that can be used in decision-making, usually by machine.

3. Computer Hardware and Image Processing

Most image processing until recently was done on standard computers, although early proposals (UNGER (1958) and UNGER (1959)) and hardware development (McCORMICK (1963) and DUFF (1973) involved use of parallelism via cellular logic (see below). However, today's commercial image processing market is dominated by special digital image processing systems: Comtal, CLI, and DeAnza are three prominent manufacturers of such devices; see the references for addresses. COMTAL's VISION ONE/20 is a self-contained system with multipurpose processors; CLI's VICOM is a peripheral micro-processor-based system. The kind of capabilities these devices enable are exemplified by:
1. pseudocolor presentations that enrich human descrimination capability (e.g., from 16 gray shades to 256 different colors);
2. image rotation, axis translation, and sizing using memories that are part of the system; and
3. image warping (sometimes called rubber-sheet deformation). These systems have found customers within the defense, space, and defense research and development domains. Several other significant markets (national governments; states/provinces, counties, and other localities; mineral resource exploration firms) have been approached and have reacted with considerably more variable acceptance of these fairly costly high-technology products.

4. Data arrays and modern computer systems

Rapid changes in computer hardware have led to many different
kinds of systems to handle large data arrays. Special processors
that function in parallel implementing the same operations on all
the elements of an array are called "Single Instruction Multiple-
Data-Stream Machines" (SIMDS). Some processors rapidly and eco-
nomically implement Fourier transformations. However, accomplish-
ing general purpose computing functions on large data arrays
remains a difficult task. Several systems with Multiple-Instruc-
tion, Multiple Data Stream capability (MIMDS) are now available.
Unfortunately, several of these parallel processor systems with
general purpose capability (in contrast to Fourier transform processors) are known to be difficult to program and even harder to
debug. This is due to the fact that a single word of a program
actually consists of control bits for the different data streams.

At lower cost, but with somewhat less general capabilities,
are a class of systems which use a conventional computer and a
peripheral array (actually a vector) processor such as the 32-bit
Floating Point Systems AP-120B (or their FPS-164 64-bit data word
system and AP-190L high performance systems), the CSP Inc. 64-bit
MAP-6400, and many others. The most expensive new systems are
the "supercomputers" such as the CRAY-1, and CYBER 205. These
employ pipelining of data to achieve very high speeds. At a
much lower cost, peripheral array processors can rapidly perform
many large data set operations under the control of their conventional host computer. A comparison sheet made available by
CSPI shows how the performance/cost ratio varies between standard large computers, a popular super-minicomputer, two supercomputers (CRAY-1 and STAR 100**), and one peripheral array processor (MAP-6400). It is reproduced below as Figure 1.

64-Bit arithmetic performance/cost comparison

	Approx. Cost ($)	100 x 100 Matrix-Matrix Multiply (SEC)	Performance Cost (Operations/Sec/$)
Array Processors			
MAP-6400	89,000*	1.0	11.0
CRAY-1	7,500,000	0.015	9.0
STAR 100**	8,000,000	0.04	3.0
Large Main Frame			
CYBER 176	4,400,000	0.42	0.5
IBM 3033	3,070,000	1.1	0.3
IBM 370/168	4,200,000	1.8	0.13
UNIVAC 1100/80	3,500,000	5.0	0.05
Supermini			
VAX-11/780	200,000	12.0	0.4

* Price of host not included.
** STAR 100 is a predecessor of CYBER 205.

Figure 1. Performance-cost ratio for MAP peripheral, CRAY and
STAR supercomputers, and five other computers

Another computing power comparison involving Goodyear's
"Massively Parallel Processor" (MPP) was made by the MITRE
Corporation and published in a technical report (see last
reference). An adaptation of a table presented there (p.4-27)
and reproduced below as Figure 2, was presented by Dr. J. L.
Potter, Goodyear Aerospace, at the 1981 IEEE Computer Society
Workshop on Computer Architecture for Pattern Analysis and
Image Database Management. The MPP is a SIMD parallel archi-
tecture with 16,384 processing elements in a 128 x 128 array.
It is discussed in some detail by POTTER (1981), where repre-

COMPUTER Operation	MPP	CDC Cyber 203	CRAY-1
Cross Correlation	100%	23%	1%
Extraction of Maximum Value	100%	25%	83%
Multispectral Classification	100%	4%	4%
Nearest Neighbor Binary Rotation	100%	22%	2%
Image Resampling	100%	11%	55%
Average	100%	17%	29%

Figure 2 Computing power comparison for MPP, CDC Cyber 203, and
CRAY-1 on a 512 x 512 8-bit image

Estimated execution speeds* for basic imagery algorithms

ITEM	SPEED (faster than real time)
Convolution (3 x 3)	6.21
Convolution (7 x 7)	1.14
Template matching (7 x 7)	142.66
Pseudo-median filter (3 x 3)	74.47
Histogram computation	0.01
Gray-scale thresholding	569.88
Region growing	39.72
Two-dimension cross correlation (13x13)	163.46
Target position determination	10485.76
Gray-scale averaging (32 x 32)	1.6384

*Assuming data rates of 100 Mbits/second

Algorithm time estimates for continuous image processing

ITEM	TIME (microseconds)
Median filter	282 per frame
Histogram	205,712 per frame
Threshold	37 per frame
Region growing	528 per frame
Coordinate search	230 per frame
Two-dimensional cross correlation	128 per target

Figure 3 Image processing algorithm timing estimates on the MPP

sentative algorithms for infrared, radar, and optical imagery, and MPP image processing execution speeds are analyzed, also for a 512 x 512 8-bit image. The image is assumed resident in fast memory (short-term image store). It is also assumed that the image will be output from there. Similar analysis was done for continuous processing (sequences of images) where 13.78 milliseconds are needed per frame. Both sets of results are summarized in Figure 3, which is adapted from POTTER (1981).

Finally, two MIMD systems, the Heterogeneous Element Processor (HEP) multiprocessing system developed by Denelcor, Inc. of Denver, Colorado for the Army Ballistic Research Laboratories and an S-1 multiprocessor supercomputer using Mark IIA SIMD scientific computers under development at the Lawrence Livermore National Laboratory, would be excellent choices for experiments in image processing. LEVINE (1982) reviews supercomputer developments in detail and indicates how pipelining of picture computations can take advantage of the properties of these multiprocessors.

5. Cellular logic

Another kind of parallel computing that is made more cost effective by recent technology changes is cellular logic (also called neighborhood processing). Cellular logic machines (CLMs) are discussed in PRESTON, et al (1979). Two are the Perkin-Elmer Diff 3 (successor to GLOPR), which has been a commercial success for blood cell-counting, and Environmental Research Institute of Michigan's cytocomputer: see STERNBERG (1981). Both possess significant speed advantages for handling large arrays of data.

Although cellular devices have been around for a long time, little detailed documentation is available describing the ways to implement (or "program") common image operations: line-finding, corner-detection, medial-axis transformation, object detection, etc.; with such systems. This impinges on the general subject of algorithm development and programming of such machines, something that is also the main area of uncertainty for all machines to handle pictorial data.

6. State of the technology

LEVINE (1980) gave the following assessment of the overall situation:
Advances in integrated circuit technology have made it possible to perform cellular logic in parallel at speeds which considerably accelerate low level image processing computations ... (and) to develop special-purpose feature extraction processors. The integration ... with conventional sequential computers, or ... with new architectures ... point to ... development of image processing computers of considerable power. Maybe it is time... to pull out of the desk drawer those totally impractical and time-consuming algorithms we have stored away and prepare for the new age.

However, several factors contrast with this positive position:
1. use of many inexpensive devices to create parallel processor systems leads to higher programming costs;
2. programming costs are increased in many systems, whether parallel, supercomputer, or peripheral array processor, due to the need to create microcode to make the system perform to full capability levels;
3. algorithms to perform image processing functions on cellular logic machines are not well described (although methods to perform several elementary image processing operations by memory-augmented cellular automata are presented in DYER and ROSENFELD (1981).)

7. Data structures and data bases

New research approaches with standard computers have used data structuring to achieve some aspects of the parallelism built into the cellular logic and array processing systems. As an example, practical methods for converting row-by-row image data into a parallel hierarchical structure emphasizing area-blocks of data have been described in detail: see KLINGER/RHODES (1979) and SAMET (1981). Methods for feature extraction on such data are also available: see ICHIKAWA (1981).

The goal of computing on images should be their use as data-sets. A realistic view of this is difficult unless the overall approach includes awareness of specific uses of image data arrays· e.g., satellite imagery; radar, sonar, and other sensor data; and radiologic imagery. In general, such uses still rely heavily on human interpretation or man-machine interaction, and make little use of individual images as components in an image data-base. That progress has been slow in that regard is apparent. NAGY and ZOBRIST (1980) discuss this:
Progress in the application of satellite and aircraft image processing algorithms to natural resource management has been slower than expected. We suspect... due to system and data-format incompatibility, the broad range of expertise required, and the sheer size of the image arrays acquired through remote sensing in relation to the available computational resources.

8. Software and functions

A Grinnel Systems image processor and display is in use with program modules developed by the Medical Imaging Science Group, University of Southern California, to provide an alternative software-based method of obtaining some useful interactive image analysis user services. Some such services, now hardwired functions in more costly commercial computer image processing systems, are:
1. Pseudocolor display
2. Zooming capability
3. Roaming capability
4. Combining images (differencing, multispectral displays)
5. Ratioing images
6. Enhancement of detail

The software system VICAR and its database extensions IBIS
(Image Based Information System) at the Caltech Jet Propulsion
Laboratory provide many other user services. In hardware systems
the Data General Eclipse AP/130 is a computer that incorporates
an array processor within an ordinary (von Neumann architecture)
machine. This yields a smaller and slower machine than those
available from Floating Point Systems and CSP, Inc., but also
provides many functions for a lower-cost, in a system suitable
for a small laboratory.

9. Summary and conclusion

In the realm of hardware we have described changes in computer
capabilities that effectively make parallel computing more
widely available and at lower costs. The implications of this
for designers concerned with computing on image data (including
data arrays from radar, sonar, and infrared sources) is a great
increase in processing speed and hence in data throughput.
Potentially, this evolutionary development could lead to interactive processing of image data, using a wide variety of software tools. These would be based on both the existing approaches
to computing on image data, and on new procedures that emphasize
user needs, for instance stereo views composed from two images
(this is data needed by surgeons and potentially available from
radiologic data as in computer tomography). In the realm of
software, many groups initially developed picture processing
techniques, while new data management systems suited to obtaining
information from pictorial data are now available at varying
stages of completeness in several university research groups.
Substantial improvements in software, particularly that for
accessing many distinct pictorial records, is needed and this
can occur only after widespread availability of parallel (vector,
array, cellular logic) computing systems to groups dealing with
image data.

References

Preston, K., et al (1979) "Basics of Cellular Logic with Some
Applications in Medical Image Processing" Proc. of the IEEE
Volume 67, May 1979, pp 826-856.

Levine, M.D. (1980) "Editorial Comments" International Association for Pattern Recognition, Volume 3, No. 1, May 1980.

Guzman, A. (1980) "Reconfigurable Data Bases" Pattern Recognition
in Practice, ed. by Gelsema, E. S. and Kanal, L. N., North-
Holland Publishing Co., 1980, pp 99-111.
Briggs, F. A., Fu, K. S. et al (1979) "PM[4]: A reconfigurable
Multiprocessor System for Pattern Recognition and Image Process-
ing, "TR-EE-79-11 Purdue University, 1979.

Duda, R. O. and Hart, P. E. (1971) Pattern Classification and
Scene Analysis, Wiley.

Rosenfeld, A. and Kak, A. C. (1971) Digital Image Processing,
Academic Press.

Pratt, W. K. (1978) Digital Image Processing, Wiley.

Alexander, P. (1978) "Array Processors in Image Analysis Applications," New Concepts Symposium on Detection and Identification of Explosives.

Klinger, A. and Rhodes, M. L. (1979) "Organization and Access of Image Data by Areas," IEEE Trans. Pattern Analysis Machine Intelligence, Vol. PAMI-1, pp 50-60, January 1979.

Samet, H. (1981) "An Algorithm for Converting Rasters to Quadtrees," IEEE Trans. Pattern Analysis Machine Intelligence, Vol. PAMI-3, pp 93-95, January 1981.

Dyer, C. R. and Rosenfeld, A. (1981) "Parallel Image Processing by Memory-Augmented Cellular Automata," IEEE Trans. Pattern Analysis Machine Intelligence,Vol. PAMI-3, pp 29-41, January 1981.

Unger, S. H. (1958) "A computer oriented toward spatial problems," Proc. IRE Vol. 46, (1959) 1744-1750.

Unger, S. H. (1959) "Pattern detection and recognition," ibid. vol. 47, 1959, 1737-1752.

McCormick,B. H. (1963) "The Illinois pattern recognition computer - ILLIAC III," IEEE Trans. EC-12, 1963, 791-813.

Duff, M. J. B. (1973) A cellular logic array for image processing, Pattern Recognition 5, 1973, 229-247.

Batcher, K. E., Design of a massively parallel processor, IEEE Trans. C-28, 1980, 836-840.

Nagy, G. and Zobrist, A. L. (1980) "Platitudes on Image Data and Geographic Information Processing," Proc. Workshop on Picture Data Description and Management, IEEE 80 CH 1530-5, 1980.

Sternberg, S. R. (1981) "Parallel Architectures for Image Processing" in Real-Time/Parallel Computing Image Analysis, ed. by Onoe, M., Preston, K., and Rosenfeld, A., Plenum, 1981.

Alexandridis, N. and Klinger, A., "Picture Decomposition, Tree Data Structures, and Identifying Directional Symmetries as Node Combinations," Computer Graphics and Image Processing I, 1978, 43-77.

Klinger, A., "Searching Images for Structure," Structured Computer Vision, Tanimoto, S. and Klinger, A. (eds.) Academic Press, New York, 1980, 151-168.

Chock, M., Cardenas, A. F., and Klinger, A., "Manipulating Data Structures in Pictorial Information Systems," IEEE Computer, November 1981.

1981 IEEE Computer Society Workshop on Computer Architecture for Pattern Analysis and Image Database Management, IEEE Catalog No. 81CH1697-2, Library of Congress No. 81-82808, IEEE Computer Society Catalog No. 378.

Potter, J. L., "Continuous Image Processing on the MPP," 1981 IEEE Computer Society Workshop on Computer Architecture for Pattern Analysis and Image Database Management, IEEE Catalog No. 81CH1697-2, Library of Congress No. 81-82808, IEEE Computer Society Catalog No. 378.

MITRE TECHNICAL REPORT MTR 79 W0030S, The Mitre Corporation, Bedford, Massachusetts, 1979.

Levine, R. D. "Supercomputers," Scientific American, vol. 246 (1982), 118-135.

COMTAL/3M, 505 W. Woodbury Road, Altadena, California 91101, (213) 797-1175 TWX 910-588-3256.

CLI Compression Labs, Incorporated, 10440 N. Tantau Ave., Cupertino, California 95014, (408) 725-0206.

DeAnza, 118 Charcot Avenue, San Jose, California 95131, (408) 263-7155.

A Methodology for Picture Indexing and Encoding

Shi-Kuo Chang

Information Systems Research Laboratory, University of Illinois
at Chicago Circle, Chicago, Ill., USA

1. Introduction

Researchers in image processing and pattern recognition have traditionally regarded pictures as two-dimensional array of pixels. Recently, researchers working on pictorial information systems have
developed the concept of logical pictures, which consist of picture
objects and picture relations. The concept of relational database has
also been used in developing pictorial database models, although there
seems to be a need to extend the relational database concept for pictorial database management. On the other hand, for many image processing problems, a hierarchical data structure seems to be the most
natural.

In traditional database systems, the use of indexing to facilitate
database accessing has been well established. Although there has been
suggestions to use picture icons as picture indices, no concrete
framework has been established for picture indexing.

The distinction of different ways of representing pictures, the various approaches for pictorial database representation, the absence of
picture indexing techniques, etc., all these problems are due to the
lack of a unified conceptual framework for picture abstraction, indexing, encoding and retrieval. In this paper, we present a methodology
for picture indexing and encoding.

The paper is divided into two parts. Part I deals with picture indexing and abstraction, and Part II deals with picture encoding. In Part
I, the concepts of picture objects, relational objects and picture
query are introduced. Examples are presented to motivate the concept
of picture indexing. Two types of abstraction operations are introduced. Type-1 abstraction performs clustering and indexing. Type-2
abstraction performs classification and cross-indexing. Conceptually,
type-1 abstraction performs generalization and integration, and type-2
abstraction performs differentiation. They can be recursively applied
to obtain various picture indices.

In Part II, we present a methodology for picture encoding. We first
discuss hypercube encoding, minimal hypercube encoding, generalized
hypercube encoding, arbitrary hypercube encoding, and the picture covering problem. The hypercube encoding technique generalizes tightly-
closed-boundary encoding and picture paging techniques. The hierarchical hypercube encoding technique is introduced. We then discuss how

micro-pictures can be associated with a hierarchical hypercube encoding. The micro-picture consists of logical picture objects, relational objects, and physical pictures. We then describe a methodology for structured picture retrieval. It is illustrated that both generalized zooming and staging techniques can be regarded as special cases of structured picture retrieval.

PART I: Picture Indexing

We first direct our attention to logical pictures, which consist of picture objects and relational objects. In Section 2, we introduce the concepts of picture objects and relational objects. In Section 3, we present picture queries, which can be used to retrieve picture objects form a logical picture. The query examples motivate the concept of picture indexing. In Section 4, we present two abstraction rules to perform abstraction operations and construct picture indices.

2. The Logical Picture

We begin by presenting examples of picture objects. A _picture object_ vi is typically represented by vi((type,tvalue), (name,nvalue), (x1,xi1), (x2,xi2),..., (xn,xin), (a1,ai1), (a2,ai2), ..., (ak,aik)), where type is the classification category of the object, name is its unique idenfitier, x1, x2,..., xn are the spatial coordinates of the object, and a1, a2, ..., ak are other attributes (e.g., resolution, average gray level, size, orientation, etc). A _picture object set_ V = {v1 v2, ..., vn}, is a set of picture objects having the same type. As an example, if the picture objects vi are pixels, then vi = ((type,pixel), (x,xi), (y,yi), (c,f(xi,yi)), where c is pixel value at point (x,y). If the picture objects vi denote average gray level over a local window area, then vi = ((type,pixel), (x,xi), (y,yi), (r,ri), (c,ci)), where r is the size of the local window (the resolution), and c is average pixel value for local area inside the window.

We can now present a general definition of picture object and picture object set. A picture object consists of a set of attribute triples: (attribute-name, attribute-value, procedure-name).

When a picture object is referenced, each attribute must be evaluated. The evaluation procedure is as follows.

(1) If attribute-value is unspecified, the procedure "procedure-name" is invoked to evaluate it.
(2) If attribute-value is specified, the procedure "procedure-name" is invoked to interpret it.

The default is not to include a procedure-name. In which case, if the attribute-value is unspecified, it cannot be evaluated.

An attribute is _real_, if in all picture objects where it occurs, its attribute-values are always specified. Otherwise it is _virtual_. A picture object is real, if all its attributes are real. Otherwise it is virtual.

A picture object usually has a _type_, which is the classification category of that object, a _name_, which is the specific and unique name of that object, a _pp_, which is the physical picture for that object, and other attributes. A picture object must have type and name attributes, but other attributes are optional. For example, v = ((type,river), (name,Kwei), (pp,*,access-routine)), refers to a picture object of type "river" whose name is "Kwei". The asterisk in the picture attribute is a pointer, and the physical picture can be accessed by invoking the access-routine.

The name of a picture object is unique among all picture objects with the same type. It can be used as an identifier to identify an object. The name attribute can be declared as a virtual attribute composed from other attributes. For example, to define a pixel object, we have w = ((type,pixel), (name=(x,y)), (x,10), (y,2), (c,5)), and the name attribute is really the combination of the x and y coordinates of the pixel. It is therefore a virtual attribute.

A picture object set is a set of picture objects having the same type. Therefore a picture object set always has a unique type.

A relational object also consists of a set of attribute triples: (attribute-name, attribute-value, procedure-name). Again, an attribute can be evaluated if its value is unspecified, and interpreted if its value is specified.

A relational object has a _type_, which specifies this relation, a _degree_, which is the number of picture objects entering this relationship, a _name_, which is unique for this relation, and other attributes. The relational object's name may also be a virtual attribute defined in terms of other attributes. Usually the name is specified by a list of (type,name) pairs for picture objects (or type of picture object sets) entering that relationship.

As an example of a relational object, we have r = ((type,over), (degree,2), (name=(type1,name1,type2,name2)), (type1,bridge), (name1,b1), (type2,river), (name2,Kwei)), where name is a virtual attribute defined as (type1,name1, type2,name2). If there is no confusion about types, we may define a relational object's name as (name1, name2). On the other hand, if we are referring to relations among picture object sets, we can define a relational object's name as (type1,type2).

A relational object set is a set of relational objects having the same type. For example, several relational objects having the same type "over" can be grouped into a relational object set "over".

A _logical picture_ consists of a collection of picture objects V, and a collection of relational objects R. In addition to logical pictures, a pictorial database may also store _physical pictures_, which will be discussed in Part II.

3. Picture Query

We can now discuss the retrieval of picture objects from logical pictures. First, we present the concept of picture query set and picture query.

A picture query set QS is a subset of a collection of picture objects V. In other words, QS is the set of picture objects to be retrieved. In the picture query language, the query set QS is usually specified by a picture query Q.

A picture predicate Q is a logical function from V to {0, 1}. Q induces a partition of V into two subsets, QS = { vi: Q(vi)=1}, and QN = { vi: Q(vi)=0}. A picture query Q uses a picture predicate to specify QS, its corresponding picture query set.

In the GRAIN system [CHANG79a], the picture predicate of a picture query is specified as a conjunction of logical clauses relating attributes and their values. The retrieval target is specified in the "get" clause, "sketch" clause, or "paint" clause. Several examples are presented below.

Query 1: The bridge over the river Kwei.

GRAIN1: get w1; w1 is "bridge"; w1 over w2; w2 is "river"; w2.name is "Kwei".

In the above query, (w1 is "bridge") is a short-hand notation for (w1.type is "bridge"). (w1 over w2) is a short-hand notation for (r.type is "over"; r.degree is 2; r.name1 is w1.name; r.name2 is w2.name). Therefore, the above query in set-theoretic notation is:

$$Q1 = \{w1: (w1.type=bridge) \land (r.type=over) \land (r.degree=2) \land (r.name1=w1.name) \land (r.name2=w2.name) \land (w2.type=river) \land (w2.name=Kwei)\}.$$

If we allow for the substitution of picture object variables by their types, the above query in GRAIN notation is:

GRAIN2: get bridge; bridge over river; river.name is "Kwei".

The database contains the following picture objects and relational objects:

```
v1((type,bridge),(name,b1),(x,10),(y,13))
v2((type,bridge),(name,b2),(x,20),(y,14))
v3((type,river),(name,Kwei),(pp,*))
v4((type,river),(name,MeiKong),(pp,*))
r1((type,over),(degree,2),(name1,b1),(name2,Kwei))
r2((type,over),(degree,2),(name1,b2),(name2,Meikong))
```

In r1 and r2, we have omitted the definition of virtual attribute name as (name1,name2).

Query 2: Little house on the prairie.

GRAIN1: sketch w1; w1 is "house"; w1.size is "little"; w1 on w2; w2 is "prairie".

or

GRAIN2: sketch house; house.size is "little"; house on prairie.

Query 3: Zoom into picture at resolution factor 2, and clip using window (0,5; 0,5).

GRAIN1: paint w1; w1 is "pixel"; w1.r is 2; $0 \leq$ w.x ≤ 5; $0 \leq$ w.y ≤ 5.

or

GRAIN2: paint pixel; pixel.r is 2; $0 \leq$ pixel.x ≤ 5; $0 \leq$ pixel.y ≤ 5.

Query 4: Display the country in Europe having cities with population over 100,000.

GRAIN1: sketch w1; w1 is "country"; w1 in w2; w2.name is "Europe"; w1 contain w3; w3 is "city"; w3.population $\geq$ 100000.

or

GRAIN2: sketch country; country in w2; w2.name is "Europe"; country contain city; city.population $\geq$ 100000.

The database contains the following picture objects and relational objects:

Node H1:

v1((type,node),(name,H1),(x1,1),(y1,1),(x2,1000),(y2,1000),(pp,*))
v2((type,continent),(name,Europe),(pp,*))
r1((type,contain),(degree,2),(name1,H1),(name2,H2))
r2((type,contain),(degree,2),(name1,H2),(name2,Europe))

Node H2:

v3((type,node),(name,H2),(x1,1),(y1,1),(x2,500),(y2,500),(pp,*))
v4((type,country),(name,France),(pp,*))
v5((type,country),(name,Germany),(pp,*))
r3((type,contain),(degree,2),(name1,H2),(name2,H3))
r4((type,contain),(degree,2),(name1,H2),(name2,H4))
r5((type,contain),(degree,2),(name1,H3),(name2,France))
r6((type,contain),(degree,2),(name1,H4),(name2,Germany))
r7((type,contain),(degree,2),(name1,Europe),(name2,France))
r8((type,contain),(degree,2),(name1,Europe),(name2,Germany))

Node H3:

v6((type,node),(name,H3),(x1,50),(y1,50),(x2,150),(y2,50),(pp,*))
v7((type,city),(name,Paris),(population,1000000),(pp,*))
r9((type,contain),(degree,2),(name1,H3),(name2,Paris))
r10((type,contain),(degree,2),(name1,France),(name2,Paris))

Node H4:

```
v8((type,node),(name,H4),(x1,140),(y1,50),(x2,200),(y2,50),(pp,*))
v9((type,city),(name,Bonn),(population,800000),(pp,*))
r11((type,contain),(degree,2),(name1,H4),(name2,Bonn))
r12((type,contain),(degree,2),(name1,Germany),(name2,Bonn))
```

In the above, the database consists of four collections of picture objects and relational objects, each being associated with a node in a picture tree PT. The concept of picture trees will be discussed in Part II. Intuitively, we can visualize a picture tree as a hierarchical tree structure with pictorial information (picture objects and relational objects) associated with each node in the tree.

Given a picture query Q, the pictorial information retrieval problem then is to find QS, the picture query set, by searching the picture tree PT. To facilitate searching, we can conceptually transform a picture tree into a picture query tree as follows. Suppose Hi is a node in a picture tree. Let Vi be the collection of picture objects which can be retrieved from Hi, PSi the collection of picture objects which can be retrieved from the subtree with root node Hi, and Pi the picture predicate corresponding to PSi. A picture query tree (QT) is a tree having the same structure as the picture tree. Each node Hk of the query tree is of the following form:

$$Hk(mk, Pk1, Pk2, \ldots, Pk(mk))$$

where mk is the number of successor nodes of Hk, and Pki is the picture predicate corresponding to PSki for successor node Hki. If mk = 0, then Hk does not have any successor node. It can be seen that PS1, the collection of picture objects retrievable from the tree with root node H1, is the union of the Vi's. In other words, PS1 = V.

Intuitively, the picture predicates Pki in the picture query tree can be used to identify subtrees of interest. An example is illustrated in Figure 1. Figure 1(a) shows the picture tree. The collection of picture objects is $V = \{vi((type,pixel), (x,xi), (y,yi), (c,f(xi,yi))): 1 \le xi \le 4, 1 \le yi \le 4\}$. The Vi's and PSi's are:

```
PS1 = V
V1 = ∅
PS2 = V2 = {v13, v14, v23, v24}
PS3 = {v11, v12, v21, v22}
V3 = ∅
PS4 = V4 = {v31, v32, v41, v42}
PS5 = V5 = {v33, v34, v43, v44}
PS6 = V6 = {v12}
PS7 = V7 = {v11}
PS8 = V8 = {v22}
PS9 = V9 = {v21}
```

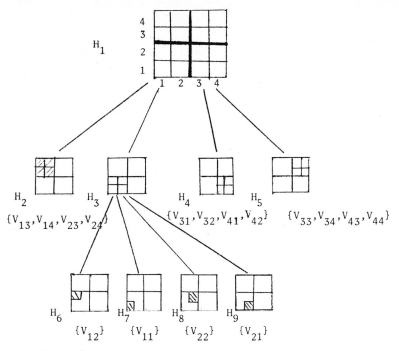

a) Picture Tree

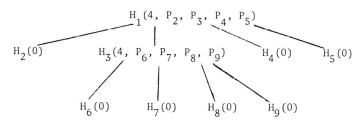

b) Query Tree

Figure 1. An Example Picture Tree a) and Query Tree b)

The picture query tree is illustrated in Figure 1(b), and the picture predicates are:

$P2 = (1 \le x \le 2 \,\wedge\, 3 \le y \le 4)$
$P3 = (1 \le x \le 2 \,\wedge\, 1 \le y \le 2)$
$P4 = (3 \le x \le 4 \,\wedge\, 1 \le y \le 2)$
$P5 = (3 \le x \le 4 \,\wedge\, 3 \le y \le 4)$
$P6 = (x=1 \,\wedge\, y=2)$
$P7 = (x=1 \,\wedge\, y=2)$
$P8 = (x=2 \,\wedge\, y=2)$
$P9 = (x=2 \,\wedge\, y=1)$

To process a query Q, the picture query tree is searched recursively. Initially, the <u>target set</u> TS is empty, and the root node is retrieved. For a node Hk, if mk > 0, then any successor node Hki with nonempty intersection of Pki and Q will be searched. Each time a node Hi is searched, TS is set to the union of previous TS and Vi. Finally, QS = Q(TS) = {v: v is in TS and Q(v)=1}.

In the above example, if the query is Q = (x ≤ 1), then only nodes H1, H2, H3, H6, and H7 need be searched. TS = {v11, v12, v13, v14, v23, v24}, and QS = {v11, v12, v13, v14}.

The above example suggests the concept of a <u>picture index</u>. In Webster's Third New International Dictionary (1971 Edition), "index" has the following definitions (among others): (1) A usually alphabetical list that includes all or nearly all items considered of special pertinence and fully or partially covered or merely mentioned in a printed or written work, that gives with each item the place where it may be found in the work; (2) Something that serves as a pointer or indicator; (3) Something in another (person or) thing that leads an observer to surmise a particular fact or draw a particular conclusion; (4) A sign whose specific character is causally dependent on the object to which it refers but independent of an interpretant. The usual concept of an index in computer science is a combination of Webster's definitions (1) and (2). If we also consider Webster's definitions (3) and (4), we can see that the picture predicates associated with a node in the picture query tree can be considered as a <u>picture index</u>, because they can be used to surmise a fact or draw a conclusion about a picture, and is at the same time dependent of the picture, but independent of any interpretations. In other words, the picture index is used to help <u>focus</u> the search process to relevant subtrees. In a picture tree, at every node we can construct a picture index based upon information contained in the subtree. The result is the picture query tree discussed above. More general abstraction operations to construct picture index is described in the following section.

4. Picture Indexing and Abstraction

Indexing is closely related to abstraction, which can be defined as the process of constructing new concepts from a given collection of concepts. In the context of this paper, we are interested in constructing new objects from a given collection of objects. The constructed abstract objects can be subject to another level of abstraction operation.

Suppose we have picture objects vi(a1,...,an, xi(n+1),..., xim), where the aj are identical for all the objects, and xij's are different. We can perform an abstraction operation, called <u>type-1 abstraction</u>, to create an <u>abstracted picture object set</u> Vln = {v1, ..., vn}, where (a1,...,an) is regarded as the common type of these objects. An <u>index object</u> vln(a1,..,an, b1,...,bm) can also be created, where a1,...,an is the name of this index object (which is also the type of the abstracted object set Vln), and b1,..., bm are other attributes extracted from v1,...,vn. This index object is a unary relation, with its name corresponding the the abstracted object set Vln. Originally the objects vi may be associated with a cretain node Hi. After the type-1 abstraction operation, we can decide where to put the index object vln, and the abstracted object set Vln. For example, we can associate the object set Vln with the original node Hi, and the index object vln with Hj, the predecessor node of Hi. The index object vln at Hj can thus be used to point to the object set Vln at Hi. When we write the index object as vln(al,...,an, bl,...,bm), the extracted attributes bl,...,bm could be interpreted as a logical predicate to characterize the set Vln.

Therefore, it can be seen that indexing and abstraction are closely related. In the above, we have assumed that objects vl,...,vn share common attributes al,...,an, which become their common type. If vl, ..., vn do not share common attributes, they may be given a new common label by extending the objects' attributes by a common labelling attribute. In fact, this is the objective of clustering analysis. Therefore, we can describe the Type-1 abstraction operation as follows.

TYPE-1 ABSTRACTION:

STEP 1: (Clustering) A set of picture objects are given a common label. This can be accomplished by either (a) identifying common attributes with identical values, or (b) extending the objects' attributes by a common labelling attribute.

STEP 2: (Decomposition) The picture objects having the same label are clustered together to form a new picture object set, with the common label as its type.

STEP 3: (Indexing) A new relational object, called the index object, is created, which contains (a) a name which is the type of the picture object set created in STEP 2, and (b) other attributes extracted from the attributes of the picture objects in the same picture object set.

The abstraction operation can be applied recursively, so that the index objects can again be clustered, decomposed, and indexed. An example of iterative abstraction is illustrated in Figure 2.

In Figure 2, we start with a collection of objects vl,...,vl2. They are clustered into four groups, and each group's objects are given a new common label gl, g2, g3, and g4, respectively. The index objects are vl3(gl,1,3), vl4(g2,4,6), vl5(g3,7,9) and vl6(g4,10,12). For example, in vl3(gl,1,3), gl is a pointer to {vl,v2,v3}, and the new attributes can be interpreted as a logical predicate ($1 \leq K \wedge K \leq 3$), to denote that the range of K is between 1 and 3. This, of course, is precisely what an ISAM index is used for. Now the index objects vl3, vl4, vl5 and vl6 can be regarded as ordinary objects, and by performing another level of clustering operation, they can be grouped into object sets, and an additional level of index objects can be constructed. As illustrated in Figure 2, the final ISAM structure consists of the object sets tl, t2, t3, gl, g2, g3 and g4.

Aggregation [SMITHJ77] can be regarded as type-1 abstraction. In aggregation, we only retain the common attributes, and the particular

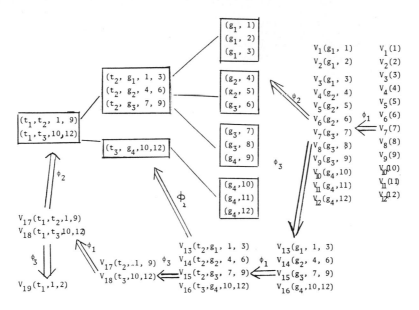

Figure 2. Type-1 abstraction example

attributes are omitted in the abstraction (in our case, the index object). However, Type-1 abstraction is more general than aggregation, because we allow for arbitrary extraction operation in Step 3 of Type-1 abstraction. Conceptually, Type-1 abstraction is applied to perform generalization and integration, although the (integrated) index object may retain the combined characteristics of the indexed object set.

In addition to type-1 abstraction, we have another abstraction operation, type-2 abstraction, where a picture object is labelled, and then decomposed into two or more picture objects.

TYPE-2 ABSTRACTION:

STEP 1: (Classification) A picture object is given a classification label. This label is added to the attribute list of that object.

STEP 2: (Decomposition) The picture object v(al,...,an, bl,...,bm, cl,...,ck) is decomposed into two objects vl(al,...,an, bl,...,bm) and v2(al,...,an, cl,...,ck). The attributes al,...,an contains at least the name of the original object v. The attributes bl,...,bm contains the new label as the type of object vl. The attributes cl,...,ck contains the old type as type of object v2.

STEP 3: (Cross-Indexing) The new objects vl and v2 are related by creating an index object, which is a relational object r12. The name of this relational object is the (type,name) pairs of vl and v2. The type of r12 is a newly created type code.

42

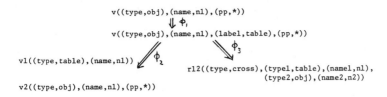

Figure 3. Type-2 abstraction example

An example of type-2 abstraction is illustrated in Figure 3. In Figure 3, an object v((type,obj), (name,nl), (pp,*)) is classified as "table". This object is then decomposed into two objects, vl((type,table), (name,nl)), and v2((type,obj), (pp,*)). The relational object for cross-indexing is rl2((type,cross), (name=(typel, namel, type2, name2)), (typel,table), (namel,nl), (type2,obj), (name2,n2)). It can be seen that icons [TANIM76] can be constructed by type-2 abstraction. Type-2 abstraction can also be applied before or after the application of type-1 abstraction. For example, we can first classify objects as tables. The logical table object and the physical table object can be separated using the decomposition rule in type-2 abstraction. The table objects can then be clustered into a table object set, using type-1 abstraction. An index can then be established to point to the table object set.

Type-1 abstraction is conceptually similar to qualified vertical decomposition, and type-2 abstraction is similar to horizontal decomposition, as discussed in [CHANG80]. Both abstraction operations can be followed by another step to realize the abstract objects as relational tables.

> STEP 4: (Realization) For each picture object set thus created, a relational table can be created, whose name is the same as the type of the picture object set and whose attributes are the same as that of the picture object set, less the type attribute.

PART II: Picture Encoding

We now turn our attention to physical pictures. A physical picture is usually given by a picture function, which is defined in Section 5. In Sections 6, we discuss minimal hypercube encoding, generalized hypercube encoding, arbitrary hypercube encoding, and the picture covering problem. The hypercube encoding technique generalizes tightly-closed-boundary encoding and picture paging techniques. In Section 7, the hierarchical hypercube encoding technique is introduced. We then discuss how micro-pictures can be associated with a hypercube encoding. The micro-picture consists of logical picture objects, relational objects, and physical pictures. The picture reconstruction problem can be regarded as the materialization of a support picture from a micro-picture. Section 8 presents the picture tree. We then describe a methodology for structured picture retrieval.

5. The Physical Picture

A 2-dimensional picture function f is a mapping, f: N x N -> {0, 1, ..., L-1}, where N represents the set of natural numbers {1,...,N}, and {0, 1, ..., L-1} is the pixel value set or gray level set. f(x,y) then represents the pixel value at (x,y) [ROSEN76].

Similarly, an n-dimensional picture function f is a mapping,

$$f: N^n \rightarrow \{0, 1, \ldots, L-1\}$$

and f(x1, x2, ..., xn) represents the pixel value at (x1,...,xn).

It is often convenient to extract from a picture those points with pixel value greater than or equal to a certain threshold. A picture point set or simply a point set extracted from a picture f with threshold t is defined by,

$$S(f,t) = \{(x,y): f(x,y) \geq t\}$$

where t is the given threshold. Similarly, for an n-dimensional picture f, the picture point set is defined by,

$$S(f,t) = \{(x1,x2,\ldots,xn): f(x1,\ldots,xn) \geq t\}$$

As an example, the picture function f is,

```
y │ 0  1  0
  │ 0  2  0
  │ 1  0  1
f └─────────
             x
```

and S(f,1) = {(1,1),(3,1),(2,2),(2,3)}. A picture f is often represented by its picture point set S(f,t) with an appropriate threshold.

Given a picture point set S, we are often interested in finding picture point sets Hi, so that their union contains the original S. The point sets Hi usually have some nice properties to facilitate encoding. One family of point sets useful for such encoding purposes is the family of n-dimensional hypercubes, defined as follows:

$$H(x1_a, x1_b ; x2_a, x2_b ; \ldots; xn_a, xn_b)$$

$$= \{(z1,\ldots,zn): xi_a \geq zi \geq xi_b , 1 \geq i \geq n\}$$

In other words, hypercubes are also regarded as point sets. A hypercube covers a point set S, if every point in S is also in H. For example, H(1,3;1,4) covers S(f,1). We also say that S(f,1) is covered by, or contained in H(1,3;1,4). An example of a 3-dimensional hypercube is given by H(1,3; 1,3; 1,3).

Given a picture function f and a point set S, f/S denotes the restricted picture function which is defined only for points in S, i.e., f/S (x1,...,xn) = f(x1,...,xn) if x is in S. f/S is called the support picture function or support picture for S.

Let F denote a family of picture functions. A picture transformation h is any mapping from F to F. The picture h(f) is called the transformed picture of f.

6. Hypercube Encoding Techniques

We are interested in techniques to find coverings of a point set S(f,t) using hypercubes. The simplest approach, called minimal hypercube (MH) encoding, is to find the smallest hypercube H containing S(f,t). The minimal enclosing hypercube H(a1,b1; a2,b2; ..., an,bn) of a point set S is given by,

aj = min {yj: for some zk, (z1,...,yj,...,zn) is in S}

bj = max {yj: for some zk, (z1,...,yj,...,zn) is in S}

For example, the minimal enclosing hypercube of S(f,1) is H(1,3;1,3). In the 2-dimensional case, the minimal enclosing hypercube is called the minimal enclosing rectangle (MER) [FREEM75].

It can be seen that H(1,3;1,3) contains many points originally not in S. Therefore the MH encoding technique gives only a crude approximation of S. To improve encoding accuracy, the generalized hypercube (GH) encoding can be employed [YANG78]. To motivate the GH encoding technique, we consider the above mentioned 2-dimensional picture f, with picture point set S = {(1,1), (3,1), (2,2), (2,3)}. The row point set S1 = {(1,1), (3,1)} is covered by MER H1 = H(1,3; 1,1). Similarly, S2 = {(2,2)} is covered by H2 = H(2,2; 2;2), and S3 = {(2,3)} by H3 = H(2,2; 3,3). The union H1 u H2 u H3 covers S.

In the 2-dimensional case, the GH encoding technique is commonly known as the tightly closed boundary (TCB) encoding [MERRI73]. In actual encoding, the TCB can be represented by (1 1 3 2 2 2 2), where the first entry is the beginning y coordinate, and the subsequent pairs of entries represent the minimal and maximum x coordinates of picture points in rows y, y+1, y+2, etc. It should be noted that if we consider column point sets, the TCB code will generally be different. In the above example, we have H1 = H(1,1; 1,1), H2 = H(2,2; 2,3), and H3 = H(3,3; 1,1). The new TCB code is (1 1 1 2 3 1 1).

We can now describe the generalized hypercube encoding technique. A GHm encoding is the union of all distinct hypercubes of the form,

$$H(x_{1},x_{1};...;x_{m-1},x_{m-1};a_{m},b_{m};...;a_{n},b_{n})$$

where

$$x_{i_{a}} = x_{i_{b}} = x_{i} \quad \text{for } 1 \geq i \geq m-1$$

and

$$a_j = \min \{y : \text{for some } z_j, (x_k, \ldots x_1, z_{m-1}, z_m, \ldots, y_j, \ldots z_n) \text{ is in } S\}$$

$$b_j = \max \{y : \text{for some } z_j, (x_k, \ldots x_1, z_{m-1}, z_m, \ldots, y_j, \ldots z_n) \text{ is in } S\}$$

When m = 1, we are simply using the smallest n-dimensional hypercube containing S as the GH code. When m = n+1, the original point set S is used as the GH code. Other intermediate values of m give GH codes of various levels of details. For example, if S = {(1,1,3), (1,1,5), (1,2,1), (1,2,4), (2,3,6)}, GH1 = H(1,2; 1,3; 1,6), GH2 = H(1,1; 1,2; 1,5) u H(2,2; 3,3; 6,6), GH3 = H(1,1; 1,1; 3,5) u H(1,1; 2,2; 1,4) u H(2,2; 3,3; 6,6), and GH4 = S. In the 2-dimensional case, GH1 is MH encoding, GH2 is TCB encoding, and GH3 is the original point set S.

As a notational convenience, a GH hypercube can be written as

$$GH(x_1, \ldots, x_{m-1}; a_m, \ldots, a_n; b_m, \ldots, b_n)$$

where (x1,...,x(m-1)) is the <u>handle vector</u>, (am,...,an) is the <u>lower bound vector</u>, and (bm,...,bn) is the <u>upper bound vector</u>.

The GH encoding technique essentially uses (n-m+1)-dimensional hypercubes with handles to cover the original point set S. A further generalization is to use an arbitrary collection of hypercubes to cover S. This technique is called <u>arbitrary hypercube (AH) encoding</u>. In AH encoding, the hypercubes may have different dimensions and different handle vectors. As an example, the picture point set S(f,t) can be covered by AH = {H(1,3;1,1), H(2,2;2,3)}.

The <u>picture covering problem</u>, of which the picture paging problem is a special case, can now be stated as follows:

(1) We are given a picture f and its associated picture point set S(f,t).

(2) We wish to find a collection of hypercubes, Hi, to cover S(f,t). If we restrict Hi to have similar (n-m+1)-dimensional handle vectors, this reduces to GH encoding problem. Otherwise, this is the AH encoding problem.

(3) The objective of finding an optimal covering is the minimization of total number of hypercubes.

A measure for the evaluation of picture coverings is based upon the minimum number of pixel gray-level changes to convert a picture into one with constant gray-level. Let h: {0, 1, ..., L-1} -> N represents the <u>histogram</u> of f, where h(i) is the number of pixels at gray-level i. We define the <u>pictorial information measure</u> PIM(f) as follows:

$$(1) \quad PIM(f) = \sum_{i=0}^{L-1} h(i)) - \max_{i} h(i)$$

46

We note that PIM(f) = 0, if and only if f is a constant picture (i.e. $f(x,y)$ = constant for all (x,y) in N x N). On the other hand, PIM(f) is maximum, if and only if f has a uniform histogram (i.e. $h(i)$ = constant, $0 \leq i \leq L-1$). Let the total number of pixels in f be $N(f)$. f has a uniform histogram if and only if PIM(f) = $N(f)$ $(L-1)/L$. In other words, PIM(f) is minimal when f is least informative, and maximal when f is most informative.

Suppose a picture point set S is divided into two disjoint subsets S1 and S2. We then have,

(2) $PIM(f/S) \geq PIM(f/S1) + PIM(f/S2)$

Therefore, if we use disjoint hypercubes Hi to cover a picture f, then the sum of PIM(f/Hi) is always less than or equal to PIM(f). In hypercube encoding, we can use <u>normalized picture information measure</u> defined as NPIM(f) = PIM(f) / $N(f)$, to decide whether the hypercube is satisfactory. For example, if NPIM(f) is less than a threshold, that hypercube need not be further decomposed. If NPIM(f) is close to maximum, and for every subpicture f/S, NPIM(f/S) is close to maximum, then the picture f is almost random and also need not be further decomposed. If we define pi as $h(i)/N(f)$, then we have

(3) $NPIM(f) = 1 - \max_i pi$

Furthermore, if we define wi as $N(f/Si) / N(f)$, then we can prove

(4) $NPIM(f/S) \geq w1 \times NPIM(f/S1) + w2 \times NPIM(f/S2)$

We can define a more general measure, PIMk, as follows,

(5) $PIMk(f) = \sum_{i=0}^{L-1} h(i)) - (\sum_{\substack{i \text{ is one} \\ \text{of the k} \\ \text{largest } h(i)'s}} h(i))$

and NPIMk is accordingly defined as,

(6) $NPIMk(f) = 1 - (\sum_{\substack{i \text{ is one} \\ \text{of the k} \\ \text{largest } pi's}} pi)$

We can again prove that NPIMk satisfies inequality (4). The picture information measures introduced above can be used to select hypercubes in picture covering. More details can be found in [SILVER82]. Results on GH encoding are reported in [YANG78], and results on picture paging, which is the pictue covering problem for 2-D pictures, can be found in [CHANG78b, REUSS78, LIU81].

7. Hierarchical Hypercube Encoding

The concepts of hierarchy is widely used in computer graphics and image processing [CHIEN80, KLING77, KLING79, McKEO77, MILGR79,

47

OMOLA79, SHAPI79, TANIM76]. The hypercube encoding technique can be applied iteratively to create a hierarchy of hypercubes. This technique is called hierarchical hypercube (HH) encoding. A hierarchical hypercube encoding is a collection of arbitrary hypercube encodings AH1, AH2, ..., AHk, satisfying the following conditions:

(1) Each AHi covers the original picture point set S.

(2) AH1 is a singleton set, i.e., AH1 consists of one hypercube covering S.

(3) Each AH(i+1) can be divided into disjoint subsets of hypercubes, such that for each subset, there exists a hypercube in AHi covering that subset.

As an example, for the picture point set S(f,t), one possible HH encoding has three levels: AH1, AH2, AH3, where AH1 = {H(1,1;3,3)}, AH2 = {H(1,3;1,1), H(2,2;2,3)}, and AH3 = {H(1,1;1,1), H(3,3;1,1), H(2,2;2,3)}. Another possible HH encoding is AH1 = {H(1,1;3,3)}, AH2 = {H(1,1;3,3)}, AH3 = {H(1,1;3,3)}. Therefore the AHi's may be identical in HH encoding.

As stated earlier, a picture is usually specified by a picture function f, together with its picture objects V and relational objects R. (V, R) can be regarded as the logical picture extracted from the physical picture f. Therefore, each hypercube Hi in a hypercube encoding can be associated with a micro-picture Ii, which contains information extracted from the support picture f/Hi. Ii, the micro-picture, consists of two parts: a logical micro-picture ILi containing picture objects extracted from the support picture and their relations, and a physical micro-picture IPi containing a transformed picture derived from f/Hi. In other words, ILi = (Vi, Ri), where Vi is a subset of V, and Ri is a subset of R. (In actual implementation, ILi could be realized as relational tables in a relational database. See [CHANG78b] where the concepts of logical and physical pictures are discussed, and relational database introduced. The translation of (V,R) into relational tables are discussed in [CHANGNS79]). For example, the logical micro-picture may contain information about the average gray level of the support picture f/Hi, the local histogram of f/Hi, and any other relevant information. The physical micro-picture may contain a resolution factor, and a picture function derived from f/Hi at that resolution.

Given a hypercube Hi and its micro-picture Ii, the reconstruction problem is to derive f/Hi, the support picture of Hi, from the micro-picture Ii. We assume that a materialization function g is given, and f'/Hi(x1,...,xn) = g(Ii, x1,...,xn) for (x1,...,xn) in Hi. Given a hypercube Hi, the associated micro-picture Ii, and the materialization function g, we can reconstruct f'/Hi. The reconstructed picture function f' is defined to be,

$$f'(x1,...,xn) = \oint_{\substack{f'/Hi \text{ is defined} \\ \text{at } (x1, \ldots ,xn)}} f'/Hi(x1,...,xn)$$

In the above, the function ϕ could be the min function, the max function, etc. $||f-f'||$ then measures the faithfulness of reconstruction, which is also a criterion for judging the adequacy of the encoding method and the micro-pictures.

8. Picture Tree and Structured Picture Retrieval

Suppose we are given HH encoding AH1, AH2, ..., AHk, and the associated micro-picture Ii for each hypercube Hi. This structure is called a _picture_ _tree_, if (1) the original picture f can be reconstructed from the micro-pictures, and (2) the original V, if specified, is contained in the union of the sets Vi.

As an example, the picture f is

```
1 1 1 2
1 1 1 2
2 2 2 2
2 2 2 3
```

The HH encoding is AH1 = {H(1,4;1,4)}, AH2 = {H(1,2;1,2), H(1,2;3,4), H(3,4;1,2), H(3,4;3,4)}. For H1 = H(1,4;1,4), its logical micropicture IL1 contains {v1((x,1),(y,4),(r,4),(c,1.68))}, indicating the average gray level of entire picture (regarded as a picture object) is 1.68. Its physical micro-picture IP1 contains ((r,2), (pp, (2, 2.25, 1, 1.5))), indicating the resolution is 2 original pixels per blurred pixel, and the subsequent numbers are average gray levels of a blurred support picture. For H2 = H(1,2;1,2), its logical micro-picture contains IL2 = {v2((x,1),(y,2), (r,2),(c,2))}, indicating the average gray level of the support picture for H2 is 2. Its physical micro-picture IP2, containing ((r,1), (pp, (2 2, 2, 2))), indicating the resolution is 1 original pixel per blurred pixel, and the subsequent numbers are average gray levels of a blurred support picture -- since the resolution is unity, the blurred picture is the support picture itself. Similarly, H3 = H(1,2;3,4), IL3 = {v3((x,1),(y,3),(r,2),(c,1))}, IP3 = ((r,1),(pp, (1,1,1,1))), H4 = H(3,4;1,2), IL4 = {v4((x,3),(y,1),(r,2),(c,2.25))}, IP4 = ((r,1), (pp, (2,3,2,2))), H5 = H(3,4;3,4), IL5 = {v5((x,3),(y,3),(r,2),(c,1.5))}, IP5 = ((r,1),(pp, (1,2,1,2))). From this example, it can be seen that a quad-tree [KLING77] is a special case of a picture tree, where only the leave nodes have associated micro-pictures, and the micro-pictures consist of only restricted physical pictures. In other words, for quad-trees, Ik is empty for all non-termial nodes Hk.

As motivated by the examples in Section 3, to facilitate pictorial information retrieval, we propose _structured picture retrieval_ as follows.

Given a picture query Q and a micro-picture Ii for hypercube Hi, it is assumed that we can compute the following:

> We can derive (TS',Q',S') from (Q,Ii), where TS' is the _partial_ _picture query set_ obtainable from (Q,Ii), Q' is the _modified_ _query_ specifying the remaining query after the processing of (Q,Ii), and S' is the set of descendent nodes Hj of Hi to be visited next.

We can now describe informally the structured picture retrieval technique as follows. We start from node H1. From (Q, I1) we can compute (TS',Q',S'). If the query Q cannot be fully answered, we will have nonempty Q'. We then retrieve all hypercubes Hi in AH2 such that {Hi} n S' is nonempty. We now use (Q',I') to compute (TS",Q",S"), where I' is the micro-picture of a descendent node Hk in Sk. If Q' cannot be fully answered, we will have nonempty Q", and we should retrieve all hypercubes Hi in AH3 such that {Hi} ∩ S" is nonempty. We proceed as above until the lowest level AHk is reached. It is assumed that any query Q can be answered, if the picture f is given. Since the picture f can be materialized from the micro-pictures in the picture tree, the above procedure can always answer Q, and QS is Q(TS), where TS is the union of the TS's. The above outlined procedure can be formally described as follows.

STRUCTURED PICTURE RETRIEVAL TECHNIQUE

STEP 1: LIST <- {(Q,H1)}, TS <- empty set.

STEP 2: Remove one tuple (Q,Hi) from LIST.
Retrieve Ii associated with Hi.
Compute (TS',Q',S') from (Q,Ii).
TS <- TS ∪ TS'.

STEP 3: For each successor node Hj of Hi, if {Hj} ∩ S' is nonempty, add (Q',Hj) to LIST.

STEP 4: If LIST is nonempty, go to STEP 2, else go to STEP 5.

STEP 5: QS <- Q(TS).

For the query tree example discussed in Section 3, the transformation (Q,Ii) -> (TS',Q',S') is as follows:

(1) TS' = Vi
(2) Q' = Q
(3) S' = {Hj: Hj is a descendent of Hi and (Pkj ^ Q) is nonempty}

This transformation (Q,Ii) -> (TS',Q',S') is a way to incorporate a knowledge model in the retrieval operation. We can then study the effects of different knowledge models on such transformation rules, and how these may affect the specification of micro-pictures.

Generalized zooming technique [CHANG79a] can then be viewed as a special case in structured picture retrieval. Vertical zoom is structured picture retrieval into lower level AHi to obtain pictures of better resolution. The vertical zoom query is $Q(a1,b1,a2,b2,r) = \{w:$ $a1 \leq w.x \wedge w.x \leq b1 \wedge a2 \leq w.y \wedge w.y \leq b2 \wedge r=w.r\}$, where a1, a2, b2 are the bounds of the zoom window, and r is resolution. Horizontal zoom is structured picture retrieval using similarity measures. For example, 2-D histogram matching technique can be used as a similarity measure [CHANG78a, CHANG79b, WARD79]. The horizontal zoom query is $Q(v,d,t) = \{w: d(v,w) \leq t\}$, where v is the prototype (template) picture object, d is similarity measure, and t is matching threshold. Similarly, the diagonal zoom query is $Q(v1,...,vn,d,t) = \{w:$ $d(v1,w) \leq t \vee d(v2,w) \leq t \vee ... \vee d(vn,w) \leq t\}$, where v1,...,vn are the template picture objects.

The staging problem is also a case of structured picture retrieval by
sequential materialization of the micro-pictures, given the query
locus which can be expressed as a query sequence. For panning, the
query sequence is Q(a11,b11,a21,b21,r),   Q(a12,b21,a22,b33,r),...,
Q(a1n,b2n,a2n,b2n,r), where (a1i,b1i,a2i,b2i) represents shifting win-
dows, and r is the common resolution factor. For zooming, the query
sequence   is   Q(a1,b1,a2,b2,r1),   Q(a1,b1,a2,b2,r2),...,
Q(a1,b1,a2,b2,rn), where (a1,b1,a2,b2) represents the common window,
and ri represents the changing resolution factor.

9. Discussions

The picture tree can be reorganized by redefining the HH encoding AH1,
AH2, ..., AHk, and recomputing the micro-pictures Ii. The set of picture queries, associated with certain weighting factors, {(Q1, w1),
..., (QL, wL)}, is called the picture query base. When a query base
is given, PT may be reorganized for optimal retrieval. When picture
function f is updated, the picture point set S(f,t) changes and PT
need also be updated. The micro-pictures associated with hypercubes
determine how much information is to be stored in a node in a picture
tree.   To   store   more detailed micro-pictures (more picture objects,
more relational objects, and higher-resolution physical pictures) at
high-level node in picture tree facilitates picture information retrieval, at the expense of increased storage overhead.   The reverse
effect is also evident. A micro-picture at Hi can be regarded as an
abstraction of f/Hi, derivable from the micro-pictures of the subtree
with root node Hi.   The problem may be stated as a transformation:
(Q,Ii,Ij) -> (I'i, I'j), where Hj is descendent node of Hi. In other
words, if we are presented with a query Q, based upon that information, we may decide to move certain information in micro-picture Ij up
to micro-picture Ii, or vice versa. We can then investigate different
ways of associating micro-pictures as picture indices with a picture
tree, as well as algorithms for picture abstraction and materialization. A support picture can be de-materialized and abstracted, and
then beamed up from a low-level node to a high-level node. Similarly,
an abstract object can be beamed down from a high-level node to a
low-level node and then materialized.

Given a query Q, the query tree can be constructed.   The retrieval
cost of a node Hk for Q is defined as (1) the cost of retrieving Hk
and all its successor nodes H'i such that Pki and Q has nonempty intersection, if mk > 0; or (2) the cost of retrieving PSk, if mk = 0.
The retrieval cost for Q is the retrieval cost of root node H1 for Q.
Two problems for picture tree manipulations can then be described:

(1) Optimal picture tree construction: Given a picture query base, we
want to construct a picture tree PT such that (a) the average retrieval cost is minimized, and (b) the storage cost is minimal among
all trees giving minimal average retrieval cost.

(2) Dynamic picture tree construction: Given a picture tree PT and a
picture query Qj, we want to modify PT dynamically so that the new
tree PT' is better in terms of retrieval cost for Qj.

With picture trees and structured picture retrieval, the recursive evaluation of queries becomes necessary. Since queries can be stored in the database as latent queries, it is possible to have one query invoke another prestored latent query. The investigation of properties of recursive queries, and techniques for recursive query evaluation, will be of interest for further study.

The above discussed structured retrieval technique can be adapted for execution on a highly parallel computer. The investigation of suitable programming languages to specify parallel processing algorithms for structured picture retrieval is another interesting research problem requiring further investigation.

Acknowledgement: This research was supported by the National Science Foundation under Grant ECS-8005953.

References

[CHANGNS79] N. S. Chang and K. S. Fu, "A Relational Database System for Images," TR-EE 79-28, Dept. of Electrical Engineering, Purdue University, May 1979.

[CHANG78a] S. K. Chang and Y. Wong, "Optimal Hist ram Matching by Monotone Gray Level Transformation," Communicatiol of the ACM, Vol. 22, No. 10, ACM, 835-840, October 1978.

[CHANG78b] S. K. Chang, J. Reuss, and B. H. McCormick, "Design Considerations of a Pictorial Database System," Internation Journal on Policy Analysis and Information Systems, Vol. 1, No. 2, Knowledge System Laboratory, UICC, pp. 49-70, January 1978.

[CHANG79a] S. K. Chang, B. S. Lin, and R. Walser, "A Generalized Zooming Technique for Pictorial Database Systems," Proceedings of National Computer Conference, AFIPS, Vol. 48, pp. 147-156, 1979.

[CHANG79b] S. K. Chang, "Ln Norm Optimal Histogram Matching," Proceedings Processing, IEEE Computer Society, pp. 169-174, August 1979.

[CHANG80] S. K. Chang and W. H. Cheng, "A Methodology for Structured Data Base Decomposition", IEEE Transactions on Software Engineering, Vol. SE-6, No. 2, March 1980, 205-218.

[CHIEN80] Y. T. Chien, "Hierarchical Data Structures for Picture Storage, Retrieval and Classification," in Pictorial Information System, (Chang and Fu, eds.), Springer-Verlag, West Germany, 1980.

[FREEM75] H. Freeman and R. Shapiro, "Determining the Encasing Rectangle for an Arbitrary Curve," Communications of the ACM, Vol.18, No. 7, ACM, pp. 409-413, July 1975.

[KLING77] A. Klinger, M. L. Rhode, and V. T. To, "Accessing Image Data," International Journal on Policy Analysis and Information Systems, Vol. 1, No. 2, Knowledge System Laboratory, UICC, pp. 171-189, January 1978.

[KLING79]   A. Klinger, "Analysis, Storage, and Retrieval of Elevation
Data with Application to Improve Penetration," U. S. ARMY Corps of
Engineers, Engineer Topological Laboratories, Fort Belvoir, Virginia,
22060, March 1979.

[LIU81] S. H. Liu and S. K. Chang, "Picture Covering by 2-D AH Encoding", Proceedings of IEEE Workshop on Computer Architecture for Pattern Analysis and Image Database Management, Hot Springs, Virginia,
November 11-13, 1981.

[McKEO77]   D. M. Mckeown Jr. and D. J. Reddy, "A Hierarchical Symbolic
Representation for Image Database," Proceedings of IEEE Workshop on
Picture Data Description and Management, IEEE Computer Society, pp.
40-44, April 1977.

[MERRI73]   R.   D. Merrill, "Representation of Contours and Regions for
Efficient Computer Search," Communications of the ACM, Vol. 16, No. 2,
ACM, pp. 69-82, February 1973.

[MILGR79] D. L. Milgram, "Constructing Trees for Region Description,"
Computer Graphics and Image Processsing 11, Academic Press, pp. 88-99,
1979.

[OMOLA79] J. Omolayole and A. Klinger, "A Hierarchical Data Structure
Scheme for Storing Pictures," Technical Report, Computer Science
Department, UCLA, 1979.

[REUSS78] J. L. Reuss and S. K. Chang, "Picture Paging for Efficient
Image Processing," Proceedings of IEEE Computer Society Conference on
Pattern Recognition and Image Processing, IEEE Computer Society, pp.
69-74, May 1978.

[ROSEN76] A. Rosenfeld and A.   C.   Kak, Digital Picture Processing,
Academic Press, N. Y., 1976.

[SHAPI79] L. G. Shapiro and R. M. Haralick, "A Spatial Data Structure," Technical Report #CS 79005-R, Dept. of Computer Science, Virginia Polytechnic Institute and State University, p. 35, August 1979.

[SILVER82] H. Silver, "An Investigation into Picture Paging Techniques", ISRL Technical Report, Department of Information Engineering,
University of Illinois at Chicago, March 1982.

[SMITHJ77] J. M. Smith, and D. C. P. Smith, "Database Abstraction:
Aggragation and Geralization", ACM Trans. on Database Systems, Vol. 2.
No. 2, pp. 105-133, 1977.

[TANIM76]   S. L. Tanimoto, "An Iconic/Symbolic Data Structuring
Scheme," in Pattern Recognition and Artificial Intelligence, Academic
Press, pp. 452-471, 1976.

[WARD79] M. Ward and Y. T. Chien, "A Pictorial Database Management
System which uses Histogram Classification as a Similarity Measure,"
Proceedings of COMPSAC 79, IEEE Computer Society, pp. 153-156, 1979.

[YANG78] C. C. Yang and S. K. Chang, "Encoding Techniques for Efficient Retrieval from Pictorial Databases," Proceedings of IEEE Computer Society Conference on Pattern Recognition and Image Processing,
IEEE Computer Society, pp. 120-125, June 1978.

Part II

Picture Representation

A General (Syntactic-Semantic) Approach to Picture Analysis[*]

K.S. Fu

School of Electrical Engineering, Purdue University
West Lafayette, IN 47907, USA

1. Introduction

Many mathematical methods have been proposed for solving pictorial pattern analysis problems [1]. They can be grouped into two major approaches, decision-theoretic or statistical approach and structural or syntactic approach [1-6]. From the point of pictorial view of pattern representation or description, we can discuss picture analysis in terms of single-entity representation versus multiple-entity representation, and suggest a combined syntactic-semantic approach on the basis of using attributed languages.

Consider a m-class pattern analysis problem. When we consider each pattern as a single entity we can use a set of n characteristic measurements (features) to represent each pattern under study. In such a case, each pictorial pattern is represented by a n-dimensional feature vector and the recognition of patterns can be accomplished by applying various techniques in discriminant analysis and statistical decision theory. Such an approach is often called decision-theoretic or statistical approach [1-3]. However, when the patterns under study are very complex or when the number of pattern classes m is very large (for example, in fingerprint identification or scene analysis problem) the number of features n required for analysis could also become very large. Consequently, the classical decision-theoretic approach often becomes ineffective or computationally infeasible in solving this kind of problem. One way to approach this kind of problem is to represent a complex pictorial pattern by its simpler subpatterns and hope that we can treat each simpler subpattern as a single entity and use decision-theoretic methods [4,5]. Of course, the relations among subpatterns must be taken into consideration. On the other hand, if each subpattern is again very complex, we may have to represent each subpattern by even simpler subpatterns, until we are sure that the simplest subpatterns, called "picture primitives," can be easily treated by simple decision-theoretic methods. By doing so, the feature extraction and selection problem (for picture primitives) will also be much simplified. Graphically, we can express such an approach in terms of a hierarchical tree structure as shown in Fig. 1.

At least two problems occur when we employ this approach for pattern representation. The first problem is the selection of subpatterns (and primitives). We may want to decompose each pictorial pattern into subpatterns and primitives based on some prespecified simple relations among subpatterns, for example, regular decomposition of an image pattern [10]. On the other hand, the patterns under study may naturally contain subpatterns which can be extracted using a segmentation technique [11]. In the latter case, each subpattern may be easily interpretable and physically meaningful [12-13]. Once a decomposition or segmentation process is carried out, the primitives are extracted and treated as single entities. Different kinds of primitive may require different sets of features for characterization [7, 12]. Primitives of the same kind can certainly be analyzed in terms of

[*]This work was supported by the NSF Grant ECS 78-16970.

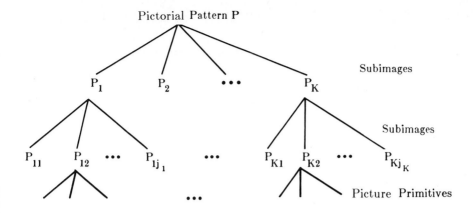

Fig. 1 Hierarchical Structural Representation of a Pictorial Pattern.

the same set of features [8,9,15].

The second problem is the additional analysis required when we use the hierarchical structure representation. If we are limited to use only one-dimensional string representation of patterns, results from formal language theory can be directly applied [16]. The problem here is how to handle the situation of context-sensitive languages. For the description of high dimensional patterns, trees and relational graphs are often more effective [5]. Efficient procedures for the analysis of tree and graph structures are thus required. Recent studies have shown that a powerful representation of patterns can be achieved by using attributes (semantic information) as well as structural (syntactic) information [17, 18]. In this paper, a brief review of these results is given. Problems for further investigation along this direction are also discussed.

2. Basic Formulation

In the decision-theoretic approach, a pictorial pattern is represented by a feature (or attribute) vector

$$\underline{X} = \left[x_1, x_2, \ldots, x_n \right]$$

For a pictorial pattern S consisting of two subpatterns X and Y with relation R between them, we can write

$$S \rightarrow XRY \tag{1}$$

Generally speaking, X, Y and relation R can be described by their feature or attribute vectors, that is,

$$A(X) = \underline{X} = \left[x_1, x_2, \ldots, x_n \right]$$

$$A(Y) = \underline{Y} = \left[y_1, y_2, \ldots, y_\ell \right]$$

57

and
$$A(R) = \left[r_1, r_2, \ldots, r_k\right]$$

where A(X) denotes the attribute vector of X. From (1), the attribute vector of S can be expressed as a function of the attributes of X, Y and R

$$A(S) = \phi(A(X), A(Y), A(R)) \tag{2}$$

For a special case, when R is a "left-right concatenation" relation, we can write

$$S \to XY \tag{3}$$

and
$$A(S) = \psi(A(X), A(Y))$$

Example 1: Let X be a straight line segment with attributes l_X and θ_X where l_X is the length of X and θ_X is the orientation (angle with respect to the horizontal axis). Similarly, we can use the attributes l_Y and θ_Y to describe straight line segment Y. After we connect Y to X to form a pattern S, the length and the orientation of S can be easily calculated by

$$l_S = l_X + l_Y \tag{5}$$

$$\theta_S = \tan^{-1}\left[\frac{l_X \sin \theta_X + l_Y \sin \theta_Y}{l_X \cos \theta_X + l_Y \cos \theta_Y}\right] \tag{6}$$

where $A(X) = (l_X, \theta_X)$, $A_Y = (l_Y, \theta_Y)$ and $A(S) = (l_S, \theta_S)$.

Example 2: Attributed Shape Grammar [19]
    Consider that a contour can be decomposed into a sequence of primitives, each is a curve segment. Let the attribute vector of curve segment C be

$$A(C) = (\vec{C}, L, \phi, Z)$$

where $\vec{C}$ is the vector length, L the total length, ϕ the total angle change, and Z a symmetry measure of C. Let the attribute of the concatenation relation CAT between two adjacent curve segments be the angle "a" between them. Thus, a contour N consisting of two curve segments C_1 and C_2 concatenated through an angle a can be expressed as

$$N \to C_1 \text{ CAT } C_2 \tag{7}$$

and
$$A(N) \to A(C_1) +_a A(C_2) \tag{8}$$

where $A(C_1) +_a A(C_2)$ denotes the following computation of attributes:

$$\vec{C}_N = \vec{C}_1 + \vec{C}_2 \tag{9}$$

$$L_N = L_1 + L_2 \tag{10}$$

$$\phi_N = \phi_1 + a + \phi_2 \tag{11}$$

and $Z_N = Z_1 + Z_2 + \frac{1}{2}\left[(\phi_1 + a)L_2 - (\phi_2 + a)L_1\right]$ $\qquad$ (12)

Similarly, if a contour S consists of two subcontours N_1 and N_2, then

$\qquad$ S → N_1 CAT N_2

and $\qquad$ $A(S) = A(N_1) +_a A(N_2)$

The operation $+_a$ is associative. That is, if

$\qquad$ S → N_1 CAT_1 N_2 CAT_2 N_3

then

$$A(S) = A(N_1) +_{a_1} A(N_2) +_{a_2} A(N_3)$$
$$= [A(N_1) +_{a_1} A(N_2)] +_{a_2} A(N_3) \qquad (13)$$
$$= A(N_1) +_{a_1} [A(N_2) +_{a_2} A(N_3)]$$

It is not difficult to see that such a representation is quite flexible and powerful in describing object contours for shape analysis. With the intro- duction of attributes, only one kind of primitive (curve segment) is re- quired.

Example 3: The PDL proposed by Shaw [20] can be extended to include attri- butes as follows:

Let the concatenation relations of +, -, x and * in PDL be represented by CAT $(+,\phi)$, CAT $(-,\phi)$, CAT (x,ϕ) and CAT $(*,\phi)$ respectively. In addition to the coordinates of head and tail we can introduce other attributes to the primitives such as shape and texture features. For example, the fol- lowing primitive X can be described by the shape of the primitive as well as the locations of its head and tail.

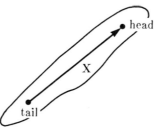

Thus the subpattern N

$\qquad$ (1) $\quad$ N → X+Y represents
$\qquad\qquad$ where $A(N) = \psi_+(A(X), A(Y), \phi)$

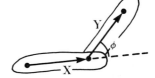

(2) $N \rightarrow X-Y$
where $A(N) = \psi_-(A(X), A(Y), \phi)$

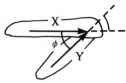

(3) $N \rightarrow X \times Y$
$A(N) = \psi_\times(A(X), A(Y), \phi)$

(4) $N \rightarrow X*Y$
$A(N) = \psi_*(A(X), A(Y), \phi)$
where $X \rightarrow X_1 + X_2$

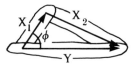

In terms of the hierarchical structure representation shown in Fig. 1, we can describe a pattern structure by a set of structural or syntax rules [5]. In general, the addition of attributes to a set of structural rules makes the pattern description more effective and flexible. Such an approach of using syntactic (structural) as well as semantic (attribute) information of patterns can be formulated in terms of attributed grammars [21, 22].

An attributed (string) grammar is a four-tuple

$$G = (V_N, V_T, P, S)$$

where V_N is a set of nonterminals, V_T a set of terminals, and $S \in V_N$ the start symbol. For each $X \in (V_N \cup V_T)$, there exists a finite set of attributes $A(X)$, and attribute x_i of $A(X)$ has a set, either finite or infinite, of possible values D_{x_i}. P is a set of production rules each of which consists of two parts, a syntactic rule and a semantic or attribute rule. The syntactic rule is of context-free form

$$N \rightarrow \alpha \ , \quad N \in V_N \text{ and } \alpha \in (V_N \cup V_T)^+$$

Let $\alpha = C_1 C_2 \ldots C_k$, $C_i \in (V_N \cup V_T)$ for $1 \leq i \leq k$. The semantic rule is a mapping

$$f: D_{C_1} \times D_{C_2} \times \ldots \times D_{C_k} \rightarrow D_N \tag{14}$$

or we can write that

$$A(N) = f(A(C_1), A(C_2), \ldots, A(C_k)) \tag{15}$$

where $A(N)$, $A(C_1)$,...,$A(C_k)$ are the attribute sets or attribute vectors of N, C_1,..., and C_k respectively.

The mapping f can be a closed-form function, that is, the attributes of N can be expressed functionally in terms of the attributes of C_1, C_2,..., and C_k. f can also be a computation algorithm which takes the attribute values of C_1, C_2,..., and C_k and any other available information as input and the attribute values of N as output. We can also include the case that (15) represents a logical or functional constraint to indicate the applicability of a certain syntactic rule.

The above definition of attributed grammar follows Knuth's formalism closely [21]; two kinds of attributes are included in the semantic rules, inherited attributes and synthesized attributes. The former are those aspects of meaning (attributes) coming from the context of a phrase (subpattern) in a string (pattern), whereas the latter are those aspects of meaning which are built up from the basic vocabulary (primitives) within the phrase. In syntactic pattern analysis, if a top-down parsing is employed to analyze pattern structures, inherited attributes are more convenient to use because they can be computed in a top-down fashion, starting from the start symbol S of the grammar. On the other hand, if a bottom-up parsing is preferred, then synthesized attributes should be used, which are computed in a bottom-up fashion.

It is noted that by deleting all semantic rules, an attributed grammar is reduced to a context-free grammar. However, if each pattern X is treated as a single entity or as a primitive and not decomposed into subpatterns, X will be characterized only by its attribute vector $A(X) = \underline{X} = [x_1, x_2, ..., x_n]$ and there is no need of structural or syntactic rules. The conventional m-class pattern classification problem using decision-theoretic approach can be expressed as follows:

Syntactic rule

$$S_1 \rightarrow X$$
$$S_2 \rightarrow X$$
$$\cdot$$
$$\cdot$$
$$\cdot$$
$$S_m \rightarrow X$$

Semantic rule

$$D_1(X) = \underset{1 \le i \le m}{\text{Max}} \{D_i(X)\}$$
$$D_2(X) = \underset{1 \le i \le m}{\text{Max}} \{D_i(X)\}$$

$$D_m(X) = \underset{1 \le i \le m}{\text{Max}} \{D_i(X)\}$$

where $D_i(X)$ is the discriminant function for class i. In this expression, each semantic rule is used as a semantic constraint to indicate the applicability of the corresponding syntactic rule. That is, when $D_j(X) = \text{Max} \{D_i(X)\}$, $1 \le i \le m$, the syntactic rule $S_j \rightarrow X$ is applied, which means that X is from class j.

3. Syntax-Semantics Trade-off

In addition to provide a more precise and flexible description of pictorial patterns, the use of attributes can also reflect the trade-off between syntactic and semantic complexities. That is, semantic (attribute) information can also be used to compensate the low syntactic complexity in pattern description. The following examples illustrate this idea.

Example 4: It is known that $L = \{a^n b^n c^n | n=1,2,\ldots\}$, which describes a set of triangles with different sizes, is a context-sensitive language $L(G_1)$ with

$$G_1: \quad S \to aSBA \qquad bB \to bb$$

$$S \to aBA \qquad bA \to bc$$

$$AB \to BA \qquad cA \to cc$$

$$aB \to ab$$

We can introduce the following attributes to the primitives and relation:

    i)   the length of primitive -- l_a, l_b, l_c

   ii)   the angle of the left-right concatenation -- θ

Let CAT(a,b) represent the relation "concatenation" between a and b. Using PDL notations, we can represent the left-right cancatention between a and b with angle θ as CAT (a,b) = (+, θ). An attributed context-free grammar G_2 can be constructed to generate L.

G_2:	Syntactic Rule	Semantic Rule
(1)	$S \to ABC$	CAT(S,A) = CAT(c,a) = (+, 120°) $l_S = l_A + l_B + l_C$
(2)	$A \to aA$	CAT(A,B) = CAT(a,b) = (+, 120°) $l_A = l_a + l_A$
(3)	$B \to bB$	CAT(B,C) = CAT(b,c) = (+, 120°) $l_B = l_b + l_B$
(4)	$C \to cC$	CAT(C,A) = CAT(c,a) = (+, 120°) $l_C = l_c + l_C$
(5)	$A \to a$	CAT(a,b) = (+, 120°) $l_A = l_a = 1$
(6)	$B \to b$	CAT(b,c) = (+, 120°) $l_B = l_b = 1$
(7)	$C \to c$	$l_C = l_c = 1$

It is noticed that in G_2 the attribute rule associated with each syntactic rule not only calculates the length of each side of the triangles generated but also imposes the constraint about the next production rule to be used in the generation. For example, after the production rule (1) is applied CAT(S,A) indicates that S must be concatenated to A. This means that the next production rule applied must be (2) or (5). Similarly, after (2) is applied, the next production rule selected must be (3), etc. Replacing the attribute or semantic rules in G_2 by the constraints of selecting the next production rule, we obtain precisely the following context-free programmed grammar G_2'.

	Core	Success	Failure
G_2':	Production	field	field
(1)	S → ABC	{2,5}	φ
(2)	A → aB	{3}	φ
(3)	B → bB	{4}	φ
(4)	C → cC	{2,5}	φ
(5)	A → a	{6}	φ
(6)	B → b	{7}	φ
(7)	C → c	φ	φ

It is noted that G_2' can be considered as a context-free (core) grammar with a control diagram [23] shown in Fig. 2. Such a control diagram can in

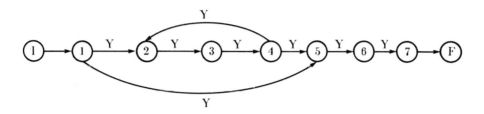

Fig. 2. Control Diagram of G_2'.

turn be interpreted as the semantic constraint for the application of syntactic rules. It is also possible to construct an attributed finite-state grammar G_3 to generate L.

G_3:	Semantic Rule	Semantic Rule
(1)	S → aA	CAT(a,b) = (+, 120°)
		$l_S = l_a + l_A$
(2)	A → bB	CAT(b,c) = (+, 120°)
		$l_A = l_b + l_B$
(3)	B → c	CAT(c,a) = (+, 120°)
		$l_B = l_c$
		$l_a = l_b = l_c = n$, n=1,2,...

Example 5: Chromosome Classification
1) Conventional syntactic approach – with the following primitives as terminals [24]:

$$V_{TM} = \{ \underset{a}{\cap}, \underset{b}{|}, \underset{c}{\cup}, \underset{d}{\}} \}$$

three kinds of chromosomes--median, submedian, and acrocentric--are segmented accordingly, and are shown in Fig. 3 together with their string representations.

The nonattributed grammars to characterize the three kinds of chromosome patterns could be as follows [5]:

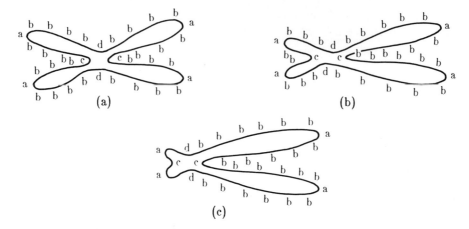

Fig. 3. Three classes of chromosomes. (a) Median chromosome z_M = cbbbabbbbdbbbbabbbcbbbabbbbdbbbbabbb. (b) Submedian chromosome z_S = cbabbbdbbbbabbbbcbbbbabbbbbdbbbab. (c) Acrocentric chromosome z_A = cadbbbbbbabbbbbcbbbbbabbbbbbdac.

$$G_{median} = (V_{NM}, V_{TM}, P_M, S)$$

$$V_{NM} = \{S, A, B, D, H, J, E, F\}, V_{TM} = \text{as above}$$

P_M: S → AA, D → FDE, H → a

A → cB, D → d, J → a

B → FBE, F → b, E → b

B → HDJ

$$G_{submedian} = (V_{NS}, V_{TS}, P_S, S), V_{TS} = V_{TM}$$

$$V_{NS} = \{S, A, B, D, H, J, E, F, W, G, R, L, M, N\}$$

P_S: S → AA, D → FDE, G → FG, L → HNJ

A → cM, D → FG, W → WE, R → HNJ

B → FBE, D → WE, F → b, G → d

B → FL, L → FL, E → b, W → d

B → RE, R → RE, H → a, N → FDE

M → FBE, J → a

$$G_{acrocentric} = (V_{NA}, V_{TA}, P_A, S), V_{TA} = V_{TM}$$

$$V_{NA} = \{A, B, D, H, J, E, F, L, R, W, G\}$$

P_A: S → AA, D → FG, G → FG, R → HDJ

A → cB, D → WE, W → WE, G → d

B → FL, L → FL, L → HDJ, W → d

B → RE, R → RE, H → a, E → b

J → a, F → b.

A close observation of the three kinds of chromosome shows that they can be easily classified by measuring the lengths of their arm pairs. The lengths of an arm pair is presented by the average of the lengths of the two arms on either side of a chromosome. If the length of the left arm pair is approximately equal to that of the right arm pair, then the pattern is a median chromosome. If they differ significantly, then it is a sub-median chromosome, or if the length of one arm pair is almost zero, then it is an acrocentric chromosome. However, since conventional grammars such as those shown above cannot incorporate attributes (numerical data) within their production rules, the classification consequently can only rely on symbolic syntax analysis which, when made to take care of numerical infor-mation contained in the input patterns, is usually not very effective and efficient.

2) Attributed grammar with synthesized attributes for chromosomes [17]. We now show that an attributed grammar with synthesized attributes can be used for chromosome description and classification. First, we remove the fixed-length restriction from terminal b, and let its length be an attri-bute. For example in Fig. 3 (a) we consider the curve between terminal d and terminal a as a single terminal b. The resulting segmentations and string representations for the chromosomes are shown in Fig. 4. Note that

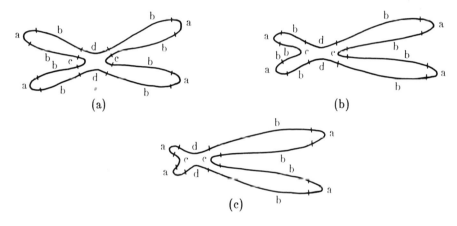

Fig. 4. Three classes of chromosomes. (a) Median chromosome z_M = dbbabcbabdbabcbab. (b) Submedian chromosome z_S = dbabcbabdbabcbab. (c) Acrocentric chromosome z_A = dbabcbabdaca.

the string representation of a median and a submedian chromosomes have be-come identical, but this is not a problem since our discrimination between them will rely on the difference of their synthesized attributes. The grammar is given as follows in which superscripts of nonterminals are used just for the purpose of discriminating identical nonterminals on the right-hand side of a syntactic rules.

A chromosome grammar with synthesized attributes:

$$G_S = (V_T, V_N, P, S)$$

$V_T = V_{TM}$ as specified previously,

$V_N = \{S, Q_1, Q_2, R_1, M_1, M_2, A, B, C, D\}$

with attribute sets as follows:

    a) $A(A) = A(C) = A(D) = A(M_2) = \phi,$

    b) $A(X) = \{l_X\},$ for $X = B, M_1, R_1, R_2, Q_1, Q_2,$

    c) $A(S) = \{l_{S1}, l_{S2}\}.$

P: 1) $S \rightarrow Q_1^1 Q_1^2;\ l_{S1} = l_{Q_1^1},\ l_{S2} = l_{Q_1^2}$

     2) $S \rightarrow Q_1 Q_2;\ l_{S1} = l_{Q_1},\ l_{S2} = l_{Q_2}$

     3) $S \rightarrow Q_2 Q_1;\ l_{S1} = l_{Q_2},\ l_{S2} = l_{Q_1}$

where nonterminal S represents the whole chromosome pattern, Q_1 or Q_2 represents an arm pair connected to a primitive d, attribute l_{S1} or l_{S2} is an arm pair length in the chromosome, and l_{Q_1} or l_{Q_2} is the average length of the two arms in the left or right arm pair:

     4) $Q_1 \rightarrow DR_1;\ l_{Q_1} = l_{R_1}$

     5) $Q_1 \rightarrow DR_2;\ l_{Q_2} = l_{R_2}$

where nonterminal R_1 or R_2 represents an arm pair, D represents the primitive d, and attribute l_{R_1} or l_{R_2} is the average length of the two arms in left or right arm pair.

     6) $R_1 \rightarrow M_1^1 CM_1^2,\ l_{R_1} = (l_{M_1^1} + l_{M_1^2})/2$

     7) $R_2 \rightarrow M_2 CM_2;\ l_{R_2} = 0$

where nonterminal M_1 or M_2 represents a chromosome arm, C represents the primitive c, and attribute l_{M_1} or l_{M_2} represents the length of arm M_1 or M_2 respectively.

     8) $M_1 \rightarrow B^1 AB^2;\ l_{M_1} = (l_{B^1} + l_{B^2})/2$

     9) $M_2 \rightarrow A$

     10) $A \rightarrow a$

11) $B \rightarrow b$; $l_B = l_b$

12) $C \rightarrow c$

13) $D \rightarrow d$

where nonterminals A, B, C, D represent primitives a, b, c, d, respectively and attribute l_B or l_b is the length of primitive b.

From Example 4 and Example 5, it can be seen that with respect to the generation of a language for picture description there exists a trade-off between the syntactic complexity and the semantic complexity [18, 25]. It is possible to construct a context-free or finite-state grammar with semantic or attribute information equivalent to a context-sensitive grammar without attributes. Thus, attributed finite-state grammar has been proposed as a normal form for pictorial pattern description [26]. Of course, in practical applications, the balance between syntactic and semantic complexities will probably also be affected by the actual implementation considerations.

4. Distance Measures Between Attributed Strings

Because of its simplicity in computation, the use of distance measures for the classification of syntactic patterns has received increasing attention recently [5]. For non-attributed strings, the Levenshtein distance between two strings is defined as the minimum number of substitutions, deletions and insertions required to transform one string to the other. Weighted Levenshtein distance and weighted distance have also been suggested and applied to practical problems [5]. For attributed strings, only the following two distance measures have recently been proposed. Their utility to practical applications still needs to be examined.

1) Let x and y be two attributed strings

$$x = a_1 a_2 \; \text{---} \; a_n$$

$$y = b_1 b_2 \; \text{---} \; b_m$$

The distance between x and y is defined as

$$d_1(x,y) = \alpha d_L(x,y) + \beta d_A(x',x'')$$

where α and β are two weighting coefficients, $d_L(x,y)$ is the Levenshtein distance between x and y. $d_A(x',x'')$ is the attribute distance between x and y after the syntactic errors (or symbolic differences) between the two strings are eliminated. Let

$$x' = a_1' a_2' \; \text{...} \; a_k' \; (= x'' = a_1'' a_2'' \; \text{...} \; a_k'')$$

Then $d_A(x',x'')$ could be defined as

$$d_A(x',x'') = \sum_{i=1}^{k} w_i \, d(A(a_i'), A(a_i''))$$

where $A(a_i')$ and $A(a_i'')$ are the attributed vectors of a_i' and a_i'' respectively. It is noted that when $k = 1$,

$$d_A(x',x'') = w_1 d(A(a_1'), A(a_1''))$$

which could be the Euclidean (or weighted Euclidean) distance between the attributed vectors $A(a_1')$ and $A(a_1'')$.

Example 6: Consider two strings

$$x = cbbabbdb$$

$$y = cbabdbb$$

with attributed vectors $A(a)$, $A(b)$ and $A(c)$. The Levenshtein distance between x and y is $d_L(x,y) = 3$ since

$$\begin{array}{cc} & \text{substitution} \\ y = cbabdbb & cbab\underline{b}bb \end{array}$$

$$\begin{array}{cc} \text{substitution} & \text{Insertion} \\ cbabb\underline{d}b & \underline{c}bbabbdb = x. \end{array}$$

The underlined symbol indicates where the error occurs. After eliminating all the symbolic errors, we obtain

$$x' = cbabb = x''$$

However $A(x') \neq A(x'')$. Let $x' = a_1' a_2' a_3' a_4' a_5'$ and $x'' = a_1'' a_2'' a_3'' a_4'' a_5''$. Thus

$$d_A(x',x'') = \sum_{i=1}^{5} w_i d(A(a_i'), A(a_i''))$$

2) In [26], a distance measure between two attributed strings x and y is defined as

$$d_2(x,y) = d_{syn}(x,y) + d_{sem}(x,y)$$

where the syntactic distance between x and y is defined as $d_{syn}(x,y) = \alpha|N_1 - N_2|$, α is a constant, N_1 is the number of productions used to generate x, and N_2 is the number of productions to generate y. The semantic distance between x and y is defined as

$$d_{sem}(x,y) = \underset{N}{\text{Min}} \left\{ \sum_{i=1}^{N} d(A(a_i'), A(b_i')) \right\}$$

where N is the length of the shorter string in {x,y}. It is noted that, in order to calculate $d_2(x,y)$ the knowledge of the grammar generating x and y is required. Also, in calculating $d_{sem}(x,y)$, all the substrings with length N of the longer string in {x,y} need to be explored.

6. Description of High-Dimensional Patterns

Besides the use of PDL, trees and relational graphs have been proposed for the description of pictorial patterns [4,5,13,14]. When we use trees or graphs for pattern description, the nodes usually represent subpatterns and the branch between two nodes represents the relation between the two corresponding subpatterns. Needless to say, both subpatterns and relations can have attributes. The following examples illustrate the use of attributed trees and attributed relational graphs for pictorial pattern description.

Example 7: Let a be a straight line segment with attributes l_a and θ_a where l_a is the length of a and θ_a is the angle of a with respect to the horizontal axis and $-30° \le \theta_a \le 30°$. That is to say that a is a more or less horizontal straight line segment with length l_a. Similarly, let b be a more or less vertical straight line segment ($240° \le \theta_b \le 300°$) with length l_b. We can then use the tree in Fig. 5(b) to represent the character E shown in Fig. 5(a). It is interesting to see that when $l_{a_2} = 0$ the character be-

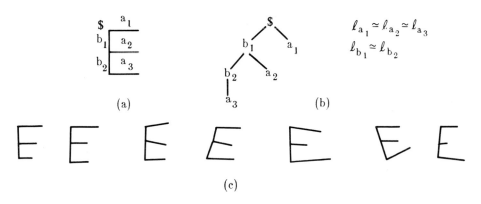

(a)   (b)

(c)

Fig. 5. (a) Character E and (b) its tree representation (c) Samples of distorted E.

comes C and primitive a_2 is essentially deleted. On the other hand, when $l_{a_3} = 0$, the character becomes F. The deletion of a_2 or a_3 causes a structural change. That is, in this case, character E is changed to C or F. Small changes in the values of l_a, θ_a, l_b and θ_b will not change the structure of pattern E, and can be used to describe the effect of noise and distortions on E. (See Fig. 5(c)).

It is noted that when the pattern structure is preserved, only semantic deformation or substitution errors are allowed[+]. When the pattern structure is not preserved, both semantic and syntactic errors can occur. A significant change of semantic information could result in a syntactic (deletion or insertion) error. On the other hand, a substitution could be

---
[+]Strictly speaking, substitution errors are the result of semantic errors or deformation (errors due to the change of semantic or attribute information).

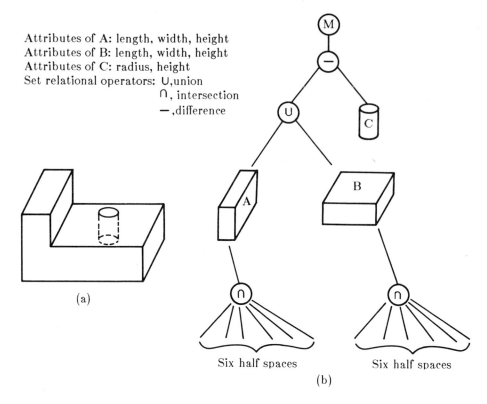

Attributes of A: length, width, height
Attributes of B: length, width, height
Attributes of C: radius, height
Set relational operators: ∪,union
∩, intersection
—,difference

(a)

Six half spaces   Six half spaces

(b)

Fig. 6. (a) Product M, and (b) its relational graph representation.

interpreted as a deletion error followed by an insertion error. Syntax-directed translation schemata has been proposed as a pattern deformation model for substitution, deletion and insertion errors [27,28]. When patterns are characterized by an attributed grammar, extension of the syntax-directed translation model has recently been made by including semantic as well as syntactic deformations [26].

Example 8: In 3D solid modeling for CAD/CAM, a manufactured product or machine part is usually represented syntactically [29]. An example is given in Fig. 6 in terms of a relational graph representation. Obviously, changes of size and/or other parameters describing the product can be made by varying the attributes of the components (primitives and subpatterns) of the product (pattern) in the graph representation.

Example 9: A 3D scene shown in Fig. 7(a) can be described by the attributed relational graph shown in Fig. 7(b). It is noted that by varying the attributes of subpatterns and relations, a variety of similar scenes can be described.

Analysis of attributed tree grammars and some special classes of attributed graph grammars has been studied recently [30-32]. Algorithms for attributed relational graph and subgraph matching have been proposed [33-35]. Distance measures between two attributed relational graphs have been proposed and some applications demonstrated [36,37]. There is no doubt that

70

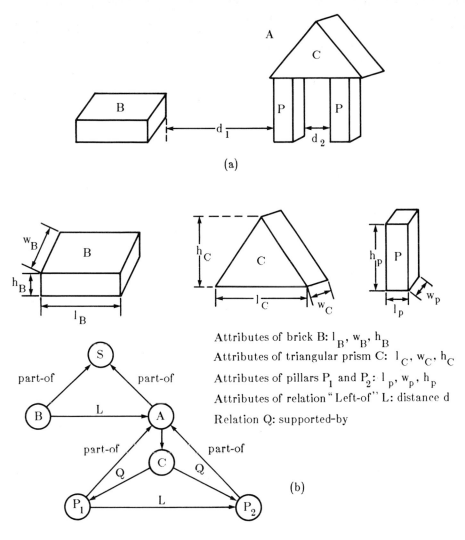

Attributes of brick B: l_B, w_B, h_B

Attributes of triangular prism C: l_C, w_C, h_C

Attributes of pillars P_1 and P_2: l_p, w_p, h_p

Attributes of relation "Left-of" L: distance d

Relation Q: supported-by

(b)

Fig. 7. (a) Scene A, and (b) its attributed relational graph representation.

more efficient and practically useful algorithms for the analysis of attributed trees and attributed relational graphs are still in demand.

6. Concluding Remarks

When the pictorial patterns under study are quite complex or when the structural or contextual information contained in the patterns is important, it is often more effective to describe each pictorial pattern in terms of its subpatterns and the relations among subpatterns. The basic subpatterns (primitives) can be characterized by their feature or attribute vectors and treated by decision-theoretic methods, and the contextual information is taken into consideration by syntactic (structural) methods. Such a general syntactic-semantic approach can be formulated in terms of attributed grammars. In addition to the representation of a pictorial pattern by a feature or attribute vector (as in the decision-theoretic approach), we can describe a pattern using a string, a tree, or a graph of attribute vectors. Contextual information is characterized by the relations among subpatterns and the grammar rules. Markovian contextual relations can be expressed as a stochastic finite-state or stochastic context-free grammar [5]. Context-sensitive or stochastic context-sensitive grammars may be required in some cases to characterize more complex contextual information. Fortunately, with the introduction of semantic or attribute information, the high syntactic complexity required can be reduced. Nevertheless, a systematic method to select appropriate syntactic and semantic complexities for a specific pattern analysis problem is still needed.

It is interesting to notice that, with the formulation introduced in this paper, relationships between pattern analysis and (rule-based) artificial intelligence can be easily established. The rules used in AI systems are, in general, of the form [38, 39]: IF E (evidence) THEN H (conclusion). Referring to Section 2, we can express the conventional one-dimensional two-class pattern classification problem as follows: Let $n = 1$, $m = 2$

E: E_1 $x_1 > t$ (threshold), or $D_1(x_1) > D_2(x_1)$

   E_2 $x_1 < t$, or $D_1(x_1) < D_2(x_1)$

H: H_1 x_1 is from class 1

   H_2 x_1 is from class 2

The decision-theoretic classification rule can then be stated as

   IF E is E_1 THEN   H is H_1

   IF E is E_2 THEN   H is H_2

It is certainly possible to extend this example to the case where $n > 1$ and $m > 2$. For the case with uncertainty, the classification rule can be expressed as

   IF E is E_1 THEN H is H_1 with $P(H_1|E_1)$

where $P(H_1|E_1) = \dfrac{P(E_1|H_1)P(H_1)}{P(E_1)}$.

In the case of a pattern S consisting of two subpatterns X and Y related by R, as shown in (1), we can express the recognition rule as

   IF X and Y, and X and Y are related by R THEN S

In order to include uncertainty, we can also express the recognition rule as

IF X, Y and R

THEN S with P(S|X,Y,R)

The last rule can be interpreted as a stochastic syntax rule with a semantic constraint.

References

1. K. S. Fu, "Recent Development in Pattern Recognition," IEEE Trans. Computers, Vol. C-29, Oct. 1980.
2. K. S. Fu, Digital Pattern Recognition, Springer-Verlag, Second Edition, 1980.
3. J. Kittler, K. S. Fu and L. F. Pau, ed., Pattern Recognition: Theory and Applications, D. Reidel Publishing Co., 1982.
4. T. Pavlidis, Structural Pattern Recognition, Springer-Verlag, 1977.
5. K. S. Fu, Syntactic Pattern Recognition and Applications, Prentice-Hall, 1982.
6. R.C. Gonzalez and M. G. Thomason, Syntactic Pattern Recognition - An Introduction, Addison-Wesley, 1978.
7. W. H. Tsai and K. S. Fu, "A Syntactic-Statistical Approach to the Recognition of Industrial Objects," Proceedings, 5th International Conference on Pattern Recognition, Dec. 1-4, 1980, Miami Beach, FL, USA.
8. R. Jakubowski, "Syntactic Characterization of Machine Parts Shapes," Cybernetics and Systems, Vol. 13, no. 1, 1982.
9. K. S. Fu and N. S. Chang, "An Integrated Image Analysis and Image Database Management System," Proc. 1981 COMPCON Fall, Washington, D.C.
10. B. Moayer and K. S. Fu, "A Syntactic Approach to Fingerprint Pattern Recognition," Pattern Recognition, Vol. 7, 1975, pp. 210-233.
11. K. S. Fu and J. Mui, "A Survey on Image Segmentation," Pattern Recognition, Vol. 13, 1981, pp. 3-16.
12. G. Stockman, L. N. Kanal and M. C. Kyle, "Structural Pattern Recognition of Carotid Pulse Waves Using a General Waveform Parsing System," Comm. ACM, Vol. 19, Dec. 1976.
13. P. H. Winston, "Learning Structural Descriptions from Examples," in The Psychology of Computer Vision, ed. by P. H. Winston, McGraw-Hill, 1975.
14. A. Rosenfeld, "Picture Processing: 1980", Computer Graphics and Image Processing, Vol. 16, May 1981.
15. J. L. Mundy and R. E. Joynson, "Automatic Visual Inspection using Syntactic Analysis," Proc. 1977 IEEE Computer Society Conference on Pattern Recognition and Image Processing, June 6-8, Troy, N.Y.
16. A. V. Aho and J. D. Ullman, The Theory of Parsing, Translation and Compiling, Prentice-Hall, 1972.
17. W. H. Tsai and K. S. Fu, "Attributed Grammar -- A Tool for Combining Syntactic and Statistical Approaches to Pattern Recognition," IEEE Trans. Syst., Man. Cybern., Vol. SMC-10, Dec. 1980.
18. K. S. Fu, "Resent Advances in Syntactic Pattern Recognition," NSF Worksnop on Structural and Syntactic Pattern Recognition, June 22-24, 1981, Saratoga Springs, N.Y.
19. K. C. You and K. S. Fu, "A Syntactic Approach to Shape Recognition Using Attributed Grammars," IEEE Trans. Syst., Man, Cybern., Vol. SMC-9, June 1979.
20. A. C. Shaw, "A Formal Picture Description Scheme as a Basis for Picture Processing Systems," Information and Control, Vol. 14, 1969, pp. 9-52.

21. D. E. Knuth, "Semantics of Context-Free Languages," _J. Math. Syst. Theory_, Vol. 2, 1968, pp. 127-146.

22. P. M. Lewis, D. J. Rosenkrantz and R. E. Stearns, _Compiler Design Theory_, Addison-Wesley, 1976.

23. H. Bunke, "Programmed Graph Grammars," in _Graph Grammar and Application to Computer Science and Biology_, ed. by V. Claus, H. Ehrig and G. Rosenberg, Springer-Verlag, 1979.

24. R. L. Ledley, et. al., "FIDAC: Film Input to Digital Automatic Computer and Associated Syntax-Directed Pattern Recognition Programming System," in _Optical and Electro-Optical Information Processing_, ed. by J. T. Tippet, et. al., MIT Press, 1965.

25. A. Pyster and H. W. Buttleman, "Semantic-Syntax-Directed Translation," _Information and Control_, Vol. 39, 1978, pp. 320-361.

26. J. W. Tai and K. S. Fu, "Semantic Syntax-Directed Translation for Pictorial Pattern Recognition," Tech. Rept. TR-EE81-38, Purdue University, Oct. 1981.

27. T. I. Fau and K. S. Fu., "A Syntactic Approach to Time-Varying Image Analysis," _Computer Graphics and Image Processing_, Vol. 11, 1979, pp. 138-149.

28. M. G. Thomason, "Stochastic Syntax-Directed Translation Schemata for Correction of Errors in Context-Free Languages," _IEEE Trans. Computers_, Vol. C-24, Dec. 1975.

29. _Computer Graphics and Applications_, Special Issue on Solid Modeling, Vol. 2, No. 2, March 1982.

30. Q.Y. Shi and K. S. Fu, "Parsing and Translation of (Attributed) Expansive Graph Languages for Scene Analysis," Tech. Rept. TR-EE82-1, Purdue University, January 1982.

31. Q. Y. Shi and K. S. Fu, "Efficient Error-Correcting Parsing for (Attributed and Stochastic) Tree Grammars," _Information Sciences_, Vol. 26, 1982.

32. A. Sanfeliu and K. S. Fu, "Tree-Graph Grammars for Pattern Recognition," submitted for publication.

33. W. H. Tsai and K. S. Fu, "Error-Correcting Isomorphisms of Attributed Relational Graphs for Pattern Analysis," _IEEE Trans. System, Man, and Cybernetics_, Vol. SMC-9, Dec. 1979.

34. W.H. Tsai and K. S. Fu, "Subgraph Error-Correcting Isomorphisms for Syntactis Pattern Recognition," submitted for publication.

35. L. Shapiro and R. M. Haralick, "Organization of Relational Models for Scene Analysis," Dept. of Computer Science, VPI & SU, September 1981.

36. A Sanfeliu and K. S. Fu, "A Distance Measure Between Attributed Relational Graphs for Pattern Recognition," submitted for publication.

37. A. Sanfeliu, K. S. Fu and J. M. S. Prewitt, "An Application of a Distance Measure Between Graphs to the Analysis of Muscle Tissue Patterns," NSF Workshop on Structural and Syntactic Pattern Recognition, June 22-24, 1981.

38. R. O. Duda, P. E. Hart and N. J. Nilsson, "Subjective Bayesian Methods for Rule-Based Inference Systems," Proc. 1976 National Computer Conference.

39. D. A. Waterman and F. Hayes-Roth, ed., _Pattern-Directed Inference Systems_, Academic Press, 1978.

Shape Design, Representation, and Restoration with Splines

Y. Ikebe and S. Miyamoto
University of Tsukaba, Ibaraki 305, Japan

ABSTRACT

The purpose of the present paper is to demonstrate several applications of
interpolation and approximation methods such as splines to picture engineering
In particular, three types of applications, i.e., shape design, shape representation, and shape restoration are discussed. Shape design is concerned with
construction of visually beautiful curves and interactive modification of the
curves. The method of B-splines gives a physically natural (minimum curvature)
curve which is locally modifiable, since it is a linear combination of basis
functions (B-splines) having local support. Bezier's method generates a
smooth curve (polynomial) by means of Bezier polygon and is appropriate for
interactive use, although a local modification may propagate throughut the
whole interval. Shape representation approximates a given irregular shape,
where a method suitable for use depends on a particular way in which data are
given. For surface approximation Coons methods are used as a standard tool,
where an entire surface is subdivided into pieses whose boundary data are
used to construct an approximating surface for the corresponding piece. When
the boundary data are given at a selected set of points, tensor product of
splines has been known to be usable. For surfaces which can be adequately
described in terms of one-parameter family of curves, the technique known as
lofting is applicable. If two families of parametric curves must be mixed
to define a given surface, one may effectively use boolean sum approximation.
Shape restoration is an approximation of an existing object, where the data
are noisy or incomplete. In this case an approximation will depend on smoothing property and the nature of data given. Moreover, in some cases, irregularly distributed data points must be incorporated. In the image restoration
the convolution property of B-splines is useful for the restoration of space-
invariant degradations. As an additional example, we mention the pattern
generation of air pollution, where spline under tension is prefered to the
ordinary cubic spline in view of the accuracy of the approximation.

1. INTRODUCTION

An overview of interpolation methods such as splines applied to picture engineering is given in this paper. Applications include problems in computer-
aided design, those in digital image processing, and a picture generation
problem in environmental science. Three categories of the problems are considered [1]: shape design, shape representation, and shape restoration.

In the problem of shape design, an original prototype does not exist, and
the primary concern is the process of design, display, and modification of
complex forms. Also the appearance of the resulting shape is important.

75

Shape representation concerns the approximation of an existing irregular bodies or surfaces for a variety of applications. For example, characteristic quantities of skulls should be calculated or gothic cathedral vaulting should be represented for stress analysis. In these examples there are different ways of providing data for interpolation. Data might be given at grid points or in functional forms. Different types of interpolation schemes should be applied according to the difference of data types.

Although the forgoing two problems concern computer graphics, similar kinds of approximation problems occur in somewhat different areas of picture engineering. Measurement of an object is sometimes difficult, inaccurate, or degraded in some fashion as in certain problems of image processing. The problem to recover a function from these incomplete data is called here "shape restoration"

2. SPLINES AND B-SPLINES

The name "spline" comes from traditional use of the draftsman's spline curve, which is a long narrow strip of wood or plastic. Lead weights called "ducks" are placed along the strip so that the curve passes through specified points. If the physical spline is regarded as a thin elastic beam, then the Bernoulli-Euler law holds [2]:

$$M(x) = \frac{E I}{R(x)} ,$$

where M is the bending moment, E is Young's modulus, I is the moment of inertia, and R is the radius of curvature. For small deflections, $R(x)$ is replaced by $1/y''(x)$. Since the ducks act as simple supports, $M(x)$ is a linear function between the supports. Namely,

$$y'' = \frac{1}{EI}(Px + Q) .$$

Integrating the above equation, we have

$$y(x) = a_3x^3 + a_2x^2 + a_1x + a_0 ,$$

i.e., $y(x)$ is a cubic polynomial between the supports.

The above argument leads to the notion of mathematical cubic splines, which is defined as piecewise cubic polynomials with second order continuity at junction points. It is known that the cubic spline has the minimum curvature property. That is, it minimizes the integral

$$\int_a^b |f(x)|^2 dx$$

on the space of functions $f(x)$ which have continuous second order derivatives on [a,b] and pass through junction points (x_1,y_1), (x_2,y_2), $\cdots\cdots$, (x_n,y_n), (i.e., $f(x_i) = y_i$, i=1,2,$\cdots$,n). This property relates closely to the minimization of potential energy of a deflected beam. Various generalizations of the cubic spline have been obtained by replacing the above integral by different functionals (cf. HATANO [3]). For example, L-splines minimize

$\|L f\|^2_{L_2}$ with a differential operator L [4], in which trigonometric splines [5], and spline in tension [6] are contained. We mention, however, another kind of generalization in relation to computer graphics.

B-splines are first introduced by CURRY and SCHOENBERG [7] which generalize the cubic spline and have properties useful in applications. The idea consists in the construction of basis functions on the space of piecewise polynomial fucntions passing through specifies points with certain order of continuity. Thus, the original cubic spline representation

$$f(x) = a_{3,i}x^3 + a_{2,i}x^2 + a_{1,i}x + a_{0,i} , \qquad x \in [x_i, x_{i+1}]$$

is converted to B-spline representation

$$f(x) = \sum_i c_i N_{i,m}(x) .$$

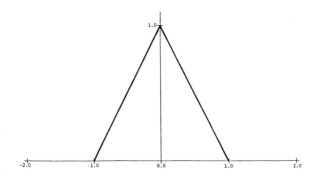

Fig.1 B-spline of order 2

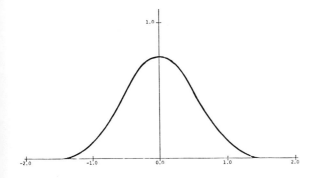

Fig.2 B-spline of order 3

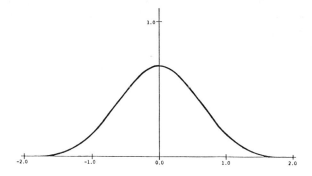

Fig.3 B-spline of order 4

Note that the former representation is local: $a_{k,i}$'s (k=1,2,3) are different
with the change of subinterval $[x_i, x_{i+1}]$, whereas the latter expression is
global: the equation is valid throughout the whole interval. C. DE BOOR has
given a method of stable evaluation of basis functions $N_{i,m}$'s based on divided
differences [8], therefore the latter representation is practically usable
as well as its theoretical interest. The notion of B-splines generalize the
cubic spline. It unifies various order of continuity into a frame of basis
functions. The basis functions are positive, "bell-shaped" (cf. Figs. 1,2,3),
having local supports. The last property is particularly useful when the
interpolated curves should be altered by interactive communications as in
computer-assisted design.

3. SHAPE DESIGN

Curves appearing in computer graphics may not necessarily be equated with
ordinary single-valued function y = f(x) [9]. For example, one might treat
objects having vertical tangents, or closed curves. The parametric form is
independent of a particular coordinate system, and is useful to represent
such an object. Therefore a plane curve is represented by a set of two functions

$$x = x(t), \qquad y = y(t) ,$$

a space curve is represented as

$$x = x(t), \qquad y = y(t), \qquad z = z(t) ,$$

and a two-dimensional surface in three-dimensional space is represented by
using two parameters:

$$x = x(t,u), \qquad y = y(t,u), \qquad z = z(t,u) .$$

Let us consider interpolation of a closed curve $(x(t), y(t))$ by B-splines. Let $x(t_0) = x_0$, $y(t_0) = y_0$, $x(t_1) = x_1$, $y(t_1) = y_1$, $\cdots\cdots$, $x(t_n) = x_n$, $y(t_n) = y_n$, $(t_0 < t_1 < \cdots < t_n)$. Since the curve is closed, assume $x_n = x_0$, $y_n = y_0$. Consider first the function $x(t)$. A general B-spline interpolation function of m-th order is given by

$$S(t) = \sum_{i=-m+1}^{n-1} c_i N_{i,m}(t) .$$

Here c_i's are constants to be determined and $N_{i,m}(t)$'s are m-th order B-splines:

$$N_{i,m}(t) = (u_{i+m} - u_i) g_m[u_i, u_{i+1}, \cdots, u_{i+m}; t] ,$$

where $g_m[u_i, u_{i+1}, \cdots, u_{i+m}; t]$ is the m-th divided difference of truncated power function [8], [10]:

$$g_m(u; t) = \begin{cases} (u - t)^{m-1}, & u \geq t \\ 0 & u < t , \end{cases}$$

The following properties of B-splines have been proved [8]:

(1) $N_{i,m}(t)$ is at most a $(m-1)$-th order polynomial on each subinterval $[t_i, t_{i+1}]$.

(2) $N_{i,m}(t) = 0$, $t \leq t_i$, $t_{i+1} \leq t$.

(3) $N_{i,m}(t)$ has $(m-2)$-th order continuous derivatives.

(4) $N_{i,m}(t)$'s are given by the recursive formula:

$$N_{i,1}(t) = \begin{cases} 1, & t_i \leq t < t_{i+1} \\ 0, & \text{otherwise} \end{cases}$$

and

$$N_{i,m}(t) = \frac{t - t_i}{t_{i+m-1} - t_i} N_{i,m-1}(t) + \frac{t_{i+1} - t}{t_{i+m} - t_{i+1}} N_{i+1,m-1}(t) .$$

(5) $\sum_i N_{i,m}(t) = 1$.

Remark   In B-spline representation, m-th order B-spline corresponds to $(m-1)$-th order piecewise polynomial functions. For example, 4-th order B-spline interpolation agrees with cubic spline interpolation [8].

Therefore the B-spline interpolation with the knot sequence (t_0, x_0), (t_1, x_1), $\cdots$, (t_n, x_n) is obtained by determining constants $\{c_i\}$ so that

$$S(t_i) = x_i , \qquad i=0,1,\cdots,n$$

is satisfied. Since there are n+m-1 constants to be determined, additional conditions on the boundary should be given. In case of a closed curve, periodic boundary condition

$$S^{(j)}(t_0) = S^{(j)}(t_n), \qquad j=0,1,\cdots,m-2$$

should be included [8]. Thus, the determination of the coefficients are reduced to a solutions of a linear equation. The function y(t) is interpolated by the same procedure. Hence it follows that

$$x(t) = \sum_{i=-m+1}^{n-1} c_i N_{i,m}(t)$$

$$y(t) = \sum_{i=-m+1}^{n-1} d_i N_{i,m}(t)$$

such that

$$x(t_i) = x_i, \qquad y(t_i) = y_i, \qquad i=0,1,\cdots,n$$

In the problem of shape design, one may control an interpolation curve by specifying and changing junction points (cf. Fig. 4). There is, however, another method of control originated by P. E. BEZIER [11], where an open polygon is used to design a curve. Bezier's approach is based on the Bernstein polynomial approximation. The basis function is given by binomial probability density functions:

$$J_{n,i}(t) = \binom{n}{i} t^i (1-t)^{n-1} , \qquad 0 \le t \le 1 .$$

The Bernstein polynomial approximation of degree n to a continuous function defined on [0,1] is [12]:

$$B_n(f(t)) = \sum_{i=1}^{n} f(\frac{i}{n}) J_{n,i}(t) .$$

Although $B_n(f) \to f$ uniformly as $n \to \infty$, the convergence is slow [12] and it is not widely used in applications. In shape design, however, aesthetic properties are prefered to the accuracy of approximation. Bezier's method specifies a set of points $(x_0,y_0)=(x(t_0),y(t_0))$, $(x_1,y_1)=(x(t_1),y(t_1))$, $\cdots$, $(x_n,y_n)=(x(t_n),y(t_n))$, where $0=t_0 < t_1 < \cdots < t_{n-1} < t_n=1$, and put

$$x(t) = \sum_{i=0}^{n} x_i J_{n,i}(t)$$

$$y(t) = \sum_{i=0}^{n} y_i J_{n,i}(t) .$$

Here the set $\{(x_i,y_i),\ i=0,1,\cdots,n\}$ defines a Bezier polygon and $(x(t),y(t))$ is the Bezier curve. Except $t = t_0$ and $t = t_n$, the curve does not, in general, pass through the vertices of the polygon [9].

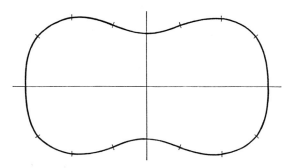

Fig.4 An example of a closed curve where 16 knots are given and cubic spline with angular parameter $(x(\theta),y(\theta))$ is used as the interpolation method

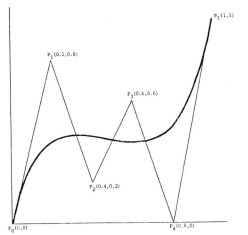

Fig.5 Bernstein-Bezier curve

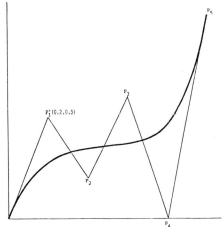

Fig.6 Modified Bezier curve (cf. Fig.5)

Figure 5 shows an example of a Bezier curve, where $P_0=(0,0)$, $P_1=(0.2,0.8)$, $P_2=(0.4,0.2)$, $P_3=(0.6,0.6)$, $P_4=(0.8,0.0)$, $P_5=(1,1)$ (we take $t = x$ for simplicity). In the interactive design process an initial polygon is specified, then positions of the vertices are altered to modify the curve. Thus, if we move $P_1 \rightarrow P_1'=(0.2,0.5)$, then we have a modified curve in Fig. 6.

81

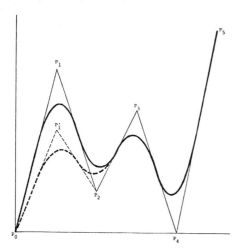 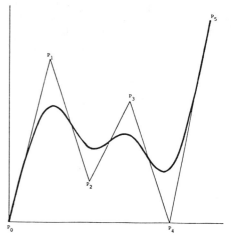

Fig.7 B-spline curve of order 3
associated with a Bezier polygon

Fig.8 B-spline curve of order 4
associated with a Bezier polygon

A modification of Bezier's method has been discussed by GORDON and RIESENFELD [12], where B-splines are used instead of the Bernstein polynomials. Namely,

$$x(t) = \sum_{i=-m+2}^{n+m-2} x_i N_{i,m}(t)$$

$$y(t) = \sum_{i=-m+2}^{n+m-2} y_i N_{i,m}(t) \, ,$$

where additional points $(x_{-m+2}, y_{-m+2}), \cdots, (x_{-1}, y_{-1}), (x_{n+1}, y_{n+1}), \cdots, (x_{n+m-2}, y_{n+m-2})$ should be added in case of the open polygon. Ordinarily, these points locate on the straight lines connecting (x_0, y_0) (resp. (x_{n-1}, y_{n-1})) and (x_1, y_1) (resp. (x_n, y_n)) [1].

Figures 7 and 8 are examples of curves with B-spline basis of order $m = 3$ and $m = 4$, respectively, where the control polygon is the same as that in Fig. 5. The method of B-splines has several advantages [9], [13].

(1) Alteration of smoothness of the curve is possible by changing the order m.
(2) The curve with low order splines (e.g. m = 3) makes closer fit than that of Bernstein polynomials.
(3) Local control of a curve is possible by changing the position of a vertex.

The last property is clear by observing that basis functions $N_{i,m}$'s have local supports. For example, comparing two curves in Fig. 7, we find that they have the same values on [0.5, 1].

82

4. SHAPE REPRESENTATION

The relationship between the type of data and approximation method to be applied is clearly exhibited in the problem of surface representation, where the data may be given at grid points, it may be given as a one family of parametric curves, or as two families of parametric curves.

Let us first consider a simple case when the surface $Q(t,u)$ should be constructed on the rectangular domain $(t,u) \in [0,1] \times [0,1]$, using two known boundary curves

$$P(t,0) = f_0(t) , \qquad P(t,1) = f_1(t) .$$

The simplest answer is the linear interpolation

$$Q(t,u) = P(t,0)(1 - u) + P(t,1)u . \tag{1}$$

In case of two boundary curves $P(0,u) = g_0(u)$ and $P(1,u) = g_1(u)$,

$$Q(t,u) = P(0,u)(1 - t) + P(1,u)t .$$

In general, interpolation of one family of parametric curves such as $P(t,u_1)$. $P(t,u_2), \cdots, P(t,u_n)$ is called lofting [14] which has been widely used in aircraft or shipbuilding industries. An example of a lofted surface is given in Fig. 9.

If four boundary curves $P(t,0)$, $P(t,1)$, $P(0,u)$, and $P(1,u)$ are given, one nught consider the sum of the above two functions:

$$Q(t,u) = P(t,0)(1 - u) + P(t,1)u + P(0,u)(1 - t) + P(1,u)t .$$

This equation does not satisfy the boundary conditions, i.e.,

$$Q(t,u) = P(t,0) + P(0,0)(1 - u) + P(1,0)u$$

$$Q(t,u) = P(t,1) + P(0,1)(1 - u) + P(1,1)u ,$$

and so on. This suggests the subtraction of certain additional terms, that is,

$$Q(t,u) = P(t,0)(1 - u) + P(t,1)u + P(0,u)(1 - t) + P(1,u)t$$

$$-P(0,0)(1 - t)(1 - u) - P(1,0)t(1 - u)$$

$$-p(0,1)(1 - t)u - P(1,1)tu ,$$

which clearly satisfies the boundary conditions. Figure 10 shows the above bilinear interpolation method applied to four boundary curves $f_0(x) = -0.75(x+1)(x-1)+0.25$, $f_1(x) = x(x-1)$, $g_0(y) = \cos(\pi/2)y$, and $g_1(y) = -0.25(y+1)(y-1)$, which are denoted by the boldest lines in the figure.

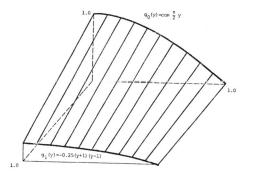

Fig.9 Lofted surface

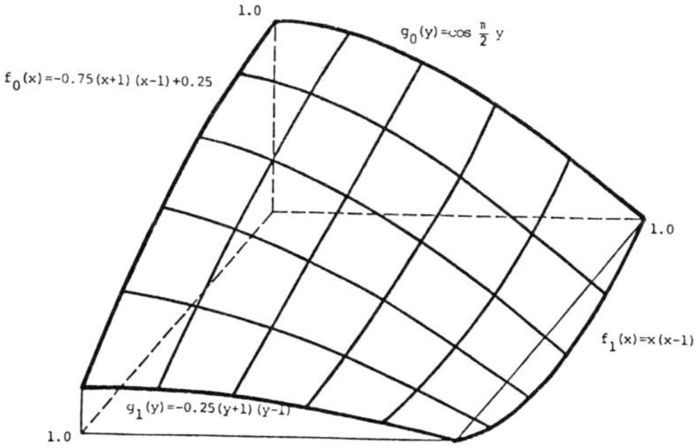

$g_0(y) = \cos \frac{\pi}{2} y$

$g_1(y) = -0.25(y+1)(y-1)$

Fig.10 Bilinear Coons interpolation of four boundary curves

$g_0(y) = \cos \frac{\pi}{2} y$

$f_0(x) = -0.75(x+1)(x-1)+0.25$

$f_1(x) = x(x-1)$

$g_1(y) = -0.25(y+1)(y-1)$

Extension to the data along mesh lines whose vertices are $\{(i,j),\ i=0,1,\cdots,M,\ j=0,1,\cdots,N\}$ is straightforward [14]:

$$Q(t,u) = \sum_{j=0}^{N} P(t,j)\phi_j(u) + \sum_{j=0}^{M} P(i,u)\phi_i(t) - \sum_{i,j} P(i,j)\phi_i(t)\phi_j(u) , \qquad (2)$$

where

$$\phi_0(t) = \begin{array}{ll} 1-t , & 0 \leq t \leq 1 \\ 0 , & \text{otherwise,} \end{array}$$

$$\phi_i(t) = \begin{array}{ll} t-(i-1) , & i-1 \leq t < i \\ (i+1)-t , & i \leq t < i+1 \\ 0 , & \text{otherwise ,} \end{array}$$

$$\phi_M(t) = \begin{array}{ll} t-(M-1) , & M-1 \leq t \leq M \\ 0 , & \text{otherwise ,} \end{array}$$

and so on.

84

In the method of Coons' surface patches (COONS [15]), surfaces are constructed piecewise as is shown above, therefore local control of the surface is easy. On the other hand, the above construction lacks the continuity of the derivatives across the boundaries. A method of achieving higher order continuity is replacement of the piecewise linear blending fucntions (1-t), t, (1-u), u, $\cdots$ by an appropriate smooth interpolation fucntions. These generalized blending functions $\{\phi_i\}$ should satisfy $\phi_i(j) = \delta_{ij}$, (δ_{ij}: Kronecker's delta) so that $Q(t,j) = P(t,j)$ and $Q(i,u) = P(i,u)$. The formula (2) with general blending function is known as boolean sum approximation. Mathematical properties of this method where investigated by GORDON [16] in relation to splines, who discussed interpolation errors in comparison with those by tensor product of splines.

As was noted earlier, the data are frequently given as a one family of parametric curves:

$$P(t,j) = f_j(t) , \qquad j=0,1,\cdots,N .$$

In this case the function $P(j,u)$ should be interpolated to use (2) by the data on the vertices $\{(i,j)\}$:

$$P(i,u) = \sum_{j=0}^{N} P(i,j)\phi_j(u) .$$

Substituting the above relation for (2), we have

$$Q(t,u) = \sum_{j=0}^{N} P(t,j)\phi_j(u) + \sum_{i,j} P(i,j)\phi_i(t)\phi_j(u) - \sum_{i,j} P(i,j)\phi_i(t)\phi_j(u)$$
$$= \sum_{j=0}^{N} P(t,j)\phi_j(u) = \sum_{j=0}^{N} f_j(t)\phi_j(u) .$$

Thus we have again the method of lofting. In particular, assume N = 1, and $\phi_0(u) = 1-u$, $\phi_1(u) = u$, then

$$Q(t,u) = P(t,0)(1 - u) + P(t,1)u ,$$

which is nothing but (1).

In case of the data given at mesh-points $\{(i,j)\}$, both $P(t,j)$ and $P(i,u)$ should be interpolated to use (2), that is,

$$P(i,u) = \sum_{j=0}^{N} P(i,j)\phi_j(u)$$
$$P(t,j) = \sum_{i=0}^{M} P(i,j)\phi_i(t) .$$

85

Substitution of these relations for (2) yields

$$Q(t,u) = \sum_{i,j} P(i,j)\phi_i(t)\phi_j(u) + \sum_{i,j} P(i,j)\phi_i(t)\phi_j(u)$$

$$- \sum_{i,j} P(i,j)\phi_i(t)\phi_j(u) = \sum_{i,j} P(i,j)\phi_i(t)\phi_j(u) \ .$$

The last expression is the tensor product of univariate interpolation. In particular, tensor product of splines is widely used [8].

In Fig. 11, two functions are considered:

$$f_0(x) = (x-1)(x+1) \ , \qquad\qquad\qquad 0 \leq x \leq 1$$

$$g_0(y) = \begin{cases} 1 & 0 \leq y \leq 0.4 \\ 250y^3 - 375y^2 + 180y - 27 & 0.4 < y < 0.6 \\ 0 & 0.6 \leq y \leq 1 \end{cases}$$

and the surface $h(x,y) = f_0(x)g_0(y)$ should be interpolated. Two families of curves $\{h(i/5,y), i=0,\cdots,5\}$ and $\{h(x,j/5), j=0,\cdots,5\}$ are given along straight lines $x = i/5$, $0 \leq y \leq 1$, $i=0,\cdots,5$ and $y = j/5$, $0 \leq x \leq 1$, $j=0,\cdots,5$, respectively. Two dashed curves passing through $(0.5,0.5)$ are generated by (2) with spline blending function. Figure 12 shows the surface by tensor product of cubic splines where the data are given at $\{(i/5,j/5), i=0,\cdots,5, j=0,\cdots,5\}$. Comparing this figure with the previous one, we find excessive undulations of the latter, since the function $g_0(y)$ is an unfavorable one for the spline, due to the rapid variation of the second derivatives.

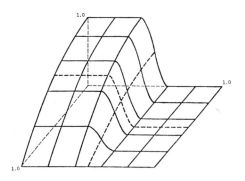 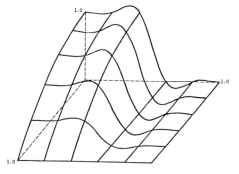

Fig.11

Spline-blended curves, bold lines are given boundary curves and dashed curves are generated by boolean sum of splines

Fig.12

Tensor product of cubic splines

In the problem of surface design, Bezier surfaces have been considered [13], [14] which is essentially an extension of Bezier's method of curve design. This method of design controls the surface by means of a Bezier polygon in three-dimensional space. Moreover the tensor pruduct of Bernstein polynomials are applied.

$$Q(t,u) = \sum_{i=0}^{M} \sum_{j=0}^{N} P(\frac{i}{M}, \frac{j}{N}) J_{M,i}(t) J_{N,j}(u) .$$

An example of a Bezier polygon in space is shown in Fig. 13, where $M = N = 3$, $P_{ij} = P(i/M, j/N)$; $P_{00} = 1.0$, $P_{01} = -0.5$, $P_{02} = 1.0$, $P_{03} = 0.0$, $P_{10} = -1.0$, $P_{11} = -0.5$, $P_{12} = 0.0$, $P_{13} = 0.5$, $P_{20} = -0.5$, $P_{21} = -0.5$, $P_{22} = -0.5$, and $P_{30} = P_{31} = P_{32} = P_{33} = 0.0$. The Bezier surface associated with this polygon is given in Fig. 14. Note that boundary curves near the four corner points of the surface are tangent to the corresponding sides of the polygon.

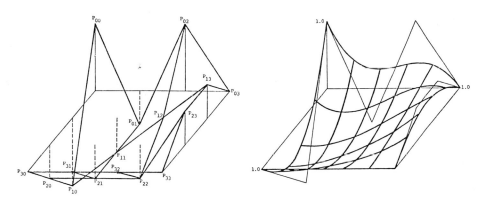

Fig.13 Bezier polygon in space

Fig.14 Bezier surface associated with the previous polygon

5. SHAPE RESTORATION

Sometimes measurement of an object include errors, noises, or some known transformations. Simple interpolation of a function with noisy data might lead to unsuccessful result. Therefore an attempt to represent an object with incomplete data or degraded data, which we call here "shape restoration" requires particular approximation schemes.

In case of noisy data least squares approximation and smoothing interpolation would be prefered to ordinary interpolation. A smoothing spline has been considered by SCHOENBERG [17] and by REINSCH [18] (cf. also DE BOOR [8]). Suppose that the data

$$y_j = g(x_j) + e_j , \qquad j=1,\cdots,N$$

are given with errors $\{e_i\}$. The variance of e_i is assumed to be estimated and is denoted by v_i^2. The problem is to estimate $g(x)$ from the data $\{y_i\}$. Consider a minimization problem with a positive parameter $p \in [0,1]$, [8]:

$$p \sum_{i=1}^{N} (\frac{y_i - f(x_i)}{v_i})^2 + (1-p)\int_{x_1}^{x_n}\left[f^{(m)}(t)\right]^2 dt$$

over all funciton with m derivatives. The solutions f_p turns out to be a spline of order k = 2m with knots at $x_2, \cdots, x_{N-1}$ and satisfying

$$f_p^{(j)}(x_1) = f_p^{(j)}(x_N) = 0 \qquad \text{for } j=m, \cdots, k-2 .$$

Algorithms to calculate smoothing splines have been discussed by REINSCH [18] and by DE BOOR [8].

Figure 15 shows an application of the smoothing spline to the approximation of a step function with noisy observations. Gaussian noise with standard deviation v_i= 0.1 are generated and added to the true funciton. We assumed m = 2 so that spline of order 4 should be used. The dashed curve in the figure is generated by subroutine SMOOTH by DE BOOR [8]. Instead of controlling the parameter p, SMOOTH minimize

$$\int \left[f^{(m)}(t)\right]^2 dt$$

subject to

$$\sum_{i=1}^{N} (\frac{y_i - f(x_i)}{v_i})^2 \leq S .$$

Control of the smoothness is possible by varying the parameter S. The curve in Fig. 15 is generated with S = 100.0 . Larger S gives a smoother curve.

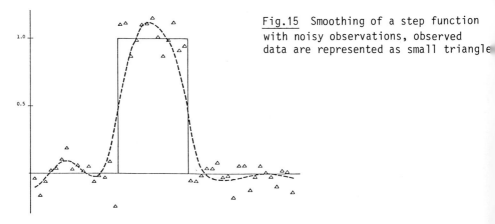

Fig.15 Smoothing of a step function with noisy observations, observed data are represented as small triangle

This method of smoothing was extended to two-dimensional reconstruction of a function as an application to a problem of image restoration [19]. An important class of picture acquisition mechanism is described by an integral relation:

$$g(x,y) = \int\int_D h(x-\xi,y-\eta)f(\xi,\eta)d\xi d\eta + n(x,y) . \tag{3}$$

Here $f(\xi,\eta)$ represent the original object, $G(x,y)$ is the obtained picture, $n(x,y)$ is an additional noise term, and $h(x,y)$ is a space-invariant point spread function [20]. The variable (x,y) and (ξ,η) are assumed to belong to some rectangular region D in two-dimensional space.

HOU and ANDREWS [19] discussed a continuous-discrete model with sampling points (x_i,y_j), $i=1,2,\cdots,I$, $j=1,2,\cdots,J$ in (x,y)-plane:

$$G = \int\int H(\xi,\eta)f(\xi,\eta)d\xi d\eta + N ,$$

which can be obtained by discretizing the continuous model (3):

$$G = (g_{ij}) = (g(x_i,y_j)), \qquad i=1,\cdots,I, \quad J=1,\cdots,J$$

$$H(\xi,\eta) = (h_{ij}(\xi,\eta)) = (h(x_i-\xi,y_j-\eta)) ,$$

$$N = (n_{ij}) = (n(x_i,y_j)) .$$

The problem is to find an estimate $\bar{f}$ of f from the measurement data. Let

$$G = \int\int H(\xi,\eta)\bar{f}(\xi,\eta)d\xi d\eta .$$

In their formulation the model is continuous-discrete, therefore some basis funciton should be chosen to obtain a finite dimensional solution. They assumed $\bar{f}$ to be represented by tensor product of splines

$$\bar{f}(\xi,\eta) = \sum_{i,j} c_{ij} N_{i,m}(\xi) N_{j,n}(\eta) .$$

The coefficients (c_{ij}) are estimated to minimize

$$Tr[(G - \bar{G})^t(G - \bar{G})] + \gamma \int\int \frac{\partial^4}{\partial\xi^2\partial\eta^2} f(\xi,\eta)d\xi d\eta , \qquad (\gamma > 0) .$$

HOU and ANDREWS [19] proved that the second term is reduced to a tensor product of almost periodic, strictly diagonally dominant, banded matrix. Therefore the resulting matrix equation has a positive definite coefficient matrix and has a unique solution. Further, they discussed other advantages of B-splines as a basis funciton: 1) to reduce quadrature error in approximating the integral, and 2) to deal with the banded matrices in spline transformed space.

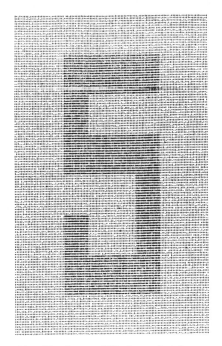

Fig.16 Image "5" degraded by additive white noise with v=0.2

Fig.17 Quantized result of Fig.16 by two levels

Fig.18 Processed image using smoothing spline with S=100

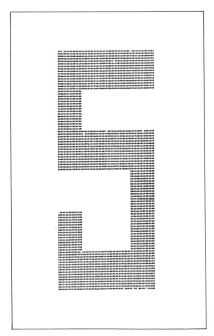

Fig.19 Quantized result of Fig.18 by two levels

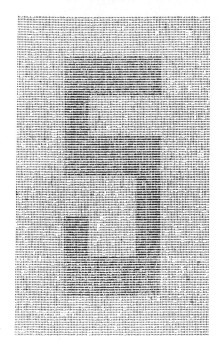

Fig.20 Processed image using smoothing spline with S=50

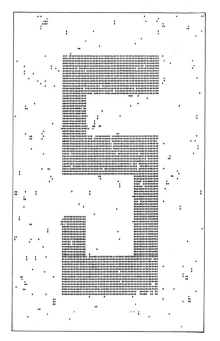

Fig.21 Quantized result of Fig.20 by two levels

Figures 16 - 21 shows results of application of one-dimensional smoothing spline to image restoration. An original function f with values 0.0 and 1.0 showing the character "5" is assumed on a plane and it is observed with Gaussian white noise with zero mean and standard deviation v = 0.2, as is shown in Fig. 16. When the observed data are quantized into two classes BLACK and WHITE:

$$\text{if } f_{ij} \geq \frac{1}{2} \left(\max_{m,n} f_{mn} + \min_{m,n} f_{mn} \right)$$

then $f_{ij} \in$ BLACK

else $f_{ij} \in$ WHITE ,

then we have a simplified image in Fig. 17. One dimensional smoothing spline are applied rowwise and then columnwise, and their pointwise mean values represent pixels in the smoothed image. Figure 18 is obtained with S = 100.0, whereas Fig. 20 is obtained with S = 50.0 . Figures 19 and 21 are the results of the quantization by the above procedure. It is clear that the noise is considerably reduced in Fig. 19; In Fig. 21, however, the smoothing parameter S is inappropriate and the result is far from satisfactory.

PEYROVIAN and SAWCHUK [21] used the convolution property of B-splines in case of uniform knots in image restoration:

$$\int N_{i,m}(x-y)N_{j,n}(y)dy = N_{i+j,m+n}(x)$$

They expanded the original object and the point spread function by B-splines. Using the convolution property, they showed that if the original image and the point spread function are approximated by B-splines, the degraded image should be expanded by B-splines of a higher order. They showed a numerical example in which a restored image using B-splines is better than that without splines.

As another example of shape restoration, we mention an application to a problem in environmental pollution. Huge amount of measurement data of air pollution are daily collected in every urban areas in Japan. The measurement stations are irregularly distributed and the data are obtained as time series. Statistical studies such as the time series analysis have been performed but advanced analyses in time and space are still required. Frequently it is desired to know or to predict pollution levels at an arbitrary place other than the measurement stations. For example, in case of the photochemical air pollution, chemical reactions occur in air and high levels of pollutant concentration arise at distant places from the sources of pollution. In such a case the present status of pollution is well grasped through charts like weather map. Therefore interpolation methods are useful to generate spatial patterns from points data of pollution levels.

It is known that ordinary cubic spline sometimes tends to have excessive undulations (cf. Fig. 12). FUJIWARA, OI, SHINDO [22] used spline under tension proposed by OONISHI [23] to interpolate data of photochemical air pollution. It was already noted that the cubic spline minimizes the integral

$$\int (\frac{d^2f}{dx^2})^2 dx \ ,$$

whereas the spline nuder tension minimizes (OONISHI [23], CLINE [24])

$$\int [(\frac{d^2f}{dx^2})^2 + \sigma(\frac{df}{dx})^2] dx \ , \qquad (\sigma > 0) \ .$$

When $\sigma \to 0$, it agrees with the cubic spline; when $\sigma \to \infty$, it is reduced to the linear interpolation.

OONISHI [23] considered two dimensional extension of the above method: the pr-blem is to find a function $z(x,y)$ which minimizes

$$\int\int_D [(\Delta z)^2 + \sigma(\nabla z)^2] dxdy \qquad (\sigma > 0) \ .$$

$$\frac{\partial z}{\partial n} = 0 \quad \text{on } \partial D \qquad (\partial/\partial n \text{ is normal derivative})$$

subject to

$$z(x_i,y_i) = z_i, \quad i=1,2,\cdots,n ,$$

where $D = (a,b) \times (c,d)$ is a rectangular domain,

$$z = \frac{\partial^2 z}{\partial x^2} + \frac{\partial^2 z}{\partial y^2} ,$$

$$(\nabla z)^2 = (\frac{\partial z}{\partial x})^2 + (\frac{\partial z}{\partial y})^2 .$$

The Euler equation is

$$\Delta^2 z + \Delta z = 0$$

with the boundary condition

$$\frac{\partial z}{\partial n} = 0 \quad \text{on } D .$$

By the discretization of D with equal interval $X_0 = a$, $X_k - X_{k-1} = h$, $k=1,2,\cdots,p$; $Y_0 = b$, $Y_\ell - Y_{\ell-1} = h$,

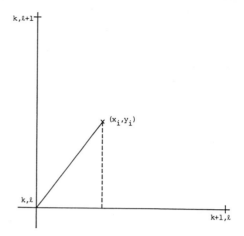

Fig.22 The point (x_i,y_i) is combined with the mesh point (X_k,Y_ℓ) by a linear relation

$\ell = 1,2,\cdots,q$, the following difference equations are obtained as approximations of the above partial differential equation:

$$(Z_{k-1,\ell} + Z_{k+1,\ell} + Z_{k,\ell-1} + Z_{k,\ell+1} - 4Z_{k,\ell})/h^2 = P_k, \tag{4}$$

$$(P_{k-1,\ell} + P_{k+1,\ell} + P_{k,\ell-1} + P_{k,\ell+1} - 4P_{k,\ell})/h^2 = P_k, \tag{5}$$

where $Z_{k,\ell}$ approximates $z(X_k,Y_\ell)$ and $P_{k,\ell}$ approximates $z(X_k,Y_\ell)$. Conditions $z(x_i,y_j) = z_i$ can be included in the system of algebraic equations by a linear interpolation. Suppose that the point (x_i,y_i) is in the subregion $[X_k,X_{k+1}]$ $\times [Y_\ell,Y_{\ell+1}]$ and the mesh point nearest to (x_i,y_i) is (X_k,Y_ℓ) as in Fig. 22, then the functional value z_i is associated with $Z_{k,\ell}$'s by the linear relation

$$z_i = Z_{k,\ell} + \frac{Z_{k+1,\ell} - Z_{k,\ell}}{h} (x_i - X_k) + \frac{Z_{k,\ell+1} - Z_{k,\ell}}{h} (y_i - y_\ell) . \tag{6}$$

If two or more points belong to the same subregion, their centroid and mean value are adopted instead. Numerical solution of (4), (5), and (6) with the discretized boundary condition gives the approximate solution of the partial differential equation.

FUJIWARA, OI, SHINDO [22] and SHINOHARA, NAITO [25] have applied the above algorithm by OONISHI. They determined the optimal value of the tension parameter σ, using a part of the observations as checking data. It was found that $\sigma \cong 1.0$ gives the least interpolation error (SHINOHARA, NAITO, [25]).

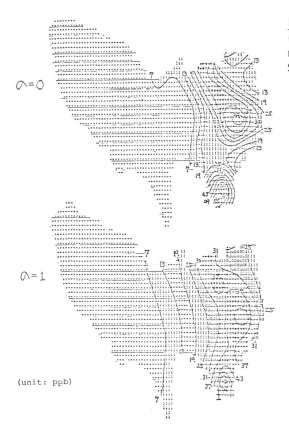

Fig.23 Spline-generated pattern of SO_2 concentration, the yearly mean in Tokyo, 1970 (from SHINOHARA, NAITO [25])

$\Lambda = 0$

$\Lambda = 1$

(unit: ppb)

Some other interpolation methods including Akima's surface fitting for irregularly spaced data (AKIMA [26]) are discussed by GOODIN, MCRAE, SEINFELD [27]. They compared several procedure by using test data and found that second degree polynomial fitting is accurate and at the same time requires small amount of computation.

Physical diffusion models have been traditionally used in this field. However, nonphysical models such as the interpolation schemes are appearing and their merits are appreciated. This type of application is considered to be promising and there is a room for further studies and experiences.

6. CONCLUSION

When a mathematical tool appears which is also useful in applications, it is first studied theoretically, then it is applied to many areas neighboring to mathematics, its generalizations are considered, further it is widespread and applications are found which are very different form its original purposes. The method of splines has been extensively studies, and we have seen a small portion of its application. Some applications described here are well-known to experts of computer graphics; others are, however, new and appearing. Thus, utility of splines can be still increased and areas of application would be enlarged.

94

ACKNOWLEDGMENT

The authors wish to express deepest appreciation to Dr. Masaaki Naito and to Dr. Ko Oi of National Institute of Environmental Science for their helpful advice and for the use of figures.

REFERENCES

1. S. C. Wu, J. F. Abel, D. P. Geenberg: Comm. ACM, 20, 10, 703-712 (1977)
2. J. H. Ahlberg, E. N. Nilson, J. L. Walsh: The Theory of Splines and Their Applications, (Academic Press, New York, 1967)
3. K. Hatano: Johoshori (Journal of Information Processing Society of Japan), 22, 1, 19-27 (1981)
4. R. S. Varga: Functional Analysis and Approximation Theory in Numerical Analysis, (SIAM Publications, Philadelphia, Pennsylvania, 1971)
5. T. Lyche, R. Winther: J. Approx. Th. 25, 266-279 (1979)
6. D. G. Schweikert: J. Math. Physics, 45, 312-317 (1966)
7. S. D. Curry, I. J. Schoenbert: Bull. Amer. Math. Soc. 53, 1114 (1947)
8. C. de Boor: A Practical Guide to Splines, (Springer, New York, 1978)
9. W. K. Giloi: Interactive Computer Graphics - Data Structures, Algorithms, Languages, (Prentice-Hall, Englewood Cliffs, N. J., 1978)
10. S. D. Conte, C. de Boor: Elementary Numerical Analysis - an Algorithmic Approach, 2nd ed. (McGraw-Hill, New York, 1972)
11. P. E. Bezier: Emploi de Machines a Commande Numerique, (Masson et Cie, Paris, 1970), Tanslated by D. R. Forrest, A. F. Pankhurst as P. F. Bezier: Numerical Control Mathematics and Applications, (Wiley, 1972)
12. W. J. Gordon, R. F. Riesenfeld: B-spline Curves and Surfaces, In Computer-Aided Geometric Design, R. E. Barnhill and R. F. Riesenfeld, eds. (Academic Press, New York, 1974)
13. D. F. Rogers, J. A. Adams: Mathematical Elements for Computer Graphics, (McGraw-Hill, New York, 1976)
14. A. R. Forrest: Computer Graphics and Image Processing, 1, 4, 341-359 (1972)
15. A. Coons: M.I.T., MAC-TR-41 (1967)
16. W. J. Gordon: J. Math. Mech. 18, 931-952 (1969)
17. I. J. Schoenberg: Proc. Nat. Acad. Sci., 52, 947-950 (1964)
18. C. H. Reinsch: Numer. Math., 10, 177-183 (1967)
19. H. S. Hou, C. Andrews: IEEE Trans. Computers, C-26, 9, 856-873 (1977)
20. A. Rosenfeld, A. C. Kak: Digital Picture Processing, (Academic Press, New York, 1976)
21. M. J. Peyrovian, A. A. Sawchuk: Appl. Opt. 17, 4, 660-666 (1978)
22. M. Fujiwara, K. Oi, J. Shindo: Symposium in Environmental and Sanitary Engineering, (in Japanese) Kyoto Univ. Aug. (1981)
23. Oonishi: J. Oceanographical Soc. Japan (in Japanese) 31, 259-264 (1975)
24. A. K. Cline: Atmospheric Technology, NCAR, 3, 60-65 (1973)
25. M. Shinohara, M. Naito: Kankyo Joho Shori (J. Information in Environmental Science, in Japanese), 9, 4, 62-64 (1980)
26. H. Akima: ACM Trans. Math. Software, 4, 2, 148-159 (1978)
27. W. R. Goodin, G. J. McRae, J. H. Seinfeld: J. Appl. Meteor. 18, 761-771 (1979)

Computer-Aided Design of 3-D Objects Using Polar Spline Representations

L.L. Schumaker*

Department of Mathematics and Center for Approximation Theory
Texas A&M University, College Station, TX 77843, USA

1. Introduction

In recent years there has been considerable interest in systems for the computer-aided design of three dimensional objects. An essential ingredient of such a system is a method for constructing mathematical representations of 3-D surfaces. The method should have the following properties:

the mathematical representation of any object should depend only (1.1)
on a finite number of parameters which can be stored in a digital
computer;

the representation should be such that perspective views (or 3-D (1.2)
views) of the object can be rapidly generated;

the representation of any object should depend on a finite number (1.3)
of control parameters in such a way that the user can interactively
modify these parameters to alter the shape of the object in a
controlled fashion.

For design purposes, it is property (1.3) which is the most important, and the most difficult to achieve. A number of presently available systems use control nets as the control parameters. In this connection, see BARNHILL & RIESENFELD [1] and BÉZIER [2] , as well as the references therein.

The purpose of this paper is to suggest a completely different approach to the problem, using polar representations and B-spline expansions. Here the coefficients of the spline expansions themselves will serve as control parameters.

2. Polar Representation of 3-D Surfaces

We begin with a simple observation. Let H be the rectangle

$$H = \{(\theta, \phi) : 0 \leq \theta \leq 2\pi , - \frac{\pi}{2} \leq \phi \leq \frac{\pi}{2} \}. \tag{2.1}$$

Then, given any positive real-valued function $r(\theta,\phi)$ defined on H, it is clear that the set of points

---

* Supported by the Humbolt Foundation at the Free University of Berlin and
  the Hahn-Meitner Institute, Berlin.

$$S = \{ (\theta, \phi, r) : (\theta, \phi) \in H \} \qquad (2.2)$$

defines a surface in three dimensions.

   In practice we shall usually only be interested in surfaces which do not have discontinuities in them. Hence, it is reasonable to require that $r(\theta, \phi)$ have the properties

r is continuous on H ; $\qquad\qquad\qquad\qquad\qquad\qquad\qquad\qquad (2.3)$
$r(0, \phi) = r(2\pi, \phi)$, all $-\dfrac{\pi}{2} \leq \phi \leq \dfrac{\pi}{2}$; $\qquad (2.4)$

$\begin{cases} r(\theta, -\pi/2) = \text{constant for} \quad 0 \leq \theta \leq 2\pi , \\ r(\theta, \pi/2) = \text{constant for} \quad 0 \leq \theta \leq 2\pi . \end{cases} \qquad (2.5)$

Property (2.3) is required if we do not want tears in the surface. Property (2.5) is introduced because of the fact that the points corresponding to $\phi = \pi/2$ and $\phi = -\pi/2$ correspond to the top and bottom peaks of the surface, respectively. Finally, condition (2.4) is required so that as we sweep around the surface with fixed ϕ, we obtain a closed line.

Definition 2.1   Let

   $\mathscr{SO}$ = { objects $\mathscr{O}$: the surface $\mathscr{S}$ of $\mathscr{O}$ has a polar representation $\quad$ (2.6)
        as in (2.2) with r as in (2.3)-(2.5) }.

We call $\mathscr{SO}$ the set of <u>starlike objects</u>.

The set of starlike objects consists of those 3-D objects for which it is possible to find a point inside the object from which every point on the surface of the object can be seen. A given starlike object may have several different representations, depending on where the origin of the polar coordinate system is placed. (Generally, most objects will have an infinite number of different such representations.)

   The set of starlike objects contains a great many members. A large subclass is formed by the objects whose surfaces are <u>surfaces</u> <u>of</u> <u>revolution</u> where r is given by

$$r(\theta, \phi) = \text{constant function of } \theta \text{ , each } -\frac{\pi}{2} \leq \phi \leq \frac{\pi}{2} . \qquad (2.7)$$

There are, of course, also a large number of non-starlike objects. The snowman shown in Figure 1 is a typical example.

   To expand the class of 3-D objects which can be represented by polar coordinates, we make the following definition:

Definition 2.2   Let

   $\mathscr{PSO}$ = { objects $\mathscr{O}$: $\mathscr{O} = \overset{N}{\underset{j=1}{U}} \mathscr{O}_j$, where each $\mathscr{O}_j$ is $\qquad$ (2.8)
        a starlike object relative to some origin e_j } .

We call $\mathscr{PSO}$ the set of <u>piecewise starlike objects</u>. Given an object $\mathscr{O}$ in $\mathscr{PSO}$, we call N* = {minimum of the N so that $\mathscr{O}$ can be divided into N starlike objects } the <u>index</u> <u>of</u> <u>the</u> <u>object</u>.

It is intuitively obvious that all physical objects are piecewise starlike, and in fact, most of them will have a relatively small index. To construct a mathematical representation of a piecewise starlike object, we must first decide how to decompose the object into starlike objects. For each of these we must choose an origin e_j, and a radius function r_j. We note that the surface of the object $\mathcal{O}$ is not generally the union of the surfaces defined by the r_j (since usually part of each surface will be inside the object). On the other hand, there always exist subsets H_j of H so that the surface S of $\mathcal{O}$ is

$$S = \bigcup_{j=1}^{N} S_j \quad , \quad \text{with} \quad S_j = \{(\theta,\phi,r_j) : (\theta,\phi) \in H_j \} ,$$ (2.9)

$$j = 1,2,\ldots,N.$$

We may call the sets of $\{H_j\}_1^N$ the <u>essential domains of</u> $\mathcal{O}$. As (θ,ϕ) moves around the boundary ∂H_j of one of the sets H_j, the point (θ,ϕ,r_j) follows a closed line in space. We call this a <u>sew line</u>.

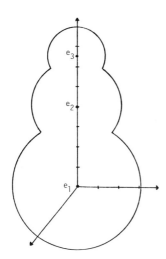

Figure 1   A piecewise starlike object

We illustrate these ideas in the following example.

<u>Example 2.3</u>   Consider the snowman in Figure 1.

<u>Discussion</u>:   The index of this object is 2. Its piecewise polar representations of index 2 are fairly complicated, however. For this object, it is easier to work with representations of index 3. For example, we may take centers

$$e_1 = (0,0,0) \quad , \quad e_2 = (0,\pi/2,4) \quad , \quad e_3 = (0,\pi/2,6.5)$$ (2.10)

and radii functions

$$r_1 \equiv 3 \quad , \quad r_2 \equiv 2 \quad , \quad r_3 \equiv 1 .$$ (2.11)

For this example, the essential domains for these functions have the form

$$H_1 = \{(\theta,\phi): 0 \le \theta \le 2\pi \;,\; \underline{\phi}_1 \le \phi \le \overline{\phi}_1 \qquad\qquad\qquad (2.12)$$
$$H_2 = \{(\theta,\phi): 0 \le \theta \le 2\pi \;,\; \underline{\phi}_2 \le \phi \le \overline{\phi}_2$$
$$H_3 = \{(\theta,\phi): 0 \le \theta \le 2\pi \;,\; \underline{\phi}_3 \le \phi \le \overline{\phi}_3 \qquad ,$$

with appropriate values of $\underline{\phi}_j < \overline{\phi}_j$, $j = 1,2,3$. Here there are two sew lines, and each of them is a circle.

Example 2.3 suggests that in many cases it may be desirable to work with piecewise polar representations of index greater than the actual index of the object being represented.

3. Perspective Display

As mentioned in the introduction, for computer-aided design it is important to be able to rapidly display the current shape of the design. In most computer systems, this is accomplished most easily by computing perspective views for display on a CRT-device.

The typical approach to displaying perspective views of 3-D objects is to define a grid of lines on the surface of the object, and then to project them onto the viewing screen. More accurately, what is usually done is to project the grid points on the surface onto the screen, and then join them together with straight lines.

There is no essential difficulty in computing perspective views of star-like surfaces with this approach. Indeed, some advantage can be taken of the fact that we are working in polar coordinates--as we move around the object it is very simple to compute the necessary transformation which defines the projection. In general, suitable perspective views can be produced only if an appropriate hidden-line algorithm is included in the system. A survey of such algorithms is given in SUTHERLAND, SPROULL & SCHUMACKER [12].

The display of perspective views of piecewise starlike objects is not significantly more difficult than the display of starlike objects. The portions of the surfaces of the various starlike pieces which are actually on the inside of the object will be eliminated by the hidden-line algorithm. Some work may be saved, however, if we have some idea of what the essential domains look like, and where the sew lines are located.

4. Tensor Product Splines

As mentioned in section 1, for computer-aided design we need mathematical representations involving a finite number of parameters. Thus, if we use polar (or piecewise polar) methods, we need an appropriate class of functions to choose the radius functions r_j from. Each r_j is defined on the standard rectangle H defined in (1.1). Recently there has been considerable interest in the problem of approximating a function of two variables defined on a rectangle by tensor product splines (see the survey [10]), and we recommend that they be used here.

First, we need to define B-splines in the θ and ϕ variables. Because of the need for periodicity in the θ direction, the construction is not the same in the two variables. We begin with the θ variable. Choose $m > 1$ and $K > m$, and let

$$0 < x_1 < x_2 < \ \ldots \ < x_K < 2\pi \ . \tag{4.1}$$

Associated with these points, define

$$y_{i+m} \ = \ x_i \ , \quad i = 1,2,\ldots,K \tag{4.2}$$

$$
\begin{aligned}
y_i &= y_{i+k} - 2\pi \ , \\
y_{K+m+i} &= y_{m+i} + 2\pi \ ,
\end{aligned}
\quad i = 1,2,\ldots,m \qquad . \tag{4.3}
$$

Let $\{N_i^m\}_1^{m+K}$ be the usual B-splines associated with the set of knots $y_1,\ldots,$ y_{2m+K} . They have the following properties (see [3,4,11]):

$$N_1^m \ (\theta) \ \text{ is a piecewise polynomial of degree } m-1 \ , \tag{4.4}$$

$$N_i^m \ \in \ C^{m-2}[0,2\pi] \tag{4.5}$$

$$N_i^m \ (\theta) > 0 \ \text{ for } y_i < \theta < y_{i+m} \tag{4.6}$$

$$N_i^m \ (\theta) = 0 \ \text{ outside of } (y_i, y_{i+m}) \ , \tag{4.7}$$

$$\sum_{i=1}^{m+k} N_i^m \ (\theta) \ = \ 1 \quad \text{ for all } 0 \le \theta \le 2\pi \quad . \tag{4.8}$$

To construct B-splines in the ϕ direction, let $\tilde{m} > 1$ and $\tilde{K} > \tilde{m}$, and let

$$\tilde{y}_1 \ < \ldots < \tilde{y}_{\tilde{m}} = -\pi/2 \ < \tilde{y}_{\tilde{m}+1} \ < \ \ldots \ < \tilde{y}_{\tilde{m}+\tilde{K}} \ < \pi/2 = \tilde{y}_{\tilde{m}+\tilde{K}+1} \tag{4.9}$$

$$< \ \ldots < \tilde{y}_{2\tilde{m}+\tilde{K}} \quad .$$

Then the associated B-splines $\{N_j^{\tilde{m}}\}_1^{\tilde{m}+\tilde{K}}$ satisfy the properties (4.4) – (4.8) on $[-\pi/2, \pi/2]$.

The following result is easy to prove (see SCHUMAKER [11]).

<u>Theorem 4.1</u> Suppose

$$s(\theta,\phi) \ = \ \sum_{i=1}^{K+m} \sum_{j=1}^{\tilde{K}+\tilde{m}} c_{ij} N_i^m(\theta) N_j^{\tilde{m}}(\phi) \ , \tag{4.10}$$

where

$$c_{i+K,j} = c_{i,j} \ , \quad
\begin{aligned}
i &= 1,2,\ldots,m \\
j &= 1,2,\ldots,\tilde{m}+\tilde{K}
\end{aligned} \quad . \tag{4.11}$$

Then

$$s(\theta,\cdot) \ \in \ C^{m-2}[-\pi/2, \pi/2] \ \text{ for all } 0 \le \theta \le 2\pi \ , \tag{4.12}$$

100

and

$$s(\cdot,\phi) \ \in \ \overset{\circ}{C}{}^{m-2}[0,2\pi] = \{f \in C^{m-2}[0,2\pi] : f^{(j)} \text{ is}$$

$$2\pi\text{-periodic}, \ j = 0,1,\ldots,m-2 \}, \tag{4.13}$$

for all $-\pi/2 \le \phi \le \pi/2$.

This result shows that B-spline expansions of the form (4.10) - (4.11) provide smooth radius functions with the desired periodicity in the θ direction. For fixed m and $\tilde{m}$, it is known that B-spline expansions of this form are capable of approximating any given smooth function to high accuracy (with enough knots). For theorems of this type, see LYCHE & SCHUMAKER [9].

The following theorem gives another important property of tensor-product B-splines which shows that they are particularly well-suited for our present application.

<u>Theorem 4.2</u>   Let s be defined as in (4.10). Given ℓ, $\tilde{\ell}$ and $\varepsilon > 0$, let

$$\hat{c}_{ij} = \begin{cases} c_{ij} + \varepsilon , & i - \ell , \ j - \tilde{\ell} \\ c_{ij} , & \text{otherwise} . \end{cases} \tag{4.14}$$

Let $\hat{s}$ be the B-spline expansion with coefficients $\{\hat{c}_{ij}\}$. Then

$$0 \le \hat{s}(\theta,\phi) - s(\theta,\phi) \le \varepsilon \text{ for all } (\theta,\phi) \in H_{\ell\tilde{\ell}} , \tag{4.15}$$

where

$$H_{\ell\tilde{\ell}} = \{(\theta,\phi): y_\ell < \theta \le y_{\ell+m} , \quad \tilde{y}_{\tilde{\ell}} < \phi \le \tilde{y}_{\tilde{\ell}+\tilde{m}} \} , \tag{4.16}$$

and

$$\hat{s}(\theta,\phi) - s(\theta,\phi) \text{ for all } (\theta,\phi) \in H \setminus H_{\ell\tilde{\ell}} . \tag{4.17}$$

<u>Proof:</u> This result follows immediately from the fact that

$$0 \le N_\ell^m(\theta) \ N_{\tilde{\ell}}^{\tilde{m}}(\phi) \le 1 \text{ for } (\theta,\phi) \in H_{\ell\tilde{\ell}} ,$$

and this B-spline vanishes otherwise.

The significance of Theorem 4.2 for our purposes is the following: if we want to increase $s(\theta,\phi)$ in the rectangle $H_{\ell\tilde{\ell}}$, then we need only increase the coefficient $c_{\ell\tilde{\ell}}$. The amount of increase of s tends to be the largest in the center of the rectangle $H_{\ell\tilde{\ell}}$, is bounded by ε, and is zero outside of this rectangle. If it is desired to increase (or decrease) s in some larger set, then we need only decide which rectangles are of interest, and increase (or decrease) the corresponding coefficients. In short, the coefficients of the B-spline expansion are themselves a set of <u>control</u> <u>parameters</u> for governing the shape of an object in polar form. We exploit this observation in the next section to outline a system for computer-aided design of 3-D objects.

In closing this section, we mention that B-spline expansions as in (4.10) are very easy to evaluate, and thus they are well-suited for display of surfaces in polar form. One factor contributing to the fact that $s(\theta,\phi)$ can be quickly evaluated at any given (θ,ϕ) is the local nature of the B-splines; indeed, we have

$$s(\theta,\phi) \;=\; \sum_{i=n-m+1}^{n}\;\sum_{j=\tilde{n}-\tilde{m}+1}^{\tilde{n}} c_{ij} N_i^m(\theta) N_j^{\tilde{m}}(\phi) \quad, \quad \text{if} \quad \begin{array}{l} y_n \;<\; \theta \;\le\; y_{n+1} \\ \breve{y}_{\tilde{n}} \;<\; \phi \;\le\; \breve{y}_{\tilde{n}+1} \end{array} . \tag{4.18}$$

Thus, only m^2 coefficients are involved in the expansion at any given point. The corresponding B-spline values can be rapidly and accurately generated using well-known recursions--see [3,4,11].

The use of tensor product B-splines is further simplified (and the associated algorithms are much faster) when the knots are chosen to be equally spaced, see [11].

5. Proposed Structure of an Interactive Design System

In the previous sections we have discussed the possibility of using tensor product B-spline expansions as radius functions for piecewise polar representations of 3-D objects. Here we outline the structure of a possible system based on these ideas. For ease of exposition, we consider first the case of designing a starlike object.

Step 1 Choose an initial design frame. By this, we mean to choose the spline parameters m, $\tilde{m}$, K, $\tilde{K}$, and knots $\{y_i\}_1^{m+K}$ and $\{\breve{y}_j\}_1^{\tilde{m}+\tilde{K}}$.

Step 2 Choose an initial design; i.e., $\{c_{ij}\}_{i=1,j=1}^{m+K,\;\tilde{m}+\tilde{K}}$.

Step 3 Display the surface.

Step 4 Decide if the surface is acceptable. If so stop. If not, then either go to step 5, or if it is felt that the desired shape cannot be accomplished within the given design frame, then go to step 6.

Step 5 Adjust the coefficients. In practice this could be accomplished by indicating areas where it is desired that the surface bulge out more (or less), along with an indication of the percentage change desired. The program should then compute which coefficients to change, and by how much. The areas to be changed could be fed into the computer using either a light pen or a joy stick.

Step 6 Refine the design frame. In order to provide a larger class of radius functions, we may increase any or all of the parameters m, $\tilde{m}$, K, and $\tilde{K}$. If K or $\tilde{K}$ are altered, we will need to choose new sets of knots. Now we return to Step 2.

Some remarks are in order. If we are designing surfaces of rotation, then the radius function should be a constant function of θ for each ϕ, and we should choose $m = 1$. In general, it is recommended that m and $\tilde{m}$ be kept relatively small. The use of linear, quadratic, or cubic splines ($m = 2,3,4$) is especially recommended.

102

The choice of an initial design is discussed in the following section. If it becomes necessary to refine the design frame, then in choosing a new initial design it is desirable to choose the coefficients so that we start out with a surface which is reasonably close to the surface obtained with the old design frame. Methods for doing this are also discussed in the following section.

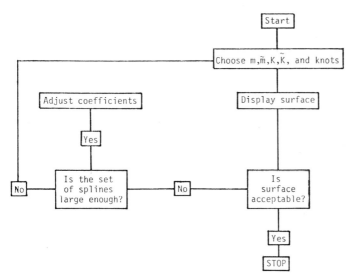

Figure 2 A possible design system

A schematic diagram of this design system is shown in Figure 2. If we desire to design piecewise starlike objects, the structure of the system is altered only slightly. First, in choosing a design frame, it is necessary to choose an index N, centers $e_1,..,.,e_N$, and spline parameters associated with each. Initial designs will be required for each of the parts of the surface. For display, it will be useful to compute the essential domains of the surface parts, and the sew lines if possible. In this regard, see Remark 4.

6. Initializing the Design

In the first two steps of the design system proposed in the previous section it is necessary to choose a design frame and an initial design. One approach to this task is to take the coarsest possible design frame; namely, $m = \tilde{m} = 1$ and $K = \tilde{K} = 0$, and the simplest possible design; namely, $r \equiv 1$. This means that the design process is to begin with a unit sphere.

On the other hand, in many cases (and in particular when we have returned to step 1 after having worked with one or more design frames) we may already be in possession of a design which has the general shape of what we want, and simply needs to be refined. In this case we should choose a finer design frame, and we should take account of the presently available design in computing a new initial design. We may express this more precisely as follows (where for simplicity we discuss only starlike objects): Suppose that the available design is given by a radius function r, and suppose we choose a new design frame with a corresponding class of splines $\mathscr{S}$. Then the initial design for the new design frame should be some spline in $\mathscr{S}$ which reasonably approximates r.

The problem of approximating a given function r on the rectangle H by splines in a given class $\mathscr{S}$ has been extensively studied--see e.g. the survey of SCHUMAKER [10]. The possibilities include interpolation, least squares, best approximation, and various direct methods. For our purposes here, the direct methods seem to be particularly well-suited. They are simple, fast, local, and deliver very good approximations. For convenience, we briefly describe how they work.

The key idea in the direct methods for tensor-product spline approximation is to compute the coefficients in a B-spline expansion as in (4.10) directly from sampled values of the function r to be approximated. In particular, with appropriate coefficients $\{a_{ip}\}_{p=1}^m$ and $\{b_{iq}\}_{q=1}^m$ and sample points

$$y_i \leq \tau_{i1} < \cdots < \tau_{ip} \leq y_{i+m} \tag{6.1}$$

$$\tilde{y}_j \leq \tilde{\tau}_{j1} < \cdots < \tilde{\tau}_{jq} \leq \tilde{y}_{j+m} \quad ,$$

we compute

$$c_{ij} = \sum_{p=1}^m \sum_{q=1}^{\tilde{m}} a_{ip} b_{jq} r(\tau_{ip}, \tilde{\tau}_{jq}) \quad . \tag{6.2}$$

Properties of approximation processes of this form are studied in considerable detail in LYCHE & SCHUMAKER [9]. It is important to note that once having chosen the sample points, we can precompute the necessary coefficients once and for all. Then the spline s approximating r can be constructed very rapidly directly from the values of $r(\tau_{ip}, \tilde{\tau}_{jq})$. It is also worth noting that if equally spaced knots are used, then the coefficients $\{a_{ip}\}$ and $\{b_{jq}\}$ can be chosen to be independent of i and j, and the whole process becomes very simple. (Methods of this type with equally spaced knots were employed in HAMMERLIN & SCHUMAKER [7] to solve Fredholm integral equations. Tables of the coefficients corresponding to equally spaced knots and m = 1,..,5 can be found there.)

7. Remarks

1) In section 4 we have described the B-splines only for simple knots. It is also possible to work with tensor products of B-splines corresponding to multiple knots. In this case the splines have reduced smoothness across knot (grid) lines. This fact can be used to advantage when it is desired to design surfaces with sharp creases or corners.

2) The direct spline approximation methods have been programmed and tested at the University of Texas, Austin. (We would like to thank Mrs. Ellin Wilson for her assistance with the programs.) Some experiments were also con-

ducted with the perspective display of 3-D objects in polar form. Piece-wise starlike objects were not treated, and the complete design system also remains to be constructed.

3) Recent research in graphics has seen the development of raster CRT meth-ods for producing shaded and colored displays of 3-D objects. For a discus-sion of this research and further references, see CLARK [6]. Actual 3-D display systems have also been developed; see CLARK [5]. These systems can also be used to display objects represented in polar form.

4) The problem of locating the line of intersection between two surfaces in space can be quite difficult, depending on the form of the surfaces. As an example of how this can be done, see LEVIN [8] where patch quadric surfaces are considered.

References

1. Barnhill, R. and R. Γ. Riesenfeld, Computer-Aided Geometric Design, Aca-demic Press, N.Y., 1974.

2. Bézier, P., Numerical Control-Mathematics and Applications, Wiley, Lon-don, 1972.

3. deBoor, C., On calculating with B-splines, J. Approximation Th. 6(1972), 50-62.

4. deBoor, C., Subroutine package for calculating with B-splines, SIAM J. Numer. Anal. 14(1977), 441-473.

5. Clark, J. H., Designing surfaces in 3-D, Comm. A.C.M. 19(1976), 454-460.

6. Clark, J. H., Hierarchical geometric models for visible surface algo-rithm, Comm. A.C.M. 19(1976), 547-554.

7. Hämmerlin, G. and L. L. Schumaker, Procedures for kernel approximation and the numerical solution of Fredholm integral equations of the second kind, Numerische Math. 34(1980), 125-141.

8. Levin, J., A parametric algorithm for drawing pictures of solid objects composed of quadric surfaces, Comm. A.C.M. 19(1976), 555-563.

9. Lyche, T. and L. L. Schumaker, Local spline approximation methods, J. Approximation Th. 15(1975), 294-325.

10. Schumaker, L. L., Fitting surfaces to scattered data, in Approximation Theory II, C. K. Chui, G. G. Lorentz, and L. L. Schumaker, eds., Aca-demic Press, N.Y., 1976, 203-268.

11. Schumaker, L. L., Spline Functions: Basic Theory, Wiley-Interscience, New York, 1981.

12. Sutherland, I. E., Sproull, R. F., and Schumacker, R. A., A characteri-zation of ten hidden-surface algorithms, Computing Surveys 6(1974), 1-55.

Application of Structure Lines to Surface Construction and 3-Dimensional Analysis

H. Enomoto, N. Yonezaki, and Y. Watanabe

Department of Computer Science, Tokyo Institute of Technology
2-12-1 Ookayama, Meguro-ku, Tokyo 152, Japan

Abstract

This paper presents a notion and properties of 'Structure Lines'. Structure lines give intrinsic geometrical features of curved surfaces or pictures based on differential geometry. They are composed of characteristic lines, division lines and edge lines, which are invariant under the rotation and parallel translation of a coordinate system.

To show the usefulness of structure lines, first we apply them to surface construction problem: With the positional information of division lines, our algorithm synthesizes a surface by 1-dimensional interpolation, i.e. combination of cross-sectional interpolation method and contour line interpolation method so that curvatures of contour lines may have the same sign in each divided region. Application to 3-dimensional analysis is also presented: 'Cusp points' are defined in terms of structure lines as sharp corners of edges for finding a key information. We present the methods of matching a stereo pair efficiently by means of them and of 3-dimensional feature extraction from the stereo pair.

1. Introduction

The researches of image processing and computer graphics are not only needed for engineering and manufacture but also interesting in the field of cognitive psychology. The combination of image processing and computer graphics has been recently advocated from the viewpoint of image understanding [1]. In those research areas the geometrical modeling becomes a very important problem.

In order to represent and recognize curved surfaces or pictures, it is necessary to assume an appropriate model and such a model should be the foundation of both representation and recognition in common. For a good representation of curved surfaces or pictures, we should extract features

106

invariant under principal operations. In the next section, we first introduce the structure lines which are completely invariant under coordinate rotation and parallel translation in terms of differential geometry. In general, they are defined as invariant features of a scalar function on n-dimensional space.

In surface design, we first give the outlines of a shape and then interpolate the space between them. We can consider structure lines as such outlines. Several methods of surface construction have already been investigated [3, 9, 10, 12]. However, none of them treats the problem of surface representation, i.e. what is the criterion of choosing the region to patch and what property the interior region has. In section 3, we present the surface construction method whose input is a surface representation by structure lines. This representation takes the surface representation problem into account. The method is mainly based on the 1-dimensional interpolation.

Three functions are needed in an image understanding system. The first is extraction of local geometrical patterns, the second is acquisition of knowledge and the third is registeration of knowledge. Feature points play an important role in feature extraction. Attension to them causes the first stage of image understanding. Knowledge acquisition on various objects and key information extraction for object recognition mainly use binocular parallax or motion parallax. In section 4, we formalize the process of feature extraction for the purpose of efficient image matching and recognition, considering feature points as cusp points defined by structure lines. We describe the method of 3-dimensional information extraction of objects which may be of curved bodies. It analyzes the difference between the structures nearing feature points on the left and right pictures of binocular stereoscopic view.

2. Structure lines [4, 5, 6, 8]

2.1 Definition of the Generalized Structure Line

A picture on the plane is considered to be a function $f(x,y)$: $R^2 \to R$, where R is the set of real numbers, or to be a curved surface $z=f(x,y)$ in R^3. This representation is generalized in n-dimensional case. A generalized structure line for a surface in R^n is now defined as follows.

(Definition 2.1) Generalized Structure Line:
Suppose some of subspace of n-dimensional space R^n is covered with a set of curves

$$C(a_1,\cdots,a_{n-1}) = \{(x_1,\cdots,x_n)\,|\,g_1(x_1,\cdots,x_n) = a_1,\cdots$$

$$,g_{n-1}(x_1,\cdots,x_n)=a_{n-1}\} \tag{2.1}$$

,where $g_1(x_1,\cdots,x_n),\cdots,g_{n-1}(x_1,\cdots,x_n)$ are smooth functions on R^n and rank$(\partial g_i/\partial x_j)=n-1$ for $i=1,\cdots,n-1$, $j=1,\cdots,n$. Provided an evaluating function $h(x_1,\cdots,x_n)$ on R^n is given, a generalized structure line $G_{c,h}$ is defined as follows.

$$G_{c,h}=\{(x_1,\cdots,x_n)\,|\ \text{for some } (a_1,\cdots,a_{n-1}),$$
$$(x_1,\cdots,x_n) \in C(a_1,\cdots,a_{n-1})$$
$$\text{and } h(x_1,\cdots,x_n) \text{ is extremal}$$
$$\text{along } C(a_1,\cdots,a_{n-1}) \ .\} \tag{2.2}$$

<Theorem 2.1> Eq. (2.3) represents the generalized structure line defined by (2.2) equivalently.

$$\begin{vmatrix} \dfrac{\partial g_1}{\partial x_1} & \cdots & \dfrac{\partial g_1}{\partial x_n} \\[6pt] \vdots & & \vdots \\[6pt] \dfrac{\partial g_{n-1}}{\partial x_1} & \cdots & \dfrac{\partial g_{n-1}}{\partial x_n} \\[6pt] \dfrac{\partial h}{\partial x_1} & \cdots & \dfrac{\partial h}{\partial x_n} \end{vmatrix} = 0 \tag{2.3}$$

Structure lines and skeleton lines are defined as special cases of a generalized structure line.

2.2 Structure Lines

(Definition 2.2) Structure Lines:

Structure lines of a surface ϕ on (x,y)-space are defined by letting $n=2$ and giving a set of curves $C(a)$ and an evaluating function $h(x,y)$ as follows.

(1) Characteristic line (C-line):

$\qquad C(a)=$ a set of contour lines, $h = \phi_x{}^2+ \phi_y{}^2$

$\quad$ (or $C(a)=$ a set of lines of force, $h = \phi_x/\phi_y$)

(2) Division line (D-line):

$\qquad C(a)=$ a set of contour lines, $h = \phi_x/\phi_y$

(3) Edge line (E-line):

$\qquad C(a)=$ a set of lines of force, $h = \phi_x{}^2+ \phi_y{}^2$

<Theorem 2.2> Equations for structure lines are respectively

(1) C-line : $(\phi_x{}^2-\phi_y{}^2)\phi_{xy} + (\phi_{yy}-\phi_{xx})\phi_x\phi_y = 0$ $\tag{2.4}$

(2) D-line : $\phi_{yy}\phi_x{}^2 + \phi_{xx}\phi_y{}^2 - 2\phi_{xy}\phi_x\phi_y = 0$ $\tag{2.5}$

(3) E-line : $\phi_{xx}\phi_x{}^2 + \phi_{yy}\phi_y{}^2 + 2\phi_{xy}\phi_x\phi_y = 0$ $\tag{2.6}$

As shown in Fig.2.1, C-lines are generalization of the ridge and valley lines, D-lines have mode informations and E-lines have edge informations in ordinary sense.

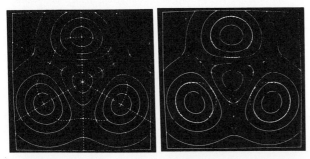

(a) Characteristic line   (b) Edge line

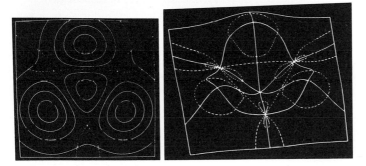

(c) Division line   (d) Perspective of structure line

Fig.2.1   Example of structure lines

The following theorem is obtained from the above definition.

<Theorem 2.3.> Let H be $\begin{bmatrix} \phi_{xx} & \phi_{xy} \\ \phi_{xy} & \phi_{yy} \end{bmatrix}$ and $e_i(i=1,2)$ be an eigenvalue of H.

(C-1) C-line is a collection of points where density of contour lines is extremal in the direction of contour line.
(C-2) C-line is a collection of inflection points of lines of force.
(C-3) C-line is a collection of points where grad ϕ = 0 or the direction of the principal axis of H coincides with the directions of grad ϕ.
(D-1) D-line is a collection of inflection points of contour lines.
(D-2) D-line is a collection of points where normal curvatures along contour lines are zero.

(D-3) D-line is a collection of points where grad ϕ = 0 or the angle between an eigenvector of H and a contour line is given by arctan $\sqrt{-e_1/e_2}$.
(E-1) E-line is a collection of points where density of contour lines is extremal in the direction of line of force.
(E-2) E-line is a collection of points where normal curvatures along lines of force are zero.
(E-3) E-line is a collection of points where grad ϕ = 0 or the angle between an eigenvector of H and grad ϕ = 0 is given by arctan $\sqrt{-e_1/e_2}$.

2.3 Global Properties of the Structure Lines

(Definition 2.3) Division Domains, Simple division Domains:
   A division domain is defined as the domain enclosed by some division lines which does not contain any other division lines internally. If all tangent vectors of the structure lines in a division domain are decided uniquely except for the points where grad ϕ = 0 and $|H| \neq 0$ (non-degenerated), this division domain is called a simple division domain.

   Fig.2.2 shows an example of simple division domains.

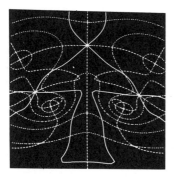

Fig.2.2 Example of simple division domains

   Extensive considerations and simulation experiments lead to some theorems and sufficiently reliable conjectures relating to global properties of structure lines.

<Theorem 2.4>
(P1) C,D and E-lines pass through every saddle point. The crossing number of C-lines with the line segment of a D-line (or E-line) from one saddle point to another is odd.
(P2) E-lines are closed except for the boundary portions.
(P3) There is at most a single maximal (or minimal) point along any straight line completely contained in the simple division domain.

110

(P4) The possible number of maximal (or minimal) points in a simple division domain D does not exceed the number of saddle points existing along the boundary of D.

(P5) The total number of maximal and minimal points is equal to the number of the simple division domains if a curved surface (or picture) is non-degenerated.

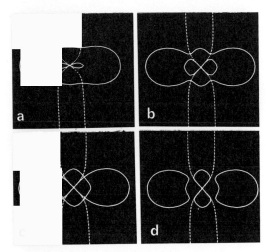

Fig.2.3   The structure lines of twin peaks of various distances

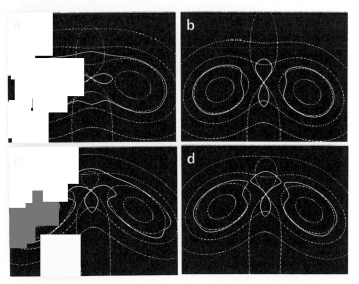

Fig.2.4   The structure lines of alingnment of oblique twin peaks

Minor variations of a surface do not change the connecting structure of the strcture lines drastically and keep almost invariant properties as shown in Figs.2.3 and 2.4, since the structure lines have the global properties described above. Fig.2.3 shows the D and E-lines for twin peaks and indicates the invariant property of D-line for distance variation between the peaks. Fig.2.4 shows similar behaviour as Fig.2.3 for alignment of oblique twin peaks. These facts are very important, when we apply the structure lines to a practical work.

2.4 Skeleton Lines

Let $X = X(u_1,u_2)$ represent a surface in 3-dimensional space, where u_1 and u_2 are parameters and parameter lines of X are lines of curvature.

(Definition 2.4) Skeleton Lines:
   Skeleton lines of a surface X in (x,y,z)-space are defined by letting $n=3$ and giving a set of curves $C(a_1,a_2)$ and an evaluating function $h(x,y,z)$ as follows.
(1) Characteristic skeleton line (CS-line):
$$C(a_1,a_2) = \text{a set of lines of curvature,}$$
$$h = \text{principal curvature.}$$
(2) Division skeleton line (DS-line):
$$C(a_1,a_2) = \text{a set of lines of curvature,}$$
$$h = \int_c P\,ds \text{ , where } P \text{ is a principal curvature and } c \text{ is a}$$
line of curvature.

\<Theorem 2.5\> Equations for skeleton lines are respectively
(1) CS-line:
$$\prod_{i=1}^{2}[(x_{iii}\cdot e)(x_i\cdot x_i) - 3(x_{ii}\cdot e)(x_{ii}\cdot x_i)] = 0 \qquad (2.7)$$

(2) DS-line:
$$\prod_{i=1}^{2}[(x_{ii}\cdot e)] = 0 \qquad (2.8)$$

,where e is a surface normal,
$$x_{iii}=\frac{\partial^3 x}{\partial u_i{}^3}, \quad x_{ii}=\frac{\partial^2 x}{\partial u_i{}^2}, \quad x_i=\frac{\partial x}{\partial u_i} \qquad (i=1,2)$$

An example of skeleton lines is shown in Fig.2.5.

Structure lines discussed previously are invariant under the transformation of (x,y) coordinate but not invariant under the transformation with respect to z-axis. To the contrary, skeleton lines have invariant properties and depend on shapes only. In general, DS-lines divide a surface into convex and concave portions and two CS-lines extract extremely curved portions. The crossing points of two CS-lines which are extracted from two different families of lines of curvature have a navel property. Furthermore, a simple division surface can be also defined as in the case of the simple division domain.

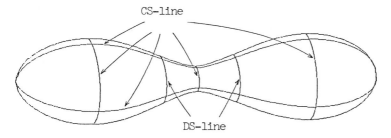

CS-line

DS-line

Fig.2.5 Example of skeleton lines

3.Application to Surface Construction [14]

In surface design, there are some fundamental problems: surface representation, surface partition and surface construction. In this section we show how the invariant properties of structure lines are applied to surface construction. Fig. 2.1 shows that the global structure of a surface represented by the structure lines and a partial surface surrounded by the structure lines is monotonic. Especially, division lines divide a surface into hill and valley regions. This shows the division lines are essential to represent a surface. So we investigate how to synthesize a surface from the informations on the division lines.

The surface construction method using division lines is basically as follows:

(1) give division lines on 2-dimensional plane,
(2) give boundary conditions on the division lines,
(3) apply the cross-sectional prediction method and
(4) apply the contour line interpolation method.

Much effort has been devoted to developing algorithms for surface synthesis from the specified boundary conditions, e.g. COONS [3] and HOSAKA [9]. However, their methods do not necessarily synthesize such a surface as has a specific property, for example a set of contour lines has the same sign of curvature. Our method utilizes this kind of property positively and synthesizes a surface in order that specific property might be hold.

Our way of considering specific property tends to select different interpolation method from past researches, i.e. our surface synthesizing method utilizes 1-dimensional interpolation.

3.1 Surface Construction Method by Contour Lines
(Contour Line Interpolation Method)

Preparation [12]

The methods of curve drawing with characteristic polygons, e.g. a Bezier curve and a B-spline curve etc., are well-known. It is shown that the curve whose curvature has the same sign is synthesized by using a convex polygon. In general, a Bezier curve of degree n is represented in the following form using Bernstein polynomial.

$$R(t) = \sum_{i=0}^{n} P_i \cdot {}_nC_i \cdot t^i (1-t)^{n-i} \quad , \quad 0 \leq t \leq 1 \tag{3.1}$$

,where P_i $(0 \leq i \leq n)$ is the i-th control point, i.e. the i-th vertex of a polygon.

Let $t \in [a,b]$ and Bernstein polynomial of degree n be in the following form.

$$B_n[P;a,b] = \sum_{i=0}^{n} P_i \cdot {}_nC_i \cdot \frac{(t-a)^i (b-t)^{n-i}}{(b-a)^n} \tag{3.2}$$

,where $P = [P_0, P_1, \ldots, P_n]$

Then the following lemma and theorem hold.

<Lemma 3.1> $B_n[P_0, P_1, \ldots, P_n; a, b]$

$$= \frac{1}{b-a} \{ (b-t) B_{n-1}[P_0, \ldots, P_{n-1}; a, b]$$

$$+ (t-a) B_{n-1}[P_1, \ldots, P_n; a, b] \} \tag{3.3}$$

<Theorem 3.1>   If $0 < u < 1$, then

$$B_n[P;0,1] = B_n[P_0^0, P_1^1, \ldots, P_n^n; 0, u] \tag{3.4}$$

$$= B_n[P_n^n, P_n^{n-1}, \ldots, P_n^0; u, 1] \tag{3.5}$$

$$,\text{where } P_i^k = \begin{cases} (1-u)P_{i-1}^{k-1} + u P_i^{k-1} & ,k=1,\ldots,n \\ P_i & ,k=0 \end{cases} \tag{3.6}$$

Theorem 3.1 indicates that the curve synthesized by $P_0,...,P_n$ coincides with the one by $P_0^0,...,P_n^n$ on $t \in [0,u]$ and with the one by $P_n^n,...,P_n^0$ on $t \in [u,1]$. Fig.3.1 shows an example.

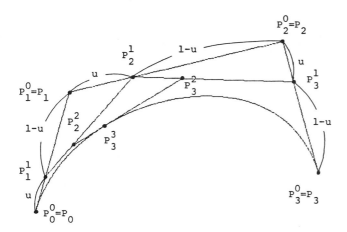

<u>Fig.3.1</u> Example of Theorem 3.1 (in case of n=3)

Let u=1/2 in the Theorem 3.1 and define $B_n^{(k)}[P;0,1]$ as the polygon derived after k-th linear interpolation. For instance,

$$B_n^{(0)}[P;0,1]=[P_0,P_1,...,P_n], \quad B_n^{(1)}[P;0,1]=[P_0^0,P_1^1,...,P_n^0],... \ .$$

Then the following theorem is proved.

<Theorem 3.2> $B_n[P;0,1] = \lim_{k \to \infty} B_n^{(k)}[P;0,1]$ $\hspace{3cm}$ (3.7)

Furthermore, the next theorem holds using Theorem 3.2.
<Theorem 3.3> The Bezier curve synthesized by a convex characteristic polygon has the same sign in curvature.

Surface Construction

The contour line at height z is represented in the following form by Bernstein polynomial.

$$R(t,z) = \sum_{i=0}^{n} P_i(z) \cdot {}_nC_i \cdot t^i(1-t)^{n-i} \hspace{3cm} (3.8)$$

The smooth movement of vertices of the polygon forms a smooth surface. Considering R as a function on (t,z)-space to (x,y)-space, a function ϕ on (x,y)-space to z exists if **R** is one-to-one. Then the Jacobian of **R** is not zero on the domain and therefore it has the same sign. Namely, if $J\mathbf{e} = \mathbf{a} \times \mathbf{b}$ in Fig.3.2, J has the same sign on the domain. This is equivalent to the fact that the contour lines do not intersect.

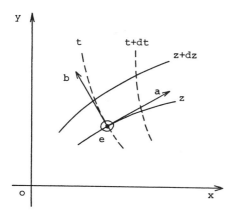

<u>Fig.3.2</u> Geometrical meaning of Jacobian of **R**(t,z)

Theorem 3.4 should be applied in order to synthesize a set of contour lines which have the same sign of curvatures and do not intersect each other.

<Theorem 3.4> If the boundary condition satisfies the following condition C, a set of contour lines whose curvatures have the same sign and which do not intersect can be synthesized. (Refer to Fig.3.3)
[Condition C]
(1) The value of height z along the boundary has the only minimal value z_{min} and has the only maximal one z_{max}.
(2) The curvatures of the contour lines on the bounbary have the same sign.

(3) If the unit vectors in the direction of the contour line on the both end points P_0 and P_n are $\mathbf{q}_0$ and $\mathbf{q}_n$ respectively, the following condition holds.

$$(\mathbf{q}_n \looparrowleft P_n-P_0 \wedge P_n-P_0 \looparrowleft \mathbf{q}_0) \vee (\mathbf{q}_0 \looparrowleft P_n-P_0 \wedge P_n-P_0 \looparrowleft \mathbf{q}_n) \qquad (3.9)$$

where $\mathbf{a} \looparrowleft \mathbf{b}$ is the relation that the counter-clockwise angle θ from $\mathbf{a}$ to $\mathbf{b}$ satisfies $0 < \theta < \pi$.
(Proof) (1) is the necessary and sufficient condition for existing the function of z. Clearly, (2) is necessary. Now provided that the first half part of the (3.9) holds, the triangle $P_0P_1P_2$ in Fig.3.4 contains the object curve.

116

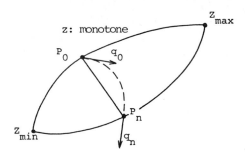

z: monotone

Z_{max}

P_0 q_0

P_n

Z_{min} q_n

Fig.3.3 Illustration of the condition C

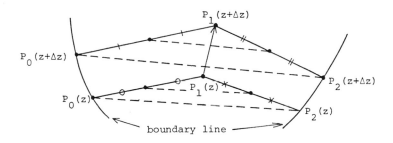

$P_1(z+\Delta z)$

$P_0(z+\Delta z)$

$P_2(z+\Delta z)$

$P_0(z)$

$P_1(z)$

$P_2(z)$

boundary line

Fig.3.4 Decision of P_1

In $C^{[1]}$-class connection if P_1 satisfies the condition (3.10) in $[z,z+\Delta z]$, the Bezier curves synthesized from the characteristic polygons $P_0(z)P_1(z)P_2(z)$ and $P_0(z+\Delta z)P_1(z+\Delta z)P_2(z+\Delta z)$ do not intersect for the following reason.

$$P_1(z)-P_0(z) \diamondsuit P_1{}'(z) \wedge P_1{}'(z) \diamondsuit P_1(z)-P_2(z) \qquad (3.10)$$

Suppose P_i^k is taken as the vertex obtained by letting $u=1/2$ in Theorem 3.1. Then $P_1^1(z)$, $P_2^1(z)$, $P_1{}'(z+\Delta z)$, $P_2{}'(z+\Delta z)$ which connect the middle points of $P_0^0 P_1^0$ and $P_1^0 P_2^0$ in z and $z+\Delta z$ respectively do not intersect and have the same sign of curvature is obtained (by Theorems 3.2 and 3.3). Similarly, it holds in case of the second half part of (3.9).

If (3.10) is not satisfied as shown in Fig.3.5, the Bezier curves which satisfy the same condition are still obtained by adding an alternative vertices, for example P_1^* and P_2^* instead of P_1, and P_3^* instead of P_2 in Fig.3.5, provided that $P_i^*{}'(z)$ (i=1,2) satisfies the following condition.

$$P_i^*(z)-P_{i-1}^*(z) \diamondsuit P_i^*{}'(z) \wedge P_i^*{}'(z) \diamondsuit P_i^*(z)-P_{i+1}^*(z) \qquad (3.11)$$

Furthermore, in the case of $C^{[2]}$-class connection, similar facts are concluded as in the above case.   Q.E.D.

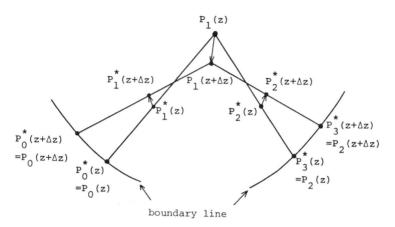

Fig.3.5 Decision of P_1^* and P_2^*

Connection of Surfaces

For a contour line at height z, let the first derivatives with respect to x at the end points $P_0=(x_0,y_0)$, $P_n=(x_n,y_n)$ be u_0,u_n respectively and the second derivatives be v_0,v_n respectively. Then the condition of smooth connection of the contour line at the end points is as follows.

$$u_0=(P_1-P_0)_y \, / (P_1-P_0)_x \tag{3.12}$$

$$u_n=(P_n-P_{n-1})_y \, / (P_n-P_{n-1})_x \tag{3.13}$$

$$v_0= \frac{n-1}{n} \cdot \frac{(P_2-2P_1+P_0)_y(P_1-P_0)_x-(P_2-2P_1+P_0)_x(P_1-P_0)_y}{(P_1-P_0)_x^3} \tag{3.14}$$

$$v_n= \frac{n-1}{n} \cdot \frac{(P_n-2P_{n-1}+P_{n-2})_y(P_n-P_{n-1})_x-(P_n-2P_{n-1}+P_{n-2})_x(P_n-P_{n-1})_y}{(P_n-P_{n-1})_x^3} \tag{3.15}$$

where n is the degree of the curve, and $(\mathbf{v})_x$ and $(\mathbf{v})_y$ are x–component and y-component of vector $\mathbf{v}$ respectively. If the boundary conditions are given in the form of the derivatives of a surface $\phi(x,y)$ with respect to x and y then u_0,u_n,v_0,v_n are

118

$$u_0 = -\phi_x / \phi_y |_{(x_0, y_0)} \tag{3.16}$$

$$u_n = -\phi_x / \phi_y |_{(x_n, y_n)} \tag{3.17}$$

$$v_0 = -(\phi_{xx}\phi_y^2 - 2\phi_{xy}\phi_x\phi_y + \phi_{yy}\phi_x^2)/\phi_y^3 |_{(x_0, y_0)} \tag{3.18}$$

$$v_n = -(\phi_{xx}\phi_y^2 - 2\phi_{xy}\phi_x\phi_y + \phi_{yy}\phi_x^2)/\phi_y^3 |_{(x_n, y_n)} \tag{3.19}$$

Fig.3.6 shows a geometrical meaning of the connection condition. At the end point P_0 it is found that (1) P_1 is on the line with incline of u_0 which passes through P_0 and that (2) P_2 is on the line which is obtained shifting $P_0 P_1$ by $\dfrac{n}{n-1} v_0 (P_1 - P_0)_x^2$ in the direction of y.

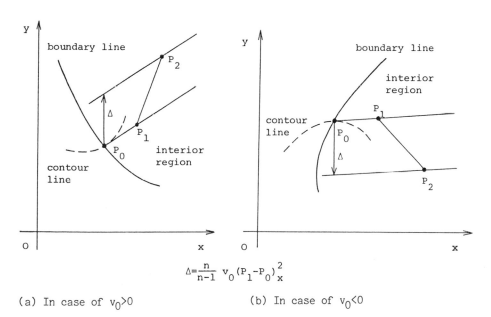

$$\Delta = \frac{n}{n-1} v_0 (P_1 - P_0)_x^2$$

(a) In case of $v_0 > 0$ (b) In case of $v_0 < 0$

Fig.3.6 The geometrical meaning of the connection condition

The present method can determine a contour line by the boundary condition. In the case of $C^{[1]}$ -class connection, each vertex of characteristic polygon can be determined uniquely. More explicitly, P_1 is determined by the boundary conditions P_0, P_2, u_0, u_2 (n=2). In the case of $C^{[2]}$-class connection, P_1 and P_2 are determined by the boundary condition $P_0, P_3, u_0, u_3, v_0, v_3$ (n=3). However, there is a case that a correct surface is not constructed as mentioned previously. In such a case we should interactively specify the internal vertices P_i ($0 < i < n$). In the case of $C^{[1]}$-class connection, we should draw the loci of P_1 and P_2 so that they can satisfy the (3.10) and then take $P_1(z)$ and $P_2(z)$ as the intersections with the tangents at $P_0(z)$ and $P_3(z)$ respectively . (Fig.3.7)

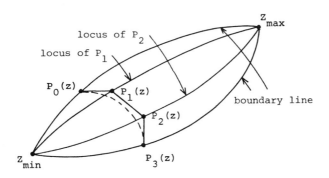

Fig.3.7 The interactive specification of P_1 and P_2

Fig.3.8(b) and (c) show the surfaces constructed by the present method using division lines and characteristic lines extracted from the original surface shown in Fig.3.8(a).

(a)Original surface and   (b)$C^{[1]}$-class connection   (c)$C^{[2]}$-class connection
its C and D lines

Fig.3.8 Surface construction by the contour line interpolation method

3.2 Surface Construction Method Based on 1-Dimensional Interpolation

Cross-Sectional Prediction Method

Concerning the property of a simple division domain, the following corollary is obtained from (P3) of Theorem 2.4.

<Corollary 3.1> If there exists a maximal (or minimal) point in a simple division domain, $\phi(x,y)$ decreases (or increases) monotonically along the line which connects the maximal (or minimal) point with any point in the domain.

With a view of surface construction, the above corollary suggests that we should interpolate the interval between the maximal (or minimal) point and the point on the division line with a monotonic function as shown in Fig.3.9. We call it "Cross-sectional prediction method".

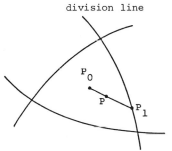

division line

(a) A division domain   (b) Prediction of the cross-section

Fig.3.9 The cross-sectional prediction method

The existence of the synthesis algorithm of this monotonic function is guaranteed by the following theorem.

<Theorem 3.6> Suppose $P_i(i=0,1,\cdots,n)$ is taken as a vertex of a characteristic polygon on 2-dimensional (x,y)-space. If the inclination of each side $a_i=P_i-P_{i-1}$ $(i=1,\cdots,n)$ has the same sign, then the Bezier curve which is synthesized by the polygon is monotonic with respect to x.

Now we present the method of synthesizing a polygon whose sides have the same sign of inclination by boundary conditions. Suppose the objective interval s and height z are normalized ($s \in [0,1], z \in [0,1]$), and let c_i, u_i, v_i $(i=0,1)$ be the values of z, z', z'' on both end points respectively. To guarantee the existence of a monotonic function, we impose the following condition to those values.

121

$$(c_0=0 \lor c_0=1) \land (c_1=0 \lor c_1=1) \land (c_0=0 \leftrightarrow c_1=1) \ (c_0=1 \leftrightarrow c_1=0)$$
$$\land(c_0=0 \to u_0 \geq 0) \land (c_0=1 \to u_0 \leq 0) \land (c_1=0 \to u_1 \leq 0) \land (c_1=1 \to u_1 \geq 0)$$
$$\land(u_0=0 \to ((c_0=0 \to v_0 \geq 0) \land (c_0=1 \to v_0 \leq 0)))$$
$$\land(u_1=0 \to ((c_1=0 \to v_1 \geq 0) \land (c_1=1 \to v_1 \leq 0)))$$

That is, both end points are not at the same height. At the lower point, the first derivation should be non-negative and if it equals zero the second derivation should be non-negative. Similar condition should hold at the high point.

In the case of $c_0=0$ and $c_1=1$,

(1) $C^{[1]}$-class connection (Fig.3.10(a)):

$$P_0=(0,0), \ P_3=(1,1)$$
$$P_1=(a_0,u_0a_0), \ P_2=(1-a_1,1-u_1a_1)$$

,where $a_i = r_i / \sqrt{u_i^2+1}$ $\qquad$ (i=0,1)

and r_0,r_1 are the parameters which satisfy $r_0>0$,$r_1>0$,$r_0+r_1<1$.

(2) $C^{[2]}$-class connection (Fig.3.10(b)):

$$P_0=(0,0), \ P_5=(1,1)$$
$$P_1=(a_0, \ u_0a_0), \ P_4=(1-a_1, \ 1-u_1a_1)$$
$$P_2=(K_0, \ d_0+u_0K_0), \ P_3=(1-K_1, \ 1-d_1-u_1K_1)$$

,where $K_i = \dfrac{-u_id_i + \sqrt{r_{i1}^2(u_i^2+1)-d_i^2}}{u_i^2+1}$

$$a_i = r_{i0} / \sqrt{v_i^2+1}$$
$$d_i = \tfrac{5}{4}a_iv_i^2$$
$$r_{i0} = \dfrac{k_i}{(u_i^2+1)(v_i^2+1)^{3/2}} \qquad (i=0,1)$$

and k_0,k_1,r_{01},r_{11} are the parameters which satisfy
$$k_0>0, \ k_1>0, \ r_{01}>k_0, \ r_{11}>k_1, \ r_{01}+r_{11}<1.$$

Similarly in the case of $c_0=1$ and $c_1=0$.

As another end point moves on the division line, a smooth surface is synthesized except for the singular points where boundary lines intersect. Fig.3.11 indicates this phenomenon.

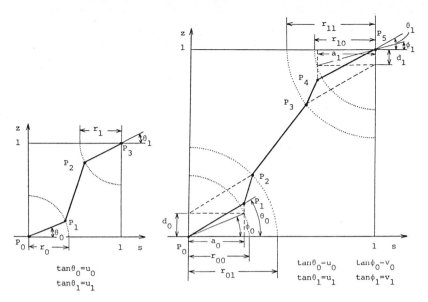

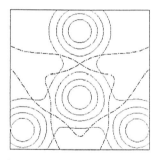

(a) $c^{[1]}$-class connection (b) $c^{[2]}$-class connection

Fig.3.10 Decision of vertices

(a) Original surface and its   (b) Constructed surface
division lines

Fig.3.11 Constructed surface by the cross-sectional prediction method

Cross-Sectional Prediction Method and Contour Line Interpolation Method

Consider the case where the division lines or boundary lines intersect.
The cross-sectional prediction method synthesizes a surface which has
discontinuity of the first derivative on the line terminating at the
intersection even if the cross-section on the line is connected in $c^{[n]}$-
class. Contour line interpolation method synthesizes a surface which has

discontinuity of the first derivative on the contour line terminating at
the point where the boundary line is not smooth even if the contour line is
connected in $C^{[n]}$-class. The former does not necessarily cause smoothness
of a surface along the contour line and the latter does not necessarily
along the cross-section. As a consequence, we can get a surface
construction by 1-dimensional interpolation, combining those methods. For
the surface constructed by the cross-sectional prediction method as shown
in Fig.3.11(b), we should correct the partial surface which do not have the
same sign of curvature or have discontinuity of the first derivative, with
the contour line interpolation method. Fig.3.12(b) shows the corrected
surface by choosing the hatched region in Fig.3.12(a). Note that the
boundary condition must satisfy the condition C in Theorem 3.4.

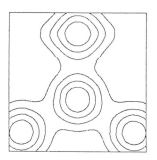

(a) The region to correct   (b) Corrected surface

Fig.3.12   Corrected surface by the contour line interpolation method

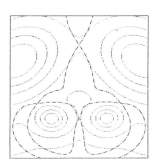
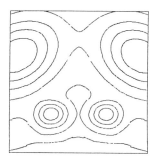

(a) Original surface and its   (b) Constructed surface
division lines

Fig.3.13   Another example of surface construction

If the object surface has a simple structure [6], surface construction
can be made easily. However ,a complicated surface must be divided into
smaller regions because the shape of a division region is more complicated.
Fig. 3.13 shows an example of a complicated surface construction.

HOSAKA et al. [10] have investigated an interactive design of free-formed surfaces and curves with characteristic polygons. The present method takes the problem of surface partition into consideration and constructs a surface to satisfy the special property that curvatures of contour lines have the same sign in each division domain. Therefore, the division lines of the constructed surface coincide with the ones of the original surface in $C^{[2]}$-class connection. This method is invariant against translation and rotation of (x,y)-coordinate. The cost of computation for surface construction is lower since it is based on 1-dimensionality. We can extend the method to the case of 3-dimensional free-formed surfaces by using skeleton lines.

4. Application to 3-Dimentional Analysis [15]

When a man recognizes an object, he attends to some feature points and makes use of binocular stereoscopic view to analyze local structures. Then he tracks one feature point to another to perceive a global structure efficiently [13]. For the purpose of object recognition by a computer, it is necessary to give it such functions as a man has. In this section, we address the development of 3-dimensional information extraction from a stereo pair using structure lines. The feature function $\phi(x,y)$ for a picture f(x,y) is obtained by applying the operator P to f. Then feature points are defined to be intersections of structure lines for $\phi(x,y)$. The matching of a stereo pair is performed by attending those points and comparing the local structures. The shift of the structure lines in both pictures is detected and used to locally extract 3-dimensional informations of the object. Moreover, the global structure is obtained by combining those local informations.

4.1 Feature Extraction of Pictures

Physiological researches using eye cameras show that eyes catch a sharp corner of edges at first. After looking at such a point, an edge is tracked to the other end of the edge. Such a feature point satisfies invariant condition under translation and rotation of picture plane. The tracking from a feature point to another is done by satisfying the invariant condition.

We now formalize the process of feature extraction using generalized structure lines in case of n=2.

(Definition 4.1) GC-line, GE-line:
For a scalar function $\phi(x,y)$ on 2-dimensional plane, a generalized C-

line (GC-line) and generalized E-line (GE-line) are defined by letting n=2 and giving a set of curves C(a) and an evaluating function h(x,y) as follows.

(1) Generalized C-line (GC-line):
   C= a set of contour lines, $h=P(\phi,\phi_x,\phi_y,...)$ (4.1)

(2) Generalized E-line (GE-line):
   C= a set of lines of force, $h=P(\phi,\phi_x,\phi_y,...)$ (4.2)
   where P is any function, which is called an operator on ϕ.

(Definition 4.2) Characteristic point:
   For a function $\phi(x,y)$, characteristic points of ϕ are points where grad $\phi=0$.

(Definition 4.3) Cusp point:
   An intersection of GC-line and GE-line is called a cusp point.

A useful cusp point is defined in case that the operator P is invariant under parallel translation and rotation. For example,

$$h = \phi_x^2+\phi_y^2 \qquad (4.3)$$

$$h = \frac{\phi_{xx}\phi_y^2 - 2\phi_{xy}\phi_x\phi_y + \phi_{yy}\phi_x^2}{(\phi_x^2+\phi_y^2)^{3/2}} \qquad (4.4)$$

The latter denotes the curvature of contour line.

Then, we have the following theorem and corollary.

<Theorem 4.1>
   In case of generalized structure lines of n=2, take C_1 and C_2 to be two families of curves forming a net on 2-dimensional plane and h to be an evaluating function. Then intersections of two families of lines defined by C_1,h and C_2,h coincide with the characteristic points of h.

<Corollary 4.1>
   For a surface ϕ defined on 2-dimensional plane, cusp points of ϕ coincide with characteristic points of h.

In view of the above theorem and corollary, the problem of finding feature points such as cusp points is the one of searching extremal points. The useful method for searching extremal points of a scalar function was proposed [7]. However, this is not necessarily effective for a gray toned picture because of noise. As an alternative, we adopt a method of detecting characteristic points using a matched filter.

Fig.4.1 shows the process of feature extraction. Feature points such as cusp points are first extracted and then edges are extracted as line feature.

126

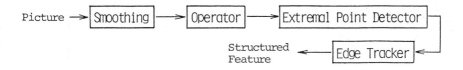

Picture → Smoothing ⟶ Operator ⟶ Extremal Point Detector ┐

Structured ← Edge Tracker ←┘
Feature

Fig.4.1 Process of feature extraction

Fig.4.2 Typical edges in a gray toned picture
(a) Original picture, (b) Edge line (Step edge), (c) Characteristic line
(Roof or spike edge)

Fig.4.2 shows typical edges in a gray toned picture: one is step edges corresponding to edge lines, and the other is roof or spike edges corresponding to characteristic lines.

Fig.4.3(b) shows an example of cusp points of a picture (a) of polyhedra in case that we choose (4.4) as an evaluating function. And (c) shows the result of tracking edges using cusp points.

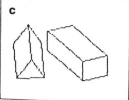

| (a) Original picture | (b) Distribution of cusp points | (c) Line drawing by edge tracking |

<u>Fig.4.3</u> Cusp points and edge tracking

4.2 Model of Stereo Vision

Fig.4.4 shows a model of stereo vision. When the matching process of feature points on a stereo pair is performed, 3-dimensional informations around the feature points can be extracted from the shift of edges on both pictures.

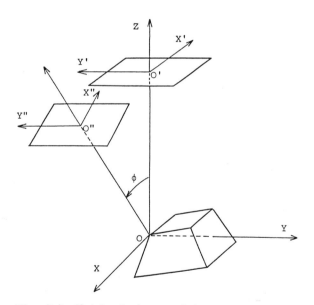

<u>Fig. 4.4</u> Model of stereo vision

In general, the picture of a 3-dimensional object is obtained by perspective projection of it to the 2-dimensional picture plane. For

128

simplicity, we assume orthographic projection and allow parallel translation, rotation and scaling on the picture plane.

Moreover, it is necessary to assume an appropriate model of surfaces. We suppose a surface is Lambertian and reflectance of it may vary with position. The object may be of a curved body. The shift in intensity of a stereo pair appears also in case of a curved surface. The assumption of Lambertian reflectance means intensities on the corresponding points are the same. In consequence the matching characteristic points and structure lines can be used to extract the 3-dimensional informations as in the case of polyhedra.

4.3 Case of Polyhedra

When we attend to feature points and edges connecting them, we can decide whether the corresponding edge of the object is convex or not even if we do not know the parallax δ. Fig.4.5 shows the way in which we decide factors of scaling and rotation using pairs of corresponding feature points (V_{Li}, V_{Ri}) $(i=0,1,2,3)$ and pairs of edges $(V_{L0}V_{Lj}, V_{R0}V_{Rj})$ $(j=1,2,3)$.

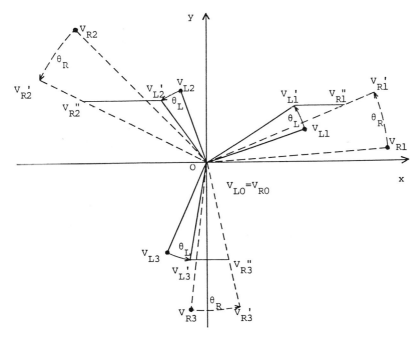

Fig.4.5 Decision of factors of scaling and rotation

Let a be the scaling factor of the right picture against the left, and θ_L, θ_R be the rotation factor of the right and left picture respectively. Then we have the following equation.

$$(V_{Lj}')_y = (V_{Rj}'')_y \qquad (j=1,2,3) \tag{4.5}$$

,where $V_{Lj}' = T_L V_{Lj}$, $V_{Rj}'' = \frac{1}{a} V_{Rj}'$, $V_{Rj}' = T_R V_{Rj}$,

$$T_L = \begin{bmatrix} \cos\theta_L & -\sin\theta_L \\ \sin\theta_L & \cos\theta_L \end{bmatrix}, \qquad T_R = \begin{bmatrix} \cos\theta_R & -\sin\theta_R \\ \sin\theta_R & \cos\theta_R \end{bmatrix}.$$

If $T_{Lj} = [x_{Lj} \ y_{Lj}]^t$ and $V_{Rj} = [x_{Rj} \ y_{Rj}]^t$, the above equation is

$$x_{Lj}\sin\theta_L + y_{Lj}\cos\theta_L = \frac{1}{a}(x_{Rj}\sin\theta_R + y_{Rj}\cos\theta_R). \tag{4.6}$$

This is a simultaneous equation with respect to θ_L, θ_R and a. At least three pairs of edges are needed for the unique solution, though optimization techniques, such as method of least-squares, are applied in case of more than four pairs. The solution of it is as follows.

$$\theta_R = \text{sign}(S_R) \cdot \arcsin(1/\sqrt{1+S_R^2})$$
$$\theta_L = \text{sign}(S_L) \cdot \arcsin(1/\sqrt{1+S_L^2}) \tag{4.7}$$
$$a = \sqrt{\frac{1+S_L^2}{1+S_R^2}} \cdot \frac{\text{sign}(S_R) \cdot x_{R1} + |S_R| y_{R1}}{\text{sign}(S_L) \cdot x_{L1} + |S_L| y_{L1}}$$

where $\quad S_R = (A_R^{-1} X_R)_3$, $S_L = (A_L^{-1} X_L)_3$

(For a vector $\mathbf{v}$, $(\mathbf{v})_3$ denotes the third component of it.

$$\text{sign}(x) = \begin{cases} 1 & x \geq 0 \\ -1 & x < 0 \end{cases}$$

$$A_R = \begin{bmatrix} x_{L1} & y_{L1} & -y_{R1} \\ x_{L2} & y_{L2} & -y_{R2} \\ x_{L3} & y_{L3} & -y_{R3} \end{bmatrix}, \quad A_L = \begin{bmatrix} x_{R1} & y_{R1} & -y_{L1} \\ x_{R2} & y_{R2} & -y_{L2} \\ x_{R3} & y_{R3} & -y_{L3} \end{bmatrix},$$

$$X_R = \begin{bmatrix} x_{R1} \\ x_{R2} \\ x_{R3} \end{bmatrix}, \quad X_L = \begin{bmatrix} x_{L1} \\ x_{L2} \\ x_{L3} \end{bmatrix}.$$

Note that this method can not be applied in case that a feature point appears as a result of projection of edges in different distance.

Let P_i be a vertex of an object and V_{Li}, V_{Ri} be projections of P_i in the left and right pictures respectively. In Fig.4.6(a), take W_L (W_R) to be the point where the straight line passing through V_{L1} (V_{R1}) and V_{L2} (V_{R2}) intersects x-axis, and W_L' (W_R') to be the point where the straight

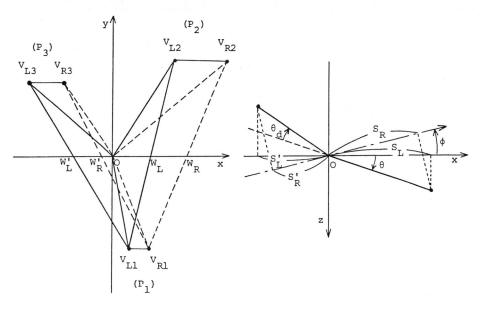

(a) Elevation of the neighbourhood
    of a vertex

(b) Plan of the neighbourhood
    of a vertex

Fig.4.6 Decision of convexity of an edge

line passing through V_{L1} (V_{R1}) and V_{L3} (V_{R3}) intersects x-axis. Fig.4.6(b) shows the plan of (a). ϕ denotes parallax and the sign of θ_d depends on convexity of the edge OP_1.

Suppose $S_L=OW_L$, $S_L'=OW_L'$ ($S_R=OW_R$, $S_R'=OW_R'$). Then we have

$$S_R/S_L = \cos(\theta+\phi)/\cos\theta = \cos\phi-\tan\theta\cdot\sin\phi ,$$

$$S_R'/S_L' = \cos\phi-\tan(\theta+\theta_d)\cdot\sin\phi . \tag{4.8}$$

Provided $D=(S_R/S_L)-(S_R'/S_L')$ and $R=(S_R/S_L)/(S_R'/S_L')$, the following equation holds.

$$D = \sin\phi \{\tan(\theta+\theta_d) - \tan\theta\} \tag{4.9}$$

When $0<\phi<\pi/2$, $|\theta|<\pi/2$ and $|\theta+\theta_d|<\pi/2$, the following conditions are equivalent.

(i) $\theta_d \lesseqgtr 0$ (ii) $D \lesseqgtr 0$ (iii) $R \lesseqgtr 1$ (4.10)

Futhermore, take A_L (A_R) and A_L' (A_R') to be the areas of the triangles $OV_{L1}V_{L2}$ ($OV_{R1}V_{R2}$) and $OV_{L1}'V_{L3}'$ ($OV_{R1}'V_{R2}'$), respectively. Then, since

$$R=(A_R /A_R')/(A_L /A_L') ,$$

we can decide whether the edge OP_1 is convex or concave, independent of factors of scaling and rotation.

For the matched stereo pair shown in Fig.4.7, factors of scaling and rotation are

$$a = 0.75, \quad \theta_R = -55 \text{ deg.}, \quad \theta_L = -48 \text{ deg.}$$

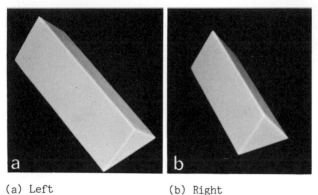

(a) Left   (b) Right

Fig.4.7 Stereo pair in different size and rotation

According to (4.10), every edge terminating at the center vertex is found to be convex.

The local 3-dimensional structure at one feature point infers the structure at the other points near the previous one consulting knowledge on the object. In the trihedral world, the decision of labeling of one line terminating at the FORK-type or ARROW-type junction [2, 11] affects the decision of labeling of the others. And the reversal figure is interpreted in two ways. In these cases, the stereo vision technique leads to efficient analysis and decides the unique interpretation.

4.4 Case of Curved Bodies

Since the relative position of both eyes is meaningful in binocular view, directional structure lines are introduced considering this fact.

(Definition 4.4) Directional Structure Line:
    A directional structure line of a surface ϕ on (x,y)-space is defined by letting n=2 and giving a set of curves C(a) and an evaluating function h(x,y) as follows.

$$C(a) = \{(x,y) \mid a = ux - vy\}, \text{ where } (u,v) \text{ is a unit vector.}$$

$$h = \phi(x,y) \tag{4.11}$$

<Theorem 4.2>
   Equation for the directional structure line with the parameter (u,v) is

$$v\phi_x + u\phi_y = 0 \quad . \tag{4.12}$$

The intensities of the left and right pictures are related with the non-linear transformation affected by shape of the object. The projections of the contour lines in intensity on the left and right picture onto the object surface coincide perfectly under assumption of a Lambertian surface. Therefore, 3-dimensional informations are obtained along all the contour lines using a stereo pair. If we take x_L and x_R to be x-coordinates of the corresponding points, the depth z of this point is

$$z = \frac{1}{\tan\phi} x_L - \frac{1}{\sin\phi} x_R \quad , \tag{4.13}$$

,where ϕ is parallax.

However, it is not necessary to compute the depths in the whole domain. The brightest point corresponds to the one where the surface normal on it coincides with the direction of illumination. In the neighbourhood of such a point, 3-dimensional informations are extracted by stereo view.

Left   Right
(a) Original pictures of spherical plaster

(b) Extracted directional structure lines

Fig.4.8 Extraction of depth information
         along the directional structure line

(c) Extracted depth from (b)

Fig.4.8(c) is an example of extracting depths along the directional structure lines (b) according to (4.13) for the stereo view (a) of a spherical plaster cast.

For any surface z=F(x,y), the shapes of the neighbourhoods of characteristic points are classified as indicated in Table 4.1. Fig.4.9 shows the front and right views of partial surfaces classified in Table 4.1

133

Table 4.1 Classification of shapes in the neighbourhood of
characteristic points

Rank $\begin{bmatrix} F_{xx} & F_{xy} \\ F_{xy} & F_{yy} \end{bmatrix}$	The shape of the neighbourhood of a characteristic point
1	Concave parabolic cylinder
1	Convex parabolic cylinder
2	Concave elliptic paraboloid
2	Convex elliptic paraboloid
2	Hyperbolic paraboloid

parabolic
cylinder

concave   convex

——·——·—— directional
         structure line

elliptic
paraboloid   concave   convex

hyperbolic
paraboloid

(left)   (right)

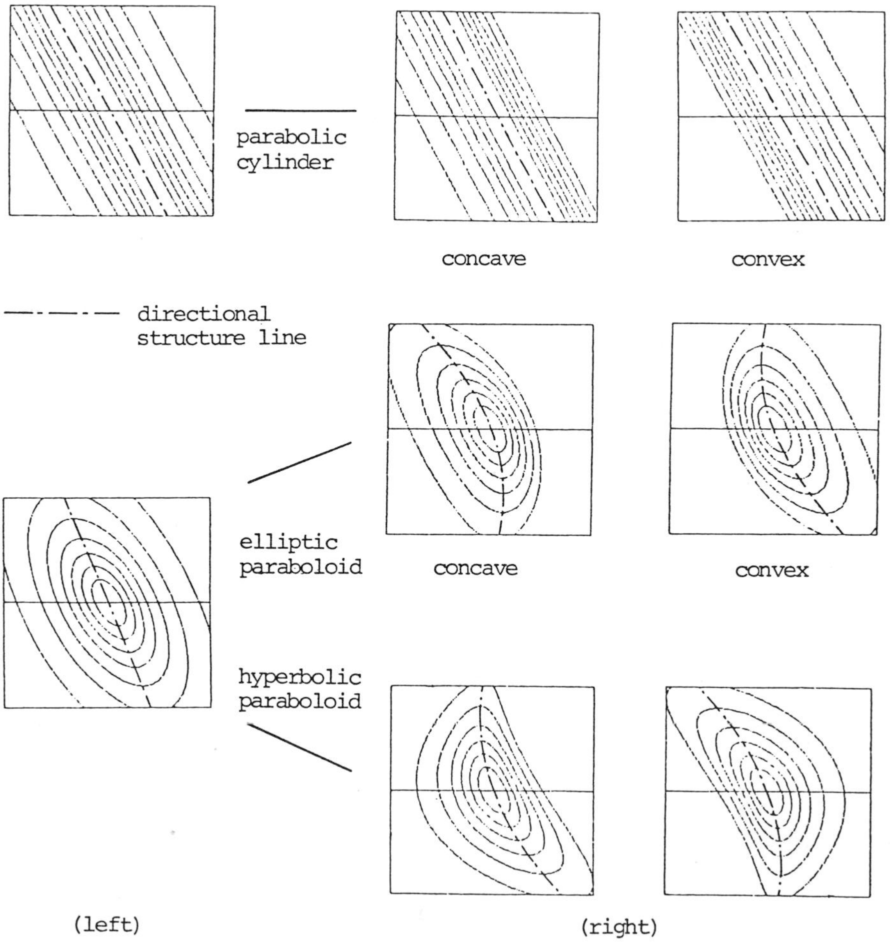

Fig.4.9 Behaviour of intensity in the neighbourhood of
a characteristic point

with front illumination. Solid lines and dot-dashed lines are contour lines of intensity and directional structure lines of them respectively. And horizontal lines indicate the direction of eye's shift. The variation of these patterns decides convexity of the surface.

Under assumption of uniform reflectance, we can decide with single view which of parabolic cylinder or elliptic paraboloid or hyperbolic paraboloid the neighbourhood of characteristic points is, when the point of sight and the light source are not in the same direction. Moreover we can perceive the convexity if we know the direction of the light source, but we can not otherwise.

In case of parabolic points, the criterion of convexity with binocular view is based on the change of intensities along the horizontal line. In case of elliptic and hyperbolic points, it is based on the change of the curvature of directional structure lines.

The reflectance of most surfaces has a specular component and a map component. In this case the corresponding points of both pictures do not necessarily correspond to the same point on the object surface. However, decision of convexities of feature points is possible as well as in a Lambertian surface.

5. Conclusions

We introduced a considerable amount of intrinsic features of images by considering their differential geometrical feature, so that feature of images were reduced to extremal portions of the family of lines. Choosing structure lines as such features of image permitted us to study not only image analysis but also image construction. Techniques which are based on ad hoc feature definition seem very attractive and popular but they often lack the mathematical elegance of its applications. However, the theory of structure lines seems to offer a strong mathematical foundation for its applications.

The combination of structure lines with syntactic methods seems promising [8]. Adopting features based on structure lines as primitives, semantic information involving spatial information can be expressed syntactically, since the semantics of the primitives is rigid and clear.

References

1. Brooks R.A.,Greiner R. and Binford T.O.: The ACRONYM Model-Based Vision System, Proc. of 6th International Joint Conf. on Artificial Intelligence, 1979, pp 105-113.

2. Clowes M.B.: On Seeing Things, <u>Artificial Intelligence</u>, Vol.2. 1971.

3. Coons S.A.: Surfaces for Computer-Aided Design of Space Forms, <u>MIT Project MAC TR-41</u>, 1967.

4. Enomoto H., Katayama T., Ito M. and Tsurumi Y.: Structure Lines of Surfaces, <u>Technical Report of the Professional Group on Pattern Recognition and Learning of the Institute of Electronics and Communication Engineers of Japan</u>, PRL72-138, March 1973 (in Japanese).

5. Enomoto H. and Katayama T.: Structure Lines of Images, <u>Proc. of 3rd International Joint Conf. on Pattern Recognition</u>, 1976.

6. Enomoto H., Katayama T. and Yoshida T.: Computer Experiment on Global Properties of Structure Lines of Images using Graphic Display and its Considerations, <u>Information Processing in Japan</u>, Vol.17, No.7, July 1976 (in Japanese).

7. Enomoto H., Katayama T. and Kawamoto E.: Searching Extremal Points of Function with Many Variables Using Linking Method, <u>Information Processing in Japan</u>, Vol.17, No.9, September 1976 (in Japanese).

8. Enomoto H., Yonezaki N. and Nitta K.: Schematic Representation and Perception of Curved Surface and Picture, <u>Proc. of Eurographics 79</u>, 1979.

9. Hosaka M.: Theory of Curve and Surface Synthesis and Their Smooth Fitting, <u>Information Processing in Japan</u>, Vol.10, No.3, May 1969 (in Japanese).

10. Hosaka M. and Kimura F.: A Theory and Methods for 3 Dimensional Free Form Shape Construction, <u>Information Processing in Japan</u>, Vol.21, No.5, May 1980 (in Japanese).

11. Huffman D.A.: Impossible Objects as Nonsence Sentences, in Meltzer B. and Michie D. (eds.) <u>Machine Intelligence 6</u>, Edinburgh University Press, 1971.

12. Lane J.M. and Riesenfeld R.F.: A Theoretical Development for the Computer Generation and Display of Piecewise Polynomial Surfaces, <u>IEEE Trans. on Pattern Analysis and Machine Intelligence</u>, Vol.PAMI-2, No.1, 1980.

13. Watanabe A. and Yoshida T.: Roles of Central and Peripheral Vision in Pattern Perception, <u>NHK Technical Monoghraph</u>, no.21, 1973.

14. Watanabe Y., Mugino S. and Enomoto H.: Surface Construction Method by Contour Lines, <u>Technical Report of the Professional Group on Pattern Recognition and Learning of the Institute of Electronics and Communication Engineers of Japan</u>, PRL80-86, February 1981 (in Japanese).

15. Watanabe Y., Imura T. and Enomoto H.: Recognition of 3-Dimensional Objects by Stereo Vision, <u>Technical Report of the Professional Group on Pattern Recognition and Learning of the Institute of Electronics and Communication Engineers of Japan</u>, PRL81-3, May 1981 (in Japanese).

Part III

Picture Computer Architecture

A Configurable Micro Array Computer for Signal and Image Processing

W.K. Giloi and U. Bruening

Technical University of Berlin, FB Informatik - CAMP Research Group
D-1000 Berlin 10, Fed. Rep. of Germany

Abstract

The increasing use of industrial robots will create a demand for inexpensive but powerful vision systems. Only multi microprocessor systems offer the opportunity of combining cost-effectiveness (through the use of VLSI components) with high performance (through parallel processing). The problem, however, is the large diversity of the image understanding procedures, ranging from array processing of gray scale matrices to sophisticated classification or decision making programs. Whereas a pipeline architecture is most adequate for vector processing (e.g. FFT), segmentation and feature extraction algorithms usually lend themselves toward parallel processing performed in a lock-step fashion by a number of general-purpose processing modules, and classification and image understanding algorithms eventually call for a machine exhibiting high-performance of scalar floating point operations. The answer to these contradicting requirements is a configurable architecture. Such an architectural design is outlined in the paper. Special considerations are given to the problem of programmability and system software that shall enable the user to program an application in an appropriate, high-level, parallel processing language, independent of the actual configuration of the system.

1. Introduction

Progress in VLSI technology provides us with powerful multiprocessors and fast VLSI memory. This development suggests to attain the desired high computing power of a computer not through the 'classical' approach of building super-fast single-processor mainframes but through a multiplicity of hardware resources and parallel processing. This view is generally accepted, albeit there may be severe pitfalls in such a concept if the wrong approach is taken.

The wrong approach, inevitably doomed to fail, is to attack the problem from a structural point of view only (as has been demonstrated by some spectacular failures). Before the hardware structure of a multiprocessor or multicomputer system can be designed, one first must have developed a clear understanding of the underlying operational principle [1], that is, the manner in which information is represented in and processed by the computer and in which the multiple hardware resources of the system are to cooperate.

The choice of an operational principle reflects the architectural goals (e.g., performance maximization, modular extensibility of the system, fault-tolerance, software simplification). The operational principle chosen then

140

implies to some extent the hardware structure of the system, i.e., the number of types of hardware resources and the communication structure by which they are connected.

This paper reports about an innovative multiprocessor architecture whose predominant feature is its configurability that allows the system to be adapted to the variety of different tasks encountered in image understanding problems. The system is a simplified version of the STARLET computer [2,3, 4,5], a data structure architecture developed at the Technical University of Berlin. Unlike the STARLET computer, which supports the construction of arbitrary, user-defined abstract data types comprising arbitrarily structured data objects, the system described in this paper supports only one structure type, the array. Therefore, it is called the micro array computer (MAC).

2. Rationale of a Configurable Array Computer

The evolving next generation of "intelligent" industrial robots will be furnished with advanced sensory systems (vision, sonar, tactile sensors). These sensory systems will require small, inexpensive, but powerful special-purpose computers that are specifically tailored to meet the requirements of high-performance digital signal processing. Vision systems, in particular, must be capable of coping with complex tasks of scene analysis, image understanding, and pattern recognition.

A computer designed for this purpose must exhibit high absolute performance as well as an outstanding performance/cost ratio for the following types of operations:
- convolution and resampling with various kernels;
- fast fourier transform (FFT) for filtering, correlation, deconvolution (homomorphic filtering), image reconstruction;
- local operations for preprocessing (enhancement) of a gray scale matrix;
- local operations for segmentation and feature extraction;
- pattern matching and classification (pattern recognition).

Whereas the first four types of operations are performed on arrays (gray scale matrices or row or column vectors thereof, respectively), the operations mentioned last are scalar by nature. Consequently, the special purpose computer should exhibit a high absolute performance as well as a high performance/cost ratio for both, vector operations and scalar operations. This rules out the "classical" approach of supercomputers for array processing, namely to equip the system with an ultra high-speed pipeline processor.

Utmost economy is attained by exploiting the recent advances in VLSI technology which lead to two major developments:
- high-speed VLSI memory (e.g., 16Kx1 bit static MOS chips with 45 ns access cycle);
- high-speed 16-bit microprocessors (e.g., MOTOROLA MC68000, 12 MHz version).

Many signal and image processing applications call for floating-point operations. The currently available microprocessors do not feature fast floating-point arithmetic. Therefore, a separate floating-point processing unit must be added that provides for high-speed floating-point processing of scalars as well as vectors. Our solution to this problem is to have a low-staged, data-flow controlled floating-point pipeline processor, realized in TTL technology. With respect to vector processing, such a pipeline cannot compete in operating speed with a highly-staged, ECL pipeline as used in supercomputers. However, it is also much less expensive and does not exhibit the performance decrease of a multi-stage pipeline when it comes to scalar operations. The pipeline processor in MAC forms a vector processing extension of a cluster of microprocessors; therefore, it is called the vector processing module (VPM).

The VPM also comprises address generators to generate the address streams needed in common vector processing as well as in FFT. The existence of the address generators renders MAC an SIMD (single instruction - multiple data) architecture. The performance gap between the LSI technology employed in the MAC and the faster MSI (ECL-based) technology used in supercomputers is reduced by a higher degree of parallel processing in MAC. That is, MAC may contain more than one pipeline processor, which may all operate simultaneously.

Besides cost, a major shortcoming of existing special-purpose array processors is inadequate and tedious programming. Existing array processors usually must be programmed in a low-level machine language. However, there is no reason why an array processor could not be furnished with an appropriate high-level programming language that features the appropriate parallel processing constructs. The reconfigurability of the hardware structure should be transparent to the programmer.

3. Modes of Operation of MAC

MAC is a configurable multi-microprocessor system whose internal communication structure is designed to maximize system performance for the following modes of operation:
- PARALLEL PROCESSING OF SETS OF INTEGER OR REAL DATA
- FLOATING-POINT FFT OF VECTORS AND MATRICES
- INTEGER OR FLOATING-POINT VECTOR ARITHMETIC (INNER AND OUTER PRODUCTS)
- INTEGER OR FLOATING-POINT SCALAR ARITHMETIC.

The MAC architecture is based on the principle of hierarchical function distribution. Operating system functions are executed by the OS machine. Application programs are interpreted by the instruction processor, and the data transforming operations in the instruction execution are jointly performed by a cluster of slave processors.

3.1 Parallel Array Processing

In this mode, the slave processors operate in parallel on a shared data object (array) in a lock-step fashion. The element types may be integer or real. Each private memory of the slave processors contains a collection of application routines that may be invoked by the master processor through appropriate procedure calls. The high-level programming language has a FOR ALL process initiation construct to initiate parallel execution of a set of activities.

Preprogrammed routines, residing in the private memory of each slave processor, may be routines for image processing and analysis (e.g., local operations, contour following, picture segmentation) or other applications. Integers are 16 bits long, packed in pairs of 2 into a 32-bit memory word; real numbers are represented in the IEEE standard, single precision representation.

3.2 Floating-Point FFT

In this mode, (row or column) vectors are subjected to the Fast Fourier Transform (FFT) to optionally obtain one of the following results:

- Fourier transform of a vector of real or complex data
- Inverse Fourier transform of a vector
- Outer product of two vectors.

In the case of a gray scale matrix, for example, the columns must be as easily accessible as are the rows (2-dimensional FFT). The basic FFT operation is the <u>FFT-butterfly</u>, carried out in MAC in a pipeline fashion.

In the following, we consider the results of an error analysis of the FFT algorithm [6]. Given $N = 2^M$ values to be transformed. Let σ_0 denote the variance of the values. Then the variance (dynamic range) of the result values is

$$\sigma_r = 2^M \cdot \sigma_0 \ .$$

That means that in the average the amplitude of the intermediate values in each of the M stages of the FFT algorithm increases by $\sqrt{2}$. That is, in the case of a fixed-point representation of the values, N/2 bits must be reserved for the amplitude increase[1]. For N ranging from 256 to 1024, this amounts to 4 to 5 bits. In the case of a floating-point representation, these bits are not lost for the accuracy of the mantissa representation.

For the variance of the result values caused by the round-off error in the representation of the original values, the following approximation formula may be used [6]

$$\frac{\sigma^2_{noise}}{\sigma^2_{signal}} \approx \frac{M}{2} \cdot 2^{-2m} \ , \quad m = \text{mantissa length.}$$

Consequently, the mantissa should be made 4 to 5 bits longer than what is the precision of the input data.

If we take the case of 8-bit gray scale values as input data, N = 256, and, thus, M = 8, a 16-bit fixed-point representation of the data may be marginally sufficient. If the number of points to be transformed is increased or if the values to be transformed are not 8-bit gray scale values but other signals, supplied by, say, a 10-bit analog-to-digital converter, then one must resort to a floating-point representation anyway.

Consequently, all FFT operations are performed on IEEE standard, single precision floating-point numbers.

3.3 Structured Data Types

MAC contains two important structured data types. The first one is the vector, which is a linear order of elements. The number of elements may vary from 2 to 2^{16} and the data sorts of the elements may be bits, integers (16 bits) and reals (24 bit mantissa, 8 bit exponent, IEEE standard).

---

[1] Of course, one can scale down the intermediate values after every two computational stages to prevent overflow. Nevertheless, by the increase in dynamic range, one loses approximately M/2 bits of accuracy.

The following functions can be performed on vectors, if the data sort of the elements permits the operation:

Reductions

MINMAX: MINMAX(<vector>) yields value and index of largest and smallest element;

VECSUM: VECSUM(<vector>) yields sum of all elements;

Outer Products

ADD: ADD(<vector>,<vector>) adds 2 vectors component-wise;

SUB: SUB(<vector>,<vector>) subtracts 2 vectors component-wise;

MUL: MUL(<vector>,<vector>) multiplies 2 vectors component-wise;

DIV: DIV(<vector>,<vector>) divides 2 vectors component-wise;

Triad Function and Inner Product

TRIADD/SUB   <vector> $\pm$ (<scalar> x <vector>)

INNER_PRODUCT   VECSUM(<vector> x <vector>)

Comparison

COMP   COMP(<vector1>,<vector2>,<relation>) compares the components of the two vectors by one of the relations, $\neq$, $<$, $\leq$, $=$, $\geq$, $>$, and generates a boolean result vector. Vector 2 can be replaced by a scalar.

The second structured data type is the digital image array (DIA). DIA is introduced to simplify the addressing functions and the internal representation of image data. For the user of MAC this is a data representation on which all vector operations mentioned above can be performed.

A DIA is a square matrix of 16 bit integers containing 2^n x 2^n elements. The column and row length n may vary from 7 to 10. The upper boundary is given by the size of the shared communication memory (2^{10} x 2^{10} x 2^4 bits $\hat{=}$ 2 MBytes).

3.4 Floating-Point and Fixed-Point Scalar Operations

Scalar operations are the 4 basic arithmetic operations and the common relational functions, to be performed on single precision floating-point numbers as well as on 16 bit fixed-point numbers.

3.5 General Performance Considerations

In the case of the general-purpose and FFT vector operations performed by the pipelined vector processing module, there are two factors contributing to the performance of the system:
(1) the "SIMD gain" (only one instruction must be fetched for a complex vector operation);
(2) the "pipeline gain" caused by the parallel activities of the various stages of the pipeline. For sufficiently long vectors, the pipeline gain approaches the value k if k is the number of pipeline stages involved.
Therefore, supercomputers like the CRAY-1 or the CYBER 200 employ highly-staged pipeline.

However, highly-staged pipelines raise the following problems:

- start time and flush time increase with the number of stages and, consequently, the performance of such a pipeline in the case of very short vectors or scalar operations is relatively poor;
- it becomes difficult to provide an effective memory bandwidth high enough to feed data into the pipeline at the rate at which the pipeline is able to process them;
- highly staged pipelines are more expensive than lowly staged ones.

In the MAC system, data are fetched from a fast communication memory, which is built with 16K static memory chips that have an access cycle of 45 ns. The memory units are dual-port memories with a high-priority and a low-priority port (cf. Figure 1). Adding the time required for the port logic and bus propagation leads to an effecitve memory access cycle of about 90 nanoseconds.

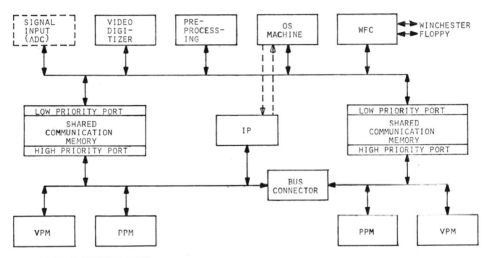

VPM VECTOR PROCESSING MODUL
PPM PARALLEL PROCESSING MODUL
IP INSTRUCTION PROCESSOR
WFC WINCHESTER FLOPPY CONTROLLER

Fig. 1 Block diagram of a MAC system with four processing modules

The most complex vector operation is the FFT "butterfly" performed on a pair of complex numbers. In that case, 10 memory accesses are required for transporting the operands and results, requiring approximately 900 ns. At the same time, the pipeline must perform 6 additions and 4 multiplications. However, since the additions and multiplications may be overlapping, only the 6 additions count. Consequently, in order to match the processing bandwidth of the pipeline to the memory bandwidth specified above, the maximum execution time per stage is about 150 ns. In the case of monadic or dyadic vector operations, respectively, one could even allow for a considerably larger clock cycle.

An execution time of 150 ns per pipeline stage can be readily obtained with standard LSI-TTL components and a lowly-staged pipeline. Table 1 lists the execution time required in the STARLET pipeline processing elements. In the STARLET computer, we have an addition/subtraction and a multiplication/division element. Each of the two elements has 3 stages.

Table 1   Typical performance of a low-cost, lowly-staged LSI-TTL pipeline

processing element	stage	operation	time
add/ subtract	1	exponent alignment and result characteristic	95 ns
	2	mantissa processing	130 ns
	3	normalization	140 ns
multiply/ divide	1	read initial value from ROM, multiplication / division	--- / 70 ns
	2	mantissa processing, multiplication / division	150 ns / 450 ns
	3	normalization	55 ns

Depending on the kind of vector operation performed, the MAC vector processing module (VPM) performs typically 5 to 10 megaflops (flops: floating-point operations per second). In order to attain a higher overall performance, several pipelines and memory modules are employed such that each pipeline of a VPM operates in connection with its dedicated memory module.

4.   Hardware Structure of MAC

4.1   General

The MAC system comprises an operating system machine (OS machine), an instruction processor (IP), a number of processing modules (VPM or PPM), and a fast communication structure through which the OS machine and the processing modules communicate. Figure 1 depicts a block diagram of a fully expanded MAC system.

The OS machine consists of a conventional microcomputer system, operating under the UNIX-7® operating system[2]. It performs the operating system functions including IO, compiles user programs, and provides the program development environment. A separate instruction processor manages the run time environment, interprets the program under execution, and initiates the VPMs or PPMs, respectively. Operating system kernel functions are:
  • management of the shared communication memory
  • IO operations.

---

[2] UNIX-7 is a trade mark of Bell Laboratories.

The program development environment provided by the master computer comprises:

- file management
- program editing
- program development library (see section 5)
- compilation.

The VPMs or PPMs, respectively, jointly perform the data-transforming operations listed in section 3. These functions take the form of <u>service</u> routines. A service routine is a reentrant program residing in the private memory space of a processing module, i.e., a <u>process</u>, to be activated whenever needed by another process in the instruction processor or in another processing module.

4.2 The Vector Processing Modules (VPM)

A VPM is a pipeline processor consisting of 5 boards, viz.:
- a general purpose MC68000-based computer board (the pipeline configurator)
- a communication and data flow control board
- a floating-point ADDER/SUBTRACTOR board
- a floating-point MULTIPLIER/DIVIDER board
- an address generator board.

The VPM performs the fixed-point or floating-point vector operations and the floating-point FFT operations in the SIMD mode of operation. Therefore, the address generator (AG) must perform either of the following address generation functions:
- addressing the elements of a vector or the rows of a matrix, respectively;
- addressing the columns of a matrix whose elements are stored in row-major order;
- addressing the data pairs of the FFT butterfly operation in the "decimation in time" mode (as well as the bit-reverse and count-down modification of the "decimation in time" addressing scheme).

Internally, the processing elements of a VPM operate asynchronously. A special hardware component, called <u>message buffer</u> (MB), is employed to synchronize their operation according to the data flow principle. An MB consists of a register and a propriatory chip accommodating a "hardware monitor" for the buffer register. The monitor monitors the state of the register and consequently generates the appropriate bus control signals indicating whether the buffer register is empty or full. If the buffer is empty, then the receiving processing element is forced into a wait state; if the buffer is full, then the sending processing element is forced into a wait state. Hence, the MB provide a communication path between sender and receiver and simultaneously synchronizes their activities according to the firing rules of the data flow schema; and no interrupt or explicit use of semaphores is required. Figure 2 illustrates the MB function.

For performance reasons, a MAC system may be equipped with 2 CMMs. Both CMMs are in the master's address space, logically separated through memory maps. Each VPM (or PPM) is connected to one of the 2 CMMs, and there is a bus-to-bus connection between the CMMs. In maximum there may be 4 processing modules in the system as depicted in Figure 1.

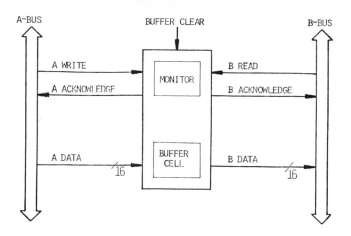

Fig. 2 Function of message buffer (MB)

The communication structure of a MAC system consists of
- the dual-port communication memory modules (CMM)
- the operating system machine bus
- the processing element bus
- interrupt lines connecting the instruction processor
  to the OS machine and to the processing elements.

4.3 The Parallel Processing Modules (PPM)

In lieu of a vector processing module (VPM), a parallel processing module (PPM) may be inserted. A PPM consists of 4 MC68000-based computer boards. The processors of a PPM operate in a conventional fashion in a MIMD mode of operation[3]; their activities are synchronized in the lock-step manner.

4.4 Preprocessing Hardware

The block diagram Figure 1 shows a component called VIDEO DIGITIZER. A video digitizer board (VDB) contains

- a fast 8-bit analog-to-digital converter (VIDEO DAC)
- a preprocessing map memory
- a frame buffer memory
- a histogram processor
- a video output.

The preprocessing map memory is a fast RAM inserted into a read-modify-write loop of the frame buffer memory. It may be loaded with arbitrary functions, to perform "on the fly" preprocessing operations such as point transformations (e.g. for contrast sharpening) or multi-level thresholding. The histogram processor calculates "on the fly" a 128 gray scale histogram of the frame buffer content. A video output allows the user to visually monitor the result of each image processing step if so desired.

---

[3] MIMD: multiple instruction stream - multiple data stream

148

5. Software Structure of MAC

MAC system operation is based on the notion of cooperating processes. There are operating system processes executed by the master processor, performing the typical operating system tasks such as IO, scheduling, HLL program translation, etc.

An application program under execution is a process in the instruction processor. In the course of program execution, this process initiates a number of service processes executed by the slave processors.

A service process consists of

- a reentrant program, residing in the private memory of its processor;
- an 'activation set' of data objects to operate upon, made available through the communication memory;
- its execution state.

Inter process cooperation requires the existence of an appropriate inter process communication (IPC) protocol. The IPC is based on the exchange of messages between processes, to initiate a process, signal a state or an exception, grant access to data objects, etc. In the case of access to shared data objects, there must be a mechanism that ensures the validity of mutual exclusion of data access.

In the MAC system, the same IPC protocols may be used as in the UPPER-system[4]. This will allow us to use on the MAC system the high-level language extension developed for the UPPER system, called PARALLEL PROCESSING PASCAL (PPP). In contrast to PASCAL proper, PPP exhibits two unique features:

- it contains constructs that reflect the IPC protocols used in the UPPER system;
- it contains a program development library that allows the user to specify and implement arbitrarily defined abstract data types, given in the form of multi-entry processes.

The first of the two features makes it straightforward and easy to synchronize the cooperation between the main process (application program) and the service processes; the second feature allows service processes to be contained in the program development library as standard library processes.

The concept of a program development library is fairly new and, as of yet, has hardly anwhere been put to practical use. However, such a library has been implemented for and is being used on the STARLET computer. Therefore, when it comes to the implementation of the MAC software, we shall be in the position to capitalize on that experience.

In PPP, there is no nesting of processes. Rather, inter process cooperation is the cooperation among peers, based upon the consumer-producer model [7]: A process requesting a service from another process becomes the consumer of that service, while the other process that provides the service becomes the producer of that service. At any arbitrary point in its execution, a process (e.g., the master process) may initiate a number of producer processes (e.g., slave processes). After initiation, the initiator may continue with

---

[4] UPPER is a distributed multicomputer system presently under construction by the CAMP group [7].

its task until a point will be reached where the service(s) requested must
be rendered. At this point, the consumer process will go into a wait state
until eventually the services have been received.

By this simple and straightforward mechanism, inter process communication
and synchronization is achieved in a most efficient, high-level manner. Process declarations and inter process communication constructs constitute a
superstructure to PASCAL proper. Inside a routine declared as a process, we
have the common block structure of PASCAL, whereas the scope control of data
objects shared in the inter process cooperation is based on the encapsula-
tion policy of abstract data types [8]. Service processes may be written in
the C language. This guarantees a relatively simple and efficient implementation. Figure 3 illustrates the structure of the MAC software.

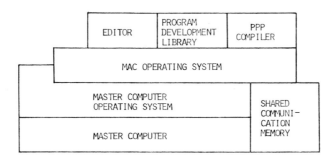

Fig. 3   Structure of MAC software

REFERENCES

1   Giloi W.K., _Rechnerarchitektur_, Springer, Berlin-Heidelberg-New York 1981

2   Giloi W.,K., Berg H.K., Introducing the Concept of Data Structure Archi-
    tectures, _Proc. 1977 Internat. Conf. on Parallel Processing_, IEEE Cata-
    log No. 77CH-1253-4C, 44-51

3   Giloi W.K., Berg H.K., Data Structure Architectures - A Major Operational
    Principle, _Proc. 5th Annual Sympos. on Computer Architecture_, IEEE Cata-
    log No. 78CH1284-9C, 175-181

4   Giloi W.K., The DRAMA Principle and Data Type Architectures, in: J. Nie-
    dereichholz(ed.), _Datenbanktechnologie_, Teubner, Stuttgart 1979, 81-100

5   Giloi W.K., Gueth W., The Realization of a Data Type Architecture, _Proc._
    Third Conference of the European Cooperation in Informatics, Springer,
    Berlin-Heidelberg-New York 1981

6   Weber J., Ein Fourier-Walsh-Spezialrechner nach dem Prinzip gesplitteter
    Arbeitsspeicher, Ph.D. Thesis, Technical University of Berlin, FB Infor-
    matik 1974 (D83)

7   Giloi W.K., Behr P., An IPC Protocol and Its Hardware Realization For a
    High-Speed Distributed Multicomputer System, Proc. 8th Annual Sympos. on
    Computer Architecture, IEEE Catalog No. 81CH1593-3, 481-493

8   Jones A.K., Liskov B., A Language Extension For Expressing Constraints
    on Data Access, CACM 21,5 (May 1978), 358-367

A Multiprocessor System for Dynamic Scene Analysis

D.P. Agrawal

Department of Electrical and Computer Engineering, Wayne State University
Detroit, MI 48202, USA

R. Jain
Department of Computer Science, Wayne State University
Detroit, MI 48202, USA

1. Introduction

Computer vision and digital image processing require a large amount of computation. A complete vision system, such as VISIONS [17], requires many number-crunching operations at the low level and sophisticated decision making at high-level. The advances in LSI and VLSI circuits have influenced researchers in computer vision and digital image processing. Many approaches for fast image processing using a network of processors have been presented [1-3,6,7,17]. However, parallelism has been applied mostly to those problems that are well defined or where use of partitioning is obvious. The problems encountered in the real world are serial in nature and it is difficult to incorporate parallelism directly.

In a parallel processor systems, only Single Instruction Multiple Data (SIMD) and Multiple Instruction Multiple Data (MIMD) characteristics are useful in providing parallelism. While outlining the general architecture of such a system, two functional modules (Processing Element and Memory Blocks) are first separately identified, and then their data path requirements are established. Most existing and proposed systems are modeled in two ways (Figs.1a and 1b) [13]. In the first system, each processing element has its own private memory, and the communication link between various processors is established through the network. Placing the network between the two types of modules provides a shared memory system (Fig.2). The first type of system can be classified as a loosely coupled system [14] and can be used conveniently in both SIMD and MIMD modes. The operating mode can be used to restructure the control patterns of the interconnection network.

Real-world (practical) problems usually require both private and shared memories and this leads to a more complex organization (Fig.2). The private memory can store the necessary instructions; the large share memory can contain the data to be used by various processors. This generalized architecture provides support for several concurrent but independent SIMD or MIMD machines [2]. Thus, the interconnection network plays an important role, and using multiple buses [15] no longer seems to be a reasonable solution in a dynamically reconfigurable multiple processor system [16,17].

One of the oldest and most frequently referred to parallel system is ILLIAC IV. Its usefulness in solving some matrix problems is well known, but it is not suitable for other complex applications in which relatively versatile intercommunication is a major concern. As the cost of the hard-

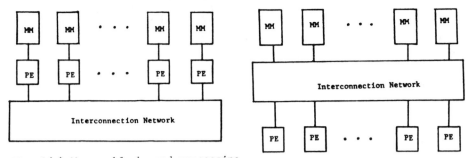

Fig. 1(a) Memory blocks and processing
elements in parallel computers

Fig. 1(b) Alternate organization

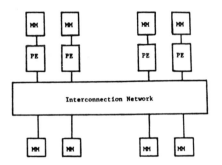

Fig. 2 Generalized architecture

ware is no longer prohibitive, it is now time to identify the basic strat-
egies in defining suitable architecture for parallel computing system so
that a given practical problem can be solved as effectively as possible.
Such tuning of the system design is expected to lead to an improved
throughput.

This paper is the result of an ongoing project at Wayne State University [18,19,37], outlined in section II.

An overview of various multiple processor systems used in image processing has been provided in the following section III and the usefulness
of pseudoparallelism has been emphasized. The section IV briefly describes the sequential algorithm used for motion analysis, and a detailed
scheme for pseudoparallel system for motion analysis is given in the section V. Various problems and their solutions are also indicated. The
performance evaluation of the proposed system is presented in the section
VI.

2. A Dynamic Scene Analysis System

Dynamic scene analysis is concerned with the analysis of a frame sequence
describing a scene. The camera may be stationary or non-stationary and
objects in the scene may be moving. The time lapse between two contiguous
frames of the sequence is assumed small so that radical changes in the
shape of objects do not take place. In our current research project, it
is assumed that the illumination in the scene remains unchanged.

153

Our long-term goal is to design and implement a system capable of recognizing objects and their motion characteristics. This system, as shown in Fig. 3, has three distinct phases: peripheral, attentive, and cognitive. The peripheral phase identifies areas in the field of view with persistant changes and extracts gross information about the moving objects and their motion characteristics [33]. The attentive phase focusses attention on the "active" image areas in order to investigate them in more detail. The attentive phase will generate symbolic/iconic structures which allow semantic interpretation of segments or images. As shown in the Fig. 3, the processes in the attentive phase will use some general knowledge sources and will be influenced by the requirements of the cognitive phase. The cognitive phase relates the observations derived from the frame sequence to the real world through a knowledge base containing information, arranged in many independent domain knowledge sources, about objects and their motion characteristics.

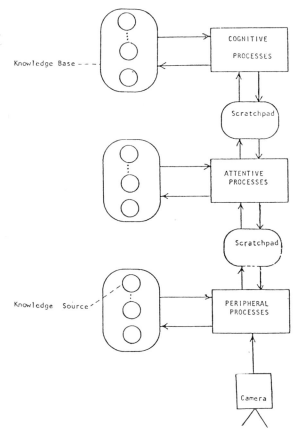

Fig. 3 Dynamic scene under standing system

Currently we are in the design phase of the system. Some of the important factors influencing our design are loose coupling of various blocks, independence of knowledge sources, distributed problem solving to combine information from different sources, an application of distributed/parallel processing wherever appropriate. This paper is mainly concerned with the application of parallel processing during peripheral and attentive phases. In this paper we consider an algorithm for segmentation of a dynamic scene and discuss our approach for designing suitable architecture for the real time implementation of the algorithm. This algorithm is mainly concerned with the peripheral and attentive phases of the dynamic scene analysis system and has limited applicability in a general scene. We consider this algorithm in our study, mainly due to our familiarity of the algorithm. Moreover, this algorithm, clearly, demonstrates the type of problems one faces in a dynamic scene analysis system. The algorithm discussed in this paper assumes stationary camera and uniform illumination. Since this algorithm analyzes moving objects, in the following we use "motion analysis" to describe the task of the algorithm.

3. Multiple Processor Systems for Motion Analysis and Pseudo-Parallelism

Architectures for several systems have been proposed for picture processing and image analysis. If communication is needed only between the neighbors; the ILLIAC-IV-like scheme of Roesser [8] works well. Davis [3] compares distinct types of architecture for image processing and advocates using pyramid architecture. In principle, a pyramid scheme, a ZMOB scheme [7], or a generalized Siegel's architecture [9] works beautifully for the image processing problem. All these efforts are directed toward defining parallel architecture for problems in which possible application of parallelism is either well known or straightforward.

In a multiple processor system, the ideal concept of "any processor can have access to any memory module" [17] is attractive theoretically, but not feasible with a system with a large number of memory modules. Moreover, this general characteristic is not required in a pipelined system in which only interconnection between a group of modules is useful. Thus, there is a need for an reconfigurable architecture [16,17] for particular applications.

The problem of motion analysis is quite different, and parallelism cannot be included directly. This makes the existing systems unsuitable for motion analysis, and a new direction or basic strategy should be sought to introduce parallelism to such a complex sequential problem. Flynn and Hennessy [21] have emphasized the concurrency determination for using any distributed system effectively. Their main concern has been the use of a proper functional language. Kieburz [22] has advocated using decomposition for problem solving. He has considered a general case using an acyclic dependence graph that determines parallelism at the subtask level. The degree of parallelism provided by such a scheme is algorithm dependent, and in the worst case of totally sequential problems like motion analysis, it may not provide any speedup.

To overcome this situation, we propose using parallelism within each subtask so that interprocessor coordination or synchronization would not be any problem. We divide the algorithm into several sequential steps and use the appropriate degree of parallelism within each step. The computation is still sequential in terms of subtasks or steps, so we call our approach "pseudo-parallel" [18,19]. Our basic strategy of tuning the architecture to a partitioned algorithm will provide effective speedup for most sequential problems as long as the interaction or forward/ backward branching is required within each partitioned step. The "pseudo-parallel" algorithm thus converts the serial algorithms into a form suitable for running in a distributed operating system environment [23,24] and the system throughput can be increased considerably by using the system in a pipelined manner.

A brief description of the algorithmic steps required in a motion analysis system is included in the next section.

4. Algorithm for Motion Analysis

In this section we describe some modules of an algorithm for extracting images of moving objects. We also indicate briefly the necessary information flow between the modules. Our aim is not to describe the algorithm in detail, but to bring out some problems associated with parallel problem solving as applied to a real time system for motion analysis. The details of the algorithm are given in Jain et al. [25].

4.1 Condensed Frame Generator: The input frames are usually obtained using a television camera. These frames have 572 by 512 pixels; each pixel represents the gray level at a point in the frame. The gray level is quantized in 256 levels. The input frames are condensed to a 96 X 128 picture obtained by grouping together four consecutive columns and six consecutive rows of the original frame. Each element of the condensed frame contains the mean and the variance of the intensities of the corresponding pixels of the raw frame. (The term frame is used for condensed frame and the term pixel is used for an element of the condensed frame.)

4.2 Difference Picture Generator: A difference picture (DP) is a binary picture generated by comparing two frames. The DP is generated by placing a 1 in each pixel for which the corresponding pixels in the two frames being compared have an appreciable difference in gray level characteristics. The difference picture for motion analysis is prepared by comparing two continuous frames of the sequence. For determining whether or not the corresponding pixels of the frames, called the previous and current frames, may be considered different, we compute

$$R = ((S_p + S_c)/2 + ((M_p - M_c)/2))^{**}2/(S_p * S_c) \qquad (1)$$

in which M and S denote the mean and variance values contained at a pixel of the condensed frame, and subscripts p and c indicate that the mean and variance is taken from the previous and current frames, respectively. If the ratio R is greater than a preset threshold, then the gray levels for this location in the previous and current frames are taken to be from different gray level distributions.

4.3 Labelling: A labelled picture is obtained by applying the algorithm given in Fig. 2 to every point (I,J) of the DP and the previous and current frames. In this algorithm DP, PREV, and CURR are difference picture, previous frame, and current frame respectively; E(P(I,J)) and SOB (P(I,J)) are boolean operators determining whether or not P(I,J) is an edge point in a binary, and gray picture, respectively.

```
IF DP(I,J)=1 THEN
   IF E(DP(I,J) THEN
      BEGIN
         DP(I,J)=2;
         IF SOB (PREV(I,J)) THEN DP(I,J)=3;
         IF SOB (CURR(I,J)) THEN DP(I,J)=DP(I,J)+2
   END;
```

Fig.4 Labelling algorithm

Edges in the DP, the previous frame, and the current frame are denoted by ED, EP, and EC, respectively. The labels 1, 2, 3, 4, and 5 in the labelled difference picture are 1 points of DP, which are $\overline{\text{(ED}}, \overline{\text{EP}}, \text{EC})$, (ED, $\overline{\text{EP}}$, $\overline{\text{EC}}$), (ED, $\overline{\text{EP}}$, EC), (ED, EP, $\overline{\text{EC}}$), and (ED, EP, EC), respectively. Note that the labelled difference picture displays edginess of points through different pictures; that is the DP, previous frame, and current frame.

4.4 Motion Detector: The difference picture contains intensity dissimilarity (change) information for the corresponding points in two frames. The dissimilarities may be caused by the lighting changes, camera noise, or motion. We consider the isolated dissimilarities caused by the noise and assume that lighting remains constant. Based on these assumptions a simple filtering scheme is used to filter entries in the DP caused by motion. All connected components that contain more than N elements (say Negnals 10) are considered the result of motion, and the '1' entries that do not belong to such a component are discarded as noise. There are several algorithms for component labelling in a picture. A component of size greater than N is called a region proposal.

4.5 Region Classifier: It has been shown that regions in a difference picture are formed from occulsion of disocclusion, (or both) of the background by a moving object. In many cases it is possible to determine whether a DP region is the result of occlusion or disocclusion, or both. These three types of regions are denoted as type O, B, and X regions. For a given region the type can be found by computing a ratio called CURPRE which equals the number as defined

$$\text{CURPRE} = \frac{\text{\# of points labelled 4 in the region}}{\text{\# of points labelled 3 in the region}} \qquad (2)$$

The CURPRE is much less than 1 for type B regions, much greater than 1 for type O regions, and near 1 for type X regions.

4.6 Object Extractor: We use region growing for O and B type regions to obtain the masks in the previous and current frames. A region is grown by taking each nonregion pixel that has a horizontal neighbor within the region and comparing its gray level with that of an adjacent region pixel. If the gray levels are similar, then the nonregion pixel is added to the region. The gray levels are taken from the previous frame for the DP regions of type B and from the current frame for the DP region of type O. A similar process is applied to the nonregion pixels that have vertical neighbors within the region. These processes are iterated until no new pixels are added to the region. The region obtained represents the pre-vious frame object mask when grown from a type B region and the current frame object mask when grown from a type O region.

The masks obtained in this way are improved by using the following re-finement processes:

a. Same Object Refinement
b. Termination Refinement
c. Gape Filling
d. Same Frame Refinement

4.7 Motion Analyzer: The outputs of the object extractor are the images of the moving objects in continuous frames. Some motion characteristics such as velocity and acceleration are easily obtained from the displace-ment of the image. Note that there is no need to save masks for all pairs of frames, and a single updated and overall mask can take care of informa-tion contained in all successive masks.

Figure 5 shows the sequential data flow diagram for the algorithm com-prising the preceeding blocks; Table 1 indicates the approximate time taken by each block. It is clear from the problem that it is impossible to use parallelism for the overall execution of the algorithm. However, parallelism can be introduced within each step, and depending on the time required for a particular step, an adequate number of processors can be assigned so that each step can effectively complete the computation in one unit of time, and pipelining achieved with synchronous transfer of infor-mation between steps. Using the subtask model in Fig. 5 and the time data in Table 1, we propose a parallel/distributed processing architecture suitable for motion analysis. A detailed scheme for such a pipelined sys-tem and its performance evaluation follow.

5. Pseudo-Parallel System Architecture for Motion Analysis

The sequence of processing steps for motion analysis and the processing time required by the individual blocks are given in Fig. 5 and in Table 1. Our objective is to design a pipelined distributed system; therefore, we should use enough processors and memory modules for each functional block such that there is an uninterrupted flow of information throughout the system. If we assume that one unit time period is the desired processing time for each block, the number of processors for individual blocks should be large enough so that the effective time delay can be matched with its sequential processing time. Thus, the number of parallel processors re-quired to make the computation time equal to one unit time can easily be obtained (Table 1). It is assumed that for every step of the algorithm, there is no restriction on the number of memory modules and that each module is large enough to store the data.

In regard to operating mode of each block, the first three blocks of Fig. 5 (condenser, D.P.G. and L.D.P.) can be computed in SIMD mode by sectionalizing the frame. In the beginning, a frame is divided into 20 sections, and each section is stored in 20 different memory modules so that 20 processing elements can work in parallel on such distributed data. In the second level, the generation of difference picture requires only 10 processors and hence, data must be distributed over only 10 memory blocks.

158

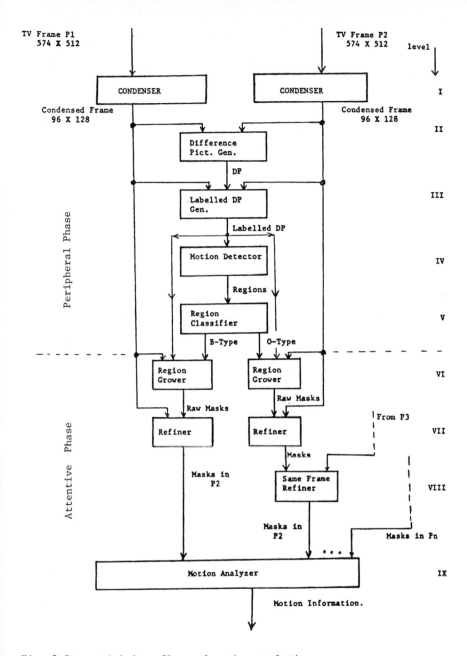

Fig. 5 Sequential data flow and motion analysis

Table 1. Characteristics of various functional blocks for motion analysis

Level No.	Functional Block	Required Processing Time[1]	No. of Processors Allocated for the Block	Data Needed Through Level Numbers	Computation Mode	Computation Time With Distributed Processing
I	Condenser	20	20	I – VII	SIMD	1
II	Difference Picture Generator	10	10	II – III	SIMD	1
III	Labelled Difference Picture	5	5	III – VI	SIMD	1
IV	Motion Detector	5	5	IV – V	MIMD	1
V	Region Classifier	0.5	1	V – VI	SISD	0.5
VI	Region Growing	3	1[2]	VI – VII	SISD	1
VII	Refinement	3	1[2]	VII – VIII	SISD	1
VIII	Same Frame Reference	1	1	VIII – IX	SISD	1
IX	Motion Analyzer	1	1	IX	SISD	1
	Total no. when not Pipelined	48.5 for uniprocessor	20		SISD/SIMD/ MIMD	8.5
	Total no. when Pipelined	48.5 for uniprocessor	45		SISD/SIMD/ MIMD	1

[1] Integer indicate their relative values
[2] Only one region to the processed for a frame pair.

This necessitates moving data and can be avoided by considering two logically adjacent memory modules of level I as a large single "macro memory" block. The resultant data of level I is stored in only 10 different memory blocks of level II, and multiple-port memory blocks [15] for such compact generation of data may be useful. This would require a procedure for memory mapping such that the macro module would contain information corresponding to sections of the picture physically adjacent to each other. Similar assumptions are made as the step moves to level III of labelled difference picture generation.

Note that 3 time unit delays are required for the region growing and refinement steps. But still, only one processor is allocated to these steps. This is done primarily because these steps may require data corresponding to a complete frame, and if three processors are to work in parallel, one copy of data is to be supplied to each processor, which imposes generation of multiple copies of data. Moreover, in motion analysis, a large volume of data is to be processed and a large portion of data is redundant. It is not always necessary to analyze all regions of each frame. For example, in the first frame, the most important region could be considered by the two blocks, and for successive frames, other regions could be analyzed.

The computation mode and required time are also shown in Table 1. A memory module allocated to a particular level is needed at two instances: when it is generated and when it is used to compute data for the next level. This is strictly true for levels II, and IV through IX. The memory space for the condenser is needed when it is generated and also in phases II, VI and VII. Similary, the labelled DP is required for level IV and VI. This enables us to calculate the minimum number of memory blocks required for a pipelined distributed system (Table 1). The effective time delay of one unit could be achieved with 162 shared memory modules and 45 processors with their own private memories.

Table 2. Information contents of various memory blocks in the proposed pipelined pseudo-parallel system for frame size of 570 x 512 (at the ith instant).

Storage Step	Total No. of Memory Modules	Size of Each Memory Module in Words	Number of Memory Modules for Frame Number									
			i	(i-1)	(i-2)	(i-3)	(i-4)	(i-5)	(i-6)	(i-7)	(i-8)	(i-9)
Original Picture	40	14592	20	20								
Condensed Picture	80	1216		10	10	10	10	10	10	10	10	
Difference P.G.	10	2432			5	5						
Labelled D.P.	20	12160				5	5	5	5			
Motion Detector	2	12160					1	1				
Region Classifier	2	12160						1	1			
Region Growing	2	12160							1	1		
Refinement	3	12160								1	1	1
Same Frame Refinement	2	12160									1	1
Motion Analyzer	1	12160										1
TOTAL	162											

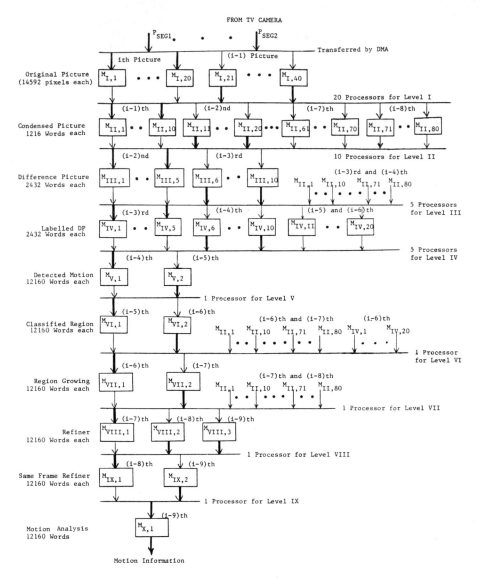

Fig.6 Architecture of the pseudo-parallel scheme (dark lines indicate
information flow at ith instant)

    The next thing to be considered is the internal structure of the sys-
tem.   The interconnection of various functional modules should be such
that an optimum performance could be achieved by proper reconfiguration of
the system.   This makes the dynamic data path requirements clear and system architecture for such a scheme can be obtained (Fig.6).   The inter-

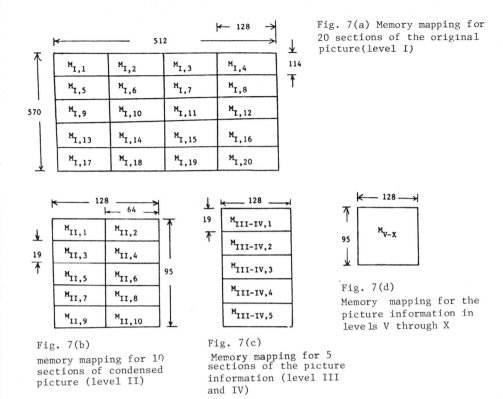

Fig. 7(a) Memory mapping for 20 sections of the original picture(level I)

Fig. 7(d)
Memory mapping for the picture information in levels V through X

Fig. 7(b)
memory mapping for 10 sections of condensed picture (level II)

Fig. 7(c)
Memory mapping for 5 sections of the picture information (level III and IV)

Fig. 7 Section of the picture frame information in various levels of the pseudo-parallel system

connection between memory modules and the corresponding processing elements are shown simply in the form of a BUS, and the private memories associated with each processor are also omitted from Fig. 6. The memory modules currently being accessed by the processing elements of each level are also identified by dark lines. In fact, it also represents the flow of information from one level to another level, and to work in a pipelined fashion, the memory modules are allocated in such a way that each group of modules at each level corresponds to one complete frame of the original picture. This partitioning of the frame at various processing levels is shown in Fig. 7. Figures 6 and 7 also provide the memory size requirement for each stage.

A more detailed diagram, illustrating the assignment of memory modules and the corresponding processing elements, is given in Fig. 8. The diagram provides much insight to the complex system architecture for motion analysis. The interconnection structure between each set of functional modules has been omitted, and its implementation could be done using a pair of generalizers [26] and Multistage Interconnection Networks [27-30]. It may also be useful to provide some additional control capability to the

163

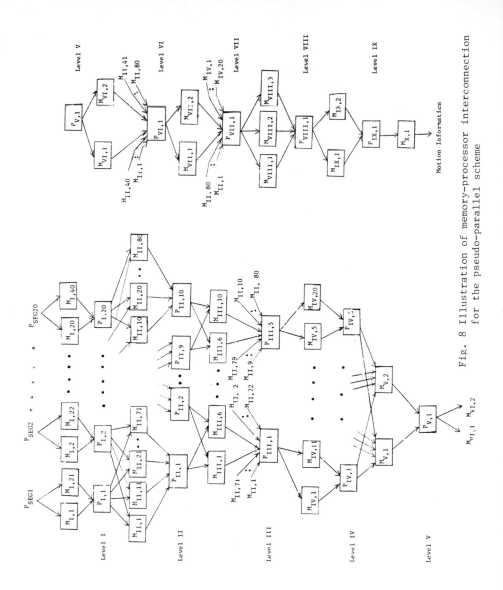

Fig. 8 Illustration of memory-processor interconnection for the pseudo-parallel scheme

network so that concatenated data corresponding to sections of the frame physically adjacent to each other, can also be logically adjacent to each other. For example, the picture is originally divided into 20 sections (Fig.7a) and the condenser of step I is expected to provide the condensed frame in 10 sections (Fig.7b); hence, two sections are to be combined. The address generation could be assigned to the additional control part to maintain adjacency for sectionalized frames of larger size.

The system can also be controlled by a distributed operating system, and there is then no need to have a central master controller. This is

164

because using pipelining dictates the synchronous flow of information from one level to the next level and the effective computation time of each stage has to be made independent of the type of actual function to be performed by the stage and is achieved by allocating enough number of processors to each level of the algorithm. Thus, there is no need to have a central controller for monitoring and guiding the sequency of the processes, as this has already been tailored in the system architecture.

6. Performance Evaluation

The "Pseudo-parallel" implementation of motion analysis presented in earlier sections provides a general design strategy for implementing a system for any other specific application. But, it also poses some interesting questions.

The first question is the degree of parallelism allowed in each step. This has been done on the basis of the data reported in an earlier work [25], and if advances made in this direction would modify the algorithm or change the time required for any level of Fig. 5, then similar alternations in Fig. 6 could be done very easily.

The other important question is the data generation time in the proposed pseudoparallel scheme. In the sequential process of Fig. 5, while moving from one level to another, a new data file is not always created, and the desired operations are performed on the old data area. Still going to the machine level, what this means is that whenever old data is not to be modified, there is no need to perform a "WRITE" operation. Hence, how do we make sure that each level of the pseudoparallel scheme of Figs. 6 and 8 takes the same amount of time taken by sequential execution on a single processor.

Another related question concerns the time required for concatenation of data whenever it is needed (such as from Fig.7a to 7b). In practice, much of the processor time is spent in doing useful computation, and storage of data is less frequently required [25]. This means that whenever data is ready for the WRITE operation, it can immediately be sent to the next level, and writing in a proper memory location can be taken care of by the next level. Thus, the processors can keep themselves busy just doing useful computations.

A similar argument can be given for concatenation, and either multiple port memory or simple memory with multiplexed inputs can be used. This should also not create any problem because rate of data transfer from each processor is small in relation to the computation time [25].

The design of data path that can be restructured is itself a problem and has been widely addressed in the literature [27-30]. This could introduce some additional time delay. Besides parallelism, one advantage of the proposed system can be easily mentioned. The processors assigned to each level have to do a very specific job, and the associated private memory should store the program needed for that part only. As a result, the private memory will be considerably smaller than the memory required in a sequential process. Another advantage of the proposed system is the absence of any synchronization problems which have been commonly observed in most distributed data base management systems. In fact, the proposed

165

system is a perfect candidate for the distributed operating system with no central master control.

To evaluate the performance of a general pseudoparallel scheme, let us assume the following:

m ≡ Total number of levels or stages in a sequential problem

t_i ≡ Time taken by the ith stage in a sequential problem, for $1 \leq i \leq m$.

6.1 Sequential Implementation: In regard to the assumptions just mentioned the total time taken in a sequential processing scheme will be

$$T_{seq} = \sum_{i=1}^{m} t_i \tag{3}$$

6.2 Pseudo-Parallel Implementation: In this scheme, there may be overhead from switching for dynamic path establishment and memory mapping. Let this be denoted by α_i such that:

α_i ≡ Total overhead in ith level of pseudo-parallel implementation.

Then, the time taken by the ith stage can be given as:

$$t'_i = (t_i + \alpha_i) = (1 + \beta_i) \, t_i \tag{4}$$

in which $\beta_i = \alpha_i / t_i$

Let K_i processors be assigned to ith stage of pseudo-parallel implementation. It may be noted that the value of K_i should be such that it is feasible to use parallelism in ith stage with K_i processors working in parallel. The time needed to complete ith stage evaluation can be given as

$$t_{pi} = t'_i / K_i \quad \text{for} \quad 1 \leq i \leq m \tag{5}$$

The total time needed for psuedoparallel implementation can be obtained as:

$$T_{pp} = \sum_{i=1}^{m} t_{pi} \tag{6}$$

6.3 PsuedoParallel Pipelined Implementation: If the overall scheme is to operate as a pipeline, then the data from each level must be moved to the next level within a fixed amount of time. This means that the effective time taken by each step should be constant, say "U". Then the effective time taken by such a system can be given by

$$T_{ppp} = U \tag{7}$$

For the pipeline to operate synchronously, we have to put additional constraint on relation (6). The number of processors allocated to each stage should be large enough so that the result of each stage is available atmost in time "U". The condition for minimum value of K_i can be given as:

$$(K_i - 1) \, U < t'_i \leq K_i \, U \tag{8}$$

Now, the speed up ratio can be easily obtained

$$\frac{T_{seq}}{T_{pp}} = \frac{\sum\limits_{i=1}^{m} t_i}{\sum\limits_{i=1}^{m} t_{pi}} \tag{9}$$

and

$$\frac{T_{seq}}{T_{ppp}} = \frac{\sum\limits_{i=1}^{m} t_i}{U} \tag{10}$$

7. Concluding Remarks

Tuning of the proposed architecture to the pseudoparallel algorithmic steps of motion analysis enables us to use parallelism in the best way possible. In fact, it can be easily conjectured that this is the only way parallelism can be introduced to the problem of motion analysis. Moreover, pipelining technique provides increased effective speed of the system, and makes the using of a distributed operating system without any central controller feasible.

The main advantage of the proposed pseudoparallel scheme is the generality of the procedure and suitable architecture for other specific applications that are basically sequential in nature can be investigated in the same way. This will require a thorough knowledge of the algorithmetic steps, the time required in solving each step of the problem, and the desired degree of speedup. This helps in balancing the computational requirements of each step. The basic philosophy can be easily used for other unexplored problems if the algorithm is modelled in the form of either Petri Nets [15] or Abstract Process Networks [32]. These models will help to identify noninteractive independent subtasks within the algorithm. Thus, the proposed pseudoparallel scheme shows great potential for its use in complex problems that have not yet been touched by other existing parallel and distributed processing systems.

References:

1. K. Batcher, "MPP-A Massively Parallel Processor," Proceedings of the 1979 International Conference on Parallel Processing, August 21-24, 1979, p. 249, also IEEE Transactions on Computers, Vol. C-29, No. 9, Sept. 1980, pp. 836-840.

2. F.A. Briggs, K.S. Fu, K. Hwang and J. Patel, "PM[4]: A Reconfigurable Multiprocessor System for Pattern Recognition and Image Processing," Proc. of NCC, AFIPS, pp. 255-266, June 1979.

3. L.S. Davis, "Computer Architecture for Image Processing," Proc. of Picture Data Description and Management, Aug. 27-28, 1980, pp. 249-254.

4. M.J.B. Duff, "Future Trends in Cellular Logic Image Processing," Proc. of Picture Data Description and Management, Aug. 27-28, 1980, pp. 294-297.

5. B. Parvin and K.S. Fu, "A Microprogrammable Vector Processor for Image Processing Application," Proc. of Picture Data Description and Management, Aug. 27-28, 1980, pp. 287-292.

6. A.P. Reeves and R. Rindfuss, "The Base 8 Binary Array Processors," Proceedings of the Pattern Recognition and Image Processing Conference," Chicago, August 6-8, 1979, pp. 250-255.

7. C. Rieger et al., "ZMOB: A Highly Parallel Multiprocessor," Proc. of Picture Data Description and Management, Aug. 1980, pp. 298-304.

8. R.P. Roesser, "Two-Dimensional Microprocessor Pipelines for Image Processing," IEEE Transactions on Computers, Vol. C-27, No. 2, February 1979, pp. 144-156.

9. H.J. Siegel et al., "An SIMD/MIMD Multiprocessor System for Image Processing and Pattern Recognition," Proceedings of 1979 Conference on Pattern Recognition and Image Processing, August 6-8, 1979, Chicago, pp. 214-220.

10. M.J. Flynn, "Some Computer Organizations and the Effectiveness," IEEE Transaction on Computers, Vol. C-21, No. 9, September 1972, pp.

11. Y. Wallach and V. Konrad, "On Block-Parallel Methods for Solving Linear Equations," IEEE Transactions on Computers, Vol. C-29, No. 5, May 1980, pp. 354-359.

12. A. Shimor and Y. Wallach, "A Multibus-oriented Parallel-processing System," IEEE Trans. on Industrial Electronics and Control Instrumentation 1978, Vol. IECE-25, pp. 137-141.

13. D.P. Agrawal and T.Y. Feng, "A Study of Communication Processor Systems," Rome Air Development Center Report, RADC-TR-310, Dec. 1979, 179 pages.

14. G.J. Lipovski, "On Some Parallel Programming Techniques," Processings of the COMPSAC '78, Nov. 13-16, 1978, pp. 781-789.

15. S.M. Ornstein et al., "Pluribus - A Reliable Multiprocessor," Proc. AFIPS 1975 National Computer Conference, pp. 551-559.

16. C.R. Vick, et al., "Adaptable Architecture for Supersystems," IEEE Computer, November 1980, pp. 17-34.

17. S.S. Reddy and E.A. Feustal, "A Restructurable Computer Systems," IEEE Transaction on Computers, Vol. C-27, No. 1, January 1978, pp. 1-20.

18. D.P. Agrawal and R. Jain, "A Novel Distributed Processing Scheme for Computer Analysis of Motion," Proceedings of the COMPCON Fall 1980, Washington, DC, Sept. 23-25, 1980, pp. 614-621.

19. D.P. Agrawal and R. Jain, "Computer Analysis of Motion Using a Network of Processors," presented, 5th International Conference on Pattern Recognition, Miami, Dec. 1-4, 1980, pp. 305-308.

20. B.J. Smith, "A Pipelined, Shared Resource MIMD Computer," Proceedings of the 1978 International Conference on Parallel Processing, August 22-25, 1978, pp. 6-8.

21. M.J. Flynn and J.L. Hennessy, "Parallelism and Representation Problems in Distributed Systems," Proc. of the 1st International Conference on Distributed Computing Systems, Alabama, Oct. 1-5, 1979, pp. 124-130.

22. R.B. Kieburtz, "A Hierarchical Multicomputer for Problem-Solving by Decomposition," Proc. of the 1st International Conference on Distributed Computing Systems, Alabama, Oct. 1-5, 1979, pp. 63-71.

23. R.Y. Kain et al., "Multiple Processor Scheduling Policies," Proc. of 1st Int. Conference on Distributed Computing Systems, Oct. 1-5, 1979, pp. 660-668.

24. L.D. Whittie, "A Distributed Operating System for a Reconfigurable Network Computer," Proc. of the 1st Int. Conference on Distributed Computing Systems, Oct. 1-5, 1979, pp. 669-679.

25. R. Jain, W. Martin and J.K. Aggarwal, "Segmentation Through the Detection of Change Due to Motion," Computer Graphics and Image Processing, Vol. 11, 1979, pp. 13-34.

26. K.M. Chung and C.K. Wong, "Construction of a Generalized Connector with $5 \cdot 8n \log_2 n$ edges," IEEE Transactions on Computers, Vol. C-29, No. 11, Nov. 1980, pp. 1029-1032.

27. M.A. Abidi and D.P. Agrawal, " On Conflict-free Permutations in Multi-stage Interconnection Networks," Proceedings of the 1979 International Conference on Parallel Processing, Aug. 1979, also appeared in Journal of Digital Systems, Vol. 4, No. 2, Summer 1980, pp. 115-134.

28. M.A. Abidi, D.P. Agrawal and J.J. Metzner, "Two Single-pass Permutations in Multi-stage Interconnection Networks," presented in 14th Annual Conference on Information Sciences and Systems, Princeton University, New Jersey, March 26-28, 1980, pp. 516-522.

29. T.Y. Feng, C.L. Wu and D.P. Agrawal, "A Microprocessor Controlled Asynchronous Circuit Switching Network," Proceeding of 6th Annual Symposium on Computer Architecture, Philadelphia, April, 23-25, 1979, pp. 202-215.

30. D.P. Agrawal, "Graph Theoretic Analysis and Design of Multistage Interconnection Networks," sent for publication.

31. C.V. Ramamoorthy and G.S. Ho, "Performance Evaluation of Asynchronous Concurrent Systems Using Petri Nets," IEEE Trans. on Software Engineering, Vol. SE-6, No. 5, Sept. 1980, pp. 440-449.

32. L.J. Mekly and S.S. Yau, "Software Design Representation Using Abstract Process Networks, IEEE Trans. on Software Engineering, Vol. SE-6, No. 5, Sept. 1980, pp. 426-435.

33. R. Jain, "Extraction of Motion Information from Peripheral Processes," IEEE Trans. on PAMI (in press).

34. A.R. Hanson and E.M. Riseman, VISIONS: A Computer System for Interpreting scenes, in Computer Vision Systems, Ed. A.R. Hanson and E.M. Riseman, Academic Press, 1978.

35. B. Kruse, "System Architecture for Image Analysis, in Structured Computer Vision," Ed. S. Taninoto and A. Klinger, Academic Press, 1980.

36. P. Narendra, "VLSI Architectures for Real-Time Image Processing," Proc. COMPON, Spring 1981, pp. 303-306.

37. D.P. Agrawal, "A Piplined Pseudoparallel System Architecture for Motion Analysis," Proc. 8th International Symposium on Computer Architecture, May 12-14, 1981, pp. 21-35.

VLSI Array Architecture for Picture Processing

P.S. Liu and T.Y. Young

Department of Electrical Engineering, University of Miami
Coral Gables, FL 33124, USA

1. Introduction

Many operations in picture or image processing are performed repeatedly over
a large number of pixels of an image, and computation time can be reduced
significantly by parallel processing. With rapid progress in VLSI technology, it will be feasible in the near future to design and fabricate VLSI
array chips for certain special image processing operations. These special
purpose chips can be connected to the host computer system through the system
bus.

With VLSI design, the major requirements are simplicity and regularity,
with a modular organization structure [1,2,3] . Only a few types of processing cells should be implemented in a VLSI array. High computation throughput can be achieved by pipelining and multiprocessing. Communication among
processing cells is a major design consideration due to the size and delay-
ing effect of the conducting paths on the VLSI chips. Therefore the data
streams and control flow of an array should be kept simple and regular, and
long distance and irregular communications should be avoided. VLSI systolic
arrays possess all the desirable features and are well suited for the tasks
of image processing [4-9]. Systolic arrays are also used for pattern analysis and matching [10 13]. Design of VLSI cellular array for image processing is examined [14]. Other types of VLSI architecture for parallel
image processing and pattern analysis have been proposed [15-20].

A systolic array consists of interconnected simple and mostly identical
processing elements (PE). A systolic array can be a one-dimensional linearly connected array, a two-dimensional orthogonally connected or hexagonally
connected array, or an array with a tree structure. One or more input
data streams are usually piped into the array in different directions. Inside the array, the elements of advancing input and internally generated
data streams meet at the processing cells, which perform usually identical
operations simultaneously on the data currently passing through. As data
streams flow deeper into the array, more PEs are engaged to calculate meaningful partial or final results. At a certain point, all PEs are engaged. The
desired results are piped out of the array in a natural manner overlapping
with remaining result computations. The results may also be stored inside
the array and then shipped out of the array after all computations are completed. For algorithms that can be executed with a systolic array, computation time is greatly reduced because of data streams pipelining and multiprocessing within the array.

An important and useful image processing operation is the image matrix multiplication [21- 22]. Let $\underline{X} = [x_{ij}]$ represents an n x n image, and

$$\underline{Z} = \underline{A} \; \underline{X} \; \underline{B}, \tag{1}$$

where both $\underline{A}$ and $\underline{B}$ are n x n matrices. In this paper, we consider VLSI systolic arrays using (1) as building blocks for several image processing operations, including DFT (discrete Fourier transform) and other image transforms, image filtering, and template matching.

Matrix multiplication can be implemented by hexagonal, rectangular or square arrays [2,4,23]. The output of a square array can be connected directly to the input of a second array, and hence it is especially suitable for the implementation of (1).

The appropriate control structure for optimal throughput of the multiplication array is discussed in some detail, taking into consideration the number of available pins for data input on a chip. The control structure is based on microprogrammed direct control [24] and modified SIMD (single instruction multiple data streams) architecture. Data flow in the array is also analyzed. It is shown that if one of the two matrices to be multiplied is a band matrix of bandwidth β, the multiplication can be implemented in a βxn array.

Arrays for image processing are described. Since the operations are based on the same principle of image matrix multiplication, a common VLSI structure is maintained, resulting in simple communication structure and regular data flow streams. The design task is thus simplified, and it may be possible to design and to use the same chips for several different image processing operations.

A few comments concerning DFT and FFT (fast Fourier transform) are in order. A two-dimensional FFT can be computed by first calculating one-dimensional row FFTs and then column FFTs. It is shown that with $n^2/2$ parallel processors, a two-dimensional FFT requires only 2 log n units of time [25]. The FFT algorithm sends the outputs of its processors back to the inputs of the same set of processors, and requires rather complicated branching or switching circuits. The proposed DFT array is slower, but it has a regular data flow and simple interconnection structure. It is noted that the best VLSI algorithm does not necessarily have the minimum number of multiplications or other arithmetic operations, an additional criterion could be weighted toward those algorithms having a minimum of branching [26]. Thus with VLSI, the choice of DFT or FFT is a matter of trade-off between computation costs and communication and control costs.

2. Arrays for Matrix Multiplication

Consider the multiplication of two n x n matrices,

$$\underline{Y} = \underline{X} \; \underline{B} \tag{2}$$

In terms of matrix elements, it may be expressed as the following recurrences:

$$y_{ij}^{(0)} = 0,$$

$$y_{ij}^{(k+1)} = y_{ij}^{(k)} + x_{ik}\,b_{kj}$$

$$y_{ij} = y_{ij}^{(n)} \tag{3}$$

The basic processing cell for the orthogonally or mesh connected square array can perform under control either a shift operation or multiplication operation which are shown in Fig.1.

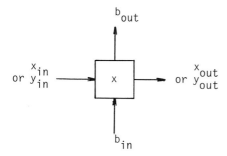

Shift operation:

$$x_{out} \longleftarrow x$$

$$x \longleftarrow x_{in}$$

Multiplication operation:

$$y_{out} \longleftarrow y_{in} + xb_{in}$$

$$b_{out} \longleftarrow b_{in}$$

<u>Fig.1</u> Basic processing cell operations

Figure 2 shows the data flow during multiplication. Initially the matrix <u>X</u> is loaded and stored into the array cells horizontally using the shift operation with each successive row delayded by one unit time if desired. The multiplication operation of matrix elements commences immediately for all cells in a row after the row is loaded.

Figure 3 illustrates two consecutive steps in the multiplication array. Consider the three cells in the middle row of the array only. For Fig.3(a), the operations of the three processing cells are as follows:

Cell 4: $y_{22} \leftarrow y_{22} + x_{21}b_{12}$

$$(= 0 + x_{21}b_{12}),$$

Cell 5: $y_{21} \leftarrow y_{21} + x_{22}b_{21}$

$$(= x_{21}b_{11} + x_{22}b_{21}),$$

Cell 6: inactive $\tag{4}$

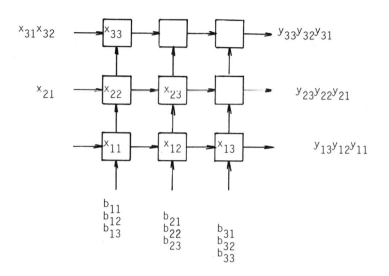

<u>Fig.2</u> Square array for matrix multiplication

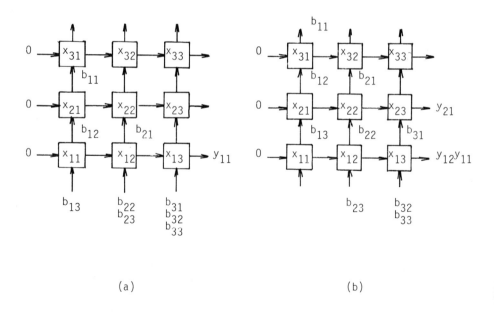

(a)   (b)

<u>Fig.3</u> Two consecutive steps of matrix multiplication with a square array.

174

The elements of the matrix $\underline{B}$ are shifted upward by one cell, and in the next step,

Cell 4: $y_{23} \leftarrow y_{23} + x_{21}b_{13}$

$$(=0 + x_{21}b_{13}),$$

Cell 5: $y_{22} \leftarrow y_{22} + x_{22}b_{22}$

$$(=x_{21}b_{12} + x_{22}b_{22}),$$

Cell 6: $y_{21} \leftarrow y_{21} + x_{23}b_{31}$

$$(=x_{21}b_{11} + x_{22}b_{21} + x_{23}b_{31}),$$

$$\text{exits } y_{21} \tag{5}$$

The major advantages of the square array are its simplicity in communication structure and regularity in data flow. With n^2 processing cells, the theoretical computation time is $(4n -2)$ units, including n units of time for multiplication, n units for loading the array, and $(2n -2)$ units for start-up delay time. The computation time is therefore $O(n)$ instead of the traditional $O(n^3)$.

A band matrix has its non-zero elements at or near the diagonal of the matrix only. Fig.4 shows an array of $\beta \times n$ cells for the multiplication of $\underline{X}$ by a band matrix $\underline{A}$ of bandwidth $\beta = 3$. It is noted that the columns of $\underline{X}$ are piped into the array simultaneously without start-up delay, and hence the computation time is only $(n + 2\beta)$ units, including the loading of $\underline{A}$. As discussed in section 5, band matrices can be used for image template matching.

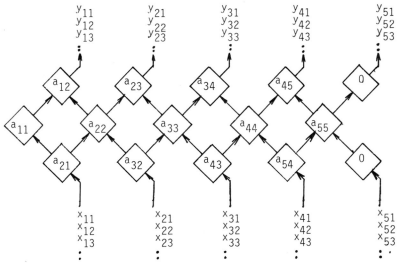

Fig.4   An array for multiplication of a matrix by a band matrix

3. Control Structure

The control structure of the multiplication array discussed in the previous section depends heavily on the number of pins available for piping the elements of $\underline{B}$ and $\underline{X}$ into the multiplication array chip. Basically, the control structure could be designed by modifying the SIMD architecture concept. When the number of input pins for $\underline{B}$ and $\underline{X}$ is not n respectively, more than one processor rows or columns would have to share the same input pin, and some processors get their data on a delayed basis. For these processors, the instructions broadcasted by the control unit should go through delay units or FIFO (first-in first-out) buffers before reaching these processors; otherwise, the instructions will be executed before the proper data are available. Due to these delays, the throughput of the multiplication array is affected.

Let k be the pin-ins for the two matrices respectively. To illustrate the basic multiplication array control structure, an example with n=4 and k=2 is shown in Fig.5. In this figure, external data are piped into the VLSI chip using 4 input pins. The elements of matrix $\underline{X}$ use input pins 1 and 2. Input pin 1 is connected directly to the leftmost processors of the bottom processor row and that of the third processor row from the bottom. Input pin 2 is connected directly to the leftmost processors of the other two processor rows. Input pin 3 is connected to buffer B1 which in turn is connected to buffer B2. Transfers of data between input pin 3 and B1 and that between B1 and B2 are carried out concurrently assuming the buffers are made of master-slave type flip-flops.

The data arrive at the input pins in the order as shown in Table 1. Each T_i is 1 unit time. For the first four unit time intervals T_0 through T_3, the single bit control line C1 is used to broadcast 4 shift commands to the bottom two processor rows and pipe in the needed x_{ij} elements for the bottom two processor rows in n=4 shifts. The x_{ij} elements for the top 2 rows are not available at the input pins until T_4. Therefore, the same n=4 shift commands issued during time intervals T_0 through T_3 are delayed n=4 unit times before they can reach the top two rows at time intervals T_4, T_5, T_6, and T_7 to load the top two processor rows. The n-unit time delay can be implemented using a FIFO stack.

Starting at T_2, the elements of $\underline{B}$ can be piped into buffers B1, B2, B3, and B4. It takes 2 shift commands broadcasted at T_2 and T_3 on the single bit control line C_2 to initially load the buffers. The first multiplication command is issued to the bottom two processor rows using the single bit control line C_3 at T_4. A shift command is also issued concurrently on control line C_2 at T_4. Since the top two processor rows are being loaded with their x_{ij}'s from T_4 through T_7, and that the multiplication commands are not needed by the top two processor rows until T_8, T_{10} and so on, the multiplication command issued at T_4 and subsequently other multiplication commands to be issued at T_6, T_8 and so on are delayed 4 unit times before they can reach the top two processor rows at T_8, T_{10}, T_{12}, etc. At T_5 a shift command is issued on control line C_2; at T_6, the shift command and the multiplication command are broadcasted concurrently on control lines C_2 and C_3. From this point on, the commands issued at T_5 and T_6 are repeated until all the resulting components of the matrix multiplication are obtained.

It should be noted that in this example, multiplications are performed at every other time intervals, and loading of the top two processor rows overlaps with the loading of the B buffers and multiplications carried out

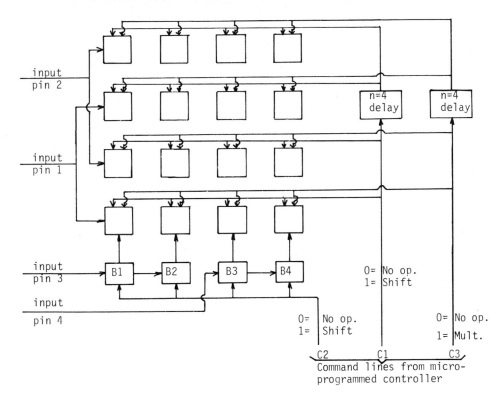

Fig.5 Control structure for matrix multiplication array

Table 1 Input-output sequence

	T_0	T_1	T_2	T_3	T_4	T_5	T_6	T_7	T_8	T_9	T_{10}	T_{11}	T_{12}	T_{13}	T_{14}	T_{15}	T_{16}	T_{17}
PIN 1	x_{14}	x_{13}	x_{12}	x_{11}	x_{34}	x_{33}	x_{32}	x_{31}										
PIN 2	x_{24}	x_{23}	x_{22}	x_{21}	x_{44}	x_{43}	x_{42}	x_{41}										
PIN 3	0	0	0	b_{11}	b_{21}	b_{12}	b_{22}	b_{13}	b_{23}	b_{14}	b_{24}	0	0	0	0	0		
PIN 4	0	0	0	0	0	0	0	b_{31}	b_{41}	b_{32}	b_{42}	b_{33}	b_{43}	b_{34}	b_{44}	0		
PIN 5												0	y_{11}	y_{21}	y_{12}	y_{22}	y_{13}	y_{23}
PIN 6												0	0	0	0	0	y_{31}	y_{41}

at the bottom two processor rows. It is also assumed that each operation involved can be completed in one unit time.

This control structure can be generalized to handle any combinations of n and k and it can be shown that a matrix multiplication takes $[n+n(3n-2)/k]$ units time to complete. Piping the results out of the VLSI chip can be handled in a similar fashion as piping in the elements of $\underline{B}$. The output sequence is partially shown in Table 1. The controller is microprogrammed, and assuming each microinstruction takes one unit time to execute, the control microprogram for the matrix multiplication is shown in Table 2.

Table 2 Control microprogram sequence

Processing cell shift control field	Processing cell multiplication control field	B buffer control field	Next μ instruction address field
1	0	0	*+1
1 n=4	0	0	*+1
1 shifts	0	1	*+1
1	0	1	*+1
0 loop	1	1	*+1 (3n-2)
0	0	1	*-1 times

*+1 means (present location +1)
*-1 means (present location -1)
The loop control field is not shown

This basic control structure can be used directly or modified to handle the image processing arrays discussed in the following sections. By changing the microprogram, the multiplication array may also be used to perform some other computations.

4. Arrays for DFT and Image Filtering

The gray levels of an n x n pixel image can be expressed as $\underline{X}=[x(i,j)]=[x_{ij}]$, and a linear image transform is defined as:

$$z_{\ell m} = \sum_{i=0}^{n-1} \sum_{j=0}^{n-1} x_{ij} f(i,j;\ell,m) \tag{6}$$

When the kernel f is separable, we have

$$f(i,j;\ell,m) = a(\ell,i)b(j,m).$$

two matrices can be defined as:

$$\underline{A} = [a(\ell,i)]$$

$$\underline{B} = [b(j,m)]$$

178

this allows (6) to be respresentated as matrix multiplications $\underline{Z} = \underline{A} \underline{X} \underline{B}$
which can be rewritten as

$$\underline{Y} = \underline{X} \underline{B}$$

$$\underline{Z} = \underline{A} \underline{Y} \tag{7}$$

Figure 6 (a) shows two square arrays in cascade, with $\underline{Y}$, the output from
the first array, piped directly into the second array. The matrix $\underline{A}$ could
be preloaded into the array as shown in Fig.6(b) if $\underline{A}$ and $\underline{B}$ do not share the
same data path. Because of pipelining from one array to the other, the
total computation time is (6n-3) units (without considering pin-number lim-
itations), compared to a sequential approach requiring $2n^3$ units of time.

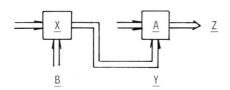

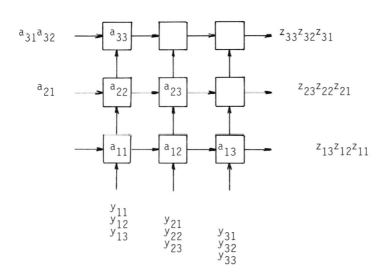

<u>Fig.6</u> Image matrix multiplication array
        (a) two square array in cascade
        (b) data flow in the second array

The class of separable image transforms,which can be represented by (7),
includes DFT, Walsh-Hadamard transform, Harr transform, and discrete cosine
transform. With two-dimensional DFT,

179

$$
\underline{A} = \underline{B} = \begin{bmatrix} 1 & 1 & 1 & 1 \\ 1 & \omega & \omega^2 & \omega^3 \\ 1 & \omega^2 & \omega^4 & \omega^6 \\ 1 & \omega^3 & \omega^6 & \omega^9 \end{bmatrix} \tag{8}
$$

where $n=4$ and

$$\omega = \exp(-j2\pi/n).$$

Two-dimensional IDFT uses $\underline{A}^{-1}$ instead of $\underline{A}$, with

$$
\underline{A}^{-1} = \frac{1}{n^2} \begin{bmatrix} 1 & 1 & 1 & 1 \\ 1 & \omega^{-1} & \omega^{-2} & \omega^{-3} \\ 1 & \omega^{-2} & \omega^{-4} & \omega^{-6} \\ 1 & \omega^{-3} & \omega^{-6} & \omega^{-9} \end{bmatrix} \tag{9}
$$

Figure 7(a) shows a standard DFT array using two square matrix-multiplication arrays as building blocks. The matrix $\underline{A}$ is given by (8), and it may be generated internally if necessary. Two variations of the standard DFT array are also shown. In Fig. 7(b), the matrix $\underline{Y}$ calculated from the first matrix multiplication is fed-back and loaded into the array to replace $\underline{A}$ for the second matrix-multiplication computation. The number of processing cells is reduced by half at the expense of more complicated communication structure and control circuit. In Fig. 7(c), the matrix $\underline{A}$ remains in the array for both matrix multiplications. A transpose array network is needed, which can be easily designed using VLSI FILO (first-in-last-out) stacks. The output is $\underline{Z}^T$ in this case.

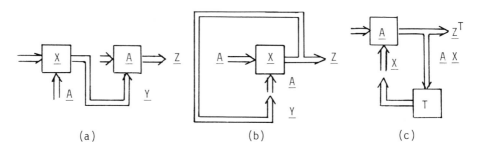

(a)　　　　　　　　　(b)　　　　　　　　　(c)

Fig.7　Architecture for DFT using square matrix multiplication array

Two-dimensional low-pass and high-pass filters are commonly used for image smoothing and image sharpening, respectively. Certain degradations in digital images such as blur caused by linear motion can be restored by inverse and Wiener filters [27]. These image enhancement and restoration techniques are DFT-based frequency domain approaches, and Fig.8 illustrates the implementation of two-dimensional filters.

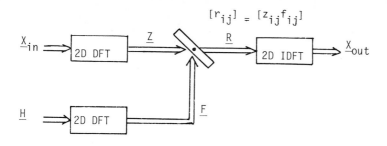

Fig.8 Implementation of two-dimensional image filters using DFT and IDFT arrays.

In the figure, the matrix $\underline{F}$ is a frequency domain filter function, and the linear array performs element-by-element matrix multiplication. If the filter is specified by its spatial domain representation $\underline{H}$, commonly referred to as a point spread function, an additional DFT array is needed as indicated in the figure. It is noted that the total computation time does not increase in this case, since the two DFTs for the image and the point spread function can be performed in parallel.

5. Image Template Matching

Template matching is a spatial domain operation that depends on the neighboring pixels only. A 3x3 template or window assigns different weighting coefficients to a pixel and its eight neighbors. By selecting the weighting coefficients properly, the templates may be used for various spatial domain tasks, including line detection, edge detection, and image smoothing by neighborhood averaging. For edge detection or line detection, each pixel, together with its neighbors, is tested against a given template pattern to determine whether it matches the pattern. Parallel processing machines for template matching have been discussed by several authors [5,28 - 30]. Here we consider template matching using matrix-multiplication arrays.

To match a 3x3 template $\underline{W} = [w(k,\ell)]$ we need to compute

$$\hat{x}(i,j) = \sum_{k=-1}^{1} \sum_{\ell=-1}^{1} w(k,\ell)x(i+k,j+\ell) \tag{10}$$

and then compare the result with a predetermined decision threshold. Equation (10) may be rewritten as

$$\hat{x}(i,j) = \sum_{k=i-1}^{i+1} \sum_{\ell=j-1}^{j+1} w(k-i,\ell-j)x(k,\ell) \tag{11}$$

If $\underline{W}$ is separable, i.e., $w(k,\ell)=a(k)b(\ell)$, or in matrix form

$$\underline{W} = \underline{a}\,\underline{b}^T, \tag{12}$$

then (11) becomes

$$\hat{x}(i,j) = \sum_{k=i-1}^{i+1} \sum_{\ell=j-1}^{j+1} a(k-i)x(k,\ell)b(\ell-j) \tag{13}$$

This means $\hat{\underline{X}} = \underline{A} \ \underline{X} \ \underline{B}$, where $\underline{A}$ consists of shifted row vectors $\underline{a}^T$ and $\underline{B}$ is composed of shifted column vectors $\underline{b}$. Since $\underline{a}$ and $\underline{b}$ are 3x1 vectors, the resulting matrices are band matrices with a bandwidth $\beta=3$. Hence, matrix multiplication can be made faster using a 3xn array instead of a square array. Shown in Fig.9 is an implementation of template matching for a sep-

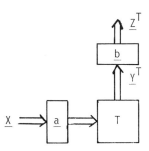

Fig.9   Template matching for a separable $\underline{W}=\underline{a} \ \underline{b}^T$

arable $\underline{W}$. The rectangular blocks are 3xn arrays of Fig.4, connected by a transpose network.

It can be shown that a 3x3 matrix $\underline{W}$ if not separable, may be expressed as

$$\underline{W} = \underline{a} \ \underline{b}^T + \underline{c} \ \underline{d}^T , \qquad\qquad \text{if det } \underline{W} = 0 \tag{14}$$

and in the worst case,

$$\underline{W} = \underline{a} \ \underline{b}^T + \underline{c} \ \underline{d}^T + e \ \underline{\Delta} , \qquad\qquad \text{if det } \underline{W} \neq 0. \tag{15}$$

In (15),

$$\underline{\Delta} = \begin{bmatrix} 0 & 0 & 0 \\ 0 & 1 & 0 \\ 0 & 0 & 0 \end{bmatrix} \tag{16}$$

is a degenerated case of a separable function, and the effect of $e \ \underline{\Delta}$ on the image $\underline{X}$ is simply to multiply $\underline{X}$ by a scalar e, which can be easily implemented as a single-pixel operation.

Almost all templates commonly used for edge detection and line detection are either separable or can be represented as the sum of two separable functions. As an example, consider the nine orthogonal templates [31] shown in Fig.10. The first four templates are for edge detection, the next four for line detection, and the last one is for averaging. The following table shows the decomposition of the templates into separable functions. Noting that $e\underline{\Delta}$ is a special case of a separable function, all nine templates are either separable or representable by (14), the latter can be implemented by using a linear array of adders and two arrays of Fig.9 in parallel.

182

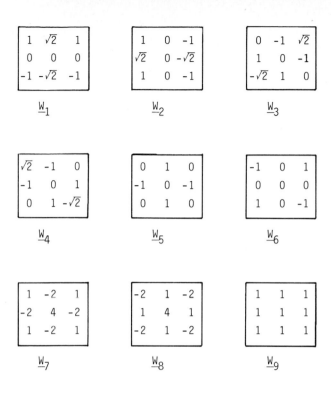

$$
\underline{W}_1 = \begin{bmatrix} 1 & \sqrt{2} & 1 \\ 0 & 0 & 0 \\ -1 & -\sqrt{2} & -1 \end{bmatrix}
\quad
\underline{W}_2 = \begin{bmatrix} 1 & 0 & -1 \\ \sqrt{2} & 0 & -\sqrt{2} \\ 1 & 0 & -1 \end{bmatrix}
\quad
\underline{W}_3 = \begin{bmatrix} 0 & -1 & \sqrt{2} \\ 1 & 0 & -1 \\ -\sqrt{2} & 1 & 0 \end{bmatrix}
$$

$$
\underline{W}_4 = \begin{bmatrix} \sqrt{2} & -1 & 0 \\ -1 & 0 & 1 \\ 0 & 1 & -\sqrt{2} \end{bmatrix}
\quad
\underline{W}_5 = \begin{bmatrix} 0 & 1 & 0 \\ -1 & 0 & -1 \\ 0 & 1 & 0 \end{bmatrix}
\quad
\underline{W}_6 = \begin{bmatrix} -1 & 0 & 1 \\ 0 & 0 & 0 \\ 1 & 0 & -1 \end{bmatrix}
$$

$$
\underline{W}_7 = \begin{bmatrix} 1 & -2 & 1 \\ -2 & 4 & -2 \\ 1 & -2 & 1 \end{bmatrix}
\quad
\underline{W}_8 = \begin{bmatrix} -2 & 1 & -2 \\ 1 & 4 & 1 \\ -2 & 1 & -2 \end{bmatrix}
\quad
\underline{W}_9 = \begin{bmatrix} 1 & 1 & 1 \\ 1 & 1 & 1 \\ 1 & 1 & 1 \end{bmatrix}
$$

<u>Fig.10</u> Orthogonal templates for edge detection and line detection

<u>Table 3</u> Decomposition of orthogonal templates

Template	$\underline{a}^T$			$\underline{b}^T$			$\underline{c}^T$			$\underline{d}^T$			e
$\underline{W}_1$	1	0	-1	1	$\sqrt{2}$	1	——			——			——
$\underline{W}_2$	1	$\sqrt{2}$	1	1	0	-1	——			——			——
$\underline{W}_3$	0	$-1/\sqrt{2}$	1	$-\sqrt{2}$	1	0	1	$-1/\sqrt{2}$	0	0	-1	$\sqrt{2}$	——
$\underline{W}_4$	1	$-1/\sqrt{2}$	0	$\sqrt{2}$	-1	0	0	$-1/\sqrt{2}$	1	0	1	$\sqrt{2}$	——
$\underline{W}_5$	1	0	1	0	1	0	0	-1	0	1	0	1	——
$\underline{W}_6$	-1	0	1	1	0	-1	——			——			——
$\underline{W}_7$	1	-2	1	1	-2	1	——			——			——
$\underline{W}_8$	1	$-1/2$	1	-2	1	-2	——			——			9/2
$\underline{W}_9$	1	1	1	1	1	1	——			——			——

Appendix   Decomposition of Templates

Consider a 3x3 template or window $\underline{W}$. If $\underline{W}$ is separable, it is easy to decompose it into $\underline{a}$ and $\underline{b}^T$ and to verify that det $\underline{W}$ = 0. In this appendix, we wish to show that

$$\underline{W} = \underline{a}\ \underline{b}^T + \underline{c}\ \underline{d}^T, \tag{A.1}$$

if and only if det $\underline{W}$ = 0 (with separable $\underline{W}$ regarded as a special case), and that if det $\underline{W} \neq 0$,

$$\underline{W} = \underline{a}\ \underline{b}^T + \underline{c}\ \underline{d}^T + e\ \underline{\Delta}, \tag{A.2}$$

where $\underline{\Delta}$ is given by (16). The following proof also yields a procedure for the decomposition of the 3x3 $\underline{W}$.

Assume that (A.1) is true. The nine elements of $\underline{W}$ may be expressed as

$$w_{ij} = a_i b_j + c_i d_j, \quad i=-1,0,1, \quad j=-1,0,1 \tag{A.3}$$

Solving for a_i and c_i, we have

$$a_i = \frac{w_{i,-1}d_1 - w_{i,1}d_{-1}}{b_{-1}d_1 - b_1 d_{-1}},$$

$$c_i = \frac{w_{i,1}b_{-1} - w_{i,-1}b_1}{b_{-1}d_1 - b_1 d_{-1}}, \qquad i = -1, 0, 1. \tag{A.4}$$

The two equations for $w_{-1,0}$ and $w_{1,0}$ in (A.3) can be solved to obtain

$$b_o = \frac{w_{-1,0}\,c_1 - w_{1,0}\,c_{-1}}{a_{-1}c_1 - a_1 c_{-1}}$$

$$d_o = \frac{w_{1,0}a_{-1} - w_{-1,0}\,a_1}{a_{-1}c_1 - a_1 c_{-1}} \tag{A.5}$$

There are two separate cases to be considered. In the first case, $b_{-1}d_1 - b_1 d_{-1}$ = 0, then according to (A.4),

$$w_{i,-1}/w_{i,1} = b_{-1}/b_1 = d_{-1}/d_1, \quad i =-1,0,1.$$ in order that a_i and c_i be finite. In other words, the first column and the last column of $\underline{W}$ differ by a constant factor only, which implies det $\underline{W}$ = 0. A similar argument can be used if $a_{-1}c_1 - a_1 c_{-1} = 0$.

We now consider the case that $b_{-1}d_1 - b_1 d_{-1} \neq 0$ and $a_{-1}c_1 - a_1 c_{-1} \neq 0$. It is noted that (A.4) and (A.5) are derived from eight of the nine equations in (A.3). The remaining equation to be satisfied is

$$a_o b_o + c_o d_o = w_{0,0} \tag{A.6}$$

Substitution of b_o and d_o by (A.5) yields

$$a_o(w_{-1,0}c_1 - w_{1,0}c_{-1}) + c_o(w_{1,0}a_{-1} - w_{-1,0}a_1) = w_{0,0}(a_{-1}c_1 - a_1 c_{-1}) \tag{A.7}$$

Using (A.4) for a_i and c_i, we obtain, after tedious but straightforward algebraic manipulations,

$$(b_{-1}d_1 - b_1d_{-1})^{-1} \det \underline{W} = 0. \tag{A.8}$$

Conversely, if $\det \underline{W} = 0$, we may choose somewhat arbitrarily b_{-1}, d_{-1}, b_1 and d_1 such that $b_{-1}d_1 - b_1d_{-1} \neq 0$. Then, a_i and c_i can be calculated from (A.4), and assuming that $a_{-1}c_1 - a_1c_{-1} \neq 0$, b_0 and d_0 can be obtained from (A.5). The resulting vector elements will satisfy (A.6) since $\det \underline{W}=0$. If it turns out that $a_{-1}c_1 - a_1c_{-1} = 0$, the first row and the last row of $\underline{W}$ must differ by a constant factor only, and the decomposition of $\underline{W}$ into (A.1) is fairly obvious in this case.

Finally, if $\det \underline{W} \neq 0$, the same decomposition procedure mentioned above can be used except that now $a_0b_0 + c_0d_0 \neq w_{0,0}$. Let

$$e = w_{0,0} - (a_0b_0 + c_0d_0) \ ,$$

and it is obvious that $\underline{W}$ is decomposed in the form of (A.2).

References

1. C. Mead, L. Conway: Introduction to VLSI Systems. (Addison-Wesley, Reading, Mass., 1980).
2. H.T. Kung: "Let's design algorithms for VLSI systems", Proc. Caltech.Conf. on VLSI, pp. 65-90 (1979).
3. T.Y. Young, P.S. Liu: Impact of VLSI on pattern recognition and image processing, in VLSI Electronics: Microstructure Science, vol. 4, N.G. Einspruch, Ed., (Academic, New York, 1982), pp. 319-360.
4. T.Y. Young, P.S. Liu: "VLSI Arrays and Control Structure for Image Processing", Proc. Workshop on Computer Architecture for Pattern Analysis and Image Database Management, pp. 257-264 (1981).
5. H.T. Kung, S.W. Song: "A Systolic 2-D Convolution Chip", Proc. Workshop on Computer Architecture for Pattern Analysis and Image Database Management, pp. 159-160 (1981).
6. H.T. Kung, R.L. Picard: "Hardware Pipelines for Multi-Dimensional Convolution and Resampling", Proc. Workskop on Computer Architecture for Pattern Analysis and Image Database Management, pp. 273-278 (1981).
7. D.W.L. Yen, A.V. Kulkavni: "The ESL Systolic Processor for Signal and Image Processing", Proc. Workshop on Computer Architecture for Pattern Analysis and Image Database Management, pp. 265-272 (1981)
8. T.J. Willet, C.W. Brooks, G.E. Tisdale: "Relaxation, Systolic Arrays and Universal Arrays", Westinghouse System Development Division, Baltimore, Maryland 21203.
9. J.M. Speiser, H.J. Whitehouse, K. Bromley: "Signal Processing Applications for Systolic Arrays", Naval Ocean Systems Center, San Diego, California, 92152.
10. B. Ackland, N. Westle, D.J. Burr: "An Integrated Multiprocessing Array for Time Warp Pattern Matching", 8th Intl.Sym. on Computer Architecture, pp. 197-215 (1981).
11. K.H. Chu, K.S. Fu: "VLSI Architecture for High Speed Recognition of General Context-Free Languages and Finite-State Languages", Tech.Report, School of Electrical Engineering, Purdue University (1981).
12. K. Hwang, S.P. Su: "A Partitioned Matrix Approach to VLSI Pattern Classification", Proc. Workshop on Computer Architecture for Pattern Analysis and Database Management, pp. 168-177 (1981).

13. M.J. Foster, H.T. Kung: "Design of Special-Purpose VLSI Chips", Computer, pp. 26-40 (1980).
14. S.L. Tanimoto, J.J. Pfeiffer,Jr.: "An Image Processor Based on an Array of Pipelines", Proc. Workshop on Computer Architecture for Pattern Analysis and Database Management, pp. 201-208 (1981).
15. C.R. Dyer: "A VLSI Pyramid Machine for Hierarchical Parallel Image Processing", Dept. of Information Engineering, University of Illinois at Chicago Circle, Chicago, Illinois 60680 (1981).
16. E.E. Swartzlander,Jr.: "VLSI Networks for Image Processing", Proc. Workshop on Computer Architecture for Pattern Analysis and Database Management, pp. 161-167 (1981).
17. B. Parvin: "VLSI Architecture for Edge Detection", School of Electrical Engineering, Purdue University, West Lafayette, Indiana 47907.
18. M.R. Lowry, M. Allan: "A General Purpose VLSI Chip for Computer Vision with Fault-Tolerant Hardware", Artificial Intelligence Laboratory, Stanford University, Stanford, California 94305.
19. P. Narendra: "VLSI Architecture for Real-Time Image Processing", Digest Spring COMPCON, pp. 303-306 (1981).
20. N.S. Chang, Y.C. Yuan: "VLSI Design and Verification of a Signal Processing Chip", Proc. Workshop on Computer Architecture for Pattern Analysis and Database Management, pp. 279-283 (1981).
21. T.Y. Young, T.W. Calvert: Classification, Estimation and Pattern Recognition, (American Elsevier, New York, Ch. 8, 1974).
22. R.C. Gonzalez, P.A. Wintz: Digital Image Processing, (Addison-Wesley, Reading, Mass., 1977).
23. K. Hwang, Y.H. Cheng: "VLSI arithmetic arrays and modular networks for solving large-scale linear system of equations", Tech. Report, School of Electrical Engineering, Purdue University,(1980).
24. P.S. Liu, F.J. Mowle: "Techniques of Program Execution with a Writable Control Memory", IEEE Trans. Computer, vol. C-27, pp. 816-827 (1978).
25. P.T. Mueller,Jr., L.J. Siegel, H.J. Siegel: "Parallel algorithms for the two-dimensional FFT", Proc. 5th International Conf. on Pattern Recognition, pp. 497-503 (1980).
26. R.W. Brodersen: Signal Processing using MOS-VLSI technology, in VLSI Electronics: Microstructure Science, vol. 2, N.G. Einspruch, Ed. (Academic, New York, 1981).
27. M.M. Sondhi: "Image restoration - the removal of spatially invarian degradation", Proc. IEEE, vol. 60, pp. 842-853 (1972).
28. M.J.B. Duff: "A cellular logic array for image processing",Pattern Recognition , vol. 5, pp. 229-247 (1973).
29. B. Kruse: "A parallel picture processing machine", IEEE Trans. Computers, vol. C-22, pp. 1075-1086 (1973).
30. R.M. Lougheed, D.L. McCubbrey: The cytocomputer - A practical pipelined image processor", Proc. 7th Annual Symp. Computer Architecture, pp. 271-277 (1980).
31. W. Frei, C.C. Chen: "Fast boundary detection - A generalization and a new algorithm", IEEE Trans. Computers, vol. C-26, pp. 988-998 (1977).

Part IV

Office Automation

High-Level Programming Support for Color/Graphics Reports

K. Saigusa

APL Support, Product Marketing, IBM Japan
2-chome, Nishi-shinjuku 6-1, Shinjuku-ku, Tokyo 160, Japan

T. Takeshita

Development No. 1, Software Development Center, IBM Japan
2-chome, Minami-Aoyama 5-17, Minatu-ku, Tokyo 107, Japan

ABSTRACT

Color/graphics capabilities of interactive terminals vastly expand potential computer applications. However, programming to utilize them fully is much more complex and time-consuming than conventional report writers handling just numbers and texts.

Based on extensive experience in developing commercial applications and system/utility support for them using APL, SAIGUSA has developed easy-to-use, flexible user interfaces and supporting functions for generating programs and parametric data for drawing graphs of statistical data, simple figures (illustrations, diagrams, maps, company logos, etc.) represented by X and Y coordinates, and titles and other texts consisting of alphanumeric and Kanji characters of different sizes and for composing graphs, figures and titles into a single graphic report. In this development, he has tried to take best advantage of APL and to integrate a number of latest programming technologies.

The GDDM/PGF (Graphical Data Display Manager/Presentation Graphic Feature) is used as base software support which produces character and graphic images on the IBM 3279 color/graphics screen as specified by a set of commands given by a user program.

1. Introduction

Color/graphics reports are easier to read and more effective for business executives, planners, scientists, engineers and almost anybody. People who have seen them are attracted to such reports, and so color/graphics capabilities help create a large number of various new applications, including those which have been totally unpredicted.

However, programming is more complex because such things as listed below have to be taken into consideration:

- Shapes, sizes, and layout of graphs and figures.
- Selection of line types, color and patterns.
- Combination of characters and graphic data.
- Composition/overlay of different graphs and figures.
- A large number of items and attributes to be specified.

    To facilitate development of applications using color/graphics displays,
SAIGUSA has developed several modules written in APL (APL defined functions):
- to generate APL functions for creating graphs of different types,
- to generate parametric data to be used by an APL function for creating
  two-dimensional figures represented by X-Y coordinates,
- to prepare strings of Kanji codes to be used by an APL function for
  writing Kanji titles and text, and
- to compose graphs, figures and text into a single report and to save as
  a procedure the input statements in this process.
A few of these APL functions use routines in GDDM/PGF (cf. Appendix) invoked
via an auxiliary processor called AP126 (cf. Appendix).

    These modules are combined into a workspace (a program written in APL)
called GRAPHAID. Any of these can be called by specifying its name in an
APL program, or by selection (by keying in its number) from the menu on the
screen entitled "GRAPH AID".

    The first one (GPGF) of the modules mentioned above has a specially de-
signed, ease-of-use interface for entering specifications to generate APL
programs for graphs.

    The second and third ones (GPAT and GTEXT) in GRAPHAID have different
interfaces which allow the user to easily specify parameters to be used by
APL functions for figures and Kanji titles at execution time and to verify
the specification input (by locking at rough images consisting of special
characters without using color/graphics) at the entry time.

    The fourth one (GGDDM) prompts the user with messages to instruct him to
provide the names of the functions and parameters (prepared by the first
three modules) and other parameters, and displays the composed graphical
report on the screen, and also it allows him to save as a procedure these
statements (including the names and parameters) which have been inputted by
him.

    Four other modules listed below have been developed under GRAPH AID, but
they are not described in this paper for lack of space:
- Data Display/Entry Facility
- Alpha-Numberic Screen Formatting Facility
- APL Function Definition Facility
- GRAPHAID Work Results

    VS APL is an IBM program product, an implementation of APL which was origi-
nally developed by KENNETH E. IVERSON. It runs under MVS/TSO, VM/CMS, VSPC
and CICS/VS. For the description of GDDM/PGF and AP126, refer to Appendix.
Whole implementation (including the original conception, design, and testing)
has been done by SAIGUSA. Because he has been too busy to write a paper,
TAKESHITA has studied his implementation and has drafted this manuscript,
which has been reviewed and corrected by SAIGUSA for conceptual and technical
accuracy.

2. Background and Objectives

It is relatively a short time since low-cost general-purpose color/graphics
display terminals were made available for office use. It has been discovered
that the color/graphics capabilities are to vastly expand end-user oriented

applications because of increased ease of identifying and recognizing high-
lights and exceptional things as well as general trends, i.e. those requiring
higher attention without examining detailed numerical data.

Basic software support packages for color/graphics presentation such as
GDDM/PGF have been released only recently. Even with this kind of packages,
it still requires a large amount of programming efforts for a user to develop
application programs to produce various color/graphics reports. Combining
strings of characters and arrays of numerical data and formatting them into a
report is not considered to be a difficult task, but combining this character
information into graphic data and with different patterns and colors very
often creates enormous programming workload.

Based on extensive knowledge of APL and commercial applications and on
long-time experience in programming real applications and utility functions
in APL, SAIGUSA has explored approaches to facilitate the development of applications taking best advantage of color/graphics capabilities. The areas
of interest which he has been studying with users' direct involvement and
feed-back are the following:

a) Types of applications to benefit from color/graphics presentations.
b) Output data and their presentations generally required in these applications.
c) Logic designing and programming required and their workload.
d) Common characteristics of software functions required on top of the
   basic color/graphics software support provided by the manufacturer.
e) Architecture and implementation techniques for packaging these additional functions and providing the user interfaces so that they can be
   readily invoked by the user to be merged with other parts of his program as subroutines to serve as main-line functions or even to work as
   self-sufficient functions.
f) Implementation, testing and maintenance of these additional functions
   - - - prototyping and enhancement into production application programs.

Mostly, the components of a business graphics report can be classified
into the three categories:

1) A graph of a standard type suitable for representing statistical data.
   This is changed as a new set of data is inputted at the execution time.
2) A figure (a simple illustration, diagram, flow chart, map, company
   trade mark/logo, etc.) which can be drawn with a set of points (X and
   Y coordinates).
3) Titles and other texts of alphanumeric and/or Kanji characters of different sizes.

With this understanding, SAIGUSA has intended to provide utility functions
(modules written in APL) and application development methodologies for reducing the need for complex programming by the user, and to demonstrate the effectiveness of these modules modifiable and so adaptable to individual user's
needs rather than to provide a complete ready-made application package.

To accomplish this, SAIGUSA has utilized powerful interactive APL capabilities for modular programming and for ease of modification and expansion, and
he has developed the effective user interfaces whose characteristics are as
follows:

- User friendly and practical.
- Multiple forms (entry screens) suitable for types of information to be
  entered.

- Compact, but extensive (avoiding information dilution).
- Menus plus fill-in-the-blank.
- Novice and expert modes. (A beginner is prompted by the next input area turning white. An expert can enter all parameters without pressing the enter key each time.)
- Visual verification at specification entry time.
- Parametric specifications to generate required functions or argument data to be used by functions at execution time.

The resulting software support is a set of interactive forms (panels) driven generators (modules written in APL) which the user can use in learning color/graphics programming potentiality, in quickly developing ad hoc graphic reports, and in using these in whole or in part to expand into sophisticated large-scale application systems. SAIGUSA's philosophy is to provide substantial programming aids and guiding methodologies, but to leave to the user the final responsibility to complete his application system.

3. Organization and Architecture

GRAPHAID is a collection of several modules written in APL. Three of them (GPGF, GPAT and GTEXT) generate APL function (APL defined functions consisting of APL statements) or data (to be given as arguments of APL functions) to display graphic reports using routines in GDDM/PGF. The Fourth one (GGDDM) is to compose the graphs, figures and titles by executing the functions generated by the first module (GPGF) and by executing GDRAW and GWRITE functions with arguments generated by the second and third modules (GPAT and GTEXT) respectively.

The information inputted by the user during the execution of GGDDM - - - namely the names of functions generated by GPGF and of the data generated by GPAT and GTEXT) and new sets of parameters specified at this time - - - can be stored as a procedure so that it can be retrieved for modification or repetitive use.

At the execution time, for actually displaying graphs, and drawing figures and texts on the screen by executing APL functions (those generated by GPGF, and pre-coded GDRAW and GWRITE functions with data prepared by GPAT and GTEXT), routines in GDDM/PGF are invoked via AP126.

After entry into VS APL by a proper log-on procedure on a terminal under an interactive subsystem, keying in 'GRAPHAID' causes the display of the screen panel shown below.

Then, the user's section of a desired module, i.e. a generator or composer (by pressing a numeric key) causes the display of the panel for input of specifications (of the first prompting message in case of the composer). In case of a generator, upon the completion of filling the blank character positions with the required pieces of information, the desired APL functions or argument data (to be used by APL functions) are generated with the names assigned for later retrieval. In the case of the composer (GGDDM), as the requested pieces of control information are entered, a graph, figure and/or text appears by itself or combined with others on the screen.

Any of these can be used stand-alone or called in by an APL program. Also, any APL coding can precede and follow the modules in GRAPHAID for pre-

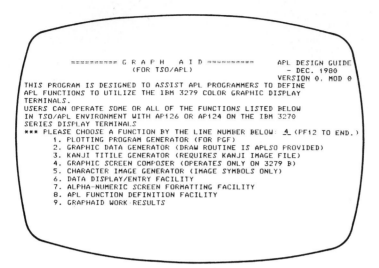

Fig.1 GRAPHAID menu panel

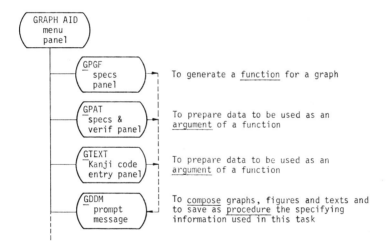

To generate a function for a graph

To prepare data to be used as an argument of a function

To prepare data to be used as an argument of a function

To compose graphs, figures and texts and to save as procedure the specifying information used in this task

Fig.2 Organization of GRAPHAID

processing or additional processing after the display of graphical reports. The user can return to the APL native mode by pressing a Program Function key.

VS APL is an implementation of APL, which runs under MVS/TSO, VSPC, VM/CMS and CICS/VS. A user program written in APL is often called an 'APL workspace', which is stored into and loaded from the public library or a private library.

For linking an APL workspace with GDDM/PGF, an APL auxiliary processor (called 'AP126') written in Assembler language is used. For setting up shared variables between the two (for exchange of data and control information), the user uses BOPEN function (written in APL). GDDM/PGF receives as input a sequence of commands with operands for specifications of color and graphics representations.

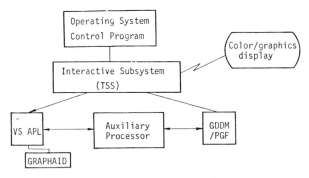

Fig.3 System environment of GRAPHAID

4. Plotting Program Generator (GPGF)

GPGF is a program module written in APL to generate an APL function to produce a graph of a statistical type using subroutines in GDDM/PGF for
- Pie charts
- Line graphs
- Surface charts
- Venn diagrams
- Histograms
- Bar charts

As shown below, a graphic report has so many attributes (graph elements):

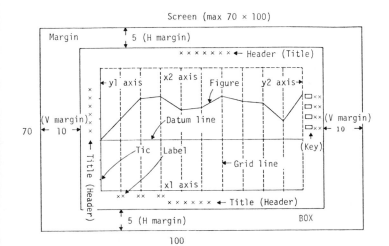

Fig.4 Graph elements

The types of graphic data representations are as follows:

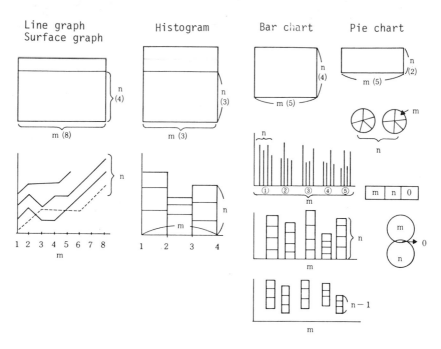

Fig.5 Types of graphic data representations

GDDM/PGF has 192 commands available for the user to specify graph attributes (graph elements and others) and other items including control information. Out of them seventy-odd commands (routines) have been selected and have been grouped into 14 categories to be used in GGDDM (for the execution of the functions generated by GPGF). The display screen is divided into 14 areas, each of which has abbreviations indicating the commands belonging to the corresponding category so that all the essential graph attributes (corresponding to GDDM/PGF routines) can be seen on a single screen for easier entry of many items and for verification of completeness of the input information by the user.

In order to prompt the beginner, the areas into which the selection indications and/or parameters may be entered turn white successively in sequence of the entry.

The 14 areas are used to specify the following, which are listed in the order of entry:
1) The names of data to be used,   2) Color, line type, marker,
3) Display of data value,   4) Legend,   5) Exchange of X and Y axes, secondary axes,   6) Labels to axes,   7) Attributes of axes,
8) Tics on axes,   9) Datum line and grid lines,   10) Titles,
11) Lables,   12) Note,   13) Header,   14) Chart area

194

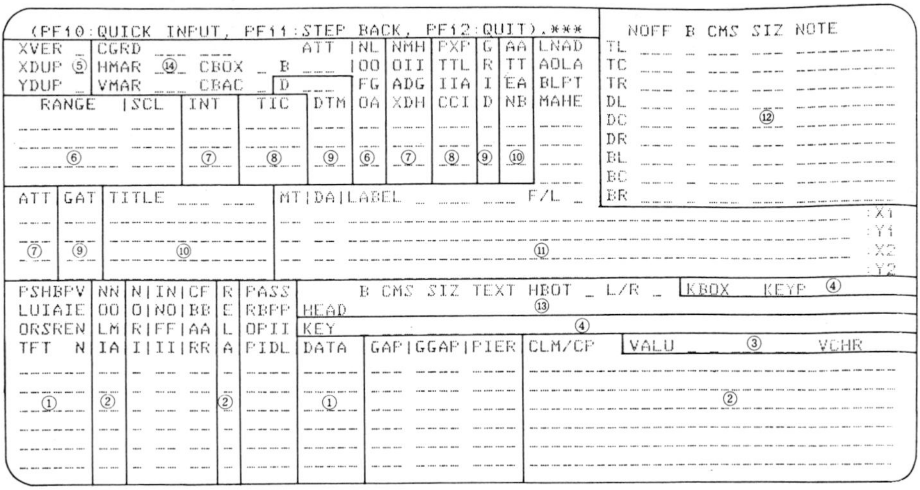

```
(PF10:QUICK INPUT, PF11:STEP BACK, PF12:QUIT).***        NOFF B CMS SIZ NOTE
XVER _ CGRD  ___  ___        ATT  |NL|NMH|PXF|G|AA|LNAD   TL ____ __ ___ ___ _____
XDUP ⑤ HMAR ⑭_ CBOX _ B ___ |00|OII|TTL|R|TT|AOLA   TC ____ __ ___ ___ _____
YDUP _ VMAR ___ CBAC _ D     FG|ADG|IIA|I|EA|BLPT   TR ____ __ ___ ___ _____
  RANGE  |SCL| INT | TIC |DTM|OA|XDH|CCI|D|NB|MAHE   DL ____ __ ___ ___ _____
_____ _____ _____ _____ ___|__|___|___|_|__|____    DC        ⑫
_____ _____ _____ _____ ___|__|___|___|_|__|____    DR ____ __ ___ ___
   ⑥     ⑦    ⑧    ⑨  ⑥  ⑦  ⑧ ⑨ ⑩      BL ____ __ ___ ___ _____
                                                     BC
ATT|GAT|TITLE ___ ___      MT|DA|LABEL ___ ___ __ F/L _   BR ____ ____ ___ ___ _____
                                                                            :X1
 ⑦   ⑨ _____   __ __ _____ ⑪_   :Y1
       ⑩                                                     :X2
                                                             :Y2
PSHBPV|NN|N|IN|CF|R|PASS        B CMS SIZ TEXT HBOT _ L/R _  |KBOX   KEYP ④
LUIAIE|00|O|NO|BB|E|RBPP|HEAD                        ⑬
ORSREN|LM|R|FF|AA|L|OPII|KEY                              ④
TFT  N|IA|I|II|RR|A|PIDL|DATA |GAP|GGAP|PIER|CLM/CP |VALU    ③    VCHR
_____ __ _ __ __ _ ____|____ ____ ____ ____ _____
 ①    ② _ __ ②  ① ____ ____ ____ ____        ②
_____ __ _ __ __ _ ____|____ ____ ____ ____ _____
```

Fig.6 Graph specification panel

The steps to use this user interface for generation of an APL program to produce a graph are as follows. (Each entry of characters is completed by pressing the Enter key, which is omitted in this paper except when it has special meanings.)

1) Specify GPGF, which causes the display of panel 1 whose first line is 'ENTER PROGRAME NAME'.
2) Enter a program name, which causes the display of Panel 2 whose first line describes the use of 3 PF keys.
3) Key in a graph type and data names.
4) Enter selection indications or parameters as guided by screen areas turning white. At the entry of each item, the user presses the Enter key, which causes the display of the same panel with the next area turned white. The entry of the last item makes the whole panel areas available for verification and correction. If the user wishes to avoid pressing the Enter key each time a new item is entered, then he presses PF10, which causes all the areas on the screen to accept any input without pressing the Entry key.
5) Verify the completeness of the information entered on the screen. Pressing the Enter key causes the generation of the program (APL function) with the name specified in step 2).

This ends the generation of the required function. If the user wishes to look at and modify the generated program (function), and to modify it, to generate sample data, and to display a graph using the modified program and the sample data, he can do so by using the 8th, 6th and 4th modules of GRAPHAID in this order. By doing so, the user can verify if the generated program works correctly as the user desires or not.

5. Graphic Data Generation

Some simple figures (such as simple illustrations, diagrams, flow charts, company trade marks/logos, etc.) other than graphs of standard types (which change with new data) can be represented by a matrix each row of which contains 1) a control (CTL) indication (1 or 0) to show whether to be connected or not, 2) X coordinate, and 3) Y coordinate.

Example

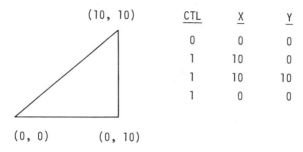

CTL	X	Y
0	0	0
1	10	0
1	10	10
1	0	0

CTL: Indicator to show whether connected or not.

GPAT is a utility function (written in APL) to allow the entry of the matrix to specify the figure and to verify the figure as the row of the matrix is entered. It generates an argument (a set of matrices) to be passed to another utility function called GDRAW which draws the figure at the execution time.

By selecting 2 in the GRAPHAID menu panel or by keying in 'GPAT' the following panel appears.

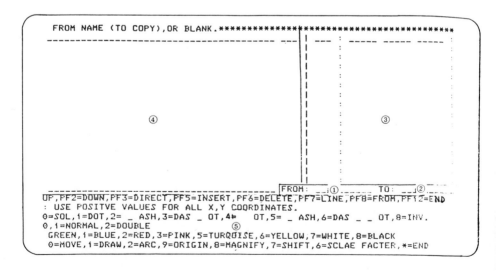

Fig.7 Figure parameter entry and verification panel

196

The five areas on the screen are used for the following purposes:
1) to specify the name of the already defined figure.
2) to give a name to the new figure to be drawn now.
3) to define the pattern (figure) to be drawn.
4) for GPAT to plot the figure defined by 3).
5) Explanation of options and PF keys which can be used in 3).

The steps to use this interface to define a figure are as follows:
1) If an existing figure is to be modified, place its (specification matrix) name after 'FROM' (; otherwise, this field is left blank). Then, the specification matrix (the name of which has just been placed) appears on the right side of the screen. If no name is specified, it is assumed that a new figure is to be defined.
2) Key in the specification matrix name in the right side area. Then, pressing the enter key causes the display of the figure on the left side.
3) Repeat the process (move the origin, reduce or magnify the figure) as shown in the bottom area; and, at the end, press PF12.
4) Enter the new specification matrix name. This completes the task of generating the specification matrix to be used by GDRAW at the execution time.

At the execution time, the GDRAW function (which corresponds to the DRAW routine in GDDM/GPF) is used with the left argument (to specify the attributes of the line) and the right argument (which is the name of the specification matrix prepared by the above task).

GDRAW function has the following syntax:

        p GDRAW Q
P(1):   line type (0: solid line 2: dotted line, 2: colored)
P(2, 3): starting point (X and Y coordinates)
P(4, 5): scaling (in X and Y directions)
P(6, ..): color

Q is the specification matrix, each row of which has a control indicator and X and Y coordinates.

For example, a triangle and circle can be expressed as follows:

0	0	0	
1	10	0	triangle
1	10	10	
1	0	0	
0	10	10	
3602	15	15	circle
1	10	10	

If the above specification matrix is named ZUI, then to draw a blue triangle and a red circle both with pattern 5 with the equal scaling starting at coordinates (10, 10), the following statement is given:

        2   10   10   1   1   51   52   GDRAW   ZU1
        ↓
     colored   starting   scaling   pattern   data
      line   point   and   matrix
                                      color

197

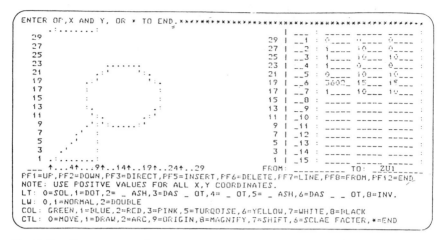

Fig.8 Sample use of G̲PAT

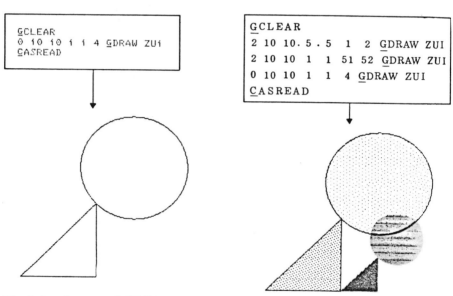

```
GCLEAR
0 10 10 1 1 4 GDRAW ZU1
CASREAD
```

```
GCLEAR
2 10 10.5 . 5   1   2  GDRAW ZUI
2 10 10  1   1  51 52  GDRAW ZUI
0 10 10  1   1   4  GDRAW ZUI
CASREAD
```

Fig.9 Sample use of G̲DRAW

6. Kanji Title Generator (G̲TEXT)

G̲TEXT is a utility program to prepare a string of 4-digit Kanji codes for use by G̲WRITE at the execution time for including Kanji font images in the graphic report. These images can be reduced or enlarged by G̲WRITE.

To use G̲TEXT and G̲WRITE, a file of Kanji font images each consisting of 16 x 16 bit matrix is required. A four-digit decimal number is given to each font image.

198

Selection of 3 in the GRAPHAID menu panel of keying in <u>G</u>TEXT causes
the display of the following panel:

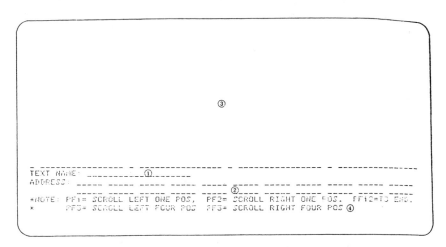

Fig.10 Kanji code entry and verification panel

```
TEXT NAME: TEXT1_____
ADDRESS: 1939  1616  1382  1468  1908  1923_

*NOTE: PF1= SCROLL LEFT ONE POS,  PF2= SCROLL RIGHT ONE POS.  PF12=TO
*      PF3= SCROLL LEFT FOUR POS  PF3= SCROLL RIGHT FOUR POS
```

Fig.11 Sample use of <u>G</u>TEXT

The four areas are used for the following purposes:
1) To give a name to the string of 4-digit Kanji codes for a text to be
generated.
2) To enter a string of 4-digit Kanji codes.
3) To display 12 x 18 bit Kanji images for verification.
4) The expanation of five PF keys

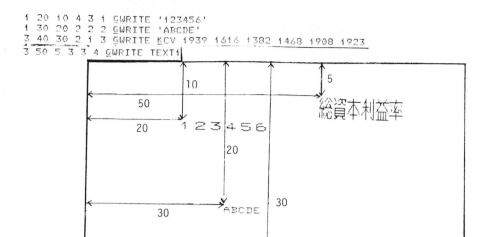

```
1 20 10 4 3 1 GWRITE '123456'
1 30 20 2 2 2 GWRITE 'ABCDE'
3 40 30 2 1 3 GWRITE KCV 1939 1616 1382 1468 1908 1923
3 50 5 3 3 4 GWRITE TEXT1
```

Fig.12 Sample use of GWRITE

The user enters the 4-digit Kanji codes of those characters of a text, verifies them with their Kanji images displayed, and enters a name to be given to it.

GWRITE function candraw alphanumeric characters specified as literal or variable name in its right argument of draw a Kanji text represented by the string of 4-digit codes whose name is also given in its right argument.
P[1]   : character type (1: AN characters, 0: Kanji test)
P[2, 3]: starting point (X and Y coordinates in the screen)
P[4, 5]: scaling in X and Y directions
P[6]   : an AN literal or the name of an AN variable of the name of a string of Kanji codes

7. Graphic Screen Composer (GGDDM)

GGDDM is a utility function to compose graphs, figures and texts (consisting of alphanumerical or Kanji characters of different sizes) in the same screen using the functions generated by GPGF and arguments prepared by GPAT and GTEXT, and to name and save as procedure the user's input (statements containing the names of the functions and arguments and additional parameters) in this process.

The saved procedure can be repeatedly used with a different set of data for repetitive jobs. And, also the saved procedures can be retrieved for modification on the screen and the modified procedures can be renamed.

200

GGDDM has the two models:
0: to define/modify a procedure
1: to draw a graphic report according to the procedure

In model 0, the following can be specified:
1: a graph
2: a figure (drawn with X and Y coordinates)
3: a text
4: a format
5: a hard copy

In mode 1, the completed procedure is executed and the complete graphic report is displayed.

A GGDDM procedure consists of the display of a graph(s) of a standard format(s) (by a function(s) generated by GPGF), the display of a figure(s) (by GDRAW), the display of an AN or Kanji text(s), input/output of messages (by GMSG), switching of screens, overlaying, reading of cursor positions, etc.

GGDDM displays several messages with blank spaces to be filled in with specifications by the user. In the description below, each message from the GGDDM is followed by its explanation.
MODE: ①, NEW PROC NAME: ②, OLD PROC NAME: ③
　　1) 0: interactive composition/modification of graphs, figures, etc.
　　　　1: execution of the completed procedure.
　　2) The name of the new procedure.
　　3) The name of an existing procedure.
CHART NAME: ④, LOC (L-XY, H-XY < 100 70): ⑤
　　4) The name of the function generated by GPGF
　　5) The position of the graph to be created by the function specified in 4).

Example:
　LOC (L-XY, H-XY < 100 70): 20 10 50 60
　will cause the display of the graph in the shaded area

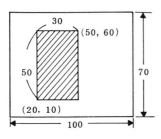

Fig.13　Example of graph area

PATT NAME: ⑥, PAR (FOR GDRAW): ⑦
　　6) The name of the specification matrix prepared by GPAT.
　　7) The parameters to be given to GDRAW.
TEXT NAME: ⑧, SIZE: ⑨, LOC (X, Y): ⑩, COL: ⑪, PS: ⑫
　　8) The name of the Kanji code string prepared by GTEXT or an alphanumeric literal surrounded by quote marks or the name of an AN variable.

9) The scaling of the text in X and Y directions.
10) The position (X and Y coordinates) on the screen.
11) The color of characters.
12) An asterisk for Kanji data.

8. A Sample Case

Assuming that the necessary log-on steps have been taken and the required
programs (APL functions) are loaded, the user keys in 'GRAPHAID' to have the
menu with the title "GRAPH AID" displayed.
   1) Generation of an APL function to produce a graph. Selection 1 causes
       the display of the following panel:

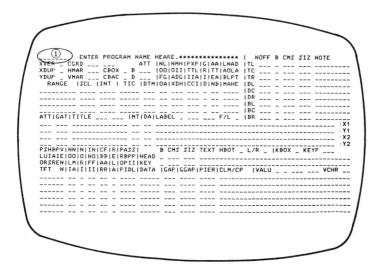

Fig.14 Graph specification panel

'PROGRAM' is keyed in. Then, the same panel with the first line replaced
with the explanation of the use of PF's appears and the area for specifications of color, line type and marker turns white.

An asterisk is placed under 'BAR' (shown vertically) and 'DATAA' is entered
under 'DATA' to declare that the data used in this graph is named 'DATAA'.

Other areas turn white one by one, prompting the user to enter information
if any. This continues till entry into all the areas has been prompted (by
turning white) or till PF10 key is pressed. Upon pressing PF10, the user is
allowed to enter the remaining items without pressing the Enter key each time
a new piece of information is put into an area.

202

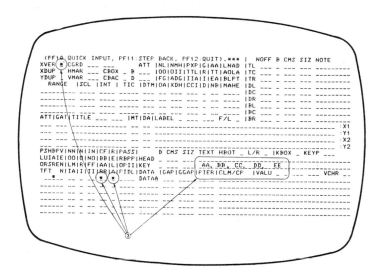

Fig.15 Graph specification panel with input by the user

An asterisk is placed beside XVER (to exchange X and Y axes), under CBAR (to combine bar charts) and under RELA (to use relative value). Then the GRAPHAID menu panel appears again.
2) Display of the function just generated

Selection of 8 causes 'FNS NAME: . . . to be displayed. When the program name 'PROGRAM' is entered, the APL defined function which was generated in 1) is displayed.

An example is as follows: ▽
1   PROGRAM Q   ▽
2   CCHRNIT   ▽
3   $\overline{\phi}$ (0 = ρQ)/'CCHAREA Q'   ▽
4   CCHSET 1 4 ρ'XVER'   ▽
5   CCHKEY 5 2 ρ'AABBCCDDEE'   ▽
6   CCHSET 2 4 ρ'CBARRELA'   ▽
7   CCHBAR DATAA   ▽
    :
Pressing PF12 causes a return to the menu panel.

3) Generation of test data

In order to verify the function which has been just generated, the user can call the 6th module in GRAPHAID by selecting 6, which displays the instruction to the user:
ENTER DATA NAME: , DIMENSION:
VALUE/RANGE: Then, the user keys in the following statements:
DATA NAME = DATAA
DIMENSION = 5 3
VALUE/RANGE = 0   1000

203

This causes the display of random numbers in a 5 × 3 matrix.

Pressing PF12 twice causes a return to the menu panel.

4) Creation and display of the graph for verification. Upon entry into
   GGDDM, it displays the message

MODE: , NEW PROC NAME: , OLD PROC NAME:

Then, the user keys in the following:

MODE: 0
NEW PROC NAME: SAM2
OLD PROC NAME: blank

Another message comes out:

CHART NAME: , LOC (L-XY, H-XY ≤ 100 70):
The user responds with
CHART NAME: PROGRAM
LOC (L-XY, H-XY ≤ 100 70):   blank
The following graphic report now appears.

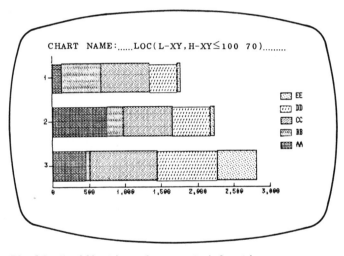

Fig.16   Verification of generated function

Pressing the Enter key is repeated till the menu panel appears.
5)   Generation of parameters for drawing a figure

    Selection of 2 (GPAT) causes the display of Figure Parameter Entry and
Verification Panel.

    Entering control digits and X and Y coordinates (specification matrix) in
the right section causes the approximate figure to appear on the left side.

204

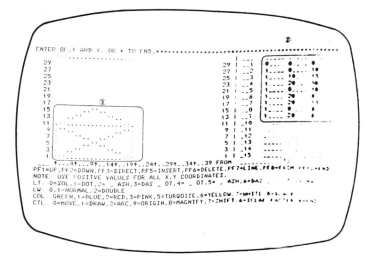

Fig.17 Figure parameter entry and verification
        panel with input by the user

    Pressing PF12 key causes 'TO: .....' field to turn white, prompting entry
of a name, to which the user responds with 'ZU1'. We then return to the
menu panel.
    6) Generation of a Kanji 4-digit code string

    Because of lack of space, the steps for generation of a string of 4-
digit Kanji codes, and for verifying the Kanji text are not described here.
    7) Composition of a graph, figure and title

    Steps similar to those in 4) are repeated. But 'SAM2' is keyed in after
'OLD NAME:' and 'PROGRAM' appears after 'CHART NAME' and 0 0 100 70 is placed
at the end of this message. After the message starting with 'CHART NAME' is
displayed and the Enter key is pressed, the message demanding the data name
and graph attributes appears:
    PATT NAME: ...., PAR (FOR GDRAW): .....
    The user keys in the next two lines
    PATT NAME: ZU1
    PAR (FOR GDRAW):   0   80   60   .3   .3   4
                        | | | |
                        | | | └──── green
                        | | └── scaling in two directions
                        | └── Pos of graph
                        └── line

    The graph containing lines with the same message on the top appear. The
user keys in the same two lines except for the first number in the second replaced by 2 indicating that shading is required. This causes the display of
the shaded graph with the same message on the top.

    Entering nothing and just pressing the Enter key causes the message re-
questing information for Kanji text to appear:

```
TEXT: .....  SIZE: .... LOC (X, Y) .....  LOC:          PS:
```
The user responds:
```
TEXT:  TEXT1 (the name of the 4-digit Kanji code string)
SIZE:  1 2  (scaling of characters)
LOC:   blank
P5:    *(P5 for Kanji is used)
```
Leaving blank the field after 'LOC:' causes a 'MOVE CURSOR ... message to
come out.

Then, the user sets the cursor to the location where the Kanji text should
appear. This completes the steps to have the following displayed:

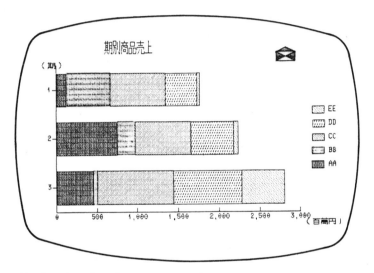

Fig.18 Completed sample graphic report

8) Printing of a hard copy

A hard copy of this can be printed. The steps for it are omitted here to
save space.

9. Concluding Remarks

In this implementation, the following programming techniques are employed;
- Modular coding
- Interactive programming
- Interactive screen dialogues
- Menus and fill-in-the-blank messages
- Program generators
- Visual verification at specification entry
- Debugging at source level
- Reuse of existing modules

Some of the significant advantages of this support for color/graphics programming are as follows:
- No need for debugging because of visual verification of specifications at the entry time.
- Short turn-around time from giving specification to getting final results.
- Ease of adding and modifying processes increases expandability and adaptability.
- Menu selection and fill-in-the-blank approaches eliminate the need to learn a large number of key words and complex syntax and reduce programming errors.
- Changes to programs at multiple levels (at specs entry, composition and execution) ease maintenance.

This has been very well received by APL customers and systems engineers supporting them, and has made outstanding contribution to expansion of the users of color/graphics display terminals at a rapid pace.

APL has proved to be highly flexible and effective to create functions to support user interfaces for color/graphics report programming. Without APL's simplicity and practicality, implementation and installation of these with limited resource in a short time would have been impossible.

SAIGUSA is still seeking for better ways. One of the pro'lems he is looking at is performance. Some tuning may be possible. For ac. ieving good performance, the GRAPHAID approaches may not be the best. For i e experienced programmers, direct use of sub-modules commonly shared in the GRAPHAID may help improve performance.

As a follow-on project, an additional module to retrieve from existing files the data which satisfy specified conditions and to produce not only conventional reports (containing character information), but also color/graphics reports has been under development since April, 1981.

SAIGUSA is now replacing the PGF by APL coding so that the user can have similar capabilities as provided by Interactive Chart Utility and Interactive Vector Symbol Utilities which are not accessible from VS APL.

Appendix

___

GDDM/PGF as an IBM program product comprised of a base component, the Graphical Data Display Manager (GDDM) and the Presentation Graphic Feature (PGF).

GDDM provides support of the following hardware functions:

- Field and character Highlighting
  - Blink
  - Reverse Video
  - Underscore
  - Color (base or extended)
  - Protected/Unprotected
  - Intensified
  - Light-pen Selectable

Software Functions

- Display or printing of:
  - Lines
  - Arcs
  - Areas
  - Annotations
- Attributes
  - Line Types (e.g., solid, thick, clashed)
  - Color shading (64 unique hues)
  - Patterns (26 unique patterns)
- Graphics functions
  - World Coordinate System
  - Two-Dimensional Windowing and Clipping
  - Support of 3277 Graphic Attachment
    (Support PRPQ non-device dependent
    Application Support Subroutines)

PGF is an optional feature available with GDDM. It provides a set of high level presentation graphics subroutines to minimize the programming of applications involving presentation charts (pie charts, line graphs, surface charts, Venn diagrams, histograms or bar charts).

The subroutines in GDDM and PGF are invoked via a "call" interface from programs written in COBOL, PL/I, FORTRAN or Assembler, and running under CICS/VS, TSO or VM/CMS.

AP126 is an auxiliary processor written in Assembler language. It provides a bridge between an APL workspace (program written in APL) and GDDM/PGF. A dyadic function $\Box$SVO in the APL workspace tells the AP126 the two variable names the first of which is to receive a command number (to identify a GDDM/PGF command) and a numeric parameter and the second of which is to receive a character parameter. The following shows a sequence of APL statements in the APL workspace:

    126 $\Box$SVO 2 4ρ 'CTLXDATX'
    CTLX $\leftarrow$ (command no.), numeric parameter
    DATX $\leftarrow$ character parameter (This is not needed in some cases)
    Return code CTLX
    Data $\leftarrow$ DATX (Null is returned in some cases)

The following basic and high-level general-purpose utility functions (programs written in APL) have been developed by SAIGUSA.
    1) Basic routines
        C Group is a set of the APL defined functions which correspond one to one to commands for GDDM/PGF.

A function of this group is linked to AP126 and passes to it the number to identify the corresponding GDDM/PGF command and the argument (attribute(s)) to be passed to GDDM/PGF.
    Examples are CASFCOL, CASFHLT, CASFINT, CASFPSS, CASQMAX,
            CASREAD, CCHAATT, CCHAREA, CCHBAR, CCHBATT,
        B Group consists of basic routines for full-screen processing common to AP124 and AP126. They are used as subroutines by high level general-purpose routines.
    Examples are BCHK, BOPEN, BCLOSE, BALARM, BATTRIBUTE, BFORMAT,
            BGET, BINTENSIEY, BLOCATION, BPOSITION, BPRINT,
            BWAIT, BWRITE

2) High-level general-purpose routine

   F Group consists of utility routines for full-screen design and processing. They are FCLEAR, FFORMAT, FGET, FMOVE, FMSG, FREAD, FSQ, FUTIL, FWRITE.

   G Group is a set of utilities handling graphic functions. Main ones are GPGT, GTEXT, GPAT, GCHAR, GGDDM and GDATA. They use 17 other routines as subroutines.

   Functions in,

   H Group handle graphic function other than those in PGF: HGRID, HPICTURE, HPICI, HRADAR, HSECTOR.

   K Group functions handles Kanji files: KOPEN, KCV.

An Approach to Image Editing and Filing

Y. Takao

Tokyo Scienctific Center, IBM Japan, Ltd.
Roppongi, Tokyo 106, Japan

Abstract

Among the various aspects of digital image manipulation tasks for business or office applications, image editing and filing can be regarded as one of the most fundamental and important elements at least from software standpoint. At Tokyo Scientific Center, IBM Japan, a prototype system has been developed to provide a practical solution to this problem, and this paper presents the concepts and functions of this prototype system, which consists of two major components, i.e. Image Editor for interactive image display/editing and Aggregate Data Manager for database management including both image and alphanumeric data.

Image Editor (IEDIT) facilitates interactive image display and editing which are commonly required by all image applications. Though one can manipulate both binary and gray-scale images with IEDIT, a novel point here is that it processes binary images in compressed forms throughout and, therefore, achieves very efficient processing, leading to its responsiveness.

Aggregate Data Manager (ADM) facilitates unified management of both image data and conventional alphanumeric data. The approach taken by ADM is that, externally, regarding "image" as one of the data-types, each image is treated as a data element like a number or a character string within the framework of a relational model of database, though, internally at physical storage level, they are managed separately due to their different characteristics. This approach makes it possible to utilize a simple and powerful relational data language for storage and retrieval of both image and alphanumeric data in a unified way.

Both IEDIT and ADM are operational under Conversational Monitor System (CMS) of IBM Virtual Machine Facility/370 (VM/370).

1. Introduction

One of the important applications of digital image processing is the manipulation of documents in image or non-coded forms. Actually, the introduction of digital images into business data processing and office systems is getting practical due to the progress of both general hardware technologies such as fast processor, large-scale main/auxiliary storage, etc. and image-oriented technologies such as all-point-addressable printer, digital image scanner, data compression techniques, etc. Also, at the same time, the needs are getting explicit expecially from the expectation of the office of the future, e.g. electronic mailing, electronic document filing, etc.

Regarding the document manipulation, the image approach provides us with several advantages compared with the conventional text or graphics approach. First, images are direct digital representation of paper documents and retain the original information with minimal deformation. This is essential when signature, seal impression, etc. are handled, and also desirable in some other situations where authentication, preciseness, etc. must be considered. Second, since image is a general vehicle for representing documents in digital forms, it allows to handle documents with any contents, e.g. texts in printed or hand-written forms, charts, drawings, photographs, etc. Therefore, image approach can be useful not only for the retention of original paper documents in digital forms but also for composition of documents with various contents. Third, since documents in image forms can be captured by a computer through scanning and this process is completely automatic without any human intervention, the data entry cost is very low compared with that of the conventional text or graphics data entry which is heavily labor-intensive. When the rising labor cost is taken into account, this point is very important in the future and image approach will be required not only for documents which cannot be coded but also for those which need not be coded even though they could be. And, last, image approach can be expected to provide a natural and efficient migration path from the current paper-based environments to the future less-paper system.

Image approach, however, has some drawbacks. A major problem is that the data volume is far bigger than the conventional alphanumeric data. As a rule of thumb, to represent the same document, the data volume of image is ten times or more compared with that of text even when the image is compressed. And, in general, as a consequence of this data volume, its processing tends to require considerable amount of processor time.

Nevertheless, the image approach is still beneficial as evidenced by the rapid growth of the facsimile market, and, especially in Japan, it is important since hand-written documents are prevalent due to its language speciality. And it is sure that digital images will play an important role to provide multi-media document environments along with text and graphics data in the near future.

This paper focuses on the editing and filing of digital images, and presents the concept and functions of a prototype system which consists of two major components, i.e. Image Editor (IEDIT) for interactive image display/editing [1] and Aggregate Data Manager (ADM) for unified image/alphanumeric database management [2].

2. Elements of Image Document Manipulation

As the first comer of digital image document manipulation system, an image-based office communication system is coming into reality through the implementation of facsimile devices and their networks. The development of these facsimile technologies has established several fundamental elements of digital image manipulation i.e. image scanner, image printer and data compression algorithms. These elements, however, suffice only simple hardcopy-based exchange of image documents, and, in order to pursue the advantages of image document manipulation and to push image applications further beyond, additional elements are required.

Although various additional elements are conceivable, image editing and filing facilities can be considered as one of the fundamental elements required for image applications in general. This will be clear when the current text processing system is considered, where text editor and document storage/retrieval facilities constitute its kernel part.

Image editing facility is indispensable for modifying or creating documents in image or non-coded forms. As for scanned documents, this image editing facility replaces the current laborious paper cut-and-paste tasks with higher quality and further flexibility. And, also, it is useful for composition of documents consisting of texts, drawings, charts, photographs, etc., since a digital image is the most general representation of documents and other types of data like texts and vector graphics data can be converted into an image form fairly easily. Functionally, image editing requires only fundamental processing techniques and, when an image is regarded as a two-dimensional array of picture elements as usual, its implementation might be straightforward. However, this conventional approach is time-consuming at least on a general-purpose computer, whereas the performance issue is critical for image editing since interactive operations are mandatory there. IEDIT solves this performance issue through "compressed image processing" approach and achieves fast response times.

Image filing can be achieved simply by using the file system supported by general-purpose operating systems, and this approach may be sufficient for personal electronic document filing. However, the problem is that, in this case, each file must be identified by a simple file name, which generally cannot convey fully descriptive information. ADM addresses this problem by providing a facility to manage both alphanumeric data and image data in a unified way within the framework of the relational model of database [3], and supports full capabilities of relational system for data definition and data manipulation. Therefore, one can establish various relationships among alphanumeric and image data, resulting in flexible query formulation based upon these relationships.

3. Image Coding and Processing

For image document manipulation, a crucial problem is the data volume. For example, since each picture element (PEL) of a binary image is "0" (white) or "1" (black) and requires 1 bit for digital representation, a single A4-page scanned at 8 PEL/mm amounts to about 4 mega-bits or 500 kilo-bytes. Consequently, in order that an image can be efficiently handled by a computer, e.g. stored into a file or transmitted over a network, data compression becomes mandatory [4,5]. On the other hand, the conventional image processing approach regards an image as a two-dimensional array of PELs and manipulates it in a PEL-by-PEL fashion. In other words, a binary image is processed based upon the uncompressed form i.e. 1 bit/PEL format, whereas, when stored on auxiliary devices like magnetic disks, it must be in the compressed form to reduce the required storage space.

Therefore, with the conventional approach, image processing such as editing requires the following five steps:

1) retrieval of compressed image data,
2) decompression of the image into a bit string,
3) processing applied to the bit string,
4) compression of the bit string,
5) storing the compressed image data.

Two performance issues exist in this approach, i.e. compression and decompression overhead and bit string manipulation which is fairly slow on a byte or word machine.

The performance may not be a crucial problem if batch processing is considered. But, in the case of image editing, interactive operations are mandatory since an image is visual in nature and its blind editing is almost impossible. And, in order to make an image editing system really interactive and usable, attentions must be paid not only to its functions and user interface but also to its performance.

IEDIT/ADM is a trial to solve the above-mentioned problems and it gives one possible solution within the framework of the current IBM general-purpose computer i.e. System/370. The approach adopted here is "compressed image processing". That is, binary images are processed in compressed forms all through and, therefore, there is no difference between the image data format for processing and that for filing.

The compression method adopted by IEDIT/ADM is one-dimensional run-length coding, where a contiguous sequence of the same color PELs called "run" is regarded as a unit and a binary image is represented by the lengths of these black/white runs. And, IEDIT processes a binary image in a run-by-run manner instead of applying PEL-by-PEL operations.

As for the selection of code words for representing run-lengths, two points must be considered, i.e. one is the code word length and the other is whether the codes should be systematic or statistical. Regarding the code word length, from the standpoint of processing on byte machines like System/370, byte-based code words are desirable, but, in this case, the compression rate becomes very low, since runs with length less than 8 usually appear frequently in scanned documents and they become expanded when they are encoded by byte-based code words. On the other hand, when bit-based code words are used for achieving higher compression rate, it becomes necessary to do the bit-by-bit processing which is fairly slow on byte machines. From these considerations, IEDIT/ADM uses 4-bit-based (half-byte-based) code words, i.e. 4, 8, 12, 16 and 20 bit code words, as a trade-off between the processing efficiency and the data compression efficiency. Regarding the second point, it is generally agreed that the statistical code system achieves better compression rate since the code words for more frequently occurring run-lengths are made shorter. However, the statistics used as a basis of code definition depend on the image contents and the optimal codes are different for each document. And, moreover, when generating or interpreting the code words, this statistical code system necessitates the time-consuming table-look-up or tree-search operations. Therefore, IEDIT/ADM uses systematic code words which correspond directly to the run-lengths and can be generated or interpreted with simple arithmetic and logical operations. The code words used by ADM/IEDIT is shown in Table 2.1.

Table 2.1 Code words for compression

Run length	Code words
0	1111 1110
1- 8	0xxx
9- 72	10xx xxxx
73- 584	110x xxxx xxxx
585-4680	1110 xxxx xxxx xxxx
4681-	1111 0xxx xxxx xxxx xxxx
line end	1111 1111 (1111)

Table 2.2 Comparison of compression rates

Doc	IEDIT	CCITT
1	14.4	13.7
2	14.6	14.9
3	7.4	7.9
4	4.3	4.7
5	7.1	7.5
6	9.2	10.0
7	4.0	4.8
8	8.3	8.2

The compression rate attained by this method has been compared with the Modified Huffman coding (CCITT standard one-dimensional method) using eight CCITT reference documents. As shown in Table 2.2, the result indicates that both are comparable except the cases of dense text documents, where the runs with length two or three appear frequently and Modified Huffman coding shows slightly higher compression rates.

With the "compressed image processing" approach, IEDIT processes binary images very efficiently and achieves fast responses adequate for interactive image editing. The major advantages attained by this approach are summarized in the following. First, the units of processing become runs instead of PELs and this contributes considerably to the processing efficiency, since the number of runs are far smaller than the number of PELs. For example, when the average value of the 8 CCITT reference documents are taken, the ratio of the number of runs to that of PELs is 1 to 70. Second, the compression and decompression overhead has been completely eliminated, which, if done, could consume considerable amount of processor time mainly to scan or build a bit string in a bit-by-bit fashion. Third, by manipulating run-lengths represented by 4-bit-based code words, the bit manipulation has been reduced considerably. Though the algorithms for compressed image processing become more or less complex compared with the PEL-by-PEL processing, it is remarkably advantageous at least from the standpoint of interactive image editing on general-purpose computers. And, though it cannot be claimed that the current image coding scheme is optimal, IEDIT/ADM will show one possible approach to balance the processing and compression efficiency.

4. Image Editor (IEDIT)

Image Editor (IEDIT) is an interactive system for image display and editing. The image editing capability provided by IEDIT is basically a digital replacement of paper cut-and-paste, but with further flexibility and convenience. Though IEDIT supports both binary and gray-scale images, the discussion here will be limited to its binary image manipulation aspects.

4.1 IEDIT User Interface

The user interface of IEDIT is command-oriented and IEDIT commands can be entered in truncated forms as far as they are unique. Command parameters are designed so that key strokes are minimized, and parameter default is extensively adopted. Further, it provides command procedure facility with which users can build their own commands by combining the basic commands provided by IEDIT. Generally, the design of user interface is an important but difficult problem especially when implementing an interactive system, since it is a human factor issue which requires various feed-backs from many users' experiences. From this reason, the design of this IEDIT user interface was done by following the text editors as paradigms as much as possible, since, among various interactive packages, they are most widely used and, therefore, can be regarded as having most refined user interface.

The interactive workstation of IEDIT is IBM 3277 Graphics Attachment (3277 GA), which consists of two display heads i.e. an IBM 3277 character display with an alphanumeric keyboard and a Direct View Storage Tube (DVST) with a joystick unit by which an arbitrary-shaped cursor on DVST can be dragged and the position coordinates on the DVST screen can be input to the host computer. IEDIT uses the 3277 character display for command entry and system information feedback, while DVST as an image display device. While editing an image, it is often required to specify points within an image, and this can be achieved by positioning the DVST cursor by joystick , though the coordinates of these points can be also specified as explicit command parameters. In

other words, though it has been mentioned that IEDIT user interface is command-oriented, it is augmented by joystick or DVST
cursor operations so that users can interact directly with the
contents of the image displayed on the DVST screen when required.

4.2 IEDIT Functions

Functions provided by IEDIT can be categorized into three groups,
i.e. image editing function, image display function and system
control function. The image editing function changes the
contents of the current image, while the image display function
achieves scrolling and zooming without affecting the image
contents. The system control function covers the other support
functions like image file read/write, etc.

The image editing function constitutes the nuclear portion of
IEDIT, and is supported through the following commands:

    EXtract
    SUppress
    REVerse
    MIrror
    ROtate
    SCale
    COpy
    MOve
    IMbed

where the uppercase letters represent the shortest acceptable
version of the command, since, in general, IEDIT allows trun-
cation of a command name.

"EXtract" simulates "paper cut" operations through digital
image manipulation. It performs the extraction or cropping of a
specified subimage and discards the outer portion, where the size
of the resultant image is reduced to that of the subimage.

"SUppress", on the other hand, is the digital replacement of
an eraser. It performs the suppression or erasure of a specified
subimage, that is, the specified portion of the image is set to
blank i.e. completely white, while the other portion is kept the
same as that of the original image.

"REVerse" changes white PELs to black and black PELs to white,
and achieves the conversion from a positive image to negative one
or vice versa. This can be applied not only to a whole image but
also to a subimage, therefore one can achieve field-wise reversal
which is useful for document make-up purposes. Since each PEL of
a binary image represents "0" (white) or "1" (black) and can be
regarded as a Boolean or logical variable, this reversal can be
restated as logical NOT operation which is fundamental in Boolean
algebra and, hence, is also fundamental in binary image processing.

"MIrror" produces a mirror image of the current one, and this operation can be regarded as the simulation of turning over or flipping the paper documents. The direction of mirroring can be specified by "Horizontal" (right to left and vice versa), "Vertical" (top to bottom and vice versa) or "Diagonal" (left to top and vice versa).

"ROtate" supports 90-degree-wise image rotation, and the angle of rotation can be specified by "Right" (-90 degree), "Left" (+90 degree) or "Down" (180 degree). Internally, this rotation is achieved by sequentially applying two different mirror operations; e.g. +90 degree rotation is achieved by taking diagonal mirror image at first and then vertical mirror image.

"SCale" allows one to magnify or reduce an image to an arbitrary size. And it also supports to change the aspect ratio of an image, since horizontal and vertical scaling factors can be specified separately. This "SCale" function is always applied to the whole image, i.e. it changes the size of the whole image, but, instead, subimage-wise scaling can be done through "MOve" or "COpy" functions described in the next.

"COpy", "MOve" and "IMbed" are all basically the digital simulation of "paper paste" operations. The difference among these functions is the way to obtain the image which is to be pasted onto the current image. "COpy" produces a replica of a specified portion of the current image, leaving the original subimage untouched. "MOve" extracts a specified portion from the current image and then makes the extracted portion cleared out, i.e. completely white. "IMbed", on the other hand, obtains the image to be pasted from a specified file.
Regarding the "paste" operation performed by "COpy", "MOve" and "IMbed", IEDIT provides four modes, i.e. REPlace, logical OR, logical XOR (exclusive OR) and logical AND. The REPlace is the direct simulation of paper pasting, i.e. pasting opaque paper patch and the overlaid portion of the current image gets invisible. The other three are the PEL-by-PEL logical operations, and, along with logical NOT (REVerse), they constitute a complete set of PEL-wise or point operations for binary images. Among these, the logical OR operation can be interpreted intuitively that it simulates overlaying a transparency where the black PELs of both overlaying and overlaid images become visible.
The target area for pasting is generally specified by its position and its size. The size of the target area can be different from that of the image to be pasted, and, in this case, the image scaling algorithm is automatically invoked in order to make the pasted image fit in the target area.
Though the target area specification can be given as explicit command parameters, one can alternatively specify it through DVST cursor operation, which is the default mode when relevant parameters are not given. When this mode is selected, IEDIT displays a box on DVST showing the frame of the image to be pasted, and one can move this box to the desired position by using the joystick. Also one can change the size and/or shape of the target area through so-called "orthogonal rubber banding", in which mode the upper-left corner of the box is fixed and the lower-right corner can be moved around by joystick operation.

The image display function consists of scrolling and zooming. Both functions regard the DVST screen as a view window to the current image in buffer, and scrolling moves this window, while zooming changes the size of this view window. Similar to the text editor, scrolling are controlled by commands such as Top, Bottom, Next, etc., and, in IEDIT, both PEL-wise and screen-wise scrolling are supported. Zooming can be done by Magnify and SHrink commands and, in order to achieve fast image display, the zooming factor is limited to integers.

The system control functions support image file read/write and system parameter settings. Image file read/write commands allow one to read/write a whole image or any subimage, to change the file names, and so forth. IEDIT provides several system parameters to control image file format, image redisplay and image processing algorithms including the scaling options to be described in the following section.

In addition to the above-mentioned basic commands, IEDIT provides macro command or command procedure facility. Its main purpose is to allow users to define their own high-level commands and to adapt IEDIT to their application requirements. But, furthermore, it can be used to define a virtual image as a sequence of cut-and-paste operations using other images. Since image data are voluminous even when compressed, this virtual image definition by a command procedure seems to be useful in many applications. And it must be noted that this notion of virtual image has become possible through the efficiency of compressed image processing.

4.3 Binary Image Scaling Algorithms

The flexible image scaling is one of the most important advantages attainable by digital approach, since, in the paper-based manual approach, it necessitates laborious photographic processes. Further, it is also important from the viewpoint of the resolution change or resampling of a digital image, which becomes mandatory when utilizing various image I/O devices with different resolutions, e.g. a scanner with 8 PEL/mm, a printer with 12 PEL/mm, etc. From these reasons, various image scaling algorithms have been proposed and evaluated [6,7].
IEDIT manipulates binary images in compressed forms, i.e. in run-length-coded forms as mentioned before, and image scaling is done as two-step processes, that is, horizontal scaling is done at first and then vertical scaling is performed. The horizontal scaling is achieved based on the run-length representation, i.e. basically by changing the length of each run according to the horizontal scaling factor [8]. The vertical scaling is achieved by mapping each horizontal scan line of the original image to that of the resultant image.

The basic image scaling algorithm adopted by IEDIT is the nearest neighbor method, and the horizontal scaling by this method can be formulated in run-length representation as follows: Let "r(i)" and "R(i)" denote the original and resultant i-th run-length respectively and "Sh" denote the horizontal scaling factor. Since run-lengths "r(i)" and "R(i)" must be integers whereas "Sh" generally is not an integer, round-off error or residual denoted by "E(i)" must be taken into account. This error E(i) is always kept between -1/2 and 1/2 and, if E(i) is not zero, it is carried over to the next run. This procedure assures that the nearest neighbor PEL values are selected as can be easily verified. The relationship among those variables is expressed as follows:

R(i) + E(i) = Sh * r(i) + E(i-1)

where   -1/2 < E(i) <= 1/2

The vertical scaling is achieved by selecting the nearest neighbor horizontal scan line from the input image and put it in the resultant image. And, when magnifying an image, this results in the replication of original scan lines.

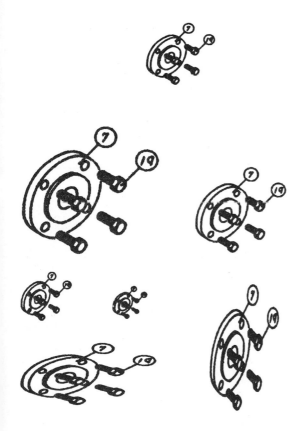

Fig.4.1   Image size and aspect-ratio changing by nearest neighbor method (The image at the top is the original)

In most cases, this nearest neighbor method gives fairly
satisfactory results as shown in Fig.4.1. However, depending
upon the scaling factor and the contents of the original image,
several undesirable effects can occur from the viewpoint of image
quality. In the followings, three problems are pointed out and
their solutions adopted by IEDIT are described.

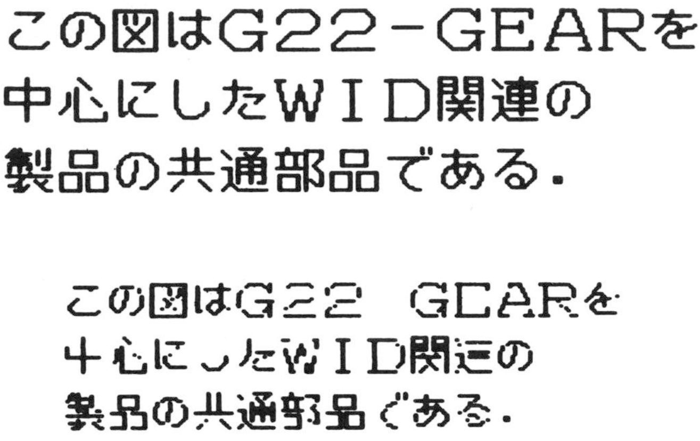

この図はG２２-GEARを
中心にしたＷＩＤ関連の
製品の共通部品である.

この図はG２２ GEARを
中心にしたＷＩＤ関連の
製品の共通部品である.

Fig.4.2 An image scaled down (4/5) by nearest neighbor method
(The upper is the original)

The first problem is that, when an image contains narrow lines
and is scaled down, the resultant image loses much information
since many original PELs are lost when selecting the nearest
neighbor PELs, as shown in Fig.4.2.
In order to remedy this shortcoming of the nearest neighbor
method, IEDIT provides the "Black PEL Preservation" option. This
method is based upon the assumption that, in most documents,
black PELs constitute informative part while white PELs represent
just background. And it preserves all the black portion of the
original image in order that the black PEL information should not
be lost. For this "Black PEL Preservation", the scaling algorithm is slightly modified regarding black-run handling and scan
line selection as follows.
The basic scheme for horizontal scaling is the same as the
nearest neighbor method except that, in order to always preserve
black-runs in this case, if the resultant black run-length
becomes zero, it is forced to one. With the same notation as
before, this can be formulated basically as follows:

$$R(i) + E(i) = Sh * r(i) + E(i-1)$$

$$\text{where} \quad \text{if } r(i) \text{ is black} \quad \text{then } R(i) \geq 1$$
$$\text{else } R(i) \geq 0$$

$$\text{therefore} \quad -3/2 < E(i) \leq 1/2$$

In this formulation, one additional consideration is required for the case that, if the original image contains a sequence of short black/white runs and is scaled down, the accumulated error can exceed the above limits. And the actual implementation is that, if the intervening white run-length becomes zero, the two black runs are merged and the resultant black run-length is recalculated so that E(i) becomes between -3/2 and 1/2.

The vertical scaling is done as follows: that is, at first, it is determined to which resultant scan line each original line corresponds in the nearest neighbor sense, and, then, if several original lines correspond to one resultant scan line, the result is built by taking logical OR of these original lines.

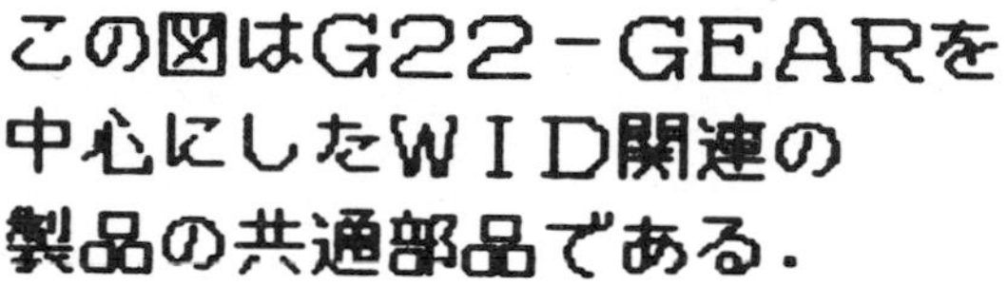

この図はG22-GEARを
中心にしたWID関連の
製品の共通部品である.

Fig.4.3 An image scaled down (4/5) by "Black PEL Preservation" method

As apparent from the above description, this "Black PEL Preservation" method is different from the nearest neighbor method only when an image is scaled down. Figure 4.3 shows the result image scaled down by this "Black PEL Preservation" method, and, compared with the nearest neighbor result shown in Fig.4.1, the improvement is clear. It must be noted, however, that this method gives far higher priority to black PELs and small white regions can be suppressed. And, when negative images, i.e. images with white information on black backgrounds, are scaled down, they should be reversed beforehand to avoid the loss of information.

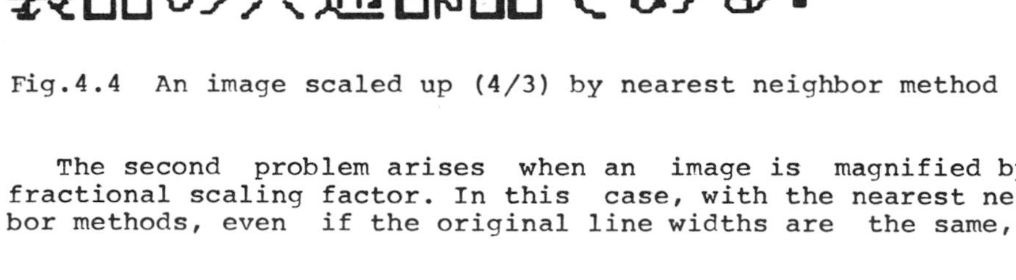

この図はG22-GEARを
中心にしたWID関連の
製品の共通部品である.

Fig.4.4 An image scaled up (4/3) by nearest neighbor method

The second problem arises when an image is magnified by a fractional scaling factor. In this case, with the nearest neighbor methods, even if the original line widths are the same, the resultant line widths can be different and this leads to the line width irregularities as shown in Fig.4.4.

In order to avoid this undesirable effects, IEDIT provides "Line Width Equality Preservation" option, which produces black lines of the same width when the original line widths are the same.

In this "Line Width Equality Preservation" method, the horizontal scaling is done by inspecting a pair of white and black runs at a time and the detail of this method is given in the following: Let "r(W,k)" and "r(B,k)" denote the original white and black run-lengths of the k-th pair and "R(W,k)" and "R(B,k)" denote the resultant run-lengths respectively. And "Sh" is the horizontal scaling factor, and "E(k)" and "E(B,k)" are round-off error produced by the k-th run-pair and k-th black run respectively. The first step is the calculation of the black run-length R(B,k), which is set equal to ceiling(Sh*r(B,k)) i.e. the minimum integer value greater than or equal to Sh*r(B,k). Then, R(W,k) is calculated by taking into account both errors produced by the previous run-pair and the current black run. The formulation is as follows:

R(B,k) = ceiling(Sh * r(B,k))

E(B,k) = Sh * r(B,k) - R(B,k)

R(W,k) + E(k) = Sh * r(W,k) + E(B,k) + E(k-1)

where   -1/2 < E(k) <= 1/2

The vertical scaling is done as follows: Let "Sv" denote the vertical scaling factor and an integer "I(Sv)" defined by ceiling(Sv). Then, each original scan line is replicated "I(Sv)" times and then put in the nearest "I(Sv)" result scan lines, where some of these lines originating from different original lines are merged by taking their logical OR. This process assures that every original scan line appears "I(Sv)" times in the resultant image though some will be merged with the neighbor lines by logical OR operation, and, therefore, the line width equality can be preserved also in the vertical direction.

Figure 4.5 shows the result of this "Line Width Equality Preservation" scaling, which is free from the line width irregularities and the quality of which is apparently superior to the nearest neighbor result shown in Fig.4.4.

The final option for quality improvement of image scaling is the smoothing of oblique edges. When an image is magnified by the nearest neighbor method, exaggerated staircase patterns appear along oblique edges which are generally not desirable. And, usually, to achieve more smooth magnification, bilinear interpolation is used, but even this method cannot eliminate rugged patterns along oblique edges. To solve this, IEDIT uses piecewise linear interpolation. This method uses four neighboring PELs for interpolation like the bilinear interpolation, but interpolation is done by using one or two plane segments in contrast to that the bilinear interpolation uses curved surface represented by a bilinear polynomial. It must be noted, here,

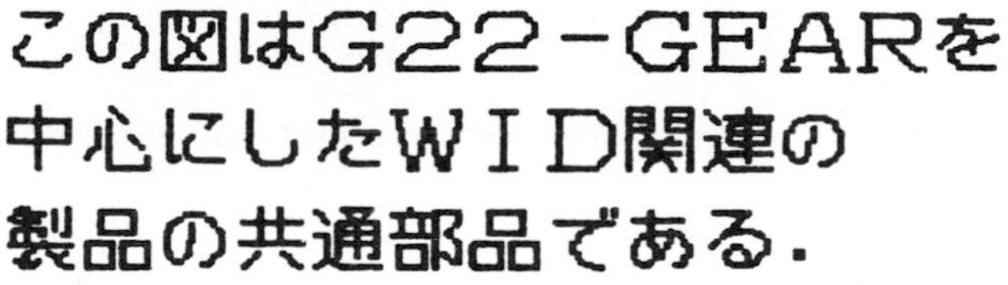

この図はＧ２２－ＧＥＡＲを
中心にしたＷＩＤ関連の
製品の共通部品である．

Fig.4.5 An image scaled up (4/3) by "Line Width Equality Preservation" method.

that, when spanning an area surrounded by four neighboring PELs with two plane segments, the selection of plane segments is not unique, and, the criteria for this selection are that 45 degree edges become smooth and eight-connectivities of black PELs are preserved.

Fig.4.6 Examples of image magnification by nearest neighbor method (left), bilinear interpolation (middle) and piecewise linear interpolation (right)

This piecewise linear interpolation can be achieved by linearly interpolating the positions of black to white and white to black transition points, and, since these transition point positions can be derived directly from the run-length representation, it can be easily formulated as run-length manipulation operations. For the comparison of the magnified image quality, Figure 4.6 shows the results obtained by the nearest neighbor method, the bilinear interpolation and the piecewise linear interpolation.

5. Aggregate Data Manager (ADM)

Aggregate Data Manager or ADM is a prototype database system which manages both alphanumeric data and image data within the framework of the relational model and facilitates interactive database access through a high-level relational data language. Externally, a database of ADM can be viewed as a collection of tables each of which consist of several columns containing numbers, character strings or images as data elements. On the other hand, internally, two-level storage approach is adopted, and alphanumeric and image data are stored separately at the physical storage level due to the difference of their characteristics.

5.1 Approaches to Image Filing

Image filing may be achieved simply by using the standard file systems supported by general-purpose operating systems. Actually, this is one of the environments, where IEDIT is used and, in this mode, it handles images stored in CMS files of VM/370. Also, in the usual text processing environments, this type of approach is taken, where each text document is stored into a file and is browsed or edited with text editors. These file systems generally provide full utilities for file management such as COPY, ERASE, RENAME, LIST and, if network is available, SEND/RECEIVE functions, and, therefore, this approach becomes practical for small-scale image filing especially at personal level. Each image, however, must be identified by a simple file descriptor, i.e. file-name and some system-supplied attributes like creation date/time, file size, etc., and, when the number of stored images is large, it becomes very difficult to manage them. A simple way to attach more descriptive information to each image is to provide header records, which is widely used in existing image processing systems. This, however, does not solve the image filing problem because the primary key to access each image is still its file-name and, even if the header information can be used for image selection, the header data are predefined and lack generality and flexibility.

In order to achieve large-scale image filing, therefore, database approach becomes mandatory, with which full descriptive information can be handled. The capabilities required here are not only to associate alphanumeric information to images but also to represent various relationships among alphanumeric and image data. And, moreover, all the available information, i.e. data themselves and the relationships among them, must be usable for data selection and retrieval. For example, consider a part catalog with part sketch images. Then, each part image will be associated with the specification data like part number, supplier name, size, etc., and it will be also associated with its sub-part images. And various conditional retrievals are conceivable, e.g. retrieving part images by giving their supplier names, retrieving part specification data by giving part images, retrieving part specification data and part images by giving their sub-part images, and so on.

Though objects are restricted to conventional alphanumeric data, existing systems for formatted database management suffice the above-mentioned requirements. Especially, relational database systems are powerful due to its general and flexible data definition and manipulation capabilities. Relational systems, moreover, provide simple data model and high-level data languages, both of them are essential in the interactive environ-

ments for end-users. Since Image manipulation necessitates
interactive operations, the above-mentioned features of relational systems will be essential for image filing or image-oriented
database management.

ADM extends the scope of the relational database system to
cover both alphanumeric data and image data. In order to handle
both of them in a unified way and to provide users with a simple
and uniform view of the database, ADM supports image data as one
of the data-types at the same level as the conventional alphanumeric data. This approach makes it possible to retain all the
advantages of the relational system, i.e. the data model
simplicity and the high-level data language with flexible data
definition and manipulation capabilities.

5.2 ADM Functional Structure

ADM functionally consists of four subsystems, i.e. Interaction
subsystem, Image Edit subsystem, Workspace subsystem and Database
subsystem as shown in Fig.5.1.

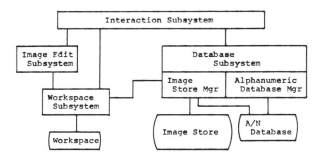

Fig.5.1 ADM functional structure

One of the design issues here is how to provide both database
manipulation and image editing functions with simplified user
interface. The approach taken by ADM is to separate these two
completely and, instead, to provide workspace for bridging the
database and image edit subsystems. With this approach, operations for these two become independent, thereby, the simplicity
of the relational data language has been retained, while full
interactivity is assured for image editing. As an alternative,
it is conceivable to provide image editing capabilities in the
form of built-in functions imbedded in the data language. This,
however, complicates the data language and prohibits the visual
editing of images. And, moreover, the relational data language
is set-oriented and a single query results in retrieving several
records at a time, but image editing operations are usually
different for each image depending upon its contents and, therefore, it seems inadequate to specify the same editing operations
for all the images retrieved.

225

The workstation of ADM is IBM 3277 Graphics Attachment terminal, and the Interaction subsystem controls the man-machine
communication through this workstation. Its major role is to
determine the class of an entered command and to dispatch an
appropriate other subsystem depending on the command class. It
also manages the physical I/O from/to the workstation and
provides I/O services to other subsystems. In addition to this
workstation, ADM uses a color image display for displaying
gray-scale images and their color composites, and it is also
controlled by this subsystem, though gray-scale images can also
be displayed on DVST using digital halftoning method.

Workspace subsystem bridges Database and Image Edit subsystems
by providing the temporary image store in which images generated
by editing or scanning are held for later storing into a database
and images retrieved from a database are held for later editing.
For users, this workspace is a collection of temporary images
which can be accessed simply by specifying their names. This
subsystem facilitates to create, erase, replace, rename and list
the images in this workspace.

Image Edit subsystem is IEDIT. Though, in the previous
section, only the binary image manipulation functions are
described, it also provides gray-scale image manipulation functions such as cut-and-paste operations, contrast modifications,
geometric transformations, overlaying two images by arithmetic or
logical operations, histogram calculation, etc., and some image
conversion functions such as gray-scale to binary conversion by
fixed thresholding or by digital halftoning, etc. Further, it
facilitates to incorporate user-defined image processing functions and to adapt ADM to various application environments.

Database subsystem controls the database-related activities
like storage/retrieval, data definition, integrity control, etc.
Since, at the physical storage level, alphanumeric and image data
are managed separately, two subsidiary components run within this
subsystem, i.e. Alphanumeric Database Manager and Image Store
Manager. The Alphanumeric Database Manager is SYSTEM-R [9],
which is an experimental relational database management system
developed at IBM San Jose Research Laboratory, and facilitates
all the data manipulation, definition and control functions
through the high-level language called "Structured Query
Language" or "SQL" [10]. The Image Store Manager controls the
storage/retrieval of image data with the aid of image index
tables stored in the Alphanumeric Database. The relationships
among alphanumeric and image data are established by storing the
logical pointers or internal identifiers of images in the Alphanumeric Database. Since SYSTEM-R is a kernel component of ADM,
"SQL" is also adopted as the data language in ADM.

5.3 ADM User Interface

For accessing an ADM database covering both image and alphanumeric data, users can utilize the full functions of "SQL" supported
by SYSTEM-R. This section will show how the data manipulation
can be achieved under ADM by giving several examples. For this

purpose, consider a database containing a table named "PARTS" which has the following structure:

```
PARTS
       | PNO | PTYPE | PMAT | PSPPL | PDESC | PDRAW |
```

where PNO is a part number, PTYPE is the part type, PMAT is the material of the part, PSPPL is the supplying company name, PDESC is the descriptive comments, and PDRAW is the image column containing the sketch drawing of the part. Using this table "PARTS", examples of both database query and update are shown below with an emphasis on the usage of image column "PDRAW".

Q1: Show the numbers, supplier names and drawings of the parts which are made of steel.

```
Select  PNO, PSPPL, PDRAW
from    PARTS
where   PMAT='steel'
```

This query results in a table displayed on a character display screen and, at the same time, the sketch drawing image of the part corresponding to the top row of the table is displayed on DVST. The image is displayed one by one and its selection can be done by scrolling the table on the character display. Also one can copy the image data currently displayed on the DVST screen to workspace for later editing. Therefore, from the standpoint of image data selection, "SQL" is used as first step screening and the actual selection is done by viewing the image contents one by one.

Q2: Show all the information about the parts which are supplied by the same company as the part whose drawing is held in workspace as IMAGE_BOLT55.

```
Select  *
from    PARTS
where   PSPPL = ( select PSPPL
                  from   PARTS
                  where PDRAW = IMAGE_BOLT55 )
```

This query contains a comparison operator for the image column "PDRAW", and ADM determines the eqaulity of images based upon the equality of the image internal identifiers. And, the assumption of Q2 is that the image named IMAGE_BOLT55 in workspace has been retrieved from the database beforehand and its internal identifier is defined, since the internal identifier is assigned when the image is stored into a database and, therefore, an image newly created in workspace by editing or scanning has no internal identifier assigned. Though sample query is not given, it is also possible to join two tables by equating image columns.

U1: In PARTS table, add the information about the part which number is 63, type is worm gear, material is copper and drawing is given by the image named IMAGE_GEAR63 in workspace.

    Insert into PARTS(PNO, PTYPE, PMAT, PDRAW):
        ⟨63, 'worm gear', 'copper', IMAGE_GEAR63⟩

U2: As for the part with part number 48, replace the drawing with the image named IMAGE_NEW48 in workspace.

    Update   PARTS
    set   PDRAW = IMAGE_NEW48
    where   PNO=48

U3: From PARTS table, drop all the information about the parts which drawings are equal to the image named IMAGE_OBS in workspace.

    Delete   PARTS
    where   PDRAW = IMAGE_OBS

When describing images in a database, there are the cases where a single number or character string is insufficient and somewhat fuzzy way is required. For this purpose, ADM provides the data-type "set", the element of which is literally an unordered set of numbers or character strings. Though its introduction violates the original relational model concept, it facilitates easy description of images. The usefulness of this "set" will become more clear when one think of information retrieval system where documents are characterized by a set of keywords. The comparison operators for this "set" data-type are "IS EQUAL TO", "COVERS ALL OF", "COVERS SOME OF", "IS COVERED BY" and their negations. Assuming the PDESC column of the PARTS table to be a "set" column, the following example Q3 shows the usage of "set" comparison.

Q3: Show the numbers, suppliers and drawings of the parts which are somehow related to all of the terms 'hexagon', 'circular hole' and 'ABC standard'.

    Select   PNO, PSSPL, PDRAW
    from   PARTS
    where   PDESC covers all of
              ('hexagon','circular hole','ABC standard')

"Set" is internally represented by a binary relation of SYSTEM-R, and a query containing set comparison operators is processed by modifying the query sentence at SQL level, and this modified query can be executed directly by SYSTEM-R.

5.4 Image Data Management

ADM adopts two-level storage approach as mentioned previously. That is, it manages alphanumeric data and image data separately at the physical storage level, and only the logical pointers or the image internal identifiers are stored in the alphanumeric database. This approach has several advantages over the single storage approach where both alphanumeric and image data are stored together. First, since only logical pointers are stored in the alphanumeric database, it achieves non-redundant storage of image data. This point is very important since image data are voluminous, whereas, generally, the same image can appear several times in a table or in several different tables within a database. Second, queries concerning only alphanumeric data can be processed very efficiently, because, in this case, image store need not be accessed. And, third, it is matched to a future hierarchical storage system, where alphanumeric data will be stored on high-speed devices and image data on low-cost mass-store like optical storage.

The Image Store of ADM are split into several areas so that the same group of images are physically clustered and selective dump/restore can be easily done for recovery purposes. This area of Image Store is called Image Store Segment (ISS) and is defined as a mini-disk supported by VM/370 operating system. The provision of ISS also makes it possible to control the level of locking in shared environment i.e. whether locking should be done at ISS level or at individual image level, in the same manner as SYSTEM-R does with its segment.

The image data-types supported by ADM are currently three, i.e. binary image, 4 bit/PEL and 8 bit/PEL gray-scale image. Binary images are stored in the compressed form described in section 2. Gray-scale images are, however, stored without any compression, since bit-based code words is essential for the efficient coding of gray-scale images and their encode/decode becomes prohibitively time-consuming. Though color image is not supported explicitly as a data-type, primitive color image manipulation can be done by interpreting the PEL intensities of gray-scale images as color codes or by combining three gray-scale images as three primary color components.

Though images are basically characterized by the above-mentioned image data-types, they are also categorized by user-defined domains. The domains are disjoint sets of images and are defined according to the application view of the image data semantics. Domains are characterized by two attributes i.e. on what ISS the member images should reside and what types of images are included, and can be created by "CREATE DOMAIN" statement as follows:

Create domain PART_SKETCH (binary) in iss PARTS

where domain named PART_SKETCH is defined which includes only binary images and the member images are stored in ISS named PARTS. If the image size is the same for all member images, the size can also be specified in addition to the image-type. Also several image-types can be specified for one domain if it allows multiple image-types. And, when defining a table in a database, image columns are characterized by these domains, though alphanumeric columns are characterized by data-types such as INTEGER, CHARACTER, etc.

The domains are internally managed by two types of system tables which reside on an alphanumeric database. One is the domain master catalog, in which each domain is described by one entry representing the domain name, domain internal identifier, residing ISS name, covering image-types and so forth. The other is the domain image index, which is created for each domain and used for the management of member images. This domain image index keeps one entry per member image and provides the information about each image such as the image internal identifier, type, size, corresponding file-id in ISS, reference count and so forth. It must be noted here that the image internal identifiers are assigned uniquely only within a domain, and, therefore, the comparison of images is valid only when they belong to the same domain since it is done based upon the internal identifiers as mentioned before.

6. Concluding Remarks

The goal of Image Editor (IEDIT) is to make the digital image processing more handy and familiar in the general computing environments. One big challenge here is how to achieve fast responses in order to fit in the interactive environments, and IEDIT provides an effective solution to this problem. When IEDIT is run on IBM System/370 model 158, the response times for the most cases are within a few seconds, and it can be concluded that image processing algorithms can be made fast enough to make image editing really interactive, provided that the objects are restricted to binary images and they are processed in appropriately compressed forms all through. The functions currently supported by IEDIT, however, cover only fundamental ones, and cannot be regarded as sufficient. And, as for its functional enhancement, further study is required to determine what and how to add within the framework of IEDIT.

Regarding ADM, its image support part is designed as a straightforward extension of the current relational database. Since a relational database system provides flexible and easy-to-use interface and this feature will become more and more important in the future end-user environments, this approach seems to be very effective. Further, as apparent from the previous descriptions, it is fairly easy to extend its scope to other types of data, e.g. text, graphics and so forth. And, in order to add other types of data, three constructs are generally required for each i.e. browser, editor and comparison operators which could be specified for conditional retrieval of the database. This extensibility seems to be essential when the future multi-media document environments are taken into account.

References

1. Takao, Y. : Image Editor (IEDIT): An Efficient Approach to Binary Image Editing. TSC Report C318-1539, IBM Japan, Ltd. (1981)

2. Takao, Y., et al : An Image-Oriented Database System. in Data Base Techniques for Pictorial Applications edited by A. Blaser, Springer-Verlag (1979)

3. Codd, E.F. : A Relational Model of Data for Large Shared Data Banks, Comm. ACM, Vol.13, No.6 (1970)

4. Huang, T.S. : Coding of Two-Tone Images. IEEE Trans. on Communications, Vol.COM-25 (1977) Nov P 1406~ 1424

5. Hunter, R., Robinson, A.H. : International Digital Facsimile Coding Standards. Proc. of IEEE, Vol.68 (1980) July 874-885

6. Arai, K., Yasuda, Y. : A System of the Facsimile Line-Density Conversion. Paper of Tech. Group, IECE Japan, Vol.IE76, No.44 (in Japanese) (1976)

7. Stucki, P. : Image Processing for Document Reproduction. in ADVANCES IN DIGITAL IMAGE PROCESSING edited by P. Stucki, Plenum Press (1979)

8. Fukinuki, T., Yoshigi, H. : Conversion of Picture Element Density in Run-Length Domain. Paper of Tech. Group, IECE Japan, Vol.IE79, No.60 (in Japanese) (1979)

9. Astrahan, M.M., et al : System R: A Relational Approach to Data Base Management, ACM Trans. on Database Systems, Vol.1, No.2 (1976)

10. Chamberlin, D.D., et al : SEQUEL2: A Unified Approach to Data Definition, Manipulation and Control, IBM Journal Res. Develop., Vol.20, No.6 (1976)

A Multiple Microprocessor System for Office Image Processing

L.M. Ni

Department of Computer Science, Michigan State University
East Lansing, MI 48824, USA

K.Y. Wong and D.T. Lee*
IBM San Jose Research Laboratory, San Jose, CA 95193, USA

1. Introduction

During the last decade, automatic office document systems have been evolved with advances in microprocessors, low cost memories, and peripherals. Text processing systems are being used to create and edit documents. Interactive computer graphics are being used to manipulate graphics in the display. Integrated systems have been developed to implement communication and processing of text and graphics [5,8]. Interactive image processing is needed in an office document system to enhance and to scale scanned pictures into a desired page format.

The image processing functions create two problems: one is the need of an on-line storage system for image database and the other is the high processing time required to produce an output image [10]. An imagery frame must be scanned through a scanner to generate a digitized format for storage and processing. If an 8.5" x 11" frame is scanned at 240 pixels/in. resolution, it generates 5 million picture elements (pixels). These large volume of pixels are usually stored in high speed disks. The image processing time, therefore, is limited by the data transfer rate between disk and main memory modules. A high speed disk usually can provide data transfer rate 1 Mbyte/sec. Transfer 5 million pixels back and forth needs 10 seconds not including the processing time. If the processing time for each pixel is 100 μsec, the total processing time will be 500 seconds. In order to achieve an acceptable response time, multiple processors are required and the overlapping between data transfer and processing are necessitated.

In addition to problems related to transferring the image between main memory and disks, the image may need also to be displayed in high resolution CRT devices, be window clipped, or be hardcopied in high resolution printers. Interactive image editing requires the functions of adding text information to an image, moving image to different part of a page, scaling image, or merging text into image. The image rescaling

---

* D.T. Lee is now with the Compute Research Center,
  Hewlett-Packard Laboratories, Palo Alto, CA 94304, USA.

algorithm is the most frequently used algorithm in an office document system. For example, an image should be able to be magnified so that detail appears more clearly, or be reduced so that more of the image is visible. Other image processing algorithms which will be used include the digital halftoning of gray-scale pictures, the dynamic thresholding for black and white images, moire suppression for halftones, and resolution translation, etc. Common characteristics of most of these image processing algorithms are partitionable and non-recursive. Therefore, they are suitable for parallel processing.

This paper presents a multiprocessor system architecture and the scheduling policies of the processors which can off-load a host computer in the image processing of office documents. Different approaches to parallel image processing were proposed by [3,5,7,11,12]. Special computer architectures for image processing have been proposed or developed in many research centers [4] such as the PUMPS [2] and the MPP [1] among many other systems. Most of these special-purpose systems are not cost-effective. We investigate a master/slave shared-bus multiprocessor system and the possible extension to a shared-resource multiple-master multiprocessor system. The attributes of such a system are its modularity, expandability, software simplification, and minimum cost. Such a system can be built with off-the-shelf processor/memory modules. Thus, the development overhead is low and implementation efforts can be greatly simplified. We describe first the system architecture and image processing requirements. Interactions between multiple resources and the optimization of certain system parameters will be analyzed via an analytical model. Based on this model, two different scheduling policies of the processors are proposed. Finally, we present an image partitioning strategy for such an image multiprocessing system. A prototype multiprocessor image processing system has been built at the IBM San Jose Research Laboratory.

2. Architecture of the Image Processing System

The brightness of an image varies continuously across the picture. In order to facilitate computer processing, an image must be digitized into an integer array. The elements of a digital image array are called <u>picture elements</u> (pixels). When the resolution is high, it requires minutes or even hours to process an image frame on a single processor. Processing the image by multiple processors will improve the performance significantly. In the ideal case, a speedup of m is expected where m is the number of processors in a system. In practice, the actual speedup may vary and is less than m.

In order to involve all processors, one approach is to partition an image in a way to allow each processor work independently of the others. An ideal partition strategy is to cut an image into a set of disjoint <u>segments</u>. Then several segments of an image can be processed concurrently on several processors. However, since many image processing algorithms

require information from neighboring pixels, i.e., neighborhood type operations, each processor has to load into its
local memeory not only a segment of image data but also the
boundary pixels information in order to reduce the inter-pro-
cessor communications.   In this study a frame of image is
partitioned into row-major pattern, because images stored in
the disk are usually in row-major format. Also, the processing times for all pixels are equal in most office document
applications. A frame of image, therefore, is partitioned into
equal-size segments.   Figure 1 shows an example of an image
frame partitioned into a row-major pattern.

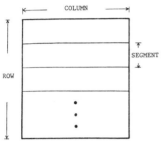

(a) An image frame

(b) The actual transfer size
for each segment is the
segment size plus the
overlapped neighboring
information

Fig.1   An image frame partitioned into a row-major pattern

Due to the large amount of pixels involved, on-line image
data is stored in disks.   The processing speed therefore is
limited by the disk data transfer rate.   A single time-shared
system bus is suitable, if only one disk controller is employed. The number of processors linked to the system bus should
be chosen to match the application need.   The major function
of the system bus is to transfer image data between distributed memories and disks.   It is a loosely-coupled multiprocessor
system because executable code of each processor has a high
degree of locality. The processor should not attempt to
access the system bus frequently, during the execution of an
image process.

The functional block diagram of the shared-bus multiprocessing image system is shown in Fig.2. Each processor has its own
memory. One of the processors, called the master processor,
is used to monitoring the operation of the multiprocessor
system.   It interprets user commands, downloads the image processing programs to other processors, partitions an image
frame, schedules image segments among processors, and super-
vises other I/O operations.   The other m slave processors perform image processing tasks.   The whole system can work as a
back-end peripheral system if the master processor is linked
to a host processor. In the prototype design, five Intel iSBC
86/12A's are employed, where one is master and the other four

234

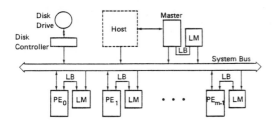

Fig.2 A single shared-bus multiprocessor system with m processors

LB: Local Bus
LM: Dual-port Local Memory

are slave processors. An IBM Series/1 minicomputer is used as the host.

The disk controller, under the supervision of the master processor, performs DMA operations, transferring image data between disks and the local memories of the processors via the system bus, which is an Intel Multibus. The Series/1 system is also equipped with scanners, printers, and CRT displays for other I/O operations. The bus arbitration logic is required in each processor to solve the bus congestion problem. The use of a single system bus imposes constraints on the maximum bandwidth of communication traffic. However, the sequential data transfer from between disk and some of the processors can overlap with image processing in other processors.

Dual-port memory is required for each processor. Currently, each iSBC 86/12A has a 32K dual-port RAM. Dual access ports permit the local processor to access the local memory directly via the Local Bus (LB). Remote processors or disks can also access the local memory via the system bus. The dual-port architecture offers two operational advantages: First, if two processors communicate through shared memory, only one must access the memory using the system bus, and the amount of system bus traffic may be significantly reduced. Second, memory is distributed on all processors. A separate memory board is therefore not needed.

The optimal number of processors required for each image processing function is algorithm dependent. An image processing algorithm can be compute-bound or I/O-bound or "near-optimal". A compute-bound application demands more processors to achieve the speed; whereas, an I/O-bound application does not need as many processors. A "near-optimal" application has the needs in between. The number of processors to be used is governed by the cost factor and performance demanded. Obviously, a fixed number of processors cannot satisfy all demands. One can use multiple master processors sharing the slave processors. Several image processing alogrithms, therefore, can be executed concurrently. The slave processors are dynamically allocatable to the master processors. Each master processor has its own system bus and disk controller. Figure 3 shows a two-bus multiprocessor system with two master processors sharing six slave processros. Two image processing algorithms can be executed concurrently in this sytem. The path selector (PS) is used to assign the slave processors to one of the master processors.

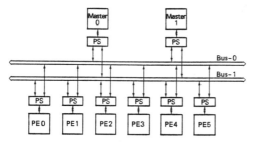

PS: Path Selector

Fig.3   The functional block diagram of a two-buses
         multiprocessor system sharing six slave processors

Cost-effectiveness is essential in this design. With system architecture that allows modular development of flexible designs from off-the-shelf PC cards, the multiprocessor system greatly extends the power of the individual microprocessor with inherent parallel structure. Principal benefits of this approach are modularity, expandability, software simplification, low development overhead, and high reliability.

3.   Operational Characteristics of the Image Processors

The assignment of a segment of an image frame to a processor initiates a process. With no ambiguity, we shall refer to a slave processor as a processor. Data transferred to the local memory consists of one image segment plus the overlapped portion (see Fig.1). An analytical model is developed to analyze the system performance with respect to two scheduling policies of the processors. Stated below are the assumptions and parameters used in modeling a single shared-bus multiprocessor system. An image frame is partitioned into s segments with fixed partitioning strategy. The data transfers therefore have fixed size. An image segment is processed in three steps. 1) Load the image from disk to one of the local memory; 2) Process the image by the local processor; and 3) Store the output image back to disk. Loading and storing of the image data require seizure of the system bus for some transfer times. The input image segment and output image segment may have different sizes (image rescaling, for example), requiring seizure of the system bus with time periods of t_i and t_o, respectively. The image data is processed locally. Very little interprocessor communication is needed. The bus time for this purpose is then ignored. Let t_p be the processing time for a single image segment. For simplicity t_p is assumed constant for all image segments.

236

Each processor must issue a bus request signal before the image data transfer can be initiated. The master processor schedules the bus request on a first-come first-serve (FCFS) basis to make an efficient use of the system bus and to avoid bus congestion. Each processor may assume one of the following four states: load, process, store and idle. The system bus has two states, either idle or busy (carry data transfer). In a uniprocessor system, to process s segments of an image frame requires $T_i(s,1)$ unit times, where

$$T_1(s,1) = s(t_i+t_p+t_o) \qquad (1)$$

The memory size of the uniprocessor is assumed to be the same as all processors. Due to the large amount of image data stored in the disk, it still has to be partitioned before processing.

Two scheduling policies of the processors are considered under this model. The 3-step schedule policy treats separately the storing of the image segment currently being processed and the loading of the next image segment processed. The 2-step schedule policy loads the next to be processed image segment immediately after finishing the storing of the previous image segment. These two scheduling policies are illustrated by the state-time diagrams shown in Fig.4 and Fig.5 for compute-bound and I/O-bound applications, respectively.

In Fig.4 and Fig.5, each image frame is partitioned into 11 segments (s=11) in a system with 4 processors (m=4). It takes $11(2t+t_p)$ to process the whole image frame on a uniprocessor, assuming that $t_i=t_o=t$. In Fig.4, t_p is assumed to be 2t. Figures 4a and 4b illustrate the state-time diagram for 3-step and 2-step policies, respectively. The execution time of both policies are the same and equal to 22t. The speed-up over uniprocessor system is 44t/22t=2. Note that the system bus is always busy for such I/O-bound tasks.

In Fig.5, t_p is assumed to be 7t. The execution times are 35t and 31t for the 3-step and 2-step policies, respectively. The corresponding speedups over uniprocessors are 2.8 and 3.2, respectively. The system bus utilization is less than 1 for such compute-bound tasks. This example clearly shows that the 2-step policy is better than the 3-step policy and compute-bound tasks have higher speedup than I/O-bound tasks.

Denote the time required to process an image frame of s segments in an m-processor system employing 3-step policy by $T_3(s,m)$. We have

$$T_3(s,m)= \lfloor s/m \rfloor T(m) + T(s \bmod m) \qquad (2)$$

where T(n) is defined by

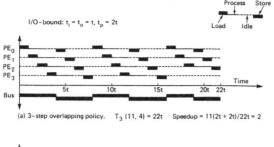

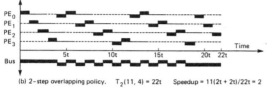

(a) 3-step overlapping policy. T_3 (11, 4) = 22t   Speedup = 11(2t + 2t)/22t = 2

(b) 2-step overlapping policy. T_2(11, 4) = 22t   Speedup = 11(2t + 2t)/22t = 2

Fig.4   The state-time diagram of a 4-processor system, where 11 image segments are processed

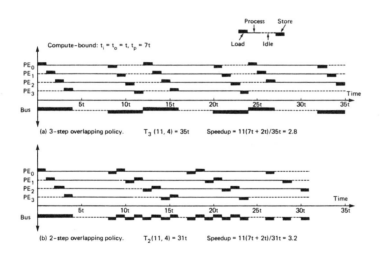

(a) 3-step overlapping policy. T_3 (11, 4) = 35t   Speedup = 11(7t + 2t)/35t = 2.8

(b) 2-step overlapping policy. T_2(11, 4) = 31t   Speedup = 11(7t + 2t)/31t = 3.2

Fig.5   The state-time diagram of a 4-processor system, where 11 image segments are processed

$$T(n) = \begin{cases} t_i + t_p + nt_o & \text{if } t_i \leq t_o \text{ and } t_p \geq (n-1)t_i \\ n(t_i + t_o) & \text{if } t_i \leq t_o \text{ and } t_p < (n-1)t_i \quad (3) \\ nt_i + t_p + t_o & \text{if } t_i > t_o \end{cases}$$

238

Note that $n \neq 0$ and $T(0) = 0$. With the 3-step policy, the s image segments are divided into groups, where each group has m segments except the last group. $T(n)$ is the processing time of n image segments processed by n processors. The speedup is dominated by the number of processors, m. When m is increased, a compute-bound problem may become an I/O-bound problem, and vice versa.

For the 2-step policy, the execution time is $T_2(s,m)=T(s)$ if $s \leq m$. When $s > m$, we have

$$T_2(s,m) = s(t_i+t_o) \tag{4}$$
$$\text{if } t_p \leq (m-1)t_i \text{ and } t_p \leq (m-1)t_o$$

$$T_2(s,m) = s(t_i+t_o) + t_p - (m-1)t_o \tag{5}$$
$$\text{if } t_p \leq (m-1)t_i \text{ and } t_p > (m-1)t_o$$

$$T_2(s,m) = s(t_i+t_o) + t_p - (m-1)t_i \tag{6}$$
$$\text{if } (m-1)t_i < t_p \leq (m-1)t_o$$

$$T_2(s,m) = s(t_i+t_o) + 2t_p - (m-1)(t_i+t_o) \tag{7}$$
$$\text{if } (m-1)t_i < t_p \leq (m-1)(t_i+t_o) \text{ and } t_p > (m-1)t_o$$

$$T_2(s,m) = \lfloor s/m \rfloor (t_i+t_p+t_o)+[(s-1) \bmod m](t_i+t_o) \tag{8}$$
$$\text{if } t_p > (m-1)(t_i+t_o)$$

Equations (4) to (7) are I/O-bound problems. If t_p approaches $(m-1)(t_i+t_o)$, it becomes "near-optimal." After the total execution time has been derived, three indices of system performance can be measured. The <u>speedup</u> is defined as the ratio of the execution time on a uniprocessor system to that on an m-processor system. The <u>bus utilization</u> is defined as the ratio of the actual data transfer time to the total execution time. The <u>processor utilization</u> is defined as the ratio of the processor being busy, which includes data transfer time and processing time, to the total execution time. Formally, we define

$$\text{Speedup} = s(t_i+t_p+t_o)/T_{2(3)}(s,m) \tag{9}$$

$$\text{Bus utilization} = s(t_i+t_o)/T_{2(3)}(s,m) \tag{10}$$

$$\text{Processor utilization} = \lfloor s/m \rfloor (t_i+t_p+t_o)/T_{2(3)}(s,m) \tag{11}$$

$$\text{or} = \lceil s/m \rceil (t_i+t_p+t_o)/T_{2(3)}(s,m) \tag{12}$$

The processor utilization may vary depending on whether that processor is assigned with an extra image segment (Eq.11) or not (Eq.12) in the last run.

It can be easily proved that the 3-step scheduling policy is never better than the 2-step scheduling policy. Consider an image frame partitioned into 2520 segments. The input and output of an image segment take the same amount of time, i.e., $t_i=t_o=t$. Let the number of processors varying from 1 to 10. Assume t_p to be 2t, 8t and 16t. The speedup versus the number of processors over the two scheduling policies is plotted in Fig. 6. It can be seen that the 2-step policy (solid line) is never worse than the 3-step policy (dash line). When the number of processors increases, the speedup

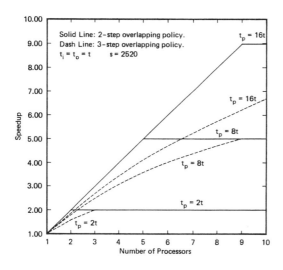

Fig.6 Comparison of two scheduling policies of processors

becomes flat and never increases. The maximum speedup equals min $\{m, 1+t_p/(t_i+t_o)\}$ where the second term is derived when the execution time is dominated by the data transfer time exclusively. When t_p is small, it is easy to achieve the maximum speed. Increasing the number of processors will turn the compute-bound problems into near-optimal problems when the maximum speedup is reached. Further increasing the number of processors will result in I/O-bound problems. The system bus may become bottleneck under such circumstances. Increasing the number of processors will not help the system performance after the system bus has been saturated.

240

The speedup factor is also affected by the number of image segments. From Figs. 4 and 5, we observed that the system performance is degraded due to the low degree of overlapping of processor usage in the beginning and ending stages of an image process. If the number of image segments is not an integer multiple of the number of processors, the residue effect will also reduce the speedup. These phenomena are demonstrated in Fig.7 with t_p equal to 2t or 7t for a 4-processor system with the 2-step scheduling policy. As the number of image segments increases, the effect of less overlapping of process usage becomes insignificant. The upper bound of the speedup factors for the two cases are 2 or 4, respectively. For an I/O-bound problem, it is easy to achieve the upper bound even with small image segments, because the bus is always busy. However, a compute-bound problem must have enough number of image segments to achieve the maximum speedup. The residue effect also slightly reduces the speedup factor. This fact suggests that the number of image segments should be an integer multiple of m. We also conclude that the optimum number of processors for a particular image processing application is $1+t_p/(t_i+t_o)$, if the number of image segments per frame is sufficiently large.

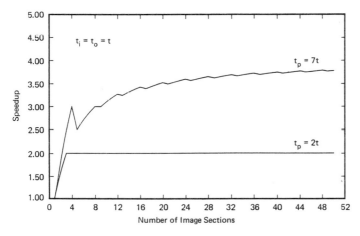

Fig.7   The speedup versus different number of image segments on a 4-processor system with 2-step scheduling policy

4.   Image Partitioning Strategies

Given an image frame, theoretically, the more image segments it can be partitioned into, the better the speedup will be. But in practice, the processor scheduler needs a certain amount of time to assign the bus to the processor. This <u>scheduling overhead</u>, d, is independent of the size of image segments. The system bus is idle during the scheduling overhead time. The time required to partition the image and to assign an image segment to a processor can be ignored, because these can be done in advance by the master processor or overlapped with the operation of other processors.

In Section 3, the analysis ignores the scheduling overhead. However, the scheduling overhead, d, can be merged into the effective data transfer time by replacing t_i and t_o by (t_i+d) and (t_o+d), respectively. Obviously, if an image is partitioned into too many segments, the scheduling overhead will greatly degrade the system performance, becasue the overhead is proportional to the number of image segments. To alleviate difficulty imposed by scheduling overhead, the following actions can be taken:

(1)   Make the processor scheduler as simple as possible.
(2)   Make the scheduling overhead relative small to the image segment transfer time. In other words, make the image segment size as large as possible.
(3)   If the image processing time, t_p is very large compared with the scheduling overhead, the scheduling overhead will become negligible.

Only the second solution is related to the image partitioning strategy. Physically, the size of an image segment can be enlarged as long as it fits in a local memory. However, if the number of image segments is small, the degree of overlapping of processor usage will decrease. An optimal choice of image segments, s, under 2-step scheduling policy is to find an s such that $T_2(s,m)$ is minized. The case corresponding to the least execution time gives the optimal number of image segments. A numerical example is illustrated to find such an optimal value of s.

Consider an image frame having size 1024 by 1024. The processing time for each pixel is 100 μsec. The data transfer time for each pixel is 1.67 μsec (in MULTIBUS, for example) via the system bus. This is a typical compute-bound task. In practice, the processing time is much greater than the transfer time for each pixel. Table 1 shows the execution time versus the number of image segments for different values of scheduling overhead, d, on a 4-processor system. In order to eliminate the residue effect, the number of segments is chosen to be an integer multiple of 4. A high scheduling overhead tends to have less image segments. Note that the size of each image segment cannot exceed the local memory capacity of a local processor.

The scheduling overhead depends on the complexity of the processor scheduling policy. For a fixed scheduling policy, the overhead is small because the image segments assigned to each processor are predetermined. However, in some applications the processing time for each image segment may be different. Thus, a good processor scheduling policy which can dynamically assign image segments to processors on a first-come first-serve basis is needed. Other factors, such as the processor speed, optimality of the object code, and image partitioning strategy, can also affect the schedule overhead.

Table 1   The execution times of a 1024 by 1024 image processed on a 4-processor system are listed with respect to different size of image segments and scheduling overheads "d"

Image size:	1024×1024 pixels
Processing time:	100 μsec/pixel
Data transfer time:	1.67 μ/sec/pixel
Processor scheduling policy:	2-step overlapping policy
Execution time:	$T_2(s,4)$ msec

Section Size (rows)	Number of Sections	d=8 msec	d=2 msec	d=0.5 msec	d=0.1 msec
1	1024	31244	28136	27359	27152
2	512	29206	27634	27241	27136
4	256	28203	27399	27198	27144
8	128	27732	27312	27207	27179
16	64	27558	27330	27273	27257
32	32	27594	27462	27429	27420

5.   System Software Developemnt

As we mentioned in previous sections, the shared-bus multi-microprocessor system is working as a loosely-coupled system. The major shared resource is the image data. Since each pixel data is processed by the same algorithm; the image processing algorithm is essentially executed in sequence but with different copies in each processor. A heavy burden on developing new parallel algorithms is thereby released. However, in order to fully utilize the system resource, the following three characteristics must hold for the image processing algorithms. First, it must be nonrecursive to avoid chained relation among pixels. Second, the processing of an image frame must be partitionable. Third, the relation among the information of different pixels must be minimized. Most of the image processing algorithms used in office document systems have these properties.

The master processor is responsible for decoding the image processing commands, setting up the image processing program for all processors, partitioning the image frame, scheduling image segments among processors, and other I/O operations. The master processor will not become system bottleneck, because most of its time is spent on scheduling slave processors while slave processors are doing image processing tasks. If the processing time of each image segment is different, the master can hold the slave processor's bus requests on a first-come fist-serve queue and dynamically allocate image segments among processors.

The slave processors are actually performing image processing tasks. The following Pascal-like program showsn how each processor is working with 2-step scheduling policy.

```
begin
     LOAD(SEG-ID);
     while SEG-ID >= 0 do
          begin
               PROCESS-IMAGE;
               STORE-LOAD(SEG-ID);
          end;
end.
```

Procedure LOAD(SEG-ID) requests the master processor for the purpose of controlling the system bus and loading the first image segment to its local memory. SEG-ID returns the identification number of the assigned image segment. Procedure PROCESS-IMAGE simply invokes the image processing program working on the local data set. After it is done, procedure STORE-LOAD(SEG-ID) is invoked to request permission from master processor to seize the system bus and store the processed image segment. For the 2-step scheduling policy, loading of the next image segment is immediately initiated afterwards. This process is repeated until all image segments have been processed. This is acknowledged by receiving a negative SEG-ID. A few interprocessor communications may occur. For example, processors may need to access a common mailbox in the master's local memory. However, these operations rarely occur and their processing time can be ignored.

Based on the above analysis, a dynamic processor scheduling operating system has been implemented [9]. The system program is coded in assembly language. By dynamic approach, it can handle non-uniform image processing time distributions efficiently. Both 2-step and 3-step scheduling policies are implemented. The scheduling system is independent of the number of processors. The user can choose the number of processors to be used. This is a very useful feature for the user, permitting comparison of the speedup on different numbers of processors. As a result, it allows processor expandability and reliability. Other features include facilities for software debugging and timing measurement.

6. Conclusion

A cost-effective shared-bus multiple microprocessor system is presented for interactive office image processing. Since the image processing algorithm is repeated thousands or millions of times on each independent data set, each processor can work on the same program independent of others. It is unlike an SIMD machine in that the processors need not execute the same instruction at the same time [6], thus permitting conditional branches in the algorithm. It is unlike an MIMD machine in that the processors do not interact. In such a loosely coupled system, interprocessor communication can be kept to a minimum amount. The processing time is limited by the data transfer rate of the disk storage. By overlapping the image transfer and processing operations, the maximum speed can be approached. The analytical results suggest that better image partitioning and processor scheduling policies do make a difference in handling pictorial information in an office environment.

References

[1] Batcher, K.E., "Design of a massively parallel processor," IEEE Trans. on Computer, Vol. C-29, No. 9, pp. 836-840, September 1980.

[2] Briggs, F.A., Dubois, M. and Hwang, K., "Throughput analysis and configuration design of a shared-resource multiprocessor system: PUMPS," Proceeding of the Eighth Int'l Symposium on Computer Architecture, May 1981.

[3] Cordello, L., Duff, M.J.B. and Levialdi, S., "Comparing sequential and parallel processing of pictures," Third Int. Joint Conf. Pattern Recognition, Coronado, CA., November 1976.

[4] Fu, K.S., "Special computer architectures for pattern recognition and image processing," Proc. 1978 National Computer Conference, pp. 1003-1013, 1978.

[5] Hartke, D.H., Sterling, W.M. and Shemer, J.E., "Design of a raster display processor for the office applications," IEEE Trans. on Computers, Vol. C-27, No. 4, pp. 337-349, April 1978.

[6] Hwang, K., Su, S.P. and Ni, L.M., "Vetor computer architecture and processing techniques," Advances in Computer, (ed. M. Yovits), Vol. 20, Academic Press, New York, 1981.

[7] Krause, B., "A parallel picture processing machine," IEEE Trans. on Computers, Vol. C-22, No. 12, pp. 1075-1087, December 1973.

[8] Myers, W., "Interactive computer graphics - flyinghigh," Parts I and II, Computer, Vol. 12, No. 7-8, 1979.

[9] Ni, L.M. and Lee, D., "A dynamic job scheduling operating system for image processing on a multi-microprocessor," *IBM Internal Report*, Department of Computer Science, San Jose Laboratory, 1980.

[10] Poon, R.K. and Wong, K.Y., "A flexible image processor using array elements," *Fifth Workshop on Computer Architecture for Non-numeric Processing*, Monterey, CA., March 12-15, 1980.

[11] Shemer, J.E. and Keddy, J.R., "Architecture of an experimental office system: The soft display work processor," *Computer*, Vol. 11, No. 12, pp. 39-48, December 1978.

[12] Stamopoulos, C.D., "Parallel image processing," *IEEE Trans. on Coimputers*, Vol. C-24, No. 4, pp. 424-433, April 1975.

Part V

Computer-Aided Design

Logic Diagram Editing for Interactive Logic Design

H. Hiraishi and S. Yajima

Department of Information Science, Faculty of Engineering
Kyoto University, Kyoto, 606 Japan

1. Introduction

The scale and the complexity of logic circuits are increasing steadily with the progress of LSI technology. In proportion to this increase, logic design is getting more and more difficult. To meet this situation, many computer aided design (CAD) systems for logic design have been developed recently.

Because logic diagrams, such as block diagrams and logic circuit diagrams, are indispensable to logic design, they are usually manipulated by logic diagram editing systems included in such CAD systems. The main purpose of these conventional editing systems is to input the circuit information to the CAD systems. After logic designers design the circuit and draw its diagram on paper, they have to input it in one of the following ways according to the input device available in their editing system:
(1) specifying the coordinates of each logic element and connection line with a tablet or a digitizer [1,2];
(2) editing logic diagrams interactively on a graphic display [3,4,5];
(3) reading logic diagrams by a scanner [6].

Therefore these editing systems only manipulate logic diagrams which are the results of the design, and are not so useful for design process of logic circuits. But requirements for this sort of system are growing higher and higher with increasing complexity of logic design. That is, a powerful new logic diagram editing system is desired, which can not only manipulate logic diagrams but also support logic design itself.

In order to realize such a logic diagram editing system, we discuss first required facilities useful for interactive logic design. Next, we describe a new logic diagram editing system LODE (A Logic Diagram Editing System for Structured Logic Design) under development in our laboratory for the purpose stated above. LODE has powerful editing facilities including automatic connection line handling and supports top-down design approach called structured logic design. It can also manipulate state transition diagrams to specify functions of circuits. Finally, we show an example of logic design using LODE and evaluate its performance.

2. Structured Logic Design and Logic Diagrams

2.1 Hierarchy in Structured Logic Design

Structured logic design [5,7,8] is a top-down, hierarchical method suitable for designing complex and/or large scale logic circuits. Structured design technique was originally invented in the field of software. As logic design is getting more and more complex with the LSI technology, structured logic design has been contrived to cope with this situation by applying structured design techinique to logic design.

The basic idea of structured logic design is divide and conquer. The first step is to divide a block (the circuit to be designed is a block) into several blocks. The second step is to design each block in detail. If some block is still too complex to design, it is partitioned into smaller blocks again. Therefore the first step is repeated until all blocks can be designed with ease, and the whole design is completed when every block is constructed only with the well-known logic elements such as NAND gates, flip-flops and registers etc. In other words, logic designers have only to deal with the blocks manageable to them in structured logic design.

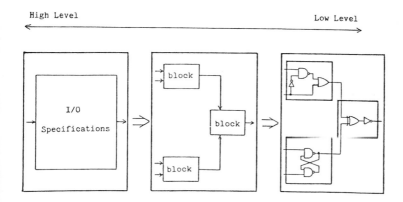

Fig.1 Structured logic design

Figure 1 shows how this process goes on. The logic circuit to be designed is given first in terms of input/output specifications. From the viewpoint of the level of abstraction, this ciruit is at the highest level and the complete design is at the lowest level. That is, advancing the design by partitioning a block means letting down the level of abstraction. Block diagrams are used in the design at a high level and logic circuit diagrams are drawn at a low level. Consequently a logic diagram editing system which can support structured logic design must manipulate both kinds of diagrams. Moreover, such a system is required to support hierarchical logic diagrams since the design process is hierarchical as stated above.

2.2 Function-Level and Structure-Level Design

In structured logic design, each block is designed after the first step of block partitioning. A logic designer passes through the following two phases in designing a block:
  Phase 1 -- function-level design
  Phase 2 -- structure-level design

In the phase 1 he designs the functions of the block and in the phase 2 he decides how it is constructed. Therefore he tries to compose the block so that it may realize the functions specified in the phase 1. He determines what logic elements are to be used and how they are to be connected together. He may also partition the block again.

We often use flow charts, timing charts, state diagrams and some languages in order to describe the function of blocks. Logic diagrams (block diagrams and logic circuit diagrams) are used to represent the structure exactly. Since conventional logic diagram editing systems manipulate the latter only, they never support the function-level design. This is a serious defect from the viewpoint of supporting the design itself.

In order to design large scale and/or complex logic circuits, consistent support for both the function-level and the structure-level design is required. Therefore a logic diagram editing system considered here should also handle the functional description of blocks. There occurs an important problem how the function of a block is described. The details are discussed later in section 3.

2.3 Editing of Logic Diagrams

In order to design logic circuits interactively, powerful editing facilities of logic diagrams are required. One of the main problems to be considered is the specification of connection lines. After the logic designer puts necessary logic elements in appropriate positions, he tries to connect them. Connection is often very troublesome in most editing systems currently used because he must specify the exact positions and/or the routes of the connection lines.

It is therefore desired that editing systems provide routing facilities. If interactive routing is possible, the logic designer has only to specify the pair of terminals to be connected together. Automatic re-routing of associated lines in case of moving and deleting logic elements etc. can also lighten his burden greatly.

In addition to the routing facilities, the following connection check facilities seem to be very useful to avoid careless mistakes in interactive logic design.
(1) Test of illeagal connections which inhibits the connection between two output terminals.
(2) Indication of unconnected terminals by displaying them in a different color.
(3) Facility of displaying several terminals with associated connection lines in a different color which are logically connected with each other.

250

2.4 Logic Simulation

Logic simulation is a powerful tool to verify logic circuits. Nowadays a number of mixed-level logic simulators, which can simulate both at the function-level and at the gate-level, have been developed.

Logic simulators usually accept the input of circuit information described in some hardware description language. However the amount of description using such a language is rather large, especially the specification of connections tends to be tiresome. And what is worse for logic designers, circuits represented in languages are not easy to understand. That is, text description of a circuit is not so suitable for designers.

For these reasons, logic diagram editing systems are required to generate input data to logic simulators. In other words, they ought to translate logic diagrams into circuit informations which are acceptable by logic simulators. Since the editing systems considered here are able to support both the function-level and the structure-level design, the circuit information can also consist of the function and the structure. Therefore it is possible to test the design at any level by using a mixed-level simulator. If the function-level simulation is performed first, it serves the detection of design errors in an early stage.

3. Features and Facilities of Logic Diagram Editing System LODE

Considering the requirements described in section 2, a new logic diagram editing system LODE [9] is being developed to fulfill them. Its main purpose is to support the logic design itself and it aimes at interactive design using computer graphics instead of using papers.

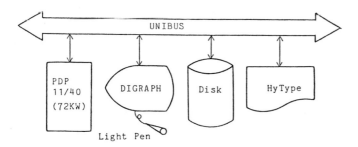

Fig.2 Hardware configuration

Figure 2 shows the hardware configuration of LODE. LODE is developed on the minicomputer PDP-11/40 with 72K word memory using extended version of MU-BASIC (Multi-User BASIC). Logic diagrams are displayed and edited on the interactive color graphic display DIGRAPH [10,11,12] which is developed in our laboratory. Black and white hard copies of logic diagrams are obtained using the Diablo HyType printer.

DIGRAPH is a television-based computer graphic display which displays pictures by 512 x 512 pixels with 8 different colors and has the merits of both random scan and raster scan displays. Although DIGRAPH utilizes a color television monitor, it is possible to manipulate DIGRAPH as a random scan graphic display device including light pen functions. That is, DIGRAPH can directly pick graphic elements using a light pen.

LODE realizes interactive logic diagram editing facilities using a light pen by making a good use of this feature of DIGRAPH. Necessary commands are given to LODE by selecting them with the light pen from the command menu displayed on the color television monitor. A diagram under editing is also displayed and a designer can point to its appropriate part directly by the light pen to modify it.

The main features of LODE are based on the discussions and the requirements in section 2. They are summarized as follows.

(1) Hierarchical logic diagrams, from high-level block diagrams to low-level logic circuit diagrams, can be manipulated in order to correspond to the hierarchy in structured logic design.

(2) To support the function-level design, LODE can handle the functional description of a block represented in a high-level language or a state transition diagram.

(3) LODE possesses routing facilities so that the logic designer can be relieved of the tedious specifications of connection lines and devote himself to his design. Furthermore, necessary re-routing caused by moving or deleting logic symbols is also maintained by LODE.

(4) LODE provides various checking facilities. They are connection check between output terminals, indication of unconnected terminals, and the facility to display the specified connection net in different color.

(5) LODE extracts circuit informations (both function and structure) from logic diagrams and provides them to a logic simulator so that logic simulation can be performed.

LODE can support the logic design much more powerfully than conventional systems due to these features.

3.1 Hierarchical Logic Diagrams

As stated before, structured logic design is advanced by repeating the division and the refinement of blocks. Rough block diagrams are used in the early stage of the design and finally logic circuit diagrams composed of well-known logic elements are drawn by logic designers. Moreover, they may utilize diagrams consisting of both blocks and logic elements in the middle of their designs.

LODE manipulates all the diagrams in use at various levels of the design. The common characteristic among these diagrams is that they are made up of symbols and lines connecting them one another. Considering this characteristic, LODE provides facilities to add, delete, and move symbols in conjunction with to draw connection lines and make changes to them automatically. Graphical representations of symbols can be also defined by using LODE.

252

Besides manipulating both block diagrams and logic circuit diagrams, LODE possesses a facility to support the process of block partitioning and block refinement. One frame on the television monitor corresponds to one block when editing a logic diagram with LODE. Consequently a block can be divided into smaller blocks by adding them to the frame and connecting them. If a logic designer decides to refine some block displayed on the screen, he has only to point the block by the light pen. The reverse of block refinement, which is called block abstraction in this paper, can be easily done as well in LODE.

LODE can not display the whole of the final design at a time since one to one correspondence between blocks and frames is kept. Hoewever, it is essentially impossible to display a large scale logic circuit on a television monitor with a limited size of screen. Consequently it is more favorable to restrict the scale of a block in this way because the logic designers can understand the blocks more easily.

3.2 Functional Description and Relation to Logic Simulator

Since block diagrams and logic circuit diagrams described above represent the structure of blocks, it is necessary to adopt other means for describing the function of blocks in order to support the function-level design as well as the structure-level design.

Flow charts, timing charts, state transition diagrams and languages etc. are usually used in practical logic design. If a logic diagram editing system is only intended for editng them and simply manipulates them like comments, it does not matter whatever is adopted. But such support of functional description is insufficient to aid the function-level design. As LODE provides functions of blocks as a part of circuit informations to a logic simulator, the exact descriptions of the functions are required. Accordingly flow charts and timing charts are not suitable and so LODE adopts state transition diagrams and languages.

State transition diagrams are similar to logic diagrams in the respect that they are also composed of symbols and lines connecting them one another. Although the symbols and the lines have a significance, they are simpler than logic diagrams in one sense because only one kind of symbol (which represents a state) is used and there are no branching points in connection lines. LODE therefore provides almost the same editing facilities for state transition diagrams as for logic diagrams. That is, the logic designer can add, delete, move symbols, connect or disconnect them etc. In this case connect means drawing a directed arc from one state to another. Furthermore, LODE provides a kind of property list associated with each connection line and/or symbol to represent input and output signals.

Functional description in some hardware description laguage is not so easy for logic designers to understand, but it is of use when describing a function by a state transition diagram is difficult. Moreover, it is suitable for representing functions in a procedural form. For these reasons LODE allows not only state transition diagrams but also languages. Considering the relation to a logic simulator, a hardware description language SHDL [13], developed in our laboratory, is adopted in LODE. The SHDL can be used for the input to an interactive simulation system ISS [14,15] and it includes the subset of PL/I for functional description.

The ISS includes a mixed-level logic simulator which can perform both function-level and gate-level simulation. LODE translates the logic diagrams and the state transition diagrams into the circuit information which is accepted by the ISS.

3.3 Routing Facilities

In logic design it is not essential how connection lines are arranged in logic diagrams, and it is much more important which terminals are connected together. Consequently logic designers need not be troubled by the routing. In order to reduce this trouble and enable them to concentrate on their designs, LODE performs the routing automatically. LODE limits connection line segments alignment with only vertical and horizontal lines.

Routing was at first studied for designing printed circuit boards and numerous routing algorithms have been proposed up to now. However, the routing for logic diagrams is different from that for printed circuit boards or master slice LSI's because the former allows intersections of vertical and horizontal lines in spite of a single layer. Furthermore, dense and short routing is required in the latter case whereas in the former case the routing easy to see is rather required. From the viewpoint of supporting the interactive logic design, fast routing algorithms are required.

Considering these characteristics of routing in logic diagrams, we have developed a new two-stage routing algorithm [16].

The first stage is a modified version of Lee's maze method [17] with depth-first search guided by some predictor function. The predictor function determines the priority of search directions. It gives the highest

O : terminal
⊗ : specified terminal   Fig.3 Example of routing

priority to the direction to the target and the second priority to the current direction of search. The direction against to the current direction is given the lowest priority, which reduces the possibility of backtracking and consequently reduces the size of search. Although this stage does not always find optimum solution (that is, the shortest pass with the least corners), it works fairly fast. Its time complexity is order n where n is a distance of two terminals to be connected if there is no obstacle.

The second stage modifies the result of the first stage. It removes loops if any and indentations as much as possible by tracing the line segments obtained in the first stage and extending them at appropriate point. Although it cannot modify the results completely, it gives reasonable connection lines in reasonable time.

In order to connect two terminals, the logic designer has only to specify them interactively using the light pen and/or the cursor. Correct routing is done as shown in Fig.3 whether the specified terminals are already connected to other terminals or not. Fig.3 (a), (b), (c) show the routing when neither of the specified terminals is connected yet, only one of them is already connected and both of them are already connected, respectively. Moreover, LODE prevents the logic designers from connecting output terminals together and it warns them if they do so by mistake.

Single delete and all delete are prepared in LODE for deleting the connection lines as shown in Fig.4. In addition, re-routing is also automatically done when a symbol is deleted or moved. The connecton lines attached to the terminals of the symbol are also deleted in the former case. As shown in Fig.5, all delete is done for each output terminal and single delete is done for each input terminal. In the latter case, the specified symbol is deleted first with associated connection lines and it is added to the new position. Then re-routing is performed so that the original connections may be maintained (refer to Fig.6).

As logic designers change connections frequently, it is very effective to support it by the facilities stated above. They contribute to smooth advancement of a logic design and shortening of time necessary for it.

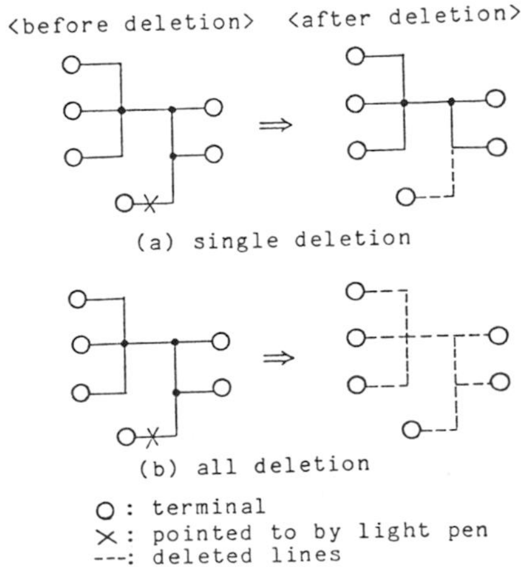

<before deletion> <after deletion>

(a) single deletion

(b) all deletion

O : terminal
X : pointed to by light pen
---: deleted lines

Fig.4 Deletion of connection lines

4. Realization of Editing Facilities and Data Structure

4.1 Logic Elements and User-Defined Blocks

When logic designers edit logic diagrams, they can use logic elements and blocks as symbols. LODE provides basic elements such as logic gates and flip-flops, and they can define any block. These symbols are stored together in the symbol library, which consists of the terminal information and display files for the symbols and is referred to by LODE when necessary.

In defining blocks, the following must be specified;
(a) as to terminals
     number, name, characteristic (input/output etc.), position;
(b) as to the graphical representations of blocks
     size, comments.
Logic designers can give necessary information to LODE by drawing a block interactively on the screen. They may append character strings as comments in the graphical representation of the block.

<before deletion>   <after deletion>

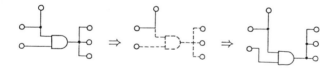

Fig.5 Deletion of a symbol

Fig.6 Moving a symbol

After the definition is completed, LODE obtains the information (a) and (b) from the picture of the block, generates necessary files and updates the symbol library. A display file and a terminal information file are created for each symbol. The former consists of relative display instructions required to display the symbol and the latter is composed in tabular form (refer to Fig.7). The first entry includes the symbol type, the number of terminals and its size. The symbol type takes a value of either "S" or "U" depending on whether the symbol is provided by LODE or by users. The size is utilized to make obstacles in routing process when the block is added to the screen. Subsequent entries consist of terminal names, characteristics and positions (in relative coordiates with respect to the symbol's origin).

The basic logic elements provided by LODE are stored in the same format as the user-defined blocks described above, except that the symbol type is "S" in this case. The symbol type "S" means that the farther block refinement is impossible.

4.2 Display File Organization

In order to display a picture on DIGRAPH, necessary display instructions (display file) must be created in the buffer area for display files and executed by it. A symbol is displayed by a number of display instructions, and so it is necessary to deal with them as a whole in manipulating the symbol. Furthermore, the same symbols often appear in a logic diagram. For these reasons, LODE realizes a symbol as a display subroutine in the display file. Therefore a display subroutine is held in common for the identical symbols.

The connection lines and the command menu are displayed on the screen when a logic diagram is being edited. Editing of a diagram is realized by changing the display file, the screen, and the contents of various data structures which are described later. As Fig.8 shows, the buffer area for the display file is divided into four regions, namely the connection line region, the symbol region, the display subroutine region and the region for working and the command menu.

symbol type	number of terminals	symbol	size
name	character-istic	Δx	Δy
¦	¦	¦	¦

Fig.7 Terminal information file

$(\Delta x, \Delta y)$ represents the terminal position in relative coordinates.

In the connection line region, the display instructions which define the start point and draw the line are created. These instructions are all ABVT's (Absolute Vector: this displays an on/off line from the current beam position to the specified position) and so four words (one word = two bytes) are always necessary per every line. The symbol region consists of the display instructions which decide the position of the symbol and call the display subroutine corresponding to it. As shown in Fig.8, every symbol requires five words. The display file stored in the symbol library is loaded in the display subroutine region if necessary.

It is true that the display file organization described above is not optimum because the created display file is not always the shortest, but it also possesses the following advantages.

(1) Faster processing is possible when a light pen hit occurs owing to the division of the buffer area into the four regions. When a light pen hit occurs, DIGRAPH executes the specified display instructions in order to

obtain the picture element pointed to by the light pen. As LODE always knows which is pointed to by the light pen (a symbol, a connection line, or a command), DIGRAPH has only to execute the display instructions in the related region.

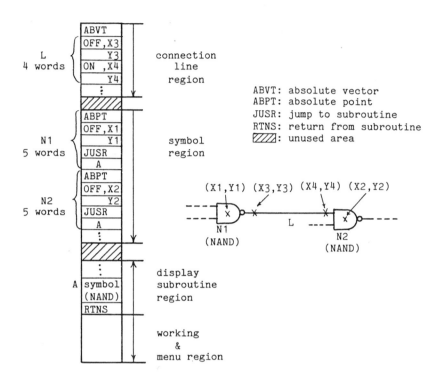

Fig.8 Display file organization

(2) LODE can obtain directly the index to the symbol or the connection line segment pointed to by the light pen from the address of the associated display instruction which is given by DIGRAPH. This is because there is one-to-one correspondence between the display file and the data structure described later.

(3) It is easy to move a symbol because only the change of (x,y) coordinates, which specify its position, is necessary.

(4) It is possible to add the display instructions to the free area effectively. As four or five words become free when a deletion is done, it is easy to place the display instructions for other lines or symbols exactly there.

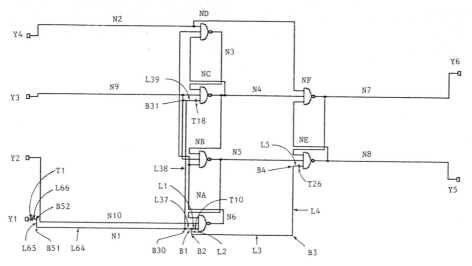

Fig.9 Sample logic diagram

Name	Module	Type	Size		Position		#Terminals	Address	Pointer
Y1	1EXT	S	1,1	−1,−1	−1	22	1	32016	1
Y2	1EXT	S	1,1	−1,−1	−1	44	1	32016	2
Y3	1EXT	S	1,1	−1,−1	−1	66	1	32016	3
Y4	1EXT	S	1,1	−1,−1	−1	88	1	32016	4
Y5	3EXT	S	1,1	−1,−1	124	38	1	31996	5
Y6	3EXT	S	1,1	−1,−1	124	76	1	31996	6
NA	3NAND	S	3,3	−2,−3	50	21	4	31868	7
NB	3NAND	S	3,3	−2,−3	50	44	4	31868	11
NC	3NAND	S	3,3	−2,−3	50	67	4	31868	15
ND	3NAND	S	3,3	−2,−3	50	90	4	31868	19
NE	3NAND	S	3,3	−2,−3	80	44	4	31868	23
NF	3NAND	S	3,3	−2,−3	80	67	4	31868	27

Fig.10 Symbol table

4.3 Data Structure

In order to edit a logic diagram, LODE requires the data on the symbols,
the connection lines, the branching points (both fan-out points and corner
points are called branching points) and the nets. In LODE these data are
managed in tabular form and each table for a sample logic diagram (refer to
Fig.9) is described below. The logic diagram consists of 6 external
terminals (Y1-Y6), 6 logic elements (NA-NF) and 10 nets (N1-N10). The
branching point number (Bi), terminal number (Ti), and line segment number
(Li) relating to the net N1 are also illustrated in Fig.9.

259

4.3.1 Symbol Table (Refer to Fig.10)

For every symbol displayed on the screen, its name, the module name, the symbol type, its size, the absolute position, the number of terminals, the starting address of the corresponding display subroutine and the pointer to the first terminal of the symbol in the terminal table are stored. External input/output terminals are also regarded as symbols with one terminal and so they are registered in this table.

	Name	Characteristic	Position		LP	NP
1	CLR	EXT INPUT	1	22	66	1
2	DATA	EXT INPUT	1	44	71	10
3	CLK	EXT INPUT	1	66	74	9
4	PR	EXT INPUT	1	88	63	2
5	QN	EXT OUTPUT	122	38	84	8
6	Q	EXT OUTPUT	122	76	81	7
7	O1	OUTPUT	54	21	36	6
8	I1	INPUT	47	23	26	5
9	I2	INPUT	47	21	67	10
10	I3	INPUT	47	19	1	1
11	O1	OUTPUT	54	44	22	5
12	I1	INPUT	47	46	30	4
13	I2	INPUT	47	44	52	9
14	I3	INPUT	47	42	31	6
15	O1	OUTPUT	54	67	21	4
16	I1	INPUT	47	69	15	3
17	I2	INPUT	47	67	55	9
18	I3	INPUT	47	65	40	1
19	O1	OUTPUT	54	90	11	3
20	I1	INPUT	47	92	6	2
21	I2	INPUT	47	90	60	6
22	I3	INPUT	47	88	16	4
23	O1	OUTPUT	84	44	51	8
24	I1	INPUT	77	46	45	7
25	I2	INPUT	77	44	78	5
26	I3	INPUT	77	42	5	1
27	O1	OUTPUT	84	67	41	7
28	I1	INPUT	77	69	10	2
29	I2	INPUT	77	67	76	4
30	I3	INPUT	77	65	46	8

Fig.11 Terminal table

4.3.2 Terminal Table (Refer to Fig.11)

Each entry consists of the terminal name, its characteristic (input or output etc.), its absolute position and two pointers (LP and NP) to the connection line table and the net table. LP points one of the connection line segments which are attached to the terminal directly. NP points the net in which the terminal is included. If it is equal to zero, it means that the terminal is not connected to other terminals yet.

260

4.3.3 Branching Point Table (Refer to Fig.12)

This table stores the data for each branching point on its degree, absolute position and the pointer LP and NP. LP and NP have the same meanings as in the terminal table. As only vertical and horizontal lines are allowed, the minimum and maximum value of the degree is two and four respectively. It is used to decide whether a fan-out symbol is displayed or not. Indices to this table are represented as negative integer in other tables to distinguish between terminals and branching points.

	Degree	Position		LP	NP
1	3	47	19	1	1
2	2	47	17	2	1
3	2	76	17	3	1
4	2	76	42	4	1
5	3	47	92	6	2
30	3	45	19	37	1
31	2	45	65	38	1
51	2	2	19	64	1
52	2	2	22	65	1
53	2	46	21	67	10

Fig.12 Branching point table

4.3.4 Connection Line Table (Refer to Fig.13)

For each line segment constructing the connection lines, the start and end points represented by the indices of terminals or branching points and two pointers to this table are stored. The pointers are utilized to express the connected lines in a circular list.

	Pointer1	Start Point	End Point	Pointer2
1	0	10	−1	37
2	1	−1	−2	3
3	2	−2	−3	4
4	3	−3	−4	5
5	0	26	−4	4
37	2	−1	−30	64
38	37	−30	−31	39
39	0	18	−31	38
64	38	−30	−51	65
65	64	−51	−52	66
66	0	1	−52	65

Fig.13 Connection line table

<u>4.3.5 Net Table</u> (Refer to Fig.14)

This table consists of the output terminal, the input terminal list and the branching point list for the nets. In case of bi-directional nets, one of the terminals in the net is selected as output terminal for convenience' sake, and the others are registered at the input terminal lists.

There is some redundancy in these tables, but it serves to facilitate editing of logic diagrams. In order to perform the routing, a frame buffer preserving the contents of the display is also utilized.

	Output Terminal	Input Terminals	Branching Points
1	1	10,26,18	1,2,3,4,30,31,32,51,52
2	4	20,28	5,6,7,8,49,50
3	19	16	9,10,11,12
4	15	22,12,29	13,14,15,16,17,22,23,24,59
5	11	8,25	18,19,20,21,60
6	7	14,21	25,26,27,28,29,45,46,47,48
7	27	24,6	33,34,35,36,61,62
8	23	30,5	37,38,39,40,41,63,64
9	3	13,17	42,43,44,57,58
10	2	9	53,54,55,56

<u>Fig.14</u> Net table

<u>4.4 Symbol Manipulation</u>

The logic designer can add, delete and move the symbols in order to edit logic diagrams. The operations which LODE executes for realizing each command are described below.

When a logic designer tries to add a symbol in a logic diagram, he must specify its name and position by the cursor first. Then LODE searches its module name in the symbol table. If it is found, the corresponding display subroutine already exists in the buffer and therefore it is not necessary to load it from the symbol library. If not found, it has to transfer the necessary display file from the library. After the required display subroutine is ready, LODE creates display instructions to call it (refer to Fig.8), updates the symbol table and the terminal table, orders DIGRAPH to display the symbol in the EX-OR mode (the exclusive-or operation between the color data in the current and new picture, is performed bit by bit) and checks if the symbol overlaps with other symbols and/or connection lines. This check is done by examining the frame buffer. If an overlap occurs, LODE abandons the symbol and erases it by displaying it in the EX-OR mode again. As $(C \oplus C') \oplus C'$ is equivalent to C, the screen can be restored to the previous one.

When a delete command is given, LODE waits until the symbol to be deleted is pointed to by the light pen. DIGRAPH searches the display instruction corresponding to the picture picked by the light pen. As a symbol is displayed using a display subroutine, this search succeeds within some display subroutine. At this time the return address is saved in the

stack of DIGRAPH and is available to LODE. The index of the specified
symbol can be obtained very easily since one to one correspondence between
the symbol index and the return address exists. When the symbol is
identified in this way, it is erased using the EX-OR mode and the
connection lines connected to its terminals are deleted. Then LODE updates
the frame buffer. Lastly the related tables are renewed.

Re-routing is necessary when a symbol is moved. However it takes much
time and the resultant logic diagram often changes completely if it is
performed from the very beginning. Consequently LODE only executes the
related re-routing in the following manner. When LODE is commanded to move
a symbol, it executes the same as it does in deleting a symbol. Then it
waits until a new position is specified and performs re-routing so that the
original connections can be kept. The terminals to be connected one another
are obtained from the net table.

4.5 Manipulation of Connection Lines

Because the scope of the light pen is rather longer than the shortest
distance between two terminals, the following approach is adopted to
specify a pair of terminals to be connected. When a logic designer gives a
CONNECT command to LODE, it requests him to point by the light pen to the
symbol which has the terminal to be connected. If some symbole is
specified, it displays the cursor at one terminal of the symbol. He has to
select YES/NO from the command menu according as the terminal indicated by
the cursor is the expected one or not. If NO is selected, LODE moves the
cursor to another terminal and waits for his respose. Thus the terminal is
interactively determined. When YES is selected, all these steps are
repeated again to choose the other terminal.

After the two terminals are designated in this way, LODE examines the
terminal table to see whether the specified terminals are already connected
to other terminals or not (refer to Fig.3). If none of them are connected
yet, the routing algorithm described in section 3 is applied to these
terminals. Otherwise, the branching points which are logically connected to
the specified terminals are taken into consideration and a pair of points
with shortest distance are selected. Then the routing algorithm is applied
to these points. LODE displays the connection lines and updates the
terminal table, branching point table, connection line table and net table.
If the degree of some branching point is changed from two into three, LODE
also displays a fan-out symbol.

In case of cutting some connection line, it is first decided which is to
be performed, single delete or all delete. Then LODE waits for the designer
to point to a connection line by the light pen and obtains its index from
the address of the display instruction which corresponds to the pointed
line. As one to one correspondence between the index and the address
exists, the index is easily found. If single delete is specified, LODE
obtains a path whose start and end points are a terminal or a branching
point of degree three or more, from the connection line table and the
branching point table. In the case of all delete, LODE finds all the lines
that connect with the specified line logically. Then LODE erases the
obtained lines and renews the related tables. It also erases fan-out
symbols if necessary.

5. Example and Evaluation

As stated before, LODE is developed in an extended version of MU-BASIC. The BASIC program area available is 16K words large, which is too small for LODE. Therefore LODE adopts an overlay structure and its total size will be about 5000 BASIC statements long. The tables necessary for editing the logic diagrams, which are described in section 4, can not be stored in the main memory on account of the small size of the program area. Consequently LODE manages them on a disk as files.

LODE does not always operate fast for these reasons. Especially the file I/O's are not so fast in BASIC. The files corresponding to the tables are copied as the working files before editing in LODE. This was performed in BASIC before and it took a fairly long time for processing some commands. For example, loading an entire new block sometimes took more than three minutes. In order to improve this response time, an assembly language subroutine for copying which is callable from LODE, is developed. Currently about one and a half minutes are required for the same operation.

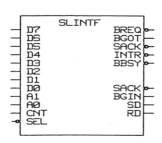

Fig.15 Circuit to be designed

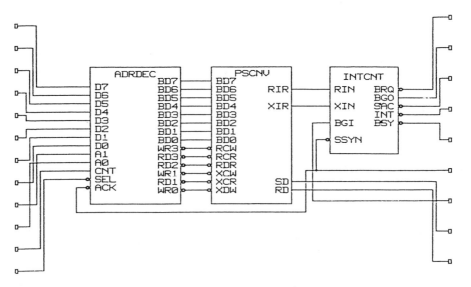

Fig.16 Logic diagram of SLINTF

264

Although the speed of LODE is not always high as described above, it can respond to basic commands (which execute only a small number of file I/O's) within a few seconds. For instance, an addition of new symbols to the screen requires about two or three seconds till the symbol appears on the screen, and routing can be done within about ten seconds at most in comparatively simple cases. As LODE often executes these basic operations when a logic designer develops his design by editing the logic diagram, LODE can support his design sufficiently. Accordingly it accomplishes its main purpose of supporting the logic design itself apart from the speed.

An example of the design using LODE and some problems are discussed hereafter. Fig.15, Fig.16 and Fig.17 show the hard copies of the logic diagrams displayed on the television monitor. The circuit to be designed is named SLINTF (refer to Fig.15), which is divided into three blocks ADRDEC, PSCNV and INTCNT as shown in Fig.16. Then the block INTCNT is designed with well-known logic elements as shown in Fig.17. It took about thirty minutes at most to edit them.

From the experience in editing them, three problems are found. The first is that it takes more time than expected to define graphical representaions of symbols. Currently a logic designer is free to place any character string for comments as a part of graphical representations. Its position is specified by the cursor, but the positioning is rather tiresome. Since characters are often put close to the terminals, it will be favorable if the cursor moves to the terminal position automatically.

The second problem occurs when specifiying the terminals to be connected. As described in section 4, the cursor is displayed at the terminals in order. Therefore it sometimes takes much time until the desired terminal is indicated by the cursor in case of a symbol with many

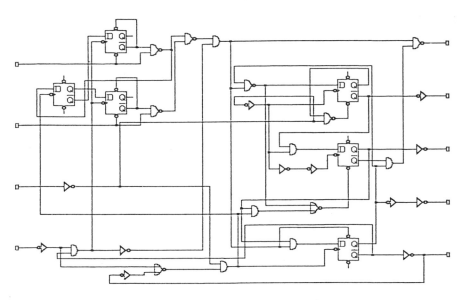

Fig.17 Logic diagram of INTCNT

terminals. Direct specification by the terminal name or the light pen may be a solution and is under consideration.

The last one relates to the routing. The routing is entirely performed automatically in LODE, and therefore it is beyond the designer's control. As it is difficult to obtain always the aesthetically pleasing routing automatically, the manual routing should be allowed. Another idea to solve this is to introduce a virtual obstacle and a virtual terminal. The former makes an area where routing is forbidden in spite of no symbol and the latter serves as a guide point. That is, the logic designer can control rather easily the result of automatic routing by using them.

6. Concluding Remarks

LODE differs from conventional logic diagram editing systms in the respect that it gives positive aid to logic design. Its ultimate goal is to enable the logic designers to carry on their work directly on the television monitor without using papers.

For this purpose, LODE manipulates the hierarchical logic diagrams corresponding to the process of structured logic design and handles functional description using a state transition diagram or the hardware description language in order to support the function-level design, which is hardly supported by conventional editing systems. LODE provides powerful editing facilities using a light pen by making a good use of DIGRAPH. Its routing facility contributes greatly to the reduction of troublesome in editing logic diagrams. Furthermore, it gives the circuit information to a logic simulator so as to test the design easily. Although it does not always run fast, it is suitable enough for practical use because it can respond to basic commands given by the light pen within two or three seconds.

There are at least three extensions which will be of use. The first is to allow manual routing as well. If the result of automatic routing is not agreeable to the logic designer, he can do it as he desires. The second is to represent a number of connection lines by a single line. This serves to reduce the number of connections to be specified and is useful especially in drawing block diagrams at a very high level. The third is to display the design hierarchy on the screen. The logic designer will be able to grasp the current state of the design easily from it.

Acknowledgement

The authors would like to express their sincere appreciation to Mr. Y. Aoki and Mr. S. Shindo who have developed editing facilities of LODE in BASIC and to Mr. N. Konda and Mr. M. Ito who have implemented routing facilities in LODE. They are also grateful to Assoc. Prof. Y. Kambayashi and Mr. H. Yasuura for their numerous suggestions and encouragement. Furthermore, thanks are due to all the members of Prof. Yajima's research group for their useful comments and discussions. This research is supported in part by the Ministry of Education, Science, and Culture of Japan under a Science Foundation Grant.

References

1. R.Rutman, Proc. 13th Design Automation Conf., pp.392-398 (1976).
2. P.Villers, Proc. 15th Design Automation Conf., pp.446-453 (1978).
3. H.M.Bayegan, Proc. 15th Design Automation Conf., pp.1-8 (1978).
4. L.C.Widdoes and T.M.McWiliams, Proc. 15th Design Automation Conf., pp.271-277 (1978).
5. W.M.VanCleemput, Digest of Papers of IEEE Compcon, Feb., pp.139-142 (1978).
6. M.Ishii, Papers of Technical Group, IECE Japan, EC80-16 (1980).
7. A.Bechtolsheim, Proc. 15th Design Automation Conf., pp.261-263 (1978).
8. K.A.Duke and K.Maling, Proc. 17th Design Automation Conf., pp.318-327 (1980).
9. Y.Aoki, Master Thesis, Dept. Information Science, Kyoto Univ. (1981).
10. H.Hiraishi, K.Kawakubo, and S.Yajima, Proc. 3rd EUROMICRO Symp., pp.66-73 (1977).
11. H.Hiraishi and S.Yajima, Trans. IPS Japan, Vol.22, No.1, pp.36-43 (1981).
12. H.Hiraishi and S.Yajima, JIP Japan, Vol.4, No.4, pp.10-18 (1982).
13. Y.Ono, Bachelor Thesis, Dept. Information Science, Kyoto Univ. (1981).
14. Y.Tsuchida, Master Thesis, Dept. Information Science, Kyoto Univ. (1981).
15. T.Sakai, Master Thesis, Dept. Information Science, Kyoto Univ. (1982).
16. N.Konda, Bachelor Thesis, Dept. Information Science, Kyoto Univ. (1981).
17. C.Y.Lee, IRE Trans. Electronic Computers, Vol.EC-10, pp.346-365 (1961).

Extended Graphic Functions of the A-IDAS System for Visual Design

H. Matsuka, S. Uno, and K. Sugimoto

Tokyo Scientific Center, IBM Japan Ltd.
Roppongi, Tokyo 106, Japan

J. Takama

Science and Engineering Faculty, Waseda University

ABSTRACT

Recently a remarkable progress was seen in computer graphics. In addition to a traditional vector-type graphic device, the debut and popularization of a raster-type color one signify the said progress. Computer graphics are expanding not only in CAD fields but also in visual application fields as landscape simulation, computer art, animation, etc. With this background, we introduce a visual design system which applys computer graphics to a visual environment planning/designing area.

This paper discusses the arrangement of requirements for a visual design system and deals with graphic functions of the A-IDAS system. In addition, the color system with the HVC (Hue, Value, Chroma) and RGB (Red, Green, Blue) is introduced for easy manipulation of natural color spectrum. Image processing techniques necessary to a visual design system are also mentioned with realistic examples. This visual design system will be a powerful tool with regard to a visual environment planning/design, especially a townscape design, a landscape design, an interior design and a thematic map production.

1. INTRODUCTION

A visual design system is a system to visualize a designed object at each design stage in a proper form to fully play the visual decision ability of a designer or a non-specialist.

The reasons why a visual design system has become a necessary tool are as follows. The users or the regional inhabitants were changing their attitudes toward demanding a qualitative improvement of environment against the buildings. Therefore, the specialists of architecture and civil engineering must explain in advance effects and impacts of the construction project upon the environments for them. In addition, if the scale of the construction project is expanded, the number of the regional inhabitants who are affected adversely increase and at the same time, their interests are complicated. This will result in the difficulty to obtain a consensus, unless the voices of these inhabitants are reflected and adjusted.

That is, a visual design system must give not only an engineering drawing or a working drawing applicable to the specialists but also a presentation material about a designed object, in which other people can easily understand and comment. It must also provide an interactive system which assesses the effects of the designed object upon the peripheral environment.

However, the conventional visual design systems, that is, analog systems such as photomontage and color simulation, are not necessarily satisfied to produce a realistical illustration or a conceptual picture for visual evaluation about the designed object.

In order to build a better visual design system, computer graphics are useful tools due to their easy utilization and easy operation. This paper introduces a visual design system which utilizes computer graphics in such visual design fields as regional environment, landscape, townscape and interior.

2. REQUIREMENTS FOR VISUAL DESIGN SYSTEM

As to the visual expression about designed information, the following requirements are sought.

(1) Visuality and reality of designed information

A wireframe picture for representing, for instance, an outline of a building or its peripheral site, etc. would be sufficient for checking its engineering specifications. However, it is insufficient in visually evaluating the beauty and harmony about the building and its peripheral site. In the future, shaded pictures and colored pictures incorporating a scenery or a texture will be important.

(2) Simplification and composition of designed information

As to information concerning the regional environment, there is information which is easily formatted and information which is not easily formatted. In addition, much effort is required to collect it. Therefore, it is desirable to establish an image database (unformatted data) together with a shape or graphic database (formatted data) by systematically storing regional environment information and to extract/process the information when necessary.

On these databases, formatted information should be collectively analyzed and processed after the assembly of its characteristics. Then only required items are expressed as a single subject (e.g. digital thematic map) and various items with different features are overlayed and expressed for indicating the mutual influence of these items (e.g. potential map for suitable location). As to unformatted information, its characteristics as an image should be analyzed, extracted and displayed as an edited information, if possible. Moreover, it is necessary to superimpose the designed shape data on this image.

(3) Manipulation and integration of designed information

In order to satisfy as various requests as possible for the designed object, it is desirable to display the analyzed data in the form of a picture or a graph and to refine the alternative plan through interactive evaluation and decision. That is, a visual design system should be accepted as one of subsystems of an interactive CAD system, based on which design information is produced as conceptual picture with visuality and reality. For this reason, it is required that the system should be designed under a general purpose CAD system which can easily be linked to various types of the subsystems, not under a turn key system designed for a specific problem.

3. BASIC FUNCTION OF THE A-IDAS SYSTEM

To build a visual design system, the A-IDAS (Advanced Integrated Designers' Activity Support) system can become an important nucleus. The A-IDAS system is a general tool for building up a specific CAD system. It supports a series of management facilities.

(1) Database management to uniformly store a designed object as 2-D/3-D geometric models (Matsuka, 1979).

(2) Graphic management to control graphic devices of a vector-type display and of a raster-type display and to convert a geometric model to 2-D picture representation.

(3) Command management to control application programs in the form of menus.

Under these facilities, various application systems such as systems building design (Matsuka, 1980.a), road design (Matsuka, 1980.b) and regional planning (Matsuka, 1981) are implemented. These systems are interactively operated as one of users of VM/CMS (Virtual Machine/Conversational Monitor System) under IBM S370/158.

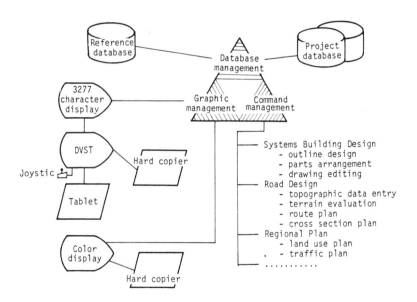

Fig. 3.1 Configuration of A-IDAS System

As shown in Fig. 3.1, the A-IDAS system has three display devices: a direct view storage tube (DVST) to display a wireframe picture, a raster type color display device to display a color image and IBM 3277 character display device to deal with menus.

270

The DVST is equipped with a tablet and a joy stick for input. The raster-type color display device has three buffer memories with 16 levels, 512 x 480 pixels, and can display the 3 pieces contents of the buffer memories simultaneously or an individual buffer. Each device has a hard copy unit.

The DVST is directly attached to the character display device via IBM 3277 Graphic Attachment. The color display device is shared with other CMS users and dedicatedly attached to a single user on demand.

In this section, the functions centering around the graphic and command managements are described, emphasizing how effective they are to build a visual design system.

3.1 Graphic Management Facility

Graphic management facility provides device-independent graphics (DIG) as an attempt to standardize graphic routines. The DIG interface is classified into basic interface for line drawings onto both DVST and color display device and special one for area drawings as well as tablet input (Uno, 1979).

Basic Interface

- Device Control: To declare device selection, device reset and device mode.

- Window and Viewport: To set the correspondence between a user coordinates and a screen coordinates. The screen coordinates system takes the range of ($0 \leq U$, $V \leq 1$) called "logical coordinates (U, V)". If the lower left corner and the upper right corner of the rectangular area in each coordinates are specified, coefficients for coordinates conversion are decided in such manner that these rectangles may correspond to each other. The rectangular becomes a scissoring boundary for output.

- Output: Output data is specified in the user coordinates system. Basic output functions provided by the DIG are move, position, draw line, draw poly-line, write alphanumeric characters, write kanji characters and end output. It is expected that curves, etc. be prepared by the user as a set of poly-line if necessary. Output is converted to data stream proper to the selected device by the DIG and is kept into the DIG buffer. End output transfers the buffer data to the actual device.

- Attribute Setting: To specify an attribute for output. Color attribute is specified by the value of R(red), G(green) and B(blue) and is effective when a color display device is selected. Line attribute represents the setting of the type of lines (solid line, dotted line, etc.) and the thickness of line. Character attribute represents character size, character spacing and rotation angle.

- Input: To request input from device. Coordinates input is only provided by the DIG. The coordinate values to be returned are already converted to the user coordinates system.

- File Control: To control two types of files: projection file (PF) and display file (DF). The PF is a device-independent data stream passed through the DIG. On the other hand, the DF is device-dependent data stream ready to be transferred to the specified device.

Special Interface

- Area Drawing: An area drawing is achieved by a hatch of a closed loop. If coordinates data of the closed loop and the inclination and interval of parallel lines are specified, the coordinates values of the crossing points between the line and the closed loop are returned one after another. Then if this line is passed through the DIG basic interface, a hatch to the loop is produced. By setting the interval of lines to "1", area painting is accomplished.

  As a new interface for an area drawing, it is possible to distribute a color spectrum (or a grey level) on the line segment. This is to similarly distribute a provided spectrum on a raster occupied by the line segment. If this function is used in combination with the area painting function mentioned above, a picture bearing a continuous color change can be displayed.

- Tablet Input: On a tablet, an arbitrary number of menus can be registered at an arbitrary position. For a menu, a definition file where its form is described should be prepared beforehand. In this file, information on the actual size of the menu, the local coordinates system (grid system), the position of each menu item, the name of an item to be returned to a program, and a subroutine linked to that item, are described. As a tablet input function, there are two different types of interface. One is for the selection of a menu, i.e. demanding an operator to select a menu item. At that time, an item name described in the definition file is returned to a program. It is possible for the program to demand execution of a subroutine linked to the item through a subroutine execution function of the DIG. The other interface is for coordinates input. In this case, coordinates values in the user coordinate system are returned to a program. The operator can select a menu item even when coordinates input is demanded. At that time, a notice to such effect that the menu was selected and an item name are returned to the program. The program may terminate processing or demand execution of a linked subroutine according to item name.

3.2 Command Management Facility

In the interactive graphics, it is necessary to provide operator interface. In the A-IDAS, this mechanism is achieved by command management.

Command management provides user-defined **hierarchical command structure.** Commands available at the current hierarchical level are displayed in the form of menu on the character display device. Thus command management looks like menu-driven system to an operator. The operator can enter into a more detailed menu of the lower level by selecting a command item from a roughly classified menu of the upper level. It is easy to return to any higher level. Menu items are classified into three types.

(1) Execution of program: a program which is declared in menu definition is executed.

(2) Entering into one level lower.

(3) Returning to one level higher.

   Besides commands displayed in the current menu, higher level commands are also accepted by keying the name. Simply entering the name, higher level menu is resumed where the entered command belongs. Or entering the name with a system command, the command is treated as if it belonged to current menu, i.e. a program is executed remaining at current level or lower level menu is encountered though it was a higher one.

   Another system command allows dynamic execution of a program. It is possible to execute application programs without registering them as a menu. Due to this function, the system becomes expandable, flexible and maintainable.

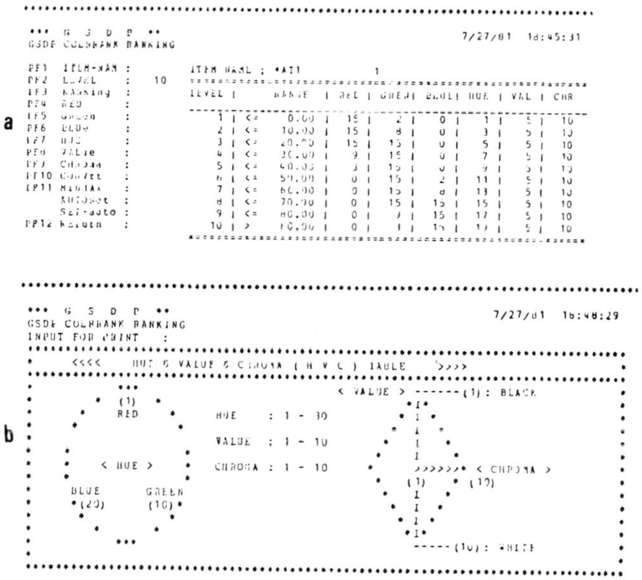

Fig. 3.2 Screen Format

(A) Primary Screen (B) Secondary Screen

   Command management supports primary and secondary screen formats (Fig. 3.2). The menu is displayed on the primary screen, whereas the secondary screen is used by an application program, permitting free display of message and data. In the case of the primary screen, the display area of the menu is composed of local commands and global commands. The global command is always displayed at each hierarchical level though it is registered ones. It is therefore recommendable to define a frequently used menu as a global command.

The A-IDAS system provides the following six standard menu groups.

(1)   Database-related menu group ("DB").

(2)   Graphic device control-related menu group ("Device").

(3)   Projection related-menu group ("Project").

(4)   Output-related menu group ("Output").

(5)   Retrieve-related menu group ("Retrieve").

(6)   Graphic edit-related menu group ("Edit").

   In addition to these menu groups, application menus for solving specific problems should be prepared.

4.   EXTENDED GRAPHIC FUNCTION FOR VISUAL DESIGN

The graphic function of the A-IDAS system can display the shape of a design-ed object in the form a black-white line drawings and a color line drawings (Uno, 1979). However, in order to produce a scenery picture with high visu-ality and reality based on a designed object or prepare a new image by over-laying various thematic images, a function is not sufficient. For this reason, a menu group related to an image processing function is added as an application subsystem of the A-IDAS so that the visual design system may be substantiated. Here, of the visual design system's functions, the important functions, i.e. color system, output of attribute data for a geometric model and image processing function are explained, citing the actual cases of a visual environment project.

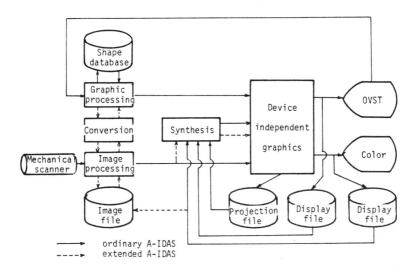

Fig. 4.1 Graphic Environment for Visual Design System

274

4.1 Color System

The color system widely used for the color display device is a RGB system.
It is unfamiliar to a user, because he does not know what RGB component a
color is composed of. He first thinks of hue, then contrast (chroma) and
brightness (value). Therefore, it is necessary to develop a mutual conversion system with the existing RGB system for the color system of such nature,
i.e. HVC (Hue, Value, Chroma).

RGB System

In the RGB system, a color system is treated as a cube having three axes as
shown in Fig. 4.2(A). Those which have the maximum intensity of only one
component are red, green and blue, those which have the maximum intensity of
two components, yellow, cyan and magenta, and those which have the maximum
and minimum intensity of three components white and black, respectively. If
each component has 16 levels of intensity, 4,096 different colors are expressed.

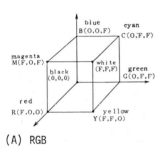

(A) RGB

Fig. 4.2 Color System

(B) HVC

HVC System

In the HVC system, hue is represented by an annulus, value by a vertical
axis and chroma or saturation by a distance from the vertical axis on the
vertical section of the cone (Fig. 4.2(B)).

Red, green and blue are arranged clockwise in the annulus. At the maximum radius of the annulus (or maxium chroma), relation between hue and RGB
component is derived by the following formula.

$$
r = \begin{cases} 1 & (0 \le h \le \pi/3,\ 5\pi/3 \le h \le 2\pi) \\ 2-3h/ & (\pi/3 \le h \le 2\pi/3) \\ 0 & (2\pi/3 \le h \le 4\pi/3) \\ 3h/\pi-4 & (4\pi/3 \le h \le 5\pi/3) \end{cases}
$$

$$
g = \begin{cases} 3h/\pi & (0 \le h \le \pi/3) \\ 1 & (\pi/3 \le h \le \pi) \\ 4-3h/\pi & (\pi \le h \le 4\pi/3) \\ 0 & (4\pi/3 \le h \le 2\pi) \end{cases} \qquad \ldots\ldots(4.1)
$$

$$
b = \begin{cases} 0 & (0 \le h \le 2\pi/3) \\ 3h/\pi-2 & (2\pi/3 \le h \le \pi) \\ 1 & (\pi \le h \le 5\pi/3) \\ 6-3h/\pi & (5\pi/3 \le h \le 2\pi) \end{cases}
$$

where h: Angle of hue (radian from red)

As to value, achromatic colors ranging from black (0) to white (1) are designated as a vertical axis of the cone. As to chroma, the maximum value of chroma is set on the circumference of an intermediate value (0.5) between black and white and the radius is designated as absolute chroma.

In addition, if this radius is regarded as a ratio against the maximum chroma, it will be possible to treat it as a column possessed by the lower plane of black color and the upper plane of white color without definition of chroma. Here an optional color will be set on the column's surface by indicating hue, value and relative chroma.

$$[R,G,B] = \begin{cases} \{(1-c)[1,1,1]/2 + c[r,g,b]\} *2v & (0 \le v \le 1/2) \\ \{(1-c)[1,1,1]/2 + c[r,g,b]\} & (1/2 \le v \le 1) \\ +\{(1+c)[1,1,1]/2 - c[r,g,b]\} *(2v-1) \end{cases} \quad \dots\dots(4.2)$$

where (r, g, b): Calculated results by formula (4.1)
         v : Value
         c : Relative chroma

The formulas (4.1), (4.2) represent a conversion formula from HVC color system to RGB color system (Photo. 4.1, 4.2). It is, however, impossible to convert from RGB color system to HVC color system from these formulas. Then as shown in Fig. 4.2(B), if it is considered that edges indicated in bold lines correspond to a hue ring of pure color in the HVC color system, it is possible to make an approximate inverse conversion (Takama, 1981).

4.2 Pictorial Output from Shape Database

The A-IDAS system has a function to display a 2-D area picture through projection of a geometric model (Matsuka, 1980.a). Here, the output representation about an attribute data of the geometric model is introduced.

As for quantitative expression about the attribute data, two types of the method are conceivable: ranking classification map for representing level-classified attribute data and graph for representing the magnitudes of the data (Matsuka, 1981).

Output of Ranking Classification Map

The classification menus for which attribute data is classified by level are shown in Fig. 3.1(A). It is possible to set colors under either RGB or HVC system against classes optionally sorted by some levels. In addition, it is possible to indicate the results in the right area of the menu screen. However, in order to determine continuous colors according to altitude; for example from a plain (green) to a mountain (dark brown) as seen in a topographic map, technical skill is required. For this purpose, an automatic coloring command for the automatic determination of a color path through color induction against a middle level is prepared (Photo 4.3). This picture shows that various delicate color ranks can simply be set by this command. Photo. 4.4 shows altitude classification map colored at the command. This map represents the color tone used in "Japan Atlas Book".

A visible and invisible area map is shown in Photo. 4.5 as an application example of topographical classification map. This map shows the results of an invisible area indicated by darker tone as viewed from the upper mountain top, computed based on a terrain model and overlayed on an altitude classification map.

It is also possible to output a ranking classification map on the DVST as a hatching pattern instead of color ranking.

Thus, an output with high quality is obtained under this system.

Output of Graph

As to the type of graph, a circular graph and a bar graph can be produced. Attribute items constituting a graph are displayed in such manner that items are expressed split or aligned widthwise (Photo. 4.6).

4.3 Image Processing from Image File

Image processing capability is extended to the A-IDAS system for producing image picture with high reality and visuality based on a designed object. This process is composed of a basic processing for image editing and application processing for scenery picture production.

Image data which are converted to digital values in multi levels of RGB components or monochromatic levels are stored as sequential data in an image file. As a basic function for processing an image data, the following menu groups are prepared.

- File-related menu group: Image data or its subset of a rectangular area, optionally specified can be read into a system working area from a sequential file on a disk or a tape, or the processed results can be written back.

- Image data analysis-related menu group: Image data in an arbitrary region of a displayed image picture are statistically analyzed for RGB, HVC, or specified color components. The statistical data such as intensity distribution, average value, standard deviation, highest frequency value, etc. are displayed on the character display device.

- Expansion/Reduction-related menu group: Original data are interpolated by expansion, or eliminated by reduction for display.

- Image data edit-related menu group: Transfer, rotation, mirror image and repetition are performed for the partial image of a displayed image.

- Color change-related menu group: Hue, value and chroma are changed for a partial image.

  Photo. 4.7 shows a marble's texture having these basic functions (reduction - repetition - color change)

- Geometric deformation-related menu group: The shape is deformed by means of a linear transformation (Affain) or perspective transformation of image data.

- Features extraction-related menu group: An image mask is formed by extracting an area from a partial image with the help of a cluster of the following color components.

(a) R, G, B
(b) R/(R+G+B), G/(R+G+B), B/(R+G+B)
(c) R-G, G-B, B-R
(d) (R+G)/2, (G+B)/2, (B+R)/2
(e) R-(G+B)/2, G-(B+R)/2, B-(R+G)/2
(f) H, V, C
(g) Horizontal, vertical, diagonal contrast

- Image synthesis: It is possible to synthesize multiple images through logical operation between background image and active image extracted by image mask with priority.

The results of the interior design using an image processing function are shown in Photo. 4.8-10.

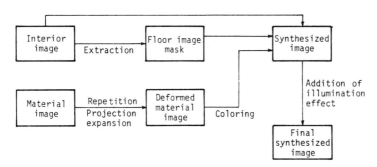

Fig. 4.3 Processing Step of Interior Design

Illumination effects are processed by the following steps. At first, the brightness of the floor area and its average value is analyzed by the image analysis menus. The difference value obtained by reducing the average value from each brightness of the floor is considered representating illumination effects. At last, the synthesized image about the floor is modified on an assumption that the positive value of the differential value represents the reflection of the illumination and the negative value shows the shadow of the illumination.

5. Conclusion

The A-IDAS system equipped with the image processing function performs its function sufficiently as a visual design system. The features are summariz-ed as follows.

(1) It is possible to produce a picture or an image of high visibility and reality under a conversational environment through the process of a mixture of shape data and image data.

(2) Specially as to color, by virtue of multi-freedom resulting from not only the RGB system but also the HVC system prepared, it is possible to

analyze and match the colors and also it is easy to put delicate color shading on a scenery picture.

(3) It is possible to easily expand the application's function under packages of database management, graphic and command management. In addition, the function can be customized by purpose.

By adding functions such as the classification of a foreground and a background based on a distance factor, color shading by light's diffused reflection effect, etc. to the existing image processing function, the visual design system will be reinforced more than over.

REFERENCES

(1) Matsuka H. and Uno S. (1979) Canonical geometric modeling for computer aided design, Data Base Techniques for Pictorial Applications, Lecture Notes in Computer Science 81, Springer-Verlag, June, Florence.

(2) Matsuka H. and Uno S. (1980.a) An application of advanced-integrated designer's activity system, Proc. of Man-Machine communication in CAD/CAM, IFIP Working Conf., October, Japan.

(3) Matsuka H. (1980.b) An application of an A-IDAS system to civil engineering plan and design, Quarterly Column, No. 77, Nippon Steel Corp. July, Japan (in Japanese).

(4) Matsuka H., Sugimoto K. and Udo M. (1981) Geo-socio data processing system, IFIP Working Conf. on ESAM, September, Italy.

(5) Uno S. and Matsuka H. (1979) A general purpose graphic system for computer aided design, Computer Graphics, Vol. 13, No. 2, pp 25-32, August, USA.

(6) Takama J., Matsuka H., Uno S., and Sugimoto K. (1981) Visual environmental graphic analysis and synthesis system, TSC report, N:G318-1536, IBM Japan (in Japanese).

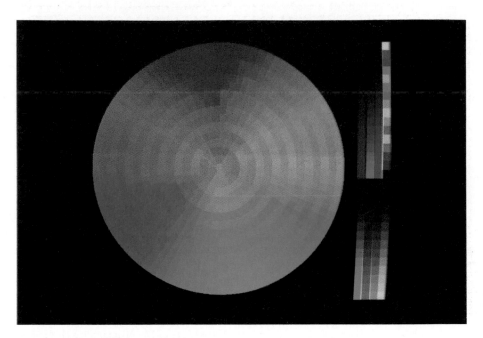

Photo. 4.1   Hue-Chroma Plane

Photo. 4.2   Chroma-Value Plane

280

Photo. 4.3   Various Ranking

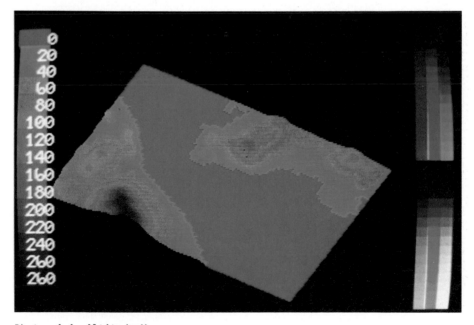

Photo. 4.4   Altitude Map

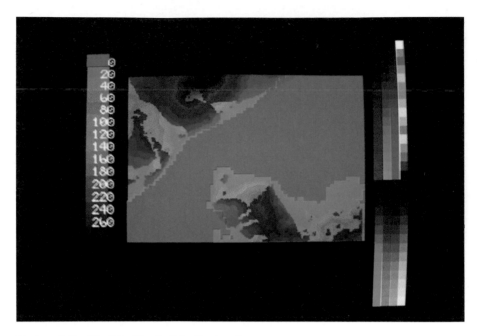

Photo. 4.5 Visible/Invisible Region Map

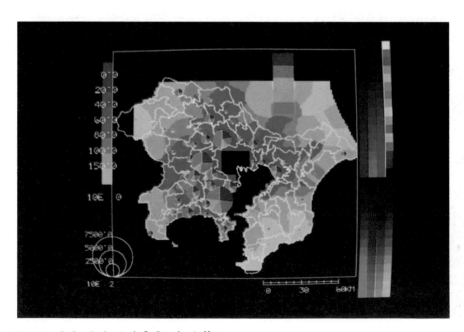

Photo. 4.6 Industrial Product Map

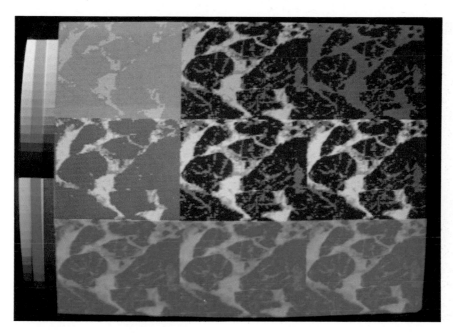

Photo. 4.7 Marble Texture

Photo. 4.8 Original Interior

Photo. 4.9 Synthesized Interior

Photo. 4.10 Illumination Effect

284

Part VI

Computer Art

Towards an Intelligent Computer Art System

M.K. Sasaki and T. Sasaki

The Institute of Physical and Chemical Research
Wako-shi, Saitama 351, Japan

ABSTRACT

The computer art systems constructed so far have no intelligence in that
they cannot understand and generate artistic pictures. This paper describes
an attempt to implement an intelligent computer art system for picture generation. A picture may be characterized by the global composition, the local
structure, the texture, the tint, etc., and processing of the global composition is discussed in this paper. Suppose the main part of a picture is
composed of separable objects which are given weights. In terms of the mean,
the variance, the covariance, and so on, of the distribution of the objects,
we may characterize beautiful arrangements of the objects mathematically.
Following this idea, we analyzed many well-known pictures from the viewpoint
of the distribution of objects and constructed two algorithms for generating
pictures of "beautiful" compositions. The algorithms were tested in several
ways, which shows that our approach is reasonable so far as it is supplemented by one or two well-established rules for good compositions.

1. Introduction

Computers are often used for generating melodies, pictures, and even sculptures [1], and nowadays many people are familiar with so-called computer art.
This fact as well as a remarkable advancement of artificial intelligence
makes many people think that computers have already got a good intelligence
of understanding art and generating art works. The actual situation is,
however, that computers have almost no aesthetic intelligence except for
that of music.

   Music is one-dimensional in structure and it is not difficult to analyze
and generate melodies by a computer [2]. On the other hand, pictures and
sculptures are, respectively, two- and three-dimensional in structure and
they are much more difficult to process by a computer than melodies. When
we use a computer as only a tool for drawing pictures with ideas in our
minds, we find the computer to be quite useful and convenient. Most works
of computer art so far were generated in this way. When, however, we want
to implement intelligence of understanding art and generating artistic pictures on a computer, we will find that the problem is quite difficult. This
paper describes our initial attack to this problem.

   It is worthwhile to note the difference between the conventional image
processing and intelligent computer art. Here, by intelligent computer art
we mean implementation of intelligent systems for computer art and generation of art works by using such systems. The conventional studies aimed at
processing given pictures for various applications, such as pattern recogni-

tion, image restoration, measurement of images, and so on. In these studies, the problems are concerned mostly with processing of local structures of images and they are well formulated in terms of mathematical languages. On the other hand, in intelligent computer art, our purpose is to generate art works on only the basis of a standard of beauty which is too vague to formulate accurately in terms of mathematical languages. Furthermore, in the case of art systems, important is not the processing of local structure but the processing of global structure of a picture.

In §2, we describe our strategy of implementing aesthetic intelligence on a computer. §3 is devoted to an analysis of pictures, most of them are well-known, to obtain basic data for beauty. Our method of generating pictures intelligently is formulated in §4. Results of experiments of our method and an improvement of the method are presented in §5.

2. Strategy

We expect that many beautiful pictures must contain some common features which make a picture beautiful and which can be described in terms of mathematical languages. Let us explain our strategy by considering music.

It is well-known that the Fourier transformation is a quite useful and powerful technique for analyzing melodies. If one calculates the Fourier spectrum $g(\nu)$ of a well-known melody, where ν is the frequency, one will find the following approximate relation to be valid in a relatively wide range of $|\nu|$:

$$|\text{Re } g(\nu)|, \ |\text{Im } g(\nu)| \ \lesssim g_0/|\nu|, \tag{1}$$

where Re and Im denote the real and imaginary parts, respectively, and g_0 is a constant. One will also find that high frequency part of $g(\nu)$ is not large. Therefore, we may consider these properties to be the most necessary conditions of good melodies. Note that some low frequency components of $g(\nu)$ may be much smaller than $g_0/|\nu|$. The difference between distinct melodies is mostly due to the difference in low frequency parts of the Fourier spectra, and the high frequency parts determine the detailed structures of melodies.

The above consideration suggests us a simple strategy of generating melodies, that is, to generate melodies so that the relation (1) may be satisfied and the high frequency part of $g(\nu)$ may not be large. Then, resulting melodies will not be so bad, although they may not be beautiful. We apply the same strategy to pictures. That is, we extract common features from beautiful pictures and generate pictures so that the features may be satisfied.

Extraction of common features from beautiful pictures requires a careful investigation of pictorial beauty. There are various properties which characterize a picture: the forms of main objects, the arrangement of the main objects and their colors, the background, the unessential objects and their relationships to the main objects, the texture, the tint, and so on. If the mutual relationships among these properties are represented by a graph, then the graph must be of a hierarchical network type. Therefore, in the analysis and generation of a picture, it is reasonable to treat the above properties several by several successively, in such a way that properties at higher level of the hierarchy are processed earlier. For example, the detailed structure and the texture of main objects should be processed after the determination of the forms, arrangement, and coloring of the main objects.

Now, which properties are the most important in a picture? When we see a picture, we see at the first sight the forms and the arrangement of the main objects and the global tone and change of the color, i.e., the global composition of the picture. The impression obtained by this first sight determines mostly whether or not the picture is beautiful. Therefore, we may think that the processing of the global composition of the picture is of prime importance for our intelligent computer art system. Fortunately, the properties characterizing the global composition are at the top level of a hierarchy of the whole properties characterizing the picture. Therefore, in processing the global composition, we need not consider the complication of processing local structure of the picture. This makes the processing of the global composition quite simple. In this paper, we consider only the processing of the global composition.

Which mathematical technique is the best for treating the global composition? We may use the technique of Fourier transformation which is often used in analyzing and processing pictures. In this case, the global composition of a picture is characterized by low frequency part of the Fourier spectrum. Fourier analysis is very useful for periodic patterns. However, periodicity is scarecely seen in the global compositions of the pictures. Furthermore, calculation of two-dimensional Fourier spectrum requires a lot of time. We, therefore, abandon the technique of Fourier transformation.

The method we use in this paper is an elementary technique of processing distributions. In order to make such a treatment possible, we assume in this paper that main objects in a picture are separable. Then, the arrangement of the main objects is nothing but the determination of their distribution on a canvas. Furthermore, coloring of the main objects and the global tone of the color can be treated from the viewpoint of the distribution. Therefore, the use of a technique of processing distributions is quite reasonable.

Let the canvas be normalized to the square $-1 \leqq x \leqq 1$, $-1 \leqq y \leqq 1$, where x and y denote the horizontal and the vertical coordinates, respectively. The scales of x- and y-axes may not be the same. If a picture is monochromatic, it is specified by a density function $f(x,y)$ which represents the gray scale of the picture at point (x,y). If a picture is colored, it is decomposed into three primary colors, red, blue and yellow, and the picture is specified by three density functions $f_R(x,y)$, $f_B(x,y)$ and $f_Y(x,y)$. In the following sections, we treat pictures as monochromatic. Thus, in this paper, we are concerned with only the density function $f(x,y)$. Note that $f(x,y)$ is a nonnegative function: $f(x,y) \geqq 0$. We normalize $f(x,y)$ as

$$\int_{-1}^{1} \int_{-1}^{1} f(x,y)\,dxdy = 1. \tag{2}$$

Let $z = z(x,y)$ be a variant which is a function in x and y. We denote the average of z for the density function $f(x,y)$ as $E(z)$:

$$E(z) = \int_{-1}^{1} \int_{-1}^{1} z(x,y)f(x,y)\,dxdy. \tag{3}$$

Let us consider the moments of the distribution:

$$E(x^i y^j) = \int_{-1}^{1} \int_{-1}^{1} x^i y^j f(x,y)\,dxdy, \quad i,j=0,1,2,\cdots. \tag{4}$$

If $f(x,y)$ is a piecewise continuous function, which is the case of actual pictures, then the distribution is determined almost everywhere by the

288

moments $E(x^i y^j)$, $i=0,1,2,\cdots$, $j=0,1,2,\cdots$. This can be proved by using the completeness of the set of Legendre polynomials. Hence, we expect that common features of beautiful pictures can be extracted by calculating the moments $E(x^i y^j)$ for well-known pictures.

3. Analysis of Pictures

We have so far analyzed the following pictures from the viewpoint of the distribution of objects in a picture:

    P1: "The birth of Venus" by S. Botticelli,
    P2: "Mona Liza" by L. Da Vinci,
    P3: "Madonna with the Goldfinch" by Raphael Sanzio,
    P4: "Liverty leading the people" by E. Delacroix,
    P5: "Grande Odalisque" by J.A. Dominique Ingres,
    P6: "The gleaners" by J.F. Millet,
    P7: "Déjeuner sur l'herbe" by É. Manet,
    P8: "The starry night" by V.V. Gogh,
    P9: "Sunday afternoon on the island of la Grande Jatte" by G. Seurat,
    P10: "White prunes in the spring" by Ogata Korin,
    P11: "Three musicians" by P. Picasso,
    P12: "The great wave, from thirty-six views of Mt. Fuji"
            by Katsushika Hokusai,
    P13: "My portrait" by M. Sasaki,
    P14: "Nemophila" by M. Sasaki.

Pictures P13 and P14 are monochromatic and they were generated by using a computer.

The analysis was performed as follows. A monochromatic version of each picture was read by a picture-digitizer which divided the canvas area into 512×512 small sections and measured the gray scale in each section. The data of gray scales obtained were then compacted by unifying 4×4 adjacent sections into one larger section. The resulting data of gray scales over 128×128 sections form the density function $f(x,y)$. The $f(x,y)$ represents everything of the monochromatic version of the picture: main objects, unessential objects, background, and so on. Since almost every part of a colored picture is painted, the monochromatic version of the picture does not exhibit a good contrast as the original colored picture does. That is, the variance of $f(x,y)$ is small for many colored pictures. The density function $f(x,y)$ is, hence, not suited for investigating the arrangement of main objects, and we construct density functions which are more suited for our analysis than $f(x,y)$ in the following way.

Let the variance of $f(x,y)$ be σ^2:

$$\sigma^2 = \int_{-1}^{1}\int_{-1}^{1} \{f(x,y)-\bar{f}\}^2 dxdy, \quad \text{with } \bar{f} = 1/4. \tag{5}$$

(Note the average of $f(x,y)$ is $\bar{f}$.) As we have mentioned above, σ is mostly much less than $\bar{f}$; a typical value of σ is $0.3\times\bar{f}$. We first construct f_1 and f_2 as

$$f_1(x,y) = \begin{cases} 4\sigma, & \text{if } f > \bar{f} + 2\sigma, \\ f - \bar{f} + 2\sigma, & \text{if } \bar{f} + 2\sigma \geqq f \geqq \bar{f} - 2\sigma, \\ 0, & \text{if } \bar{f} - 2\sigma > f, \end{cases} \tag{6}$$

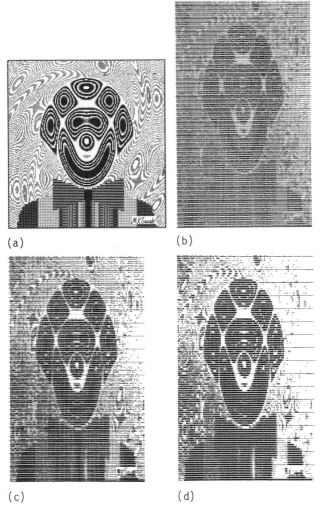

(a)

(b)

(c)

(d)

Fig.1 Picture P13 and corresponding density functions f, f_1, and f_2.

$$f_2(x,y) = \begin{cases} 2\sigma, & \text{if } f > \bar{f} + \sigma, \\ f - \bar{f} + \sigma, & \text{if } \bar{f} + \sigma \geqq f \geqq \bar{f} - \sigma, \\ 0, & \text{if } \bar{f} - \sigma > f. \end{cases} \qquad (7)$$

The f_1 and f_2 are then normalized as

$$\int_{-1}^{1} \int_{-1}^{1} f_i(x,y)\,dx\,dy = 1, \quad i=1,2, \qquad (2')$$

which we use for our analysis. The net effect of the transformation $f \to f_i$, $i=1,2$, is to magnify the variation of f. For example, Figs.1b, 1c, and 1d show the density functions f, f_1, and f_2, respectively, for the picture P13 which is illustrated by Fig.1a.

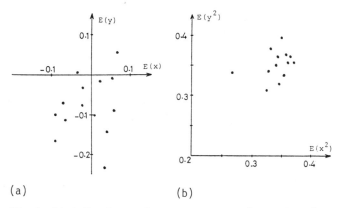

(a)   (b)

Fig.2 Distributions of $E(x)$, $E(y)$, $E(x^2)$, and $E(y^2)$ for $f_1(x,y)$.

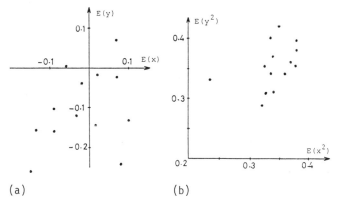

(a)   (b)

Fig.3 Distributions of $E(x)$, $E(y)$, $E(x^2)$, and $E(y^2)$ for $f_2(x,y)$.

We have calculated moments of various degrees using the density functions $f_1(x,y)$ and $f_2(x,y)$ for each picture. Figures 2a and 2b show $E(x)$, $E(y)$, $E(x^2)$, and $E(y^2)$ calculated for the pictures P1, $\cdots$, P14 by using $f_1(x,y)$, and those calculated by using $f_2(x,y)$ are shown in Figs.3a and 3b. We see that $E(x) \sim 0$ indicating that the distributions are almost balanced with respect to the y-axis. On the other hand, $E(y) \sim -0.1$ indicating that the center of the vertical distribution is slightly below the center of canvas. Figures 2 and 3 also show that $E(x^2) \sim E(y^2) \sim 0.33 \sim 1/3$. Note that the uniform distribution, i.e. $f(x,y) = 1/4$, gives the values $E(x) = E(y) = 0$, and $E(x^2) = E(y^2) = 1/3$. If the distribution is random, $E(x)$ and $E(y)$ are distributed around 0 and $E(x^2)$ and $E(y^2)$ around 1/3.

Table I Results of analysis of pictures. Note that not σ^2 but σ is shown as the variance. The x_c and y_c denote $1/(1+4x^2)$ and $1/(1+4y^2)$, respectively. The numbers on the left side in the rightmost column are $E(z_i)$'s in the uniform and the random distributions, and those on the right side are their approximate variances in the random distribution (i is the degree of the moment).

	data for pictures using $f_1(x,y)$		data for pictures using $f_2(x,y)$		uniform/random distribution	
	average	variance σ	average	variance σ	average	$\dfrac{i}{i+1}\sqrt{\dfrac{1}{2i+1}}$
$E(x)$	-0.0069	0.0562	-0.0102	0.0834	0.0	0.2887
$E(y)$	-0.0794	0.0728	-0.1251	0.1176	0.0	0.2887
$E(x^2)$	0.3409	0.0249	0.3424	0.0364	0.3333	0.2981
$E(y^2)$	0.3502	0.0246	0.3560	0.0362	0.3333	0.2981
$E(x^3)$	-0.0031	0.0326	-0.0047	0.0493	0.0	0.2835
$E(y^3)$	-0.0451	0.0413	-0.0702	0.0665	0.0	0.2835
$E(x^4)$	0.2072	0.0204	0.2090	0.0285	0.2	0.2667
$E(y^4)$	0.2170	0.0195	0.2232	0.0294	0.2	0.2667
$E(x^5)$	-0.0010	0.0231	-0.0023	0.0352	0.0	0.2513
$E(y^5)$	-0.0314	0.0290	-0.0481	0.0461	0.0	0.2513
$E(x^6)$	0.1494	0.0168	0.1511	0.0232	0.1429	0.2377
$E(y^6)$	0.1584	0.0153	0.1643	0.0235	0.1429	0.2377
$E(x^7)$	0.0003	0.0182	-0.0007	0.0276	0.0	0.2259
$E(y^7)$	-0.0243	0.0225	-0.0366	0.0351	0.0	0.2259
$E(x^8)$	0.1169	0.0143	0.1186	0.0196	0.1111	0.2156
$E(y^8)$	0.1251	0.0123	0.1306	0.0194	0.1111	0.2156
$E(x^9)$	0.0012	0.0152	0.0003	0.0229	0.0	0.2065
$E(y^9)$	-0.0200	0.0185	-0.0296	0.0284	0.0	0.2065
$E(x^{10})$	0.0961	0.0124	0.0977	0.0170	0.0909	0.1984
$E(y^{10})$	0.1036	0.0102	0.1086	0.0164	0.0909	0.1984
$E(xy)$	-0.0071	0.0153	-0.0091	0.0235	0.0	
$E(x^2y)$	-0.0287	0.0229	-0.0448	0.0372	0.0	
$E(xy^2)$	-0.0040	0.0146	-0.0056	0.0215	0.0	
$E(x^2y^2)$	0.1187	0.0102	0.1211	0.0154	0.1111	
$E(xy_c)$	-0.0047	0.0673	-0.0071	0.1006	0.0	0.2887
$E(yx_c)$	-0.0771	0.0774	-0.1217	0.1239	0.0	0.2887
$E(x^2y_c)$	0.3371	0.0273	0.3367	0.0390	0.3333	0.2981
$E(y^2x_c)$	0.3499	0.0249	0.3552	0.0364	0.3333	0.2981

Table I shows the average values of $E(x^i)$ and $E(y^i)$, $i=1,2,\cdots,10$, calculated by using $f_1(x,y)$ and $f_2(x,y)$, respectively, and their variances. (The average of $E(x^i)$ or $E(y^i)$ means the averaging over the pictures P1, $\cdots$, and P14). For comparison, we have appended the average values of $E(x^iy^j)$'s and their variances for the uniform and the random distributions. (Note that the variance of $E(x^iy^j)$ for the uniform distribution is 0, hence we have shown only the variances for the random distribution.) Table I indicates that the distribution of the objects in a picture is never random, and the distribution is not much different from the uniform distribution except that the center of the distribution is slightly below the center of canvas.

We also showed in Table I the average values of $E(xy)$, $E(x^2y)$, $E(xy^2)$, $E(x^2y^2)$, $E(x/(1+4y^2))$, $E(y/(1+4x^2))$, $E(x^2/(1+4y^2))$, and $E(y^2/(1+4x^2))$ calculated by using $f_1(x,y)$ and $f_2(x,y)$, respectively, and their variances. In Table I, $E(x^i/(1+4y^2))$ and $E(y^i/(1+4x^2))$ are written as $E(x^iy_c)$ and $E(y^ix_c)$, respectively, and they denote moments of the distributions in the central regions along x- and y-axes, respectively. In many pictures, important objects are arranged mostly in the central region of the canvas. Therefore, we have investigated the distribution in the central region in some details by calculating $E(x^iy_c)$ and $E(y^ix_c)$, $i=1,2$. The $E(xy)$ and $E(x^2y^2)$ represent the characteristic of distribution along the diagonal lines of the canvas.

The average values of $E(x^iy_c)$ and $E(y^ix_c)$, $i=1,2$, mean that the distributions of objects in the central regions along x- and y-axes are also similar to the uniform distribution. However, the variances of $E(xy_c)$ and $E(x^2y_c)$ are slightly greater than those of $E(x)$ and $E(x^2)$, respectively, indicating that the distribution in the central region along the x-axis is rather various. On the other hand, smallness of $E(xy)$ and its variance indicates that the distribution along one diagonal line of the canvas is well balanced by that along another diagonal line.

Finally, let us emphasize that the variance σ for each moment $E(x^iy^j)$, with i and j even integers, is about one-tenth of the average of the moment. Therefore, the pictures we have investigated are not much different from each other if the distribution of objects is concerned.

4. Automatic Arrangement of Objects

As we have seen in the previous section, distributions of the objects in many well-known pictures have a common feature that each moment of low degree is close to a common value. Assuming that this is the most necessary condition of beautiful arrangement of objects, let us formulate an automatic method of arranging objects.

Although we have calculated many moments in the previous section, we use in this section only the moments $E(x^iy^j)$, $E(x^iy_c)$ and $E(y^jx_c)$, with $i,j \leq 2$. The use of $E(x^iy_c)$ and $E(y^jx_c)$ is to specify the distribution of objects in the central regions along x- and y-axes in some details. The reason of discard of $E(x^iy^j)$ with $i \geq 3$ and/or $j \geq 3$ is that these moments are related strongly to the distribution of objects near the fringe of canvas and they are related only weakly to the distribution of objects in the central region of the canvas.

Let z_i, $i=1,2,\cdots,12$, be x, y, x^2, y^2, xy, x^2y, xy^2, x^2y^2, $x/(1+4y^2)$, $y/(1+4x^2)$, $x^2/(1+4y^2)$, and $y^2/(1+4x^2)$, respectively. The value of $E(z_i)$ will change from picture to picture, and we may assume that the distribution of $E(z_i)$ is well described by the normal distribution $N(E(z_i);\mu_i,\sigma_i)$:

$$N(E(z_i);\mu_i,\sigma_i) = \frac{1}{\sqrt{2\pi}\sigma_i}\exp\left\{-\frac{(E(z_i)-\mu_i)^2}{2\sigma_i^2}\right\}, \tag{8}$$

293

where μ_i and σ_i are, respectively, the average and the variance of the distribution of $E(z_i)$. Let us consider the following function B which is the product of $N(E(z_i);\mu_i,\sigma_i)$, $i=1,\cdots,12$:

$$B(E(z_1),\cdots,E(z_{12})) = \prod_{i=1}^{12} N(E(z_i);\mu_i,\sigma_i)$$

$$= (\prod_{i=1}^{12}\frac{1}{\sqrt{2\pi}\sigma_i}) \exp\{-\sum_{i=1}^{12}\frac{(E(z_i)-\mu_i)^2}{2\sigma_i^2}\}. \tag{9}$$

If the objects are beautifully arranged on the canvas, then the value of each $E(z_i)$ is close to μ_i hence the value of B is large. On the other hand, if the value of B is small, then at least one of $N(E(z_i);\mu_i,\sigma_i)$'s is small. This means that at least one of the conditions $E(z_i) \sim \mu_i$, $i=1,\cdots,12$, does not hold hence the corresponding arrangement is not beautiful. Therefore, we may formulate the necessary conditions for beautiful arrangement by the largeness of the function B. In this sense, we call B the beauty function.

Following the above formulation of beautiful arrangement, we can easily formulate a method of automatic arrangement of objects. That is, we arrange objects so that the beauty function B may be as large as possible. Note that, since each σ_i is a constant, the maximum of B is obtained when

$$G(E(z_1),\cdots,E(z_{12})) = \sum_{i=1}^{12} c_i^2(E(z_i)-\mu_i)^2, \quad c_i \equiv \frac{1}{\sqrt{2}\sigma_i}, \tag{10}$$

is the minimum.

Let us consider the above method of automatic arrangement in details. Suppose we want to arrange n objects on the canvas, and let the positions of the objects be $(x_1,y_1),\cdots,(x_n,y_n)$. Here, by the position of an object we mean a representative coordinate, say the center of mass, of the object. Note that we have assumed the objects in a picture to be separable. Then, each $E(z_i)$ can be regarded as a function in $2n$ variables $x_1, y_1, \cdots, x_n$, and y_n. Therefore, our problem is to find a set of vectors $\{(x_1,y_1),\cdots, (x_n,y_n)\}$ which minimize G. This problem is well-investigated mathematically and computationally, and we can use a well-tested computer program to solve the problem.

Although our method of automatic arrangement is very simple in principle, we must consider the following complications in actual programming:

1) In many cases, we want to fix the positions of some objects.
2) In many cases, we want to fix the relative positions of some objects.
3) The objects should be drawn inside the canvas.
4) The minimization routine often fails to search the minimum point or even a local minimum point when the number of variants is large.

The first problem is easy to solve: we have only to program the minimization routine in such a way that it minimizes G by moving the positions of specified objects only. The second problem disappears if we treat a set of objects whose relative positions are fixed as a larger object. In order to ensure this, our current program inputs an object by a set of representative points as well as the weight of the object.

The third problem is also easy to solve. We modify G so that the objects may not be arranged outside the canvas. The modification should be such that the objects are little moved by this modification when they are inside the canvas. This requirement is satisfied by the following modification:

$$\tilde{G}(E(z_1),\cdots,E(z_{13})) = G(E(z_1),\cdots,E(z_{12})) + c_{13}^2 E(z_{13})^2,$$

$$z_{13} = \max[\,|x|-0.95,0\,] + \max[\,|y|-0.95,0\,].$$

(11)

That is, z_{13} is zero inside the square $-0.95 \leqq x \leqq 0.95$, $-0.95 \leqq y \leqq 0.95$, and it becomes larger and larger if the point (x,y) goes farther and farther from the square.

The fourth problem is serious if we want to arrange a large number of objects simultaneously. In most actual cases, however, the number of objects to be emphasized in a picture is not many: the number is typically 3 or 4. The other objects are less important in a picture. We, therefore, arrange the important objects first and then determine the positions of less important objects successively.

The following algorithm summarizes our method described above.

ALGORITHM A (to arrange n objects on the canvas).

> *Input*: A set of n objects $(O_1,\cdots,O_n)$ and their weights $(w_1,\cdots,w_n)$, where the positions of $O_1,\cdots,O_k$ ($0\leqq k<n$) are specified by the user and $O_{k+1},\cdots,O_n$ are ordered so that $w_{k+1} \geqq \cdots \geqq w_n$.
> *Output*: Positions of $O_{k+1},\cdots,O_n$.

Step 1: Set the objects $O_1,\cdots,O_k$ as specified by the user.
Step 2: Determine the positions of objects $O_{k+1},\cdots,O_{k+\ell}$, $\ell\leqq5$, so that $\tilde{G}$ may be minimized, where the positions of $O_1,\cdots,O_k$ are fixed and $E(z_1),\cdots,E(z_{13})$ are calculated from the distribution of $O_1,\cdots,O_k,O_{k+1},\cdots,O_{k+\ell}$. If $k+\ell = n$ then stop else $m \leftarrow k+\ell$.
Step 3: *Comment* the positions of $O_1,\cdots,O_k,\cdots,O_m$ have been determined. Determine the positions of objects O_{m-1},O_m,O_{m+1} so that $\tilde{G}$ may be minimized, where the positions of $O_1,\cdots,O_{m-2}$ are fixed and $E(z_1),\cdots,E(z_{13})$ are calculated from the distribution of $O_1,\cdots,O_{m+1}$.
Step 4: $m \leftarrow m+1$; If $m = n$ then stop, else go to Step 3.

In algorithm A, the number of objects to be arranged simultaneously is 5 at most, hence the number of variants in the minimization routine is 10 at most.

5. Experiment and Improvement of Algorithm

In this section, we first test our simple algorithm given in the previous section to know whether or not the algorithm can arrange objects well and to know the fault of the algorithm. We then improve the algorithm slightly and test the improved algorithm. Note that algorithm A guarantees only some necessary conditions for beautiful arrangement of objects and not the satisfactory conditions. Hence, arrangements generated by algorithm A are not guaranteed to be beautiful, although they will not be so bad.

The objects we have used in our experiments are squares and triangles of various sizes and weights. A square is represented by coordinates of its four corners, and a triangle by coordinates of its three corners. Each object in pictures generated is represented as a set of concentric squares or triangles the number of which is proportional to the weight of the object (cf. Figs.4 ~ 7).

We have determined the parameters μ_i and c_i, $i=1,\cdots,12$, in G in two ways. In one parametrization, for which G is represented as G_B for simplicity, the values of μ_i and c_i are as follows:

$$\begin{aligned}
\mu_1 &= 0.0, & c_1 &= 10, & (\ z_1 &= x &), \\
\mu_2 &= -0.080, & c_2 &= 7, & (\ z_2 &= y &), \\
\mu_3 &= 0.280, & c_3 &= 40, & (\ z_3 &= x^2 &), \\
\mu_4 &= 0.300, & c_4 &= 35, & (\ z_4 &= y^2 &), \\
\mu_5 &= 0.0, & c_5 &= 50, & (\ z_5 &= xy &), \\
\mu_6 &= -0.025, & c_6 &= 30, & (\ z_6 &= x^2 y &), \\
\mu_7 &= 0.0, & c_7 &= 35, & (\ z_7 &= xy^2 &), \\
\mu_8 &= 0.080, & c_8 &= 70, & (\ z_8 &= x^2 y^2 &), \\
\mu_9 &= 0.0, & c_9 &= 8, & (\ z_9 &= xy_c &), \\
\mu_{10} &= -0.100, & c_{10} &= 6, & (z_{10} &= yx_c &), \\
\mu_{11} &= 0.280, & c_{11} &= 40, & (z_{11} &= x^2 y_c &), \\
\mu_{12} &= 0.320, & c_{12} &= 35, & (z_{12} &= y^2 x_c &).
\end{aligned}$$

In another parametrization, for which G is represented as G_{NB}, the values of μ_i and c_i are the same as those for G_B except that $\mu_3 = 0.24$, $\mu_4 = 0.25$, $\mu_{11} = 0.22$, and $\mu_{12} = 0.25$. Most of these values were determined by refer- ring to the data in Table I, in particular, the data obtained by using the density function $f_1(x,y)$. However, the values of μ_3, μ_4, μ_{11} and μ_{12} were determined to be considerably smaller than the corresponding values in Table I. The reason will become clear soon.

Figure 4 shows two pictures generated by algorithm A. In these pictures, triangles were set at corners of the canvas as background and squares were arranged by computer using G_B for the beauty function. We have also tested G_B in the case where no object was set as background, and found that the resulting pictures were not good because the objects were too widely distri- buted on the canvas. This means that not only the main objects but also the background plays an important role in determining the value of beauty function. In fact, the effect of background in pictures shown in Fig.4 is rather weak and we were necessary to choose the values of μ_3, μ_4, μ_{11} and μ_{12} to be rather small.

Figure 5 shows two pictures generated by algorithm A, where the computer arranged every object in a picture by using G_{NB} for the beauty function. Since no object was set as background in these pictures, we were necessary to choose the values of μ_3, μ_4, μ_{11} and μ_{12} to be even smaller than those for pictures shown in Fig.4. We think that the pictures shown in Figs.4 and 5 are not bad: the distributions of objects are well-balanced and stable. However, our pictures are never attractive, showing the necessity of improve- ment of algorithm A.

The global composition of picture was investigated by many artists and scholars [3], and ancient Greek philosopher Plato summarized the essence of global composition concisely in the words "variation in unification." This summary is considered to be true even at present. In addition to the unifi- cation and variation, the focus is considered to be very important in the picture. Criticizing the pictures shown in Figs.4 and 5 from the above con- siderations, we can easily see the largest faults of the pictures. That is, each picture generated by algorithm A does not have focus and the arrange- ment of objects lacks variation. These faults are emphasized by that the objects we have used are only squares and triangles which are similar to each other.

We can introduce variation into the picture by various ways, for example, by introducing asymmetry, unbalance, or contrast into the arrangement of ob- jects. Any book of art which discusses the global composition shows many examples of famous compositions, such as the reversed-triangular composition or the L-shaped composition. The use of such a well-known composition is another way of introducing variation into the picture. We can introduce the focus into the picture by emphasizing one or two objects strongly. A simple

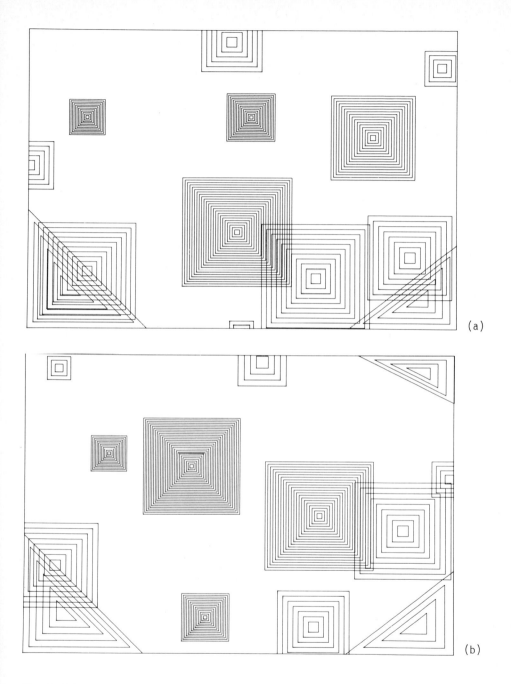

(a)

(b)

Fig.4 Pictures generated by algorithm A using G_B for beauty function.

Fig.5 Pictures generated by algorithm A using G_{NB} for beauty function.

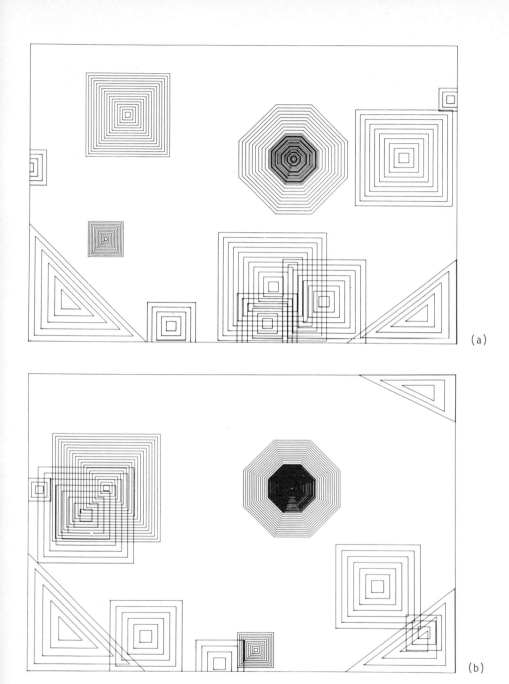

(a)

(b)

Fig.6 Pictures generated by algorithm B using G_B for beauty function.

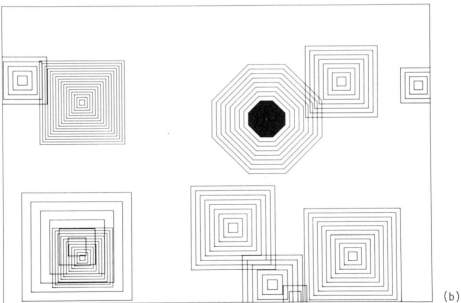

Fig.7 Pictures generated by algorithm B using G_{NB} for beauty function.

implementation of these methods is to treat the methods as built-in rules in our intelligent computer art system. The following algorithm summarizes the improvements mentioned above.

ALGORITHM B (an improved version of algorithm A).
   Input: A set of n objects $(O_1, \cdots, O_n)$ and their weights $(w_1, \cdots, w_n)$, where the first k objects $O_1, \cdots, O_k$ $(0 < k < n)$ are to be arranged by built-in rules and other objects $O_{k+1}, \cdots, O_n$ are ordered so that $w_{k+1} \geqq \cdots \geqq w_n$.
   Output: Positions of $O_1, \cdots, O_n$.
Step 1: Apply one or several built-in rules and arrange objects $O_1, \cdots, O_k$.
Step 2: The same as Step 2 in algorithm A.
Step 3: The same as Step 3 in algorithm A.
Step 4: The same as Step 4 in algorithm A.

We have tested algorithm B under almost the same conditions as those for algorithm A. The differences between the previous and the present tests are only that two squares in each of the previous pictures shown in Figs.4 and 5 were changed to octagons, increased in weight, and arranged at a golden-section point. Being changed in its form and increased in its weight, an object is stressed in the picture and it can focus our attentions. That an object is arranged at a golden-section point is nothing but the application of a built-in rule. By making other conditions be the same as those for algorithm A, we can see how much the algorithm B improves the algorithm A.

Figure 6 shows two pictures generated by algorithm B. The triangles were set at corners as background, and G_B was used for the beauty function. Figure 7 shows similar pictures without background, where G_{NB} was used for the beauty function. We see that the pictures generated by algorithm B are much better than those generated by algorithm A. From these tests, we may conclude that the beauty function approach based on the distribution of objects is reasonable so far as it is supplemented by well-established rules.

6. Future Works

Our method described in this paper is quite elementary and the pictures shown in Figs.6 and 7 are still not so good. We have many things to do for implementing human-like intelligence for art on a computer. In particular, we are interested in the following problems at present:

1) Improvement of the beauty function.
2) Inclusion of colors.
3) Detailed analysis of rules for the global composition.

As for the beauty function, an extensive improvement must be made on not only the values of μ_i and c_i, $i=1, \cdots, 12$, in G but also the function form itself of B. As we have seen in Figs.4 and 5, the beauty function B defined by (9) cannot generate pictures manifesting both unification and variation. The variation can, in principle, be represented by the correlation functions for the distribution of objects. In our beauty function (9), the correlation is represented by only $E(xy)$, $E(x^2y)$, $E(xy^2)$ and $E(x^2y^2)$ which are not enough to represent complicated correlations. Hence, a better form of the beauty function which can represent both unification and variation must be searched for.

The color is quite important in the picture, and a formulation of beauty in colored pictures is absolutely necessary in our work. Note that our data presented in Table I were obtained by treating every picture as monochromatic, and they are not well justified. Therefore, the data themselves must

be renewed. Inclusion of colors will make the beauty function quite different from (9), because the beauty function must then describe three distributions corresponding to three primary colors. In particular, correlations
among different colors are new and important quantities which we have not
seen in this paper.

Even if we will succeed in searching for a very good beauty function,
well-established rules for generating good pictures will be indispensable in
our intelligent computer art system. For example, in picture P2, the face
of Mona Liza is an extremely strong focus in the picture because of a strong
psychological effect it causes in our minds. Since our beauty function is
based on the distribution of objects, it cannot represent such psychological
effects caused by delicate and detailed structures of a picture. We will be
able to generate truly good pictures only after the success of manipulating
various well-established rules for art by a computer.

Acknowledgements

The authors thank Prof. H. Kawano of Metropolitan College of Technology,
Tokyo, Prof. K. S. Fu of Purdue University, Prof. A. Klinger of University
of California, Los Angeles, and Dr. R. A. Kirsch of National Bureau of Standards, Washington D.C., for valuable discussions, criticisms, and biblio-
graphy. Thanks are also due to Dr. T. Yatagai, an authors' colleague, for
his help in handling a picture-digitizer.

References

1. J. Reichardt, The Computer in Art, Studio Vista:London/Van Nostrand
   Reinhold Company:New York, 1971.
2. The BYTE Book of Computer Music, edited by C. P. Morgan, BYTE Books,
   1979.
3. J. M. Parramon, Así se Compone un Cuadro, Instituto Parramon Ediciones,
   Barcelona España; *translated into Japanese and published by Graphic-sha
   Publishing, Co.*, 1981.
4. G. Stiny and J. Gips, Algorithmic Aesthetics, University of California
   Press, 1978.

Index of Contributors

Agrawal, D.P. 152
Bruening, R. 140
Chang, S.-K. 33
Enomoto, H. 106
Fu, K.S. 56
Giloi, W.K. 140
Hiraishi, H. 248
Ikebe, Y. 75
Jain, R. 152
Klinger, A. 24
Kunii, T.L. 2

Lee, D.T. 232
Liu, P.S. 171
Matsuka, H. 268
Miyamoto, S. 75
Ni, L.M. 232
Saigusa, K. 188
Sasaki, M.K. 286
Sasaki, T. 286
Schumaker, L.L. 96
Sugimoto, K. 268
Takama, J. 268

Takao, Y. 210
Takeshita, T. 188
Uno, S. 268
Watanabe, Y. 106
Wong, K.Y. 232
:Yajima, S. 248
Yamaguchi, K. 2
Yonezaki, N. 106
Young, T.Y. 171

The Computer in Optical Research

Methods and Applications

Editor: B. R. Frieden
1980. 92 figures, 13 tables. XIII, 371 pages
(Topics in Applied Physics, Volume 41)
ISBN 3-540-10119-5

Contents: *B. R. Frieden:* Introduction. – *R. Barakat:* The Calculation of Integrals Encountered in Optical Diffraction Theory. – *B. R. Frieden:* Computational Methods of Probability and Statistics. – *A. K. Rigler, R. J. Pegis:* Optimization Methods in Optics. – *L. Mertz:* Computers and Optical Astronomy. – *W. J. Dallas:* Computer-Generated Holograms.

Image Reconstruction from Projections

Implementation and Applications

Editor: G. T. Herman
1979. 120 figures, 10 tables. XII, 284 pages
(Topics in Applied Physics, Volume 32)
ISBN 3-540-09417-2

Contents: *G. T. Herman, R. M. Lewitt:* Overview of Image Reconstruction from Projections. – *S. W. Rowland:* Computer Implementation of Image Reconstruction Formulas. – *R. N. Bracewell:* Image Reconstruction in Radio Astronomy. – *M. D. Altschuler:* Reconstruction of the Global-Scale Three-Dimensional Solar Corona. – *T. F. Budinger, G. T. Gullberg, R. H. Huesman:* Emission Computed Tomography. – *E. H. Wood, J. H. Kinsey, R. A. Robb, B. K. Gilbert, L. D. Harris, E. L. Ritman:* Applications of High Temporal Resolution Computerized Tomography to Physiology and Medicine.

Springer-Verlag
Berlin
Heidelberg
New York

Picture Processing and Digital Filtering

Editor: T. S. Huang
2nd corrected und updated edition. 1979.
113 figures, 7 tables. XIII, 297 pages
(Topics in Applied Physics, Volume 6)
ISBN 3-540-09339-7

Contents: *T. S. Huang:* Introduction. – *H. C. Andrews:* Two-Dimensional Transforms. – *J. G. Fiasconaro:* Two-Dimensional Nonrecursive Filters. – *R. R. Read, J. L. Shanks, S. Treitel:* Two-Dimensional Recursive Filtering. – *B. R. Frieden:* Image Enhancement and Restoration. – *F. C. Billingsley:* Noise Considerations in Digital Image Processing Hardware. – *T. S. Huang:* Recent Advances in Picture Processing and Digital Filtering. – Subject Index.

Two-Dimensional Digital Signal Processing I

Linear Filters

Editor: T. S. Huang
1981. 77 figures. X, 210 pages
(Topics in Applied Physics, Volume 42)
ISBN 3-540-10348-1

Contents: *T. S. Huang:* Introduction. – *R. M. Mersereau:* Two-Dimensional Noncursive Filter Design. *P. A. Ramamoorthy, L. T. Bruton:* Design of Two-Dimensional Recursive Filters. – *B. T. O'Connor, T. S. Huang:* Stability of General Two-Dimensional Recursive Filters. – *J. W. Woods:* Two-Dimensional Kalman Filtering.

Two-Dimensional Digital Signal Processing II

Transform and Median Filters

Editors: T. S. Huang
1981. 49 figures. X, 222 pages
(Topics in Applied Physics, Volume 43)
ISBN 3-540-10359-7

Contents: *T. S. Huang:* Introduction. – *J.-O. Eklundh:* Efficient Matrix Transposition. – *H. J. Nussbaumer:* Two-Dimensional Convolution and DFT Computation. – *S. Zohar:* Winograd's Discrete Fourier Transform Algorithm. – *B. I. Justusson:* Median Filtering: Statistical Properties. – *S. G. Tyan:* Median Filtering: Deterministic Properties.

Digital Pattern Recognition

Editor: K. S. Fu
2nd corrected and updated edition. 1980.
59 figures, 7 tables. XI, 234 pages
(Communication and Cybernetics,
Volume 10)
ISBN 3-540-10207-8

Contents: *K. S. Fu:* Introduction. – *T. M. Cover,
T. J. Wagner:* Topics in Statistical Pattern Re-
cognition. – *E. Diday, J. C. Simon:* Clustering
Analysis. – *K. S. Fu:* Syntactic (Linguistic)
Pattern Recognition. – *A. Rosenfeld,
J. S. Weszka:* Picture Recognition. – *J. J. Wolf:*
Speech Recognition and Understanding. –
K. S. Fu, A. Rosenfeld: Recent Developments
in Digital Pattern Recognition. – Subject
Index.

Digital Picture Analysis

Editor: A. Rosenfeld
1976. 114 figures, 47 tables. XIII, 351 pages
(Topics in Applied Physics, Volume 11)
ISBN 3-540-07579-8

Contents: *A. Rosenfeld:* Introduction. –
R. M. Haralick: Automatic Remote Sensor
Image Processing. – *C. A. Harlow,
S. J. Dwyer III, G. Lodwick:* On Radiographic
Image Analysis. – *R. L. McIlwain, Jr.:* Image
Processing in High Energy Physics. –
K. Preston, Jr.: Digital Picture Analysis in
Cytology. – *J. R. Ullmann:* Picture Analysis in
Character Recognition.

Nonlinear Methods of Spectral Analysis

Editor: S. Haykin
1979. 45 figures, 2 tables. XI, 247 pages
(Topics in Applied Physics, Volume 34)
ISBN 3-540-09351-6

Contents: *S. Haykin:* Introduction. –
S. Haykin, S. Kesler: Prediction-Error Filtering
and Maximum-Entropy Spectral Estimation.
– *T. J. Ulrych, M. Ooe:* Autoregressive and
Mixed Autoregressive-Moving Average
Models and Spectra. – *E. A. Robinson:* Itera-
tive Least-Squares Procedure for ARMA
Spectral Estimation. – *J. Capon:* Maximum-
Likelihood Spectral Estimation. –
R. N. McDonough: Application of the Maxi-
mum-Likelihood Method and the Maxi-
mum-Entropy Method to Array Processing.
– Subject Index.

T. Pavlidis
Structural Pattern Recognition

1977. 173 figures, 13 tables. XII, 302 pages
(Springer Series in Electrophysics,
Volume 1)
ISBN 3-540-08463-0

"…The book is well written and illustrated.
An excellent feature of the book is that the
author has tried to give detailed listings of
the various algorithms so that they can be
implemented in most high level computer
languages without too much difficulty."
Math. Reviews

Syntactic Pattern Recognition, Applications

Editor: K. S. Fu
1977. 135 figures, 19 tables. XI, 270 pages
(Communication and Cybernetics,
Volume 14)
ISBN 3-540-07841-X

Contents: *K. S. Fu:* Introduction to Syntactic
Pattern Recognition. – *S. L. Horowitz:* Peak
Recognition in Waveforms. – *J. E. Albus:*
Electrocardiogram Interpretation Using a
Stochastic Finite State Model. – *R. DeMori:*
Syntactic Recognition of Speech Patterns. –
W. W. Stallings: Chinese Character Recogni-
tion. – *Th. Pavlidis, H.-Y. F. Feng:* Shape Dis-
crimination. – *R. H. Anderson:* Two-Dimen-
sional Mathematical Notation. – *B. Moayer,
K. S. Fu:* Fingerprint Classification. –
J. M. Brayer, P. H. Swain, K. S. Fu: Modeling of
Earth Resources Satellite Data. – *T. Vámos:*
Industrial Objects and Machine Parts
Recognition.

Springer-Verlag
Berlin
Heidelberg
New York